WORK, INC.

A Philosophical Inquiry

Work, Inc.

A Philosophical Inquiry

Edmund F. Byrne

Temple University Press
Philadelphia

To
Paul Proteus, a "company man,"
who appreciated the workers of Ilium
in *Player Piano*,
the first novel by
Indianapolis-born Kurt Vonnegut

Temple University Press, Philadelphia 19122
Copyright © 1990 by Edmund F. Byrne. All rights reserved
Published 1990
Printed in the United States of America

The paper used in this publication meets the minimum
requirements of American National Standard for Information
Sciences—Permanence of Paper for Printed Library Materials,
ANSI Z39.48-1984

Library of Congress Cataloging-in-Publication Data
Byrne, Edmund F., 1933–
Work, Inc. : a philosophical inquiry / by Edmund F. Byrne.
     p.   cm.
Includes bibliographical references.
ISBN 0-87722-688-1 (alk. paper)
1. Work ethic.   2. Job security.   3. Corporations—Social aspects.
4. Distributive justice.   5. Social contract.   I. Title.
HD4905.B96   1990
331'.01'1—dc20

89-20144
CIP

Acknowledgments

Much of what is of value in this book I owe to:

Jim Wallihan, whose ongoing encouragement, instruction, advice, and friendship were an inspiration throughout this project;

Peter d'Errico for helping me understand various legal complexities and transformations of the American corporation;

Ellen K. Thomas, Charles Ellinger, and especially Ed Archer for teaching me many things about employment and labor law;

Two anonymous reviewers, Rhonda Lee, Caroline Whitbeck, and especially Anne Donchin, for contributing valuable insights at important points in the development of this book;

The members of IBEW Local No. 481 (especially Jerry Payne, Jeff Lohman, and Tom O'Donnell), Charles Deppert of IAM District 90 and the Indiana AFL-CIO, Bob Thornberry of the Indiana Federation of Teachers, and the Indiana Labor Roundtable for helping me appreciate the challenges to, and the dedication and persistence of, the American labor movement;

Working people who have taken my Philosophy of Work course on campus, for sharing with me their insights and experiences, including John Freeman, Barbara Klein, Carol Lough, William Russell, Sandra Sullivan, Allen F. Sutherland, and especially Carolyn MacAvoy;

Frank DiSilvestro, for encouraging me to develop a correspondence course on Philosophy of Work, and the many working people near and far away who, in taking this course, have shared with me their insights and experiences, especially Mark Alberts, Jamie Ashley, William C. Baker, Charles D. Carlton, Michael Davis, Barbara Govert, David Grau, Margaret Harms, Ernest W. Ketcherside, William Kindberg, Jack Martin, Paul Paradiso, Nancy Roberts, Leonard Springer, Francine Waskowicz, and Katherin White;

Steven Michaluk, for sharing with me the day-to-day challenge of empowering the unemployed to assess their skills and find appropriate employment;

William M. Plater, John Barlow, and Michael Burke for providing me with an academic schedule conducive to research;

Terry Mills and the University Library staff, for their fine bibliographical ferreting;

Jane Cullen of Temple University Press, for her early, continuing, and un-

v

daunted faith in the merits of this project; Jennifer French and Trudie Calvert, for making it better than it might have been.

An earlier version of Chapter 1 and part of Chapter 9 appeared as "Globalization and Community," in *Technological Transformation*, ed. Edmund F. Byrne and Joseph R. Pitt (Dordrecht: Kluwer Academic Publishers, 1989), pp. 141–61. Copyright © 1988 by Edmund F. Byrne.

An earlier version of parts of Chapters 1, 7, and 9 appeared as "Building Community into Property," *Journal of Business Ethics* 7 (1988): 171–83. Copyright © 1987 by Edmund F. Byrne.

An earlier version of parts of Chapters 2 and 8 appeared as "Utopia without Work? Myth, Machines and Public Policy," in *Research in Philosophy and Technology* VIII, ed. Paul T. Durbin (Greenwich, Conn.: JAI Press, 1985), pp. 133–48. Copyright © 1985 by, and quoted with permission of, JAI Press, Inc.

An earlier version of parts of Chapters 3 and 8 appeared as "The Labor-Saving Device: Evidence of Responsibility?" in *Technology and Contemporary Life*, ed. Paul T. Durbin (Dordrecht: D. Reidel, 1988), pp. 63–85. Copyright © 1988 by D. Reidel Publishing Company (now Kluwer Academic Publishers). Published under rights reserved by the author.

An earlier version of a part of Chapter 4 appeared as "Displaced Workers: America's Unpaid Debt," *Journal of Business Ethics* 4 (1985): 31–41. Copyright © 1985 by D. Reidel Publishing Company (now Kluwer Academic Publishers). Published under rights reserved by the author.

An earlier version of part of Chapter 8 appeared as "Microelectronics and Workers' Rights," in *Philosophy and Technology II*, Boston Studies in the Philosophy of Science, ed. Carl Mitcham and Alois Huning (Dordrecht: D. Reidel, 1985), pp. 205–16. Copyright © 1986 by D. Reidel Publishing Company (now Kluwer Academic Publishers). Published under rights reserved by the author.

An earlier version of a section of Chapter 8 appeared as "Robots and the Future of Work," in *The World of Work: Careers and the Future*, ed. H. F. Didsbury, Jr. (Bethesda, Md.: World Future Society, 1983), pp. 30–38. Copyright © 1983 by, and published with permission of, the World Future Society.

An earlier version of some material appears in Edmund F. Byrne, *Philosophy of Work: A Study Guide* (Bloomington: Indiana University Extended Studies Program, 1986). Copyright © 1986 by the Trustees of Indiana University. Published with permission.

"The United Fruit Company," by Pablo Neruda, is reprinted by permission of Grove Press, a division of Wheatland Corporation, Copyright © 1961 by Ben Belitt.

A statement by Marvin Minsky in Chapter 8 is from *Robotics*, ed. Marvin Minsky (New York: [Doubleday] Anchor, 1985), published with permission of DOUBLEDAY, a division of Bantam, Doubleday, Dell Publishing Group, Inc.

John Dewey is quoted in Chapter 9 with permission of the Southern Illinois University Press.

I am responsible for the shortcomings of the book. I am not sure I could have done any better. The wine is very old, but it is stored in many new bottles. From some I have drunk deeply, others I have only tasted, of others I know only the bouquet. There are others, no doubt, I have not even found, or having found have perhaps not appreciated as would the connoisseur.

Indianapolis, Indiana
May 30, 1989

Contents

Introduction

"WE HAD A social contract, and now we don't. The social contract has been broken. Government, business, and labor —each had its role and each understood its responsibilities to the others. All three together, cooperating, for the betterment of all. That's how it was, but no more."

This, quite commonly, is how people in the labor movement explain to themselves and to anyone else who will listen what has been happening in recent years in the United States and elsewhere. They do not mean that it was always so. It obviously was not. Before the Depression, business-hired goons or even government-supplied troops were widely used instruments of labor relations. But at long last it became clear, at least according to the preamble of the National Labor Relations Act, that industrial peace required a more humane approach. The use of violence as a means of controlling workers was not thereby brought to an end. But collective bargaining and dispute resolution became the established ways for employers and employees to resolve their differences and arrive in the long run at mutually satisfactory agreements. And thus, as monitor and guarantor of these processes, government became an indispensable third party in labor relations. The social contract was set. It matured during World War II; and, in spite of numerous patrician attempts to undermine its impact, it endured, even flowered, for decades thereafter. But it was fatally flawed from the outset.

In particular, it was flawed by the assumption, accepted by each of the three principal parties to it, that its parameters were predominantly national, with little if any particular commitment to communities (or, on labor's side, even to "locals" as such). So in one industry after another, corporate enterprise has been able to exploit geographical vulnerability with only token opposition. Vertical, and now even horizontal, integration is becoming commonplace; in the process traditional understandings are giving way to competition both among local unions and among communities in response to corporate demands for concessions.

What remains of the old social contract? Over time each branch of the federal government has found ways to diminish its importance, with the strongly probusiness executive branch of the 1980s finally taking charge of funeral arrangements. At the wake, both business and government compete to see which can divest itself more thoroughly of social welfare responsibilities. Meanwhile, perhaps not coincidentally, some social and political philosophers have been turn-

3

ing to the long-neglected concept of a social contract to define the conditions for justice!

As this slice of history exemplifies, work is not done in a vacuum. A truism, perhaps. But because of certain probusiness myths, it is actually controversial. Ever-burgeoning data collected and statistics generated by dutiful bureaucracies do suggest that work is not done in an economic vacuum. An abundance of statutes, processes, and publications clearly indicate that it is not done in a legal vacuum either. And as election campaigns heat up from time to time, one is reminded that work is not done in a political vacuum. These signs of context notwithstanding, there has been a concerted effort in the United States to pretend that work is carried out in a *social* vacuum.

The principal proponents of this unreal account are a host of mythical dragons that serve the interests of the major corporations far better than their creators can imagine. One such dragon will be found at work, for example, in the courts and other government agencies that subscribe to the narrow tenet that law and economics are one. What is lost by coming under the influence of this dragon is the flesh and blood of people whose values and aspirations are reduced to the periodic printing of a paycheck. More dehumanizing, but harder to articulate, is the resulting destabilization and ultimate disintegration of community. The once localized degradation of deep-pit miners who slept at the very entrance to their workplace has now been generalized into a definition of human value as a narrowly economic function of increasingly volatile corporate needs and interests.

In view of this wide-reaching corporate hegemony over the value and significance of human beings, one has cause to wonder how the official definition of a corporation has come to be a mere caricature of the complex realities with which we all deal. Forget about price fixing, toxic waste, product dumping, defective products, bribery, industrial espionage, insider trading, leveraged buyouts, and all the other real-world problems that find their way eventually into the popular media. A corporation, according to another touted dragon, is just a legal fiction that enables people to get on with the business of getting rich without worrying unduly about the side effects of their endeavors. But a corporation is nothing more than a legal fiction only to someone whose field of vision does not include organizations and the power that organizations exert. For if a corporation is anything, it is a center of power, surpassing by far the power of a city in ancient times or, for that matter, the power of many nation-states today. There are reasons for suggesting that pragmatically constituted places like Panama and Monaco are legal fictions; but only the epistemological purist would challenge the reality of Switzerland or Brazil or Canada. Why, then, should reality be denied to such incomparably more powerful organizations as General Motors, International Business Machines, Mitsubishi, or Shell Oil?

The reality of corporations is, in fact, routinely denied in the United States

—not, to be sure, by ordinary people but by judges adept at the fine art of making the obvious indefensible. Especially helpful for this purpose is yet another dragon. This one simply says that a corporation is a person. The Fourteenth Amendment to the U.S. Constitution was adopted after the Civil War to assure the rights of all persons to protection of the law. But for the better part of a century the U.S. Supreme Court applied this amendment only to corporate "persons" to protect their "life, liberty or property" against the attempts of local government to regulate their behavior. In countless other respects, however, the law of the land (e.g., that regarding securities and antitrust) considers a corporation to be a commodity that can be brought into being or abolished, bought, sold, or restructured.[1]

This reduction of the corporation to a species of property makes sense if considered only in the abstract; but when balanced against the alternative tradition that awards corporations personhood, a glaring (but never mentioned) contradiction becomes apparent. For as those alert to the technicalities of surrogate mothering know well, it is unconstitutional to buy and sell persons—by virtue of that other postbellum amendment, the thirteenth, that constitutionalized Abraham Lincoln's emancipation of the slaves. So in the United States (as distinguished from Lewis Carroll's Wonderland, where things can be whatever they are said to be), a corporation cannot consistently be both a person and a commodity. But just as physicists see light alternatively as waves or particles, so judges accommodate the interests of corporations by viewing them alternatively as persons or commodities—the Thirteenth Amendment notwithstanding.

It will be argued in this book, at least implicitly, that corporations are not reducible to their assets and liabilities any more than a government is merely its annual budget, that they are organizations, that these organizations do things, and that they are socially responsible for what they do.

I do not take this position casually. For it is constantly on the defensive in a capitalist society. Some academicians, and some politicians as well, do defend it (explicitly or otherwise). But however brilliant their defense, corporations continue to make and break rules regarding work. Still more to the point, while social and political philosophers continue to focus their attention on nation-states and their interrelations, corporations are becoming the primary seats of power in our world. This development calls for a significantly different and for the most part unprecedented shift of attention if the traditional concerns of social and political philosophy are to be made relevant to these current issues regarding work:

1. Regardless of how working people evaluate work, in particular their own, those who control businesses, not to mention economic systems, tend to value that work only as a means to ends (especially wealth and power) that they envision as attainable without dependence on work.
2. A managerial dream of profits without payrolls is in fact coming true

across a wide spectrum of jobs, thus creating a critical need for humane public policy with regard to displaced workers.

3. Public policy with regard to displaced workers, especially in the United States, is (in the absence of a union contract) individual-oriented; but the process of displacement affects in varying degrees not only workforces as a whole but entire communities and grows for the most part out of unilateral corporate decisions with regard to new technologies and global production strategies.

4. Opportunities and compensation for work depend less on the bargaining power of workers, as determined by such factors as class, sex, race, and level of organization, than they do on employer-calculated advantages of the location and the labor-intensity of a workplace.

Workers, especially through unions, have attempted in various ways to respond to these threats to their livelihood. But their strategies are typically aimed at "cutting losses," and so, compared to the gravity of the challenge, they are at best inadequate. What jobs there will be, especially for the unskilled or inappropriately skilled, may pay too little to provide a decent living.

At issue is a fundamental question of human dignity and social responsibility, which until recently most theoreticians have sidestepped because of the extreme unlikelihood of an economy not based on human toil. The twentieth century has seen the development of various systems of unemployment compensation and welfare maintenance. But in spite of such social cushions, the new technology is worrisome to the extent that it involves what some have called "the collapse of work."[2] What part, if any, should work play in people's lives? If people are not going to be working, what are they going to do? How, if at all, are they to support themselves? And who or what is responsible for finding and implementing answers to these questions?

A basic assumption of this book is that work, including work done "for a corporation," is done in a community. Attached to this assumption are three subsidiary claims: (1) that corporations are themselves collective entities whose leaders (like those of nation-states) make decisions that they know will have an impact on people's lives; (2) that this impact is not only on individuals but on other collective entities, including not only other corporations but also communities; and that, accordingly, (3) attention to corporate impact must be not only corporate (or governmental) but communitarian as well.

To elaborate this community-oriented aspect of work, I will draw upon a wide variety of sources ranging from the popular press to technical philosophical reflection. From this perspective, the views of those more philosophically inclined are but indicators of public concern and are considered as such along with those whose expertise is derived more empirically from workforce and workplace details. None of these sources is privileged, but all are appreciated to the extent that they help clarify the meaning and value of work in this corporation-dominated world. So, although this book is an example of what is sometimes called applied philosophy, the philosophy that is here applied to work has not been found only in learned texts.

Given this middle-range orientation of my approach, I will not be putting forward a thorough exposition of social contract theory. For purposes of this study, it is enough to stipulate at the outset that a social contract is an empirically discernible but ultimately hypothetical agreement that encompasses the basic terms and conditions in reference to which a stable group of interacting human beings assess the legitimacy and propriety of their interactions. In saying that it is empirically discernible I do not mean that it is an *actual* contract (as between two parties with respect to a mutual exchange) but that its essential terms and conditions are disclosed by the ways in which people count upon one another and express recrimination when their expectations are frustrated. In saying that it is hypothetical, however, I do not rule out the possibility of its being subject to reform in light of an arguably better, even if not *ideal,* dispensation.³ What is most distinctive about a social contract is that it constitutes the framework for cooperation within which a community carries on its affairs.

I will not propound a rigorous philosophical defense of the communitarian aspects of my approach, desirable though that might be. Nor (leaving aside very technical studies of the possibility of cooperation) can I direct the reader to any recent efforts to carry out such a defense. The concept of community has, until quite recently, been largely disregarded in Anglo-American philosophy. Some say philosophers have not taken the concept of community seriously in recent times because in the past it was overused, or because it is too vague or too ambiguous to serve any useful purpose. In addition, there is a serious practical concern about being interpreted as favoring some sort of fascist uniformity. So philosophers, for these and other reasons, attempt to build their justifications of social arrangements on the rights of individuals. They often acknowledge, however, that the individual is ultimately a social being. This cautious concession is typically defended by finding unqualified egoism unacceptable from the perspective of an impartial observer or a perfectly rational social contractor.

John Rawls, for example, seeking to provide hypothetical social contractors no more information than necessary to arrive at acceptable and attractive principles of social justice, uses meticulously individualist assumptions as his starting point. But he tells the reader well into his renowned treatise on justice that the success of his individual-based theory depends on explaining "the value of community" and that "everyone's conception of the good as given by his rational plan is a subplan of the larger comprehensive plan that regulates the community as a social union of social unions." But in lieu of elucidating the notion of a social union he muses about "the community of humankind," which involves "the co-operation of many generations (or even societies) over a long period of time." Local concerns are left in limbo as Rawls gives as examples such "forms of life" as "science and art . . . families, friendships, and other groups" which have no definite size, no spatial or temporal limits, "for those widely separated by history and circumstance can nevertheless cooperate in realizing their common nature." On this view, work is not merely work but a (non-Marxist) contribution: "The division of labor is overcome not by each becoming complete in himself, but by willing and meaningful work within a just social union of social unions in which all men can freely participate as they so incline." This scenario, with its overtones of utopian togetherness, tells us nothing of substance about the concatenation of social unions that is a community.[4]

In a word, one cannot look to Rawls for a detailed account of the value and significance of a local community. To provide such an account would be a worthy project by itself, one which I hope to pursue in a subsequent study. But in the present work, the complex realities of human beings sharing their lives in a community will be observed somewhat more kaleidoscopically as the context in which workers' rights are determined.

What is at issue here is this: there is a serious value conflict between the traditional instrumentalist view of work (embodied in the "work ethic") and the commitment of corporations to "laborsaving" strategies ranging from automation to globalization. Some accept this conflict as a small price to pay for progress. But progress thus understood is indistinguishable from Darwinian survival of the fittest. And even if capitalism is inevitable, is it obvious that it must forever be wedded to laissez-faire individualism? As all sorts of cooperative ventures and even mixed economies make manifest, it need not be. Nor should it be, because individualism is an ineffectual response to the local/global problems of unemployment.

In support of this position, I will draw upon recent work in political philosophy to propose a community-based account of workers' rights. This will require a kind of bifocal perspective in which the interests of transnational corporations are given no greater weight than those of local workers and communities on the one hand and of our entire globe on the other. This multivalent balancing of equities is in accord with the efforts of governments throughout the world to ameliorate the impact of corporate decisions on workers and communities. But a just solution to these emerging problems about work in the world, I shall argue, cannot be attained without taking into account human communities which are globally distributed but locally defined.

It is not my purpose here to develop a philosophical theory of justice, the accomplishment of which has been a growth industry since the appearance of Rawls's treatise on the subject in 1971. In particular, I offer no theory on the origin or development of our concept of justice.[5] Justice, for the purposes of this study, is very important, important enough to be deemed at least a necessary condition for maximization of human well-being in the world. As for what rules and obligations are implied by a commitment to justice, I offer no reflective account. But the subject matter of this book is such that my focus is inevitably upon what is known as distributive justice, that is, the ethically acceptable distribution of goods among all who are for any reason entitled to share in them.

To deal with distributive justice regarding work in the world, I take as a starting point Rawls's much discussed principles of justice, especially his so-called difference principle, to the effect that gains for some are justifiable only if they produce some gains for the least advantaged as well. I do not endorse any particular justification of this principle, either Rawls's or anyone else's.[6] But I take it to be ideologically intermediate between libertarian distrust of, and socialist identification of justice with, social welfare.

Enterprise-oriented sentiment in the United States is much more at home with the libertarian stance, including its unbounded reliance on the efficacy of individual initiative. Once characterized as liberalism, this tradition has in recent years been relabeled *libertarian* to set it apart from the revisionist doctrine, defended by Rawls, that the public sector has to take responsibility for people's basic needs.[7] So a liberal is now defined as one who subscribes to this welfarist heresy (a usage exploited in the 1988 U.S. presidential election campaign). John Rawls is just such a liberal, in intent if not successfully in execution, and so provides a convenient "talking point" for issues with regard to workers' rights.

Rawls is to some extent supportive of my principal claim, namely, that questions about workers' rights must be founded on a community-sensitive ethic. This is largely because of his insistence that the principles of justice he espouses are attainable only in a well-ordered society which thrives as a social union of social unions. Some take this to be an adequate basis for communitarian concerns.[8] But at the same time, one must take into account criticisms of Rawls to the effect that by basing his entire argument on individualist premises, congenial to libertarians, he cannot reason his way to a legitimately communitarian concept of community.[9]

More problematic is whether Rawls's approach is helpful when it comes to the more global dimensions of work in the world today. For a start, he offers little guidance on the conflict between an obligation to work and an inability to find employment. Yet work is widely considered to be obligatory, especially by virtue of a cross-cultural "work ethic." The least advantaged (among others) depend upon employment for survival; and this dependency has global implications, especially in view of the many constraints imposed upon mobility. Rawls can be interpreted as supporting a work ethic either as a "natural duty" or as an obligation of conscience. Yet, in spite of his reliance on government for redistribution of wealth and his constraints on efficiency, he would apparently let the market determine employment decisions. This surely has an impact not only on future generations (with which Rawls is concerned) but also on distant people (whom he systematically disregards). We live in an increasingly global economy; so Rawlsian (or any other) visions of justice must somehow take this basic condition of our being-in-the-world into account and not leave it to the vagaries of international law.

In spite of the efforts of Charles Beitz and others, no merely "globalized" contractarian theory of justice can respond adequately to the complex value questions that arise in regard to work.[10] For the problems at issue are not only workplace-specific and community-centered but also global in their ramifications. So it is important at the outset to disavow the tendency to speak generically about "society" and imply that all statements one makes about it apply uniformly to comparable entities everywhere. In particular, nothing said in this book about a society will refer exclusively or even primarily to a nation-state (acknowledged or asserted) but should at all times be understood as including both the macro-lens perspective of the community and the wide-angle perspective of the entire globe.

What is needed for this purpose is a more nuanced vision of justice that is communitarian as well as global. This to some might sound suspiciously like the opening sentence of some corporate report to shareholders. But, as will be seen, it has little in common with such a unidimensional outlook. For this study has as one of its principal objectives to challenge corporate hegemony with regard to laborsaving strategies in light of the values of personal fulfillment, community well-being, and global justice.

This project, then, will not result in a new theory of justice of the sort that would be of interest to professional philosophers. It will, as I see it, do little more in this respect than reiterate the assertions of others as to the importance of including community in one's account of justice. But this point is made by both supporters and critics of Rawls, between whom I have no reason to choose but from all of whom we can learn. Because the concept of a social contract is so familiar to people interested in the labor movement, I will address questions regarding corporate/community justice as problems to be solved by the terms of a social contract. I will do so, furthermore, with John Rawls's philosophical use of the social contract as the point of departure for my own, more mundane analysis. In so doing, I have no desire to improve upon or, what would be still more presumptuous, replace Rawls's theory with something philosophically superior. However, because of my focus on work in its many ramifications I do take a stand, at least implicitly, on one issue regarding Rawls's version of contract theory. This has to do with necessary preconditions for just results.

Influenced by the German idealist Immanuel Kant, Rawls assumes that individual bias is directly proportional to the level of one's information and that, accordingly, a social contract is more likely to be just the less the contractors know "what's in it" for them. So he severely limits their knowledge and attributes to them only enough motivation to arrive at a contract. I partly agree and partly disagree with this approach.

I agree with Rawls and others that impartiality is a precondition for fairness in an adjudicatory process—in other words, the sort of thing a judge or arbitrator might handle. Such impartiality, however, is not only inappropriate but is precluded by the role of representative. This includes anyone representing a group with defined interests who negotiates with others who represent others' interests, for example, in collective bargaining or in efforts to enter into a treaty between nations or a joint venture between corporations.[11]

A basic flaw in Rawls's model is that he reduces the role of a representative to that of a neutral. This flaw is fundamental and is responsible for many of the criticisms directed against his methodology. I do not for this reason, however, reject his methodology, because bargaining to contract is so basic to the thinking of people concerned with American labor, whom I envision to be among my readers. So I redefine the role of a social contractor as that of an *interested* representative, that is, one who represents certain known interests of a group of similarly situated individuals.[12]

In particular, I will be emphasizing the considerations that should be on the mind of one called upon to represent workers in negotiating a social contract. Such a representative will have the interests of workers, all workers, in mind and will be responsible for defending these interests. In the process of seeking the best possible benefits for workers, however, this representative also needs to take into account the interests of others as articulated and defended by their representatives. In and through the frank exchange of views between and among interested representatives, a representative of workers seeks the most favorable agreement that knowledge and circumstances will allow. There is a time and a place for disinterested impartiality; this, however, is not that time or place. This is, rather, the occasion for honorable confrontation aimed at a fair distribution of goods, or distributive justice. The attainment of this objective is by no means assured in a world where power rules. But to the interested representative, to seek any less would by definition constitute a failure of responsibility as a representative.[13] So I leave to others the defense of others' interests. In this book will be found only an elaboration of the interests of workers and their communities as perceived by an action-oriented reasoner.[14]

"In action-oriented reasoning," as described by Onora O'Neill,

> we do not have to suppose that there is some Archimedean point, which affords the only correct perspective on all human predicaments and possibilities. We have only to assume that the agents and agencies in a particular

context have a 'moral starting point'—the grid of categories of some outlook or milieu—which allows them to raise at least some questions whose
answers may provide reasons for shifting the starting point.[15]

Toward this end a series of topics will be considered, each of which is approached as a body of information that a workers' representative should know
about to represent adequately the interests of workers. The different topics are
interrelated, then, by virtue of their potential use. But they are also interrelated
cumulatively inasmuch as they contribute to increasingly theoretical considerations. The introductory chapter (Chapter 1) offers an initial statement of the
issue in terms of geographical relocation of a workplace. The succeeding ten
chapters explore a variety of related issues, first setting work in the context of a
community (Part I: Chapters 2–4), then examining various aspects of work in a
modern corporation (Part II: Chapters 5–8), and, finally, setting the corporation
and its workers in the context of community (Part III: Chapters 9–11).

The three chapters of Part I examine work-related values as a function of the
community in which the work is carried out. The focus of attention here is a
dragon known as "the work ethic." It is often appealed to as a basic norm in many
modern societies. But this normativity is shown to be unreliable to the extent that
a community prefers play (Chapter 2), ambiguous inasmuch as it may relate to
diverse and even mutually incompatible objectives (Chapter 3), and suspect to
the extent that a society ignores its *quid pro quo* implications (Chapter 4).

The discussion in Part I assumes that a community, however established, does
exist, has values, and formulates and enforces rules with regard to work. To the
extent that this community is heir to a common tradition, it may be expected to
perpetuate that tradition as it sets forth its work policies. But as is exemplified
by the struggle in Poland to legitimize Solidarity, a community is not always
free to determine its own work policy. Outside the Soviet sphere, for an increasingly large segment of the working population, transnational corporations are the
principal determining factors. In short, few workers today can look only to their
community to learn the terms of their social contract; they must look also to their
corporate employer.

It would be presumptuous to try to cover all there is to say about the relationship between a corporation and its employees. The issues addressed here,
however, are more circumscribed: meaningful work (Chapter 5), unions (Chapter 6), equal opportunity (Chapter 7), and obsolescence through automation
(Chapter 8). These topics, each in its own way controversial, are not exhaustive
(workplace health and safety, for example, might have been added to the list).
But the controversy surrounding each of them is clouded by smoke from one or
another fire-breathing dragon, such as liberty (regarding unions) and competition
(regarding automation).

The community may, of course, seek to influence how corporations in their midst treat their employees, their consumers, and citizens in general. But the corporation is likely to be more powerful than the community seeking to regulate its behavior. So the analyses in Part II regarding "worker and corporation" are, like those in Part I, incomplete if considered in isolation. Neither, however, is an admission of impotence so long as their respective isolation can be surmounted. Thus will these investigations lead ineluctably to the emerging issue of corporate-community relations.[16]

In Part III this relationship is taken up in earnest, not to canonize the status quo but to encourage intensifying community influence. First to be considered here are ways to tame certain legal dragons (in particular, private property and eminent domain) that have enabled corporations to subdue community influence (Chapter 9). Then the ideological dragons that defend corporate dominance (such as progress and competition) are challenged (Chapter 10). And, finally, a well-meaning but no less troublesome dragon endorsed by social and political philosophers (global justice) is confronted for not recognizing the rights of workers in the context of their community (Chapter 11).

I will attempt to show that from the perspective of a workers' representative the following guidelines for policy with regard to work are fundamental:

1. Work (but not necessarily a job) is essential to human fulfillment.
2. Workforce restructuring, usually decided by a corporate entity, never benefits the workers "restructured," seldom benefits the community or communities affected, and may not benefit even the restructuring corporation.
3. The way in which and the extent to which workforce restructuring is carried out is a function of human choice; so effective value-inclusive policies can and should be implemented to protect workers from the ill-considered excesses of workforce restructuring.
4. As a necessary condition of such effective value-inclusive policies, corporations must not be exempted from, but must be responsive to, moral and legal determinations of social responsibility.
5. In sum, there is critical need for a new social contract that will redefine corporate interests in relation to the primordial concern of any community to maintain the social welfare of its people, including workers and their families.

A summary account of what I will be arguing appears as Conclusions at the end of the book.

Chapter

1

Corporations and Communities

THERE IS A gut-level feeling, especially among those most immediately affected, that a plant closing or any other traumatic workforce restructuring must be unjust. But the instincts of corporate decision makers and their libertarian supporters engender no such feeling. As a result, at least in a capitalist society, anyone who doubts the propriety of this most literal form of moving and shaking is assumed to have the burden of proof. So be it, then. The question must be asked: Under what conditions, if any, is a workforce restructuring unjust?

A person eager to be fair might answer that a workforce restructuring is unjust if the interests of any party involved in the restructuring are seriously undermined. And this answer is of some polemical use. But its theoretical force is diminished inasmuch as these restructurings affect a wide range of persons and institutions other than those most immediately and obviously "involved," with some benefiting more, at least proportionally, than others are harmed. These beneficiaries of the workforce restructuring might, in turn, be located far from those who are harmed. Moreover, even if they are members of some society, they may not be in any ordinary sense members of the same society. This is especially the case with regard to workers whose employer is a transnational corporation engaged in globalization.

Globalization is the cumulative consequence of corporate plant location decisions made on the basis of an assessment of the most favorable business climates in the world, as determined by such factors as government tax policies and workplace health and safety regulations, infrastructure, the status of unions, the compatibility of available technology and local workforce skills, and local wage levels. In short, it is a global strategy for identifying and exploiting the means and relations of production most advantageous to the owner. How, then, against this global background can the justice or injustice of a workforce restructuring be determined?

Among Anglophone social and political philosophers (at least those who

14

think of themselves as liberal) it is widely assumed that questions of justice are best handled by applying some version of a social contract theory, especially (in recent years) that of John Rawls. And at first glance one might suppose that Rawls's conception of justice as fairness is applicable beyond the confines of a nation-state. But it is not as easy as that. Rawls neither draws nor allows for any distinction between nation-states as they are separately contracted into existence; and in this way he actually discourages a global agenda by blurring the distinguishing characteristics of any society with regard to both time and space.

Rawls's contractors are expected to arrive at principles of justice without knowing to which generation they belong or to what level of civilization and culture their society has attained. But the history of conquest and enslavement is enough to suggest that *time* is a factor in deciding the justice of workforce restructuring. As for *space,* the contractors must decide about justice while oblivious of their society's boundaries and its degree of penetration into or by another society or societies (leaving all of this unquestioningly to international law). But technology transfer in general and plant relocation in particular frequently affect two or more geopolitically distinct places very differently. To establish conditions of justice with regard to workforce restructuring, then, one surely needs to take into account a people's geopolitical position in space and time.

For example, do they inhabit a fertile crescent or an exhausted desert region? Are there exploitable minerals under their land or off their shores, and, if so, have these minerals been discovered, are they recoverable, and is there yet, or still, a market for them? Do they have technology appropriate to their environment? How close are they to an advancing glacier, or to a nuclear power plant, or to the opposite edges of tectonic plates? How does their technocultural system compare to that of others with whom they may come into contact? What are the terms of their moral understandings among themselves? Are endogenous or exogenous norms of conduct more just? According to which, or whose, criteria? Answers to these questions aside, do these people actually govern their own lives or are they subject to more powerful others?

As questions such as these suggest, allegedly "global" principles of justice that do not take into account local differences are at best irrelevant and at worst contributors to perpetuating the discrepancy between rich countries and poor countries.[1] In other words, an undifferentiated global interpretation of justice risks overlooking the moral significance of subglobal groups, be they nation-states or local communities or even families.

Rawls expresses strong support for individual-sustaining community, but he does not acknowledge the vulnerability of a community to global intrusions. Instead, he endorses the concept of national sovereignty by simply declaring that if representatives of nations were to meet behind the veil of ignorance, they would come up with the principles that constitute the law of nations, including the equalizing rights of self-determination and self-defense.[2] To the more sophisticated globalist, such perfunctory consideration of the components of global justice is clearly inadequate. Charles Beitz, for example, rightly argues that national self-sufficiency is a myth in a world in which an extremely unequal distribution of resources leaves some nations economically dependent on others. He also points out, without going into details, that intrusions by corporate entities are particularly responsible for the diminished significance of national borders. Having so stated the problem, Beitz proposes that Rawls's difference principle, which requires tending to the needs of the least advantaged, be applied globally. This, he believes, can be done even in the absence of a world government.[3] These matters will be considered in some detail in Chapter 11. Here at the outset it is enough to guard against the danger of thinking about justice in such exclusively global terms that local factors are obscured. For this purpose, Julius Stone's notion of a justice-constituency is helpful.

A justice-constituency, according to Stone, involves "the claimants and beneficiaries of justice in concrete times and places, with their biological endowments and social environments, and their limited and tentative envisionings of the future." It is typically coterminous with a nation-state, he says, but might just as well be a "postulated justice-constituency of mankind."[4] I would add, with a view to problems regarding work, that it often involves a social unit less complex than a nation-state.

Consider in particular the question of workforce restructuring. To the extent that only a company's global strategy is deemed to be at issue, and the denationalized leaders of a nation-state are compliant, the interests of more localized justice-constituencies are disregarded. With this in mind, I shall use the term *community* to mean abstractly just such a geographically localized complex of legitimate interests and concretely the human beings who assign these interests moral priority.[5]

It would, of course, be an oversimplification to say that each and every workforce restructuring involves two communities, one that experiences a plant closing and the other a plant opening. But this oversimplification does suggest a device for describing the often conflicting interests at stake in a transnational restructuring, namely, as a kind of journey. Imagine that those harmed are at the "point of departure" of a plant relocation and those somehow benefiting are at the "destination." Using this imagery, I propose to consider first communities at a point of departure of a workplace restructuring (exemplified by situations in the United States) and then some communities at a destination. My objective is to suggest, first, that community interests constitute a moral and also arguably a legal basis for limiting workforce restructuring, and second, that justice will prevail in the transnational arena only if it calls for a community-oriented limit on corporations.

Corporation and Community in America

The relationship between corporation and community in America is, at bottom, very straightforward. Corporations go where they want and do, for the most part, what they like. Communities attempt to deal with this one-sided relationship as well as they can. But workforce restructuring is considered a business necessity. What results is a dependency relationship, as can be seen in a rust-belt state like Indiana; but people are becoming less tolerant in this regard.

The Reign of "Business Necessity"

Even the staunchest defenders of American business concede that some workforce restructuring over the last several decades has harmed some communities. They excuse this harm, however, by appealing to "business necessity." Against this excuse, communities have little recourse, especially when the decision in question is said to be required to meet global competition. Even unions, however reluctantly, have generally been cooperative. The United Auto Workers' (UAW) agreement with auto manufacturers in 1949 was open to "technological progress," as were mine worker contracts negotiated by John L. Lewis, and longshoremen's contracts that acquiesced in new crating technology. Now come robots, expert systems, artificial intelligence, and, before long, automatic factories. Unemployment and social disruption are inevitable side effects. But whether plants are closed or automated, the adequacy of business necessity as a justification goes largely unchallenged.

Plant closings are commonly defended as a matter of business necessity. Many labor-intensive plants have been closed in recent years in the United States, especially in areas that developed industrially at an earlier stage in our history: the so-called rust belt. Why is this the case? Some blame rising labor costs (hence the emphasis on wage "concessions" in the 1980s). Others, including experts at the International Labor Organization (ILO), prefer to blame "the importance of technological innovation as a means of [meeting] competition." [6] The pressure of competition may generate a desire to innovate. But it may also inspire a company to find an environment in which "cheap labor" is available rather than one in which innovation can most easily be introduced. The consideration that tips the balance may be an opportunity to "get out from under" a union.

Unions, meanwhile, lobby for "domestic content" legislation, and bumper stickers say "Buy American." But the consumer, however patriotic, is finding it difficult to satisfy high-technology needs with American-made products (except for those with military applications). Zenith is the only U.S. company still manufacturing television receivers; and most of the components of an IBM-PC are manufactured abroad. The dispersal of manufacturing capability that these examples suggest is duplicated in many different industries.

Auto and truck manufacturing is, of course, a much discussed example of this trend.[7] Auto imports into the United States have more than doubled from under 1.5 million units in 1976 to well over 3 million units in 1987. During most of that period, the percentage of U.S. models manufactured abroad constituted around 5% of the total number of imports, but in 1987 it was over 11%. In 1987 over 30% of all autos registered in the United States were manufactured by foreign-owned companies (up from 15% in 1971). The following year, only 29% of the 41.4 million autos sold in the United States were imported by foreign-owned companies. The decline is attributed to a weaker dollar; but the same economics bring about a comparable increase in "transplants" (autos manufactured in U.S. plants that are owned partly or wholly by foreign companies, principally Japanese). In cars domestically produced by the Big Three, 25% of the parts are imported, and by 1995, according to U.S. Department of Commerce estimates, this will rise to 29%.

In this shifting economic climate, U.S. manufacturers look to foreign production and sales for increased profits. Ford Motor Company failed to come up with a uniform multinationally manufactured "world car" that would be invulnerable to any local labor unrest. But a weaker dollar inspired U.S. auto manufacturers to expand overseas production, especially in Europe, because earnings from sales there were converted at a higher rate of exchange. As a general trend, the production of vehicles is taking place more and more in other parts of the world. In 1978, North America (including Canada and Mexico) was responsible for 40% of the 42 million vehicles produced worldwide; but in 1987 this region produced only 28.5% of the world's total of just under 45 million vehicles. The number of vehicles produced in North America declined by 15.4% while production in Europe rose 9.7% and in Asia, 39.2%.

Of course, many of the "foreign" companies whose imports into the United States upset the balance of trade are themselves American-based companies or at least are the beneficiaries of heavy investments made by American-based companies. So xenophobic rhetoric is not entirely appropriate with regard to imported goods that "compete" against domestic products and thereby contribute to the "trade imbalance" that has brought the United States to the status of being the world's largest debtor nation. For example, by 1970 General Electric (GE) owned the single largest block of shares in the Japanese electronics firm Toshiba (223 million) as well as 40% of its subsidiary, Toshiba Electronics Systems Co., Ltd. It has twenty-four licensing agreements with both companies and a total of over sixty with Japanese firms to make products that are sold all over the world under the GE label. It buys its microwave ovens and its room air conditioners from

Pacific Rim manufacturers. In 1985 GE spent $1.4 billion to import products sold in the United States under the GE label.[8]

In the late 1970s, at the very time that U.S. Steel was accusing Japanese competitors of "dumping" their products in this country, it was busily investing in overseas operations linked directly to that very competition: partial ownership of eleven foreign companies operating on five continents. Between 1972 and 1978, while U.S. banks were redlining American-made steel, Chase Manhattan and Citicorp were responsible for 90% of $538 million invested in the South African Iron and Steel Corporation. Between 1975 and 1977 alone Chase Manhattan increased its investment in Japanese steel from $59 million to over $204 million; Chemical Bank of New York went from $15 million to $82 million; and Citibank increased its loans to Japanese steel from $59 million to over $230 million.[9]

The list of U.S. companies that are dependent on foreign companies for products is growing daily. Domestic growth is occurring mainly in service, especially at the lower end but also on a more advanced level: so-called network companies that distribute outsourced products. Included here are such well-known names as Nike, Dictaphone, Emerson, Schwinn, Ocean Pacific Sunwear, and Sulzer (marine diesel engines). Manufacturing accounted for 30% of the U.S. gross national product in 1953 but for only about 21% in 1985, with durable goods alone declining from 17.8% to 12%—a drop of 30% in both cases.[10]

Similar stories can be told of industry after industry: earth-moving equipment, industrial and office machines, bearings, forgings, compact-disk players, semiconductors, and (still to come) optical-disk computer memories. Where once we had manufacturing strength, we now might have what *Business Week* has called "the hollow corporation": a service-oriented company that does everything from designing to distribution but whose products are manufactured abroad.[11]

What will be the long-term results of this transformation of the U.S. economy? Some observers see the shift from manufacturing to service as a progressive move beyond drudgery. Others, including leaders of Japanese industry, watch in disbelief as we lose not only money but, arguably, the long-term ability to make money.[12] Such concerns, however, are salient only if one takes into account interests other than those of financial investors when formulating industrial policy. To a stockholder it matters little where a company's profits are generated. Such geographical details are important only to those whose livelihood is locally constrained, the would-be employees and host community of a profit-making enterprise. As even middle management personnel are coming to realize, the rights of these constituencies are limited at best. But why should stockholders be the only investors who matter? Employees also make investments in a work site, as does the host community. Should not a company be required to take these investments into account when it decides the future of that work site?

At present, businesses come and go according to the latest paradigm of a good business climate. Typically, they concede neither to workers nor to surrounding townspeople any effective control over the terms and conditions of their stay. Whatever the issue, be it workplace health and safety, wages and benefits, imminent layoffs, or even a plant closing, secrecy is sacred in corporate America. And so long as other corporations are not thereby shut out of the market, courts consider this to be an entirely appropriate way of doing business. Absent some "right-to-know" legislation, they seldom agree that workers might actually be entitled to "management level" information that affects their jobs.[13]

Automation is a second approach to work-force restructuring that is justified by appealing to business necessity. For several decades, the comparatively low cost of production abroad has somewhat blunted management's interest in automation as the key to making profits without payrolls. But some analysts of the corporate exodus to foreign shores see problems ahead and are looking with renewed interest to automation as an answer to the pitfalls of globalization.[14]

Disregarded in this projected solution is any concern about workers. In fact, this very silence on the subject of workers exemplifies the traditional attitude of management that labor is simply a cost of doing business and so should be reduced as much as possible.[15]

Indiana: A Crossroads of Corporate America

In the abstract, the purpose of workforce restructuring is to save labor, which means cutting the costs associated with paying labor. Concretely, workforce restructuring is inherently, even if not intentionally, hostile to anyone whose labor is thereby "saved." So it is easy to see how an a posteriori analysis of this process might lead to the claim that management tilts cost-cutting decisions whenever possible in the direction of cutting payrolls.[16] If this is meant as a criticism, however, it usually falls on deaf ears in corporate headquarters, legislatures, and courtrooms. Under American labor law corporate cost-cutting is good business, unless (in rare instances) it is found to have been motivated by antiunion animus. Generally speaking, then, the secondary effects of a restructuring on the host community are treated as a subject for regret but not for liability.

The corporation/community issue here at stake is easy to illustrate in a rust-belt state like Indiana, which has lost 18% of its manufacturing jobs since 1980.

Especially hard hit by closings are the steel mills in the area southeast of Chicago. Contrary to common belief, some mills that have been closed were not unprofitable. But they were unionized. Take, for example, Inland Steel's massive sixteen-hundred-acre facility at Indiana Harbor Works. Boasting the largest, fully integrated mill in the country, it provided employment for some four thousand salaried personnel and fourteen thousand bargaining unit workers (not counting corporate staff in Chicago). Once "a great place to work" (to quote a sign since removed), it became in the early 1980s a center of restructuring and relocation. The bargaining unit has already been reduced by four thousand employees. Now, Inland is abandoning not only its dated bar mills in one plant but also a flow technology plant and is building a state-of-the-art plant in another part of the state. It wants its Harbor Works employees to accept pay cuts, elimination of many job classifications, and restructuring of maintenance distinctions.[17]

The American steel industry, of course, has long been thought of as mature, mostly obsolete, and no longer competitive. This characterization is less accurate today than a decade ago, but it is still true enough that displacement of workers in this industry does not come as a surprise. But what about industries that are still growing? Consider a few examples of plant closings in the vicinity of Indianapolis —each of which involves a more or less "model" company.

For many years International Business Machines (IBM) was the major employer in the quiet college town of Greencastle. Recently, as a part of corporate restructuring in response to global competition, it closed its Greencastle facility, a parts warehouse. To soften the blow, it offered transfers to its employees, many of whom were long settled in the community; and in an act of corporate generosity it offered to "donate" the warehouse facility to the city and "lend" it one of its managers to assist in picking up the pieces. In the year following the closing, the city persuaded a number of smaller, and more diversified, companies to locate there. The outcome is encouraging in comparison to the debacle initially contemplated. But new employees are not generally as highly skilled or compensated as their predecessors. As a result, houses formerly owned by IBM management people have been purchased by others who want to live within easy driving distance of the Indianapolis airport. No one talks about what it cost the community to attract IBM in the first place.[18]

Columbus, Indiana, is the world headquarters of Cummins Engine Company. Long cited as a paradigm of the socially responsible enterprise, Cummins has more recently acquired a reputation as a company that knows how to cut costs to the bone to keep competition out. While providing more than half of all diesel engines sold for trucks and heavy equipment in North America (but only 2 to 3% of the global market), Cummins paid world-renowned architects to design each of thirty major buildings in Columbus. Of its 19,500 employees worldwide, as many as 11,000 were on the payroll in the Columbus area as recently as 1980 (including, incidentally, a business ethicist). Then came the worry that a Japanese competitor would move into its bailiwick. Management responded by launching a $1 billion program to expand its product line, just when a worldwide recession dropped its engine sales from 125,000 in 1981 to only 85,000 in 1982. Over the next three years it sought, and achieved half of, a 30% reduction in costs via greater efficiency from suppliers and employees. In the third quarter of 1986 the company reported a loss of over $100 million, at which point management announced the closing of two Columbus area facilities to effect a 45% reduction in its local workforce. Most of this reduction has been accomplished by firings and forced early retirements—not of unionized hourly workers but of union-"exempt" middle management employees. Those fired who agreed to sign a waiver not to sue were given several months' severance pay. A dismissed employee who did sue was stopped short by a summary judgment in favor of Cummins because employment-at-will was the unqualified rule in Indiana at the time. Other companies, impressed by this tough-minded response to competition, hoped to lure Cummins's top management into their fold. Then the luster began to wear off as brisk sales of new products did not translate into profits, both because they were underpriced to ward off the Oriental enemy and because the depleted workforce had to be put on overtime to meet greater than expected demand. The Japanese were kept at bay. But domestic competition, notably from a rejuvenated Caterpillar, began taking market share, and rumors of takeovers began to foretell the demise of yet another "independent" company. Those still employed along with the rest of the community continue to find positive things to say about Cummins, but the myth about its singularly benevolent role in their lives is gone forever. Company-community relations will never be the same again.[19]

Arvin Industries, an automotive parts manufacturer employing sixteen thousand people worldwide and thirty-two hundred in Indiana, is the second largest employer both in Columbus and in nearby Franklin and also has plants in Greenwood and North Vernon. In 1986 it acquired another parts manufacturer, Maremont Corporation, and thereby came to have excess production capacity. Early in 1988 it announced that it would be closing at least two plants. To keep their jobs, workers at its Greenwood plant agreed to roughly 15% reductions in pay and benefits. At its forty-five-year-old plant in Franklin, where eight hundred lower-seniority employees had already been furloughed, high-seniority employees still on the job were told they would have to follow Greenwood's example and accept even deeper cuts to keep their plant open. They rejected the offer by a vote of 310 to 73 and then celebrated their solidarity in a local tavern. The city government talks about diversification and retraining as one eighty-employee Japanese plant goes up and another is expected.[20]

These top management responses to "business necessity," finally, are not aimed at mere profitability. Plants so targeted may be profitable without being moved or automated. But the investor-oriented bias of the corporation drives management to seek not just profit but maximum profit. Cummins Engine, for example, increased its sales significantly in 1987 and 1988; but the very cost-cutting that won it kudos from brokerage houses prevented it from turning a profit, so management had to take on some debt to maintain cash flow. Analysts and bankers, who had tried to be as open to long-term considerations as the

Japanese routinely are, decided that a short-term long-term wait was about all they could tolerate, so they took this midwestern star out of their firmament of "recommendeds." These being the harsh rules of the game in the U.S. business arena, it is understandable, but not excusable, that even our most benign corporations are driven to interpret the right of private property as a license to use or abuse a community as it sees fit.

This license, if such it is, extends the old Roman rule that the owner of property may use or abuse (*jus utendi et abutendi*) *just that property* as the owner sees fit. Running counter to this expanding hegemony, however, is the tendency in modern times for an owner's control over property to be limited by various social constraints. Imposed at least in principle for the public benefit, these constraints can be detrimental to the interests of an individual property owner. But they seldom interfere with the mightiest property owners of all time, the major corporations, whose use of property is limited only by "business necessity." This can be seen, for example, in a 1987 decision of the U.S. Supreme Court which requires a governmental unit to compensate a private owner for even minimal interference with the owner's use of property.[21]

As more and more communities are devastated by workforce restructuring, they are raising the decibels of disapproval to a crescendo, and companies have had to respond with something more than sympathy. Faced with the serious threat of a well-organized boycott of its products in the Los Angeles area if it closed the last of its West Coast plants in Van Nuys, California, General Motors (GM) opted instead to close its plant in Norwood, Ohio. The town of Norwood, having just invested in considerable infrastructure to placate GM, is suing the auto manufacturer for $318.3 million alleging breach of contract. The Newell Co. faces a $614.6 million breach-of-contract lawsuit for closing a glassmaking facility in Clarksburg, West Virginia. Kenosha, Wisconsin, turned reminders of promises into commitments from Chrysler Corporation. Chrysler's 1988 profits generated in Wisconsin (some $20 million, or less than half the total compensation of the chairman of the board) would go into a housing and reeducation fund for the fifty-five hundred workers left jobless when the old American Motors plant closed at the end of that year, and laid-off workers would be given full seniority if they transferred to another plant.[22]

These community reactions are manifestations of a new realization that something is wrong with a relationship in which one party, the community, is invariably the beggar, and the other, the corporation, is the chooser. The importance to the corporation of salvaging a "good-guy" image provides some leverage. But as people discovered in Youngstown, Ohio, where three steel plants closed in three years (1978–80), there is little recognition in the law that something is wrong with such unilateral decision making.

In fact, corporate indifference to a community's well-being is often taken for granted even by people who are supposed to represent the community. For example, upon learning that an international air freight hub would be buying out a competitor's facilities and leaving Indianapolis, instead of expanding its facility locally as previously announced, the city's deputy mayor declared: "It's a business decision. When someone makes a business decision, somebody gains, someone loses. In this case we lose." [23] Not everyone is so sanguine about these comings and goings. Goaded by job-conscious unions and especially by targeted companies, state legislatures have been responding with statutes designed to repel raiders. [24] In response to such moves, the raiders and those whose interests they represent complain that such interference is unconstitutional. After all, where in the Constitution is it stated that communities have any rights?

One answer, according to the U.S. Supreme Court, is that "community standards" may determine what constitutes obscenity. This limited endorsement of a community's right to protect itself from perceived harm has not, however, been extended to even more devastating instances. So Colt Industries sued the city of Los Angeles for interfering with its gun business when the city council responded to mass killings involving semiautomatic weapons by passing an ordinance that would limit people's access to these instruments of destruction. Public opinion did not support the gun manufacturer, however, and as both politicians and the gun lobby tried to measure the shifting winds, the arms manufacturer withdrew its suit. This was not the propitious moment to argue that a community does not even have a right to life when corporate interests are at stake. But nothing of substance has been conceded on the point.

How did we ever come to accept such total disregard of the human effects of corporate hegemony? Leaving the sources of power aside, the effect of that power is expressed in the corporatist way in which we have institutionalized our "rugged individualist" notion of freedom. In special cases (such as those that involve subcontracting or only partial closing) the National Labor Relations Board (NLRB) might require meaningful notice to allow workers an opportunity to question whether the move is necessary ("decision-bargaining"). More often it may require notice only to allow workers an opportunity to negotiate the terms of their displacement ("effects-bargaining"). [25] But the Supreme Court's top priority in all these cases is still managerial rights, which it, like others in the judicial system, typically associates not with the reality of a giant corporation but with the nostalgic fiction of a nineteenth-century entrepreneur. [26] As a result, freedom in America is now more the prerogative of corporations than of people.

This may not be what British philosopher John Locke had in mind when he justified acquisition through labor. But he did ease the consciences of colonizers by pointing out to them that since Native Americans had not developed the bountiful land they inhabited, whereas they, the newcomers, were doing so, their labor gave them clear and exclusive title to what they developed. This pro-development theory of property has so totally dominated American thinking that the constraints on eminent domain have served mainly the interests of business without regard to its impact on communities. That could change—partly, as will be seen, because of an emerging sense of community rights, but also because of the more elemental responses of frustrated ethnocentrism.

In Franklin, Indiana, where jobs with Japanese companies are opening up as Arvin Industries talks of leaving, older workers see themselves as having fought World War II in vain. Similar sentiments are being expressed elsewhere, in Indiana and beyond, and on all levels of the workforce hierarchy. The impact of foreign companies—economically, politically, and culturally—is debated in print and in election campaigns. The title of a recent book, *Buying into America*, pulls the strings of xenophobia with a rational pick.[27] States have spent anywhere from $80 to $125 million to have a foreign-owned plant built on their soil. This comes to some $50,000 per job; but criticism of this practice is labeled racist. The Japanese still invest less than the British and the Dutch in the United States, and the total foreign investments constitute only a very small percentage of our total economy. But talk of being taken over abounds.

There is more reason for concern in some areas than in others. In Indiana, for example, the Japanese control twenty-three of thirty-six foreign-owned concerns with assets of a billion dollars. Inland Steel's new plant (noted above) involves a joint venture with the Nippon Steel Corporation to build a $400 million mill to finish cold-rolled sheet steel in less union-conscious New Carlisle. But does any of this influence state government? Leaving actual cash layouts aside, Sony Corporation almost single-handedly persuaded the legislature to abolish an unenforced unitary tax.[28] But the proverbial worm may have turned. Moved by criticism of the incumbent administration's expensive hospitality to Japanese companies, Indiana voters in 1988 elected a Democrat governor for the first time in a generation.

Nationally, the number of foreign takeovers of American companies is increasing and, some say, will eventually mushroom. In 1986, 329 companies valued at over $23 billion were acquired; and in 1987 the dollar value of such acquisitions increased well over 150%. U.S. merchants worry about losing market share and political influence to foreign companies, especially the Japanese, which spend over $300 million a year to encourage favorable treatment by policy makers.[29] Experts encourage U.S. companies to export, and foreign companies in the United States are doing just that.[30]

An unlikely microcosm of this competitive quest for opportunities is the emerging role of Native Americans as both entrepreneurs and providers of cheap labor right on the doorstep of the developed world. Despoiled of all choice lands for the sake of Lockean development and relegated for a century to so-called reservations on the basis of treaties with the United States government, these foreign nations in our midst are becoming desperate subscribers to the doctrine of laissez-faire. Relatively untouchable on their lands by state laws, they first catered to people's love of gambling, then added peripheral tourist facilities— all employing only their own people. Now they are providing companies with tax-free arrangements for manufacturing plants in exchange for jobs. State officials, deprived of taxing or regulatory authority because of a system their federal counterparts so cleverly set up long ago, are perplexed. But the treaties do not say that an Indian nation may not participate in the blessings of capitalism.[31]

Generally speaking, concerns about "foreign intruders" are not entirely without foundation. But the object of the concerns is inconsequential compared to the situation of people in other countries whose very lives may depend on the decisions of foreign corporations.

Corporations and Communities Abroad

A transnational corporation accused of being unjust because of some local workforce restructuring might defend its decision by appealing to a global concept of justice. In the abstract this appeal is at least prima facie persuasive. On utilitarian grounds it might even be beyond challenge if the calculus of benefits shows that harm done to a point-of-departure community represents a comparatively insignificant component of otherwise advantageous consequences. But a utilitarian moral accounting might be less supportive if it considered more carefully the effects on a community to which a plant is moved.

Having already suggested why the rights of a point-of-departure community should justify constraints on workforce restructuring, I shall now drop the other shoe and suggest that restructuring should also be constrained by the rights of destination communities.

For this purpose, one might try to move Rawls's principles of justice out of their unisocietal confines onto the complex matrix of the multisocietal globe. For, by not locating the original contract anywhere in particular, Rawls's abstract approach would seem to allow it to be applicable everywhere. But, unfortunately, such a purportedly generic formula for justice tends to reflect the cultural (not to mention the political and economic) preferences of its creator.[32] And like the legendary Trojan horse, a model for social justice concocted in the Northern Hemisphere is bound to arouse the suspicions of people inhabiting the other half of the planet. For they have come to know us first as their conquerors and then as usurpers of their resources; and, as Scottish philosopher David Hume once argued, conquest and usurpation provide a very poor basis for a wholesome social contract. To minimize this risk of being exploited by outsiders, the eighteenth-century French philosopher Jean-Jacques Rousseau recommended that the object of a social contract be a self-contained community that can meet its own needs with resources needed by no others.[33]

Such isolated autonomy exists only in the abstract. In the actual world, inter- and transsocietal interaction is ever possible and, in a technologically advanced global village, inevitable. What matters, if "on-site" justice is to be attainable, is how the terms and conditions of such interactions are established. I take it as basic that justice cannot be assured if any of the interested parties is not adequately represented in making this determination. And adequate representation presupposes full participation in all negotiations with all relevant information on the table. So the workers of a specific community would hardly be well represented if the terms and conditions of a hypothetical social contract are arrived at by parties who are oblivious of their community's interests. Leaving aside the seemingly basic question of whether they would have anything to think about or discuss that would be even remotely relevant to all actual communities, their chances of hitting upon some good ideas for their own community are slim.

These obstacles notwithstanding, it is just such an abstract process that Rawls would have them rely on to "get it right" for their community. The contractors would meet, not knowing their generation or their place in society; but they would know that they belong to a particular society (a remarkable grant of wisdom to which many people in the actual world attain only with great difficulty if at all). Thus minimally informed about relevant details, they would ascend beyond utilitarianism to transcendental rationality and arrive at Rawls's principles of justice as fairness. The veil of ignorance would then be partially lifted for a constitutional convention. "They now know," says Rawls, "the relevant general facts about their society, that is, its natural circumstances and resources, its level of economic advance and political culture, and so on."[34] With only this additional knowledge, he assures us, they could draft a constitution. Then, with a bit more vital information, they would establish institutions; and, finally, with access to all the facts, they would start making just decisions in their actual, flesh-and-blood community. Having thus gradually regained their forgotten space-time coordinates, they would thereafter devote themselves to building a fair "social union of social unions."

This mythical process of deduction, uncongenial even to many philosophers, will hardly appeal to a workers' representative who knows that workforce restructuring is being routinely endorsed on grounds that have nothing to do with a community's interests. Moreover, the interests of communities are as varied as are the space-time coordinates in which they are located. So a well-informed representative of workers will need to know many different stories about many different communities. The following are examples of such stories. In none of them, it may be noticed, is there anything approaching consensus among the inhabitants about what constitutes their society, what everyone's place in it is or, what is still more basic, who is or is not included as a member.

PALENQUE, PROVINCE OF CHIAPAS, IN SOUTHERN MEXICO, 1987

You are a Mayan. Centuries ago your ancestors were dominant in this part of the world and relied upon human sacrifice, among other things, to maintain preeminence in their world. But long ago they were conquered by Zapotecs, then Toltecs, and then definitively by Spanish conquistadors; and now you are only two hundred in number. Impressive ruins outside of town suggest the former greatness of your people. But you yourself live in extreme poverty. You and your people are at the margins of the predominant society in Mexico because its values are based on the imported European culture, which attributes no value to anything "Indian" unless it is respectably pre-Columbian. You do not have reliable running water so you risk dying of some form of intestinal disease. Besides, advancement of the lumber and oil industries is decimating the rain forest and thereby destroying the water table. As if by design, the resulting desiccation is also destroying the ruins of your ancestral city.[35]

CAPE BRETON ISLAND, NOVA SCOTIA, 1976

You live in the poorest part of Canada, the Maritime Provinces, whose people have for generations felt, with good reason, that they are neglected by the federal government. Like others before you, you and your family have (until now) managed to eke out a living by subsistence farming and fishing, especially since the demise of coal mining in this region. Your humble cottage is on land within a ten-mile-square area that the provincial government has just made subject to Special Development Control; but you were already on the verge of losing your land because you cannot afford the rapidly increasing taxes assessed to pay off the $270 million debt incurred for these projects, mostly from France. The increased value of your land is due to $500 million worth of industrial construction nearby, in and around the Strait of Canso, including a deep port with variable-sized docks up to a size able to accommodate 380,000-ton supertankers delivering crude oil from the Middle East, a $30 million common user terminal, a $223 million refinery to be built by American John Shaheen, and a $300 million refinery to be built by Greek Aristotle Onassis, to be followed, reportedly, by a petrochemical plant and maybe oil wells to recover proven reserves offshore. Each of the refinery builders is to receive $35 million in government-guaranteed and subsidized loans. The port itself was built almost entirely by imported labor using materials prefabricated in the United Kingdom. It is said that locals will be hired for unskilled and semiskilled construction jobs but are not considered capable of being retrained for the highly technical jobs that will be created by the oil refinery. As one writer puts it: "Canadians will be getting . . . very little out of [this development]. The people making the money will be the foreign financial interests."[36]

EAST TIMOR, 1976

You are one of the more advantaged mountain people who are being systematically slaughtered by Indonesian troops, armed and supplied by the United States, that have invaded this country (once under Portuguese control) to preserve it as an enclave for Western democracy. Your life expectancy is minimal because someone has told the soldiers that a member of your family favored the opposition party. Your interest in this territory is deemed expendable in view of its strategic importance to the oil industry, both because tankers pass nearby and because there are believed to be significant deposits of oil offshore.[37]

REPUBLIC OF KOREA (SOUTH KOREA), 1980

You are a thirteen-year-old female. In dutiful obedience to your father, who exercises patriarchal authority over all members of his family, you are working in one of the thirty-five electronics assembly plants in the Masaan Export Processing Zone (EPZ) controlled by transnational corporations. Ninety percent of your fellow workers are young females like yourself. You work eighteen hours a day, seven days a week, for less than $180 a month. Throughout your working day you peer through a microscope as you work to meet your quota. Although you wear gloves, you routinely suffer acid burns on your fingers. Within a year of your initial employment you will suffer permanent vision damage. Soon you will no longer be able to do this work, which provides you with no skills that are transferable to other kinds of work in your country.[38]

TAIPEI, TAIWAN, 1987

You used to work on an assembly line in a converted upstairs apartment with dim light and no air conditioning, but now you are a bank employee. Your husband is a quality-control manager at a textile company. Together you earn $1,500 a month and, after paying all expenses, have $500 left. But your extra money is a problem for you because consumer goods are expensive, credit is not readily available, ordinary interest is very low, and the domestic stock market is highly speculative. Your country's economy is already almost totally dependent on foreign-based, especially American, transnational companies. These companies typically exploit cheap labor in Taiwan to manufacture products for export back to their domestic market. As a result, America's trade deficit with Taiwan ($15.7 billion in 1986) is due largely to products made in Taiwan for such companies as Sears, K-Mart, J. C. Penney, Wilson Sporting Goods, Mattel, Schwinn, Hewlett-Packard, IBM, Texas Instruments, Digital Equipment, and—Taiwan's biggest exporter—General Electric.

The American government is pressuring Taiwan to be more accommodating to American imports, but each Taiwanese would have to spend an average of $7,500 (twice the average per capita income) on American goods to overcome the trade deficit. Partly because of the protectionist policies of the Taiwanese government, your country's cash reserve ($35 billion in early 1987) will soon be the largest in the world. If the Taiwan currency is not significantly devalued, foreign companies may begin placing their orders elsewhere. Meanwhile, the political autonomy of your country vis-à-vis mainland China remains unresolved. Under the circumstances, you and your husband agree with others of your generation that you might as well spend your money now while it is still worth something.[39]

DOMINICAN REPUBLIC, 1980

You are an employee of a United States–based transnational corporation that operates a plant in the La Romana Economic Free Zone (EFZ), which is essentially a regime of exception from regulation by the national government. This means, for example, that in spite of provisions to the contrary in your nation's constitution, you and your fellow workers are not allowed to form a union. In fact, shotgun-carrying police guards see to it that you do not; and high fences topped with barbed wire discourage "outside agitators" from attempting to assist you in this regard. You are paid fifty cents an hour, with capital raised locally in support of the enterprise.[40]

TUPECAMARU, OUTSIDE LIMA, PERU, 1987

You are a direct descendant of the once powerful Incas, about whose language and customs you know little (unlike your relatives in the high country). You are a poor entrepreneur. Under existing law, you cannot incorporate or obtain either credit or title to the land on which you operate your business. Your home was built illegally on land to which you cannot get legal title. The "informal sector" of the economy, of which your endeavors are a part, accounts for 60% of the total economy and owes nothing, whereas the "formal sector" accounts for only 40% and owes $11 billion. In fact, illegals are responsible for a total of $8.7 billion worth of housing, including more than half of the homes built in Lima. Not recognized by the government as a community of human beings, however, the illegals are not provided with water or electricity. But they have themselves erected a water tank, and now the government has run an electric line to operate a pump—thus, arguably, officially recognizing the existence of the illegals. But half a million laws and regulations, devised mostly by unelected bureaucrats, continue to protect the vested interests of the country's old families.[41]

NIGERIA, 1985

You are an Ibo, a member of the principal tribe in the eastern part of what is now called Nigeria, where, it turns out, there are quite respectable oil reserves.

For three centuries your ancestors were targets of the slave trade. Then in 1914, a century after the abolition of slavery, the British combined under one colonial administration an area of over seventy-six thousand square miles inhabited by some four hundred tribes speaking 250 different languages. Relieved of colonial administration in 1960, the new Federal Republic of Nigeria, with no reason for unity other than that imposed from without, erupted in a civil war (1967–70) pitting your people against the Hausa-Falani, the predominant northern tribe, and the western Yorubas, resulting in 2 million dead, 3 million wounded, and terrible social and psychological damage. The population, which stood at about 60 million at the time of independence, is now around 100 million. The capital city of Lagos, then at 1 million, has grown eightfold. Twenty percent of the workforce is now unemployed; and of those working, 80% earn one-sixteenth the income of better-paid professional workers. You, like many of your peers, had been employed by the government. But the military junta, which replaced the constitutional government in 1984, has turned to mass firings to reduce the government debt. So even educated workers like yourself serve as scapegoats for an economy designed and controlled by transnational corporations that have established themselves especially to exploit extractive industries: UAC, UTC, British Petroleum, Shell, John Holt, Royal Niger Company, and National African Company. Like many others who dream of living in a country whose people do not pay with their poverty the price of transnational profits, you feel that the basic question before people in Nigeria is "If to be, what to be and why to be." [42]

NORTHERN MEXICO, 1988

You are in any one of eight cities bordering on the United States—Tijuana, Mexicali, Nogales, Piedras Negras, Ciudad Juarez, Nuevo Laredo, Reynosa, or Matamoros. Officially, your town is part of the United States of Mexico. But your town is for all practical purposes controlled by the *maquiladoras,* which are border factories built by American-based companies to process raw materials for exportation into the United States as finished products. The factories have come here to take advantage of cheap labor: 360 sewing and sorting operations in Tijuana alone. If you are a very young Mexican female, you may be employed in one of the "in bond" factories (since 90% of their employees are so characterized). If you are a Mexican male, you are probably unemployed; but if you are married you may console yourself with your traditional patriarchal perquisites. You may also be involved in a secondary occupation such as prostitution or smuggling workers, drugs, oil, or cattle to the north or consumer goods or military equipment to the south, perhaps to bolster some revolutionary movement.

On the other hand, you may be a North American plant manager, in which case your lifestyle is very atypical. You do not speak Spanish so you require your employees to learn English in U.S. border towns. You are obviously benefiting from these arrangements, as is your company and its investors. But it is difficult to identify a society in whose founding social contract you might have been represented. Still less would Japanese companies have been represented, yet they have recently opened a number of plants in Tijuana and Juarez (where it all began) and may surpass your company's exploitation of this low-cost labor market.[43]

SANTIAGO, CHILE, 1947

You are renowned poet and diplomat Pablo Neruda. You reflect on the state of affairs in your country and have this to say:

> When the trumpets had sounded and all
> was in readiness on the face of the earth,
> Jehovah divided his universe:
> Anaconda, Ford Motors,
> Coca-Cola Inc., and similar entities:
> the most succulent item of all,
> The United Fruit Company Incorporated
> reserved for itself: the heartland and coasts of my country,
> the delectable waist of America.
> They christened their properties:
> the "Banana Republics"—
> and over the languishing dead,
> the uneasy repose of the heroes
> who harried that greatness,
> their flags and their freedoms,
> they established an *opera bouffe:*
> they ravished all enterprise,
> awarded the laurels like Caesars,
> unleashed all the covetous, and contrived
> the tyrannical Reign of the Flies—
> Trujillo the fly, and Tacho the fly,
> the flies called Carias, Martinez,
> Ubico—all of them flies, flies
> dank with the blood of their marmalade
> vassalage, flies buzzing drunkenly on the populous middens;
> the fly-circus fly and the scholarly
> kind, case-hardened in tyranny.
>
> Then in the bloody domain of the flies
> The United Fruit Company Incorporated
> unloaded with a booty of coffee and fruits
> brimming its cargo boats, gliding
> like trays with the spoils
> of our drowning dominions.
> And all the while, somewhere, in the sugary

hells of our seaports,
smothered by gases, an Indian
fell in the morning:
a body spun off, an anonymous
chattel, some numeral tumbling,
a branch with its death running out of it
in the vat of the carrion, fruit laden and foul.[44]

These space-time cameos illustrate that abstract planning would not readily translate into just arrangements given the way the traditional concept of private property allows for unbridled injustice in the world. A stock solution to this problem, of course, is to limit rights over private property. But how might this be done on a global scale? Perhaps by globalizing, somehow, Rawls's requirement that a society be so arranged that no other arrangement would be more advantageous to the least advantaged group. On a global scale, for example, the least advantaged group might be said to consist of the set of all populations with significant numbers of exploited workers and/or disfranchised potential workers. But this interpretation of the least advantaged group would be too vacuous so long as neither communities nor corporations nor their interrelations are taken into account.

As one long-trusted company after another resorts to "downsizing" and corporate flight, the loyalty of their employees, including those on the management level, is shattered.[45] Equally disillusioned are communities that had come to think of these enterprises as permanent fixtures in their midst. But why should communities have been so trusting in the first place? For it is usually they that are controlled by the corporations, and not the other way around. Some companies, like the now defunct railroad car manufacturing Pullman Company, literally own the town where they are located and rule it like a feudal lord. Others, like the rubber companies in Akron, the steel mills in Gary, and transnational corporations everywhere, exercise a more diffuse control over the communities where they locate a plant.[46]

Such unilateral corporation-community relationships are common; relationships characterized by truly cooperative attention to mutual interests are not. Frank Lorenzo bought his way into being principal owner of the largest airline in America and then quickly dismissed a third of "his" workforce. Later, in a televised interview, he said he was so affected by the thought that all those people were being "let go" that he had to get away from it all for a weekend. This story is so heartrending it should be a cover article in every checkout-counter gossip sheet. But a key question remains unanswered: why should we have allowed someone, however compassionate, to run roughshod over people's lives just because he "owned" them and, as an added justification, knew deep down that what he was doing was right?

This is not good enough. In this age of brutal workforce restructuring, social justice requires more than empty, inefficacious expressions of regret.[47] What is infinitely more important is that corporations are not just commodities; they are organizations for which someone is responsible, and they hold people's lives in their hands. They *are* people's lives. They must accordingly be made to respect communities as much as they respect stockholders.[48] This is especially true when the community in question is a time-place coordinate of the globally least advantaged.[49]

PART I

Worker and Community

2

Work and Play:
The Obscurity of Obligation

SHOULD A WORKERS' representative
acknowledge that people have an obligation in principle to work? There is certainly strong support for an affirmative answer, especially among those who employ workers; and working people themselves seem inclined to agree. But people have often accepted an obligation to work only in conjunction with such factors as their traditions, cultural priorities, and available technology. In other words, people's acknowledgment of an obligation to work has been more circumstantial than principled. So there are good reasons to proceed cautiously and not agree too readily to an unqualified obligation to work. To make this point, I will discuss, in order, the development of philosophical opposition to forced labor; objections to including a work obligation in a social contract; and a certain ambivalence about work in utopian speculation.

Forced Labor in Fact and in Philosophy

Philosophers, who are known to thrive on disagreement, do agree now that forced labor should not be encouraged. Some might hesitate to say it is morally reprehensible regardless of circumstances, but none will defend it in principle. This unanimity of opinion would not merit mention except for the singular fact that it is a relatively new star in the philosophical firmament, thanks mainly to the modern value of freedom. So basic is freedom now taken to be that just about any practice can be put on the philosophical defensive by questioning whether it diminishes our freedom. Before freedom, however, there was slavery; and philosophers contributed their expertise to showing that that was a good thing. Philosophers, then, have been consistent supporters of the claim that work should not be made obligatory for all, either because slaves need masters or because no one should have to be a slave. In this respect, they reflect a long-standing history of rationalization.

Combine a longing for leisure with a passion for well-being and you create

37

a dilemma: how to satisfy the latter without sacrificing the former? One answer is to persuade others to do the work. But their willingness to work is a function of their level of need, or at least perceived need. The less their need, the less susceptible they may be to persuasion; and their recalcitrance, in turn, returns the burden of work to those who prefer to be at leisure. How, then, are they to achieve progress (as they perceive it) without sacrificing leisure? A solution frequently turned to throughout history has been to forget about persuasion and simply force others to do the work—in a word, forced labor. There are many different ways to establish a system of forced labor, one of them being to keep one's prisons populated and see to it that idle hands do not turn them into devil's workshops. Somewhat less moralistic is the practice of capturing and using as slaves other human beings whose only fault is that they are less powerful. This practice has been widespread in the course of our species' ascendancy from the status of animals. Since we think of ourselves as moral animals, however, we need to justify actions that appear to violate the nobler sentiments we espouse.

The ancient Mayas, for example, believed that they needed the blood of human sacrifice to appease their gods.[1] The Mayas and the Zapotecs, among others, forced captives to play a deadly game of pelote, sometimes with a victim's head, to keep the gods at bay. Others resorted to cannibalism because, they believed, they needed to eat the flesh of their enemies in order to maintain their own strength. Captors and captives alike understood the rules when they went to war with one another. So they had nothing to complain about when a better-armed conqueror such as Hernando Cortés subdued the lot of them in the sixteenth century (or, for that matter, when the current "revolutionary" government of Mexico finds it difficult to fit indigenous people into its social planning).[2] These variations on the motives for conquest, of course, in no way compromise the claim that the practice of slavery has been widely pursued—and widely approved.

Aristotle (fourth century B.C.) wrote approvingly of slavery in his *Politics*.[3] Concerned more with determining the nature of a nation-state and of citizenship therein, he took the more liberal (for his time) position that women—at least those who were Greek—were in a slightly higher category than slaves. Faced also with the fact that Greeks sometimes fell into slavery, he cleverly distinguished between slaves who are such by nature (in general, all non-Greeks) and those who are such only "by law." Household management (the original "home economics") involved primarily tending to one's living property, that is, one's slaves. The art of acquiring slaves, however, he classified under hunting, which could have as its objective either wild beasts or humans suited for slavery. These latter, he warns, can be troublesome if they fail to accept their slavish nature either before or after capture.

A less "biologically" based justification than that of Aristotle depended on viewing war as a kind of lottery. According to this approach, the taking of slaves was justified if those becoming masters had in fact duly won the war that put the slaves-to-be in their subordinate situation. This simple test provided a tidy way to apply the maxim: *to the victor go the spoils.* Anyone who supports the idea that every person is entitled to respect will question the validity of a master-slave "contract" to which one party has consented only because the sole alternative offered was to be put to the sword. But the more stalwart libertarian would rather tolerate slavery than bend on the sacred principle of "freedom of contract."

The singular consideration, on this view, is what two free wills arrive at independently of any of the surrounding circumstances, however pertinent these might appear to be to a governmental interloper seeking to maximize public sector power. Deemed irrelevant by the libertarian purist is the criticism, long recognized in civilized codes of consumer law, that such an arrangement is unconscionable, hence a contract in name only and, in the interest of public policy, best found null and void.[4] Motives for seeking captives, however, have been so many and varied that the spoils-to-the-victor rule turns out to be no more than a necessary condition for the establishment of slavery. The quest for a sufficient condition is advanced by the claim that the slave trade prospers whenever some people see an opportunity for great gain at other people's expense. According to social historian David Brion Davis, masters on the march all over the world have rationalized enslaving others by appealing to the idea of progress: the progress of civilization, the progress of a religion, the progress of moral virtue, the progress of economic empire. Thus, says Davis, "The early expansion of Islam, of Christianity, and of mercantilist Europe involved the enslavement of millions of pagans and infidels for their own supposed benefit as well as for the benefit of a 'superior civilization.' "[5]

Religious or humanistic convictions certainly motivated many abolitionists in their efforts to establish a more civilized concept of progress. But changing economic needs and the availability of alternative technology are perhaps even more responsible for the decline of slavery. For there is some correlation between the date when a given part of the world abolished slavery and the arrival there of mechanization and/or industrialization. New York State abolished slavery in 1827; France and Denmark in 1848; the United States by proclamation in 1861 and, after a bitter civil war, by constitutional amendment in 1865; Brazil in the 1880s; Saudi Arabia in 1962; and the Sultanate of Muscat and Oman as recently as 1970. Of course, legal emancipation may simply mark a shift to more subtle forms of economic subjugation. Great Britain, for example, outlawed the slave trade in 1807 and emancipated many colonial slaves in 1834; but 1834 is also the year in which its Parliament passed the Poor Laws that imposed forced labor on many of its own citizens. And the emancipation of slaves in the United States created not an instant utopia but, in Davis's words, "an exploitive system of tenancy, crop liens, and declining agricultural self-sufficiency."[6]

Forced labor, in short, has long been recognized as a way for the powerful to transfer the burden of work from themselves to others, by virtue of whose efforts they maximize their leisure. It is not obvious, however, just what should be included under the heading of forced labor or what attitude one ought to have about it. It is generally thought to include the practice of slavery. But as noted above, such social practices as those associated with prisoner productivity must surely be included under the heading of forced labor; and, as will be seen, even less obvious candidates for inclusion have been proposed. The question of listing candidates for the category cannot, however, be easily separated from normative questions about the propriety of the practice, in whatever form.

In this respect, philosophers sometimes rank ethical theories according to how strongly they condemn slavery. John Rawls, for example, faults utilitarianism for justifying slavery under certain circumstances. Scholars committed to utilitarian principles, he says, may still toy with the idea that in some circumstances slavery is a defensible practice—in ancient Athens, for example, where slaves served as the underpinning of great cultural advances.[7] He thinks his own theory of justice is superior in that it does not support so retrogressive a conclusion. But he allows implementation of the requirements of justice to be delayed so long as conditions are unfavorable, thereby subordinating proclaimed values to historical circumstances. This tolerance is supported by the arguments of economists who focus on the bottom line and find it to have been in the black (no pun intended) in certain slave economies. Others say that, economic considerations aside, slavery is immoral because of the destructive effect it has on the psychology and culture of those enslaved. And still others challenge the methodological device of separating economic and moral considerations. At the other extreme, some practices that few would associate with slavery are sometimes attacked as constituting forced labor.

Take income taxes, for example. The libertarian philosopher Robert Nozick has argued that taxation of earnings from labor is on a par with (if not identical to) forced labor.[8] In so doing he presumably wants to show that welfarist ("end-state") philosophers are inconsistent in supporting taxation while at the same time opposing forced labor as an appropriate means to some socially desirable end. But his underlying motive is to challenge the justifiability of any nonconsensual government structure beyond the "minimalist" state that would limit itself to protecting individual liberty. In proceeding with this agenda, however, he abandons two commonsense meanings of liberty by finding that it is consistent with wage slavery but not with the democratic processes of a more-than-minimal state.

Granted, some individuals may flourish more than others under identical institutional arrangements, including those of chattel slavery. Granted, also, well-intended institutional arrangements, such as taxation, may not benefit those who are taxed. But to defend the one institution in principle in spite of abundant facts to the contrary and to attack the other because of circumstantial factual abuses suggests a bias indifferent to facts.

In particular, what is taken from the laborer in taxes may be returned in the form of benefits (e.g., roads, dams, and treatment plants), which everyone needs but no one can have without the cooperation of the entire community. But forced labor by definition takes without giving anything in return, directly or indirectly. Taken in this absolute sense, forced labor has seldom existed on the face of the earth. Even in the Nazi death camps those still able to work were afforded a place to sleep at night. Chained rowers on the Roman galleys were given enough food and water to sustain them in their monotonous endeavor. The inmates on a penal farm can at least count off another day toward their eventual release. So in some respects the difference between forced labor and unpleasant employment is one of degree rather than of kind. There is, however, clearly a difference in purpose between feeding a rower enough to keep a ship going and paying a rower enough so that he might live a satisfactory life before and after his hours at the oars. Yet even the most obvious line of demarcation, namely, the theoretical or legal freedom to quit in one situation but not in the other, may be quite meaningless in a given case. Granted, not all slaves have lived out their work lives without any amenities; but it is also the case that many workers are maneuvered into a situation that requires them to choose between taking a particular job or starving. So Nozick's rationalization of wage slavery is based on an unwarranted comparison between empirical findings and theoretical assertions when he argues that a person who "agrees" to take the only work available to avoid starvation is acting freely.[9] Freedom thus understood is merely a recognition of necessity; and if such usage is endorsed, democracy and tyranny are indistinguishable, at least in the so-called private sector.

These speculations on the meaning of forced labor show, in a sense, that philosophy is too serious to leave to philosophers. For human beings over the course of history have dedicated themselves to the task of getting others to do their work; and they have not always sought to achieve this objective by means of moral persuasion. What sets apart the Israelites who made bricks for a hard-hearted pharaoh is that they had Moses to lead them out of bondage. The account of this liberation in Exodus is a remarkable statement of the case against forced labor. Indeed, even to have recognized certain work arrangements as constituting what we today call forced labor is a significant advancement in human ideals. This aversion to forced labor is, of course, entirely consistent with the aspiration for leisure. And in the absence of any pressing social need, one might harbor both without upsetting either the universe or one's neighbors. But as will become clearer below, the order of priorities may be determined by circumstances.

As we will see in the next chapter, Christian attitudes with regard to work were ambivalent up through the high Middle Ages, when there was apparently a

large surplus of laborers. All of this eventually changed. Jacques Le Goff cites
a variety of medieval regulations and learned opinions that, borrowing from the
Justinian code, condemn idle and able-bodied beggars.[10] Social historian Karl
de Schweinitz, on the other hand, finds that in England, at least, the change of
policy came about quite suddenly in the first half of the fourteenth century. In
quick succession, he notes, western Europe was decimated first by famine and
then by the Black Death, which swept across the continent from Constantinople
in 1347 and by 1349 had eliminated over a third of the population of England.
The resulting sharp reduction in the labor supply led to the Statute of Laborers
(1349), which accommodated English landowners' need for agricultural workers
by forbidding the able-bodied to beg, travel, or demand more than customary
wages and requiring them to labor for their livelihood. Or, as de Schweinitz puts
it, "The King and his lords saw begging, movement and vagrancy, and the labor
shortage as essentially the same problem, to be dealt with in one law." [11]

This simplistic appraisal did not prevail. For the problem of poverty had
many causes, including not only plague but also crop failures, the dissolution of
monasteries, reorientation of arable land to sheep raising to serve the new cloth
industry, chronic inflation, and the failure to reintroduce veterans of a protracted
war into society. So at the time of King Henry VIII provision was made for those
truly in need (Statute of 1531). But able-bodied loafers were subject first to public whipping in the nude, then to whipping plus loss of part of one's right ear,
then if still not willing to "put himself to labor like as a true man oweth to do,"
to "pains and execution of death" (Statute of 1536). Then under Elizabeth I a
new official known as overseer of the poor was empowered to put poor people to
work and to imprison those who refused or performed unsatisfactorily (a somewhat primitive approach to vocational training). Meanwhile, on the Continent,
Emperor Charles V was issuing decrees to outlaw begging.[12] It was in this context
that Protestant reformers put forward their views about the obligation to work, as
we shall see.

In the centuries that followed, people thought of additional ways to coerce
other people into doing the work they wanted done. In some instances the coercion was indirect, through such devices as land enclosure and then workhouses
in England; long-term indenture contracts in the colonial period and immediately
after the Civil War in the United States (and in the twentieth century in Southeast
Asia and Latin America); and the assessment of a hut tax payable only through
work under various colonial regimes in Africa. Direct coercion was applied to
obtain agricultural workers in the pre–Civil War U.S. South and, more recently,
in the USSR.

At the very dawn of the Industrial Revolution, Georg W. F. Hegel developed
a singularly nonrevolutionary way to explain the modern idea of freedom and
what it means philosophically. In his *Phenomenology of Spirit*, he applies a logic

of opposites to the imaginary situation known as the state of nature to show that the roles of slave and master are inherently reversible. This reversal, however, is only attitudinal. In the very process of doing the work, the person subjected to "alienated labor" comes to recognize how much the other depends on his (or her) doing the work, and thus the relationship of dependency is reversed—not in the reality of economic trade-offs, but in the worker's consciousness. This clever ploy enabled Hegel to view work, especially creative work, as self-expression that leads to self-discovery, thereby challenging the traditional view that art only imitates nature. To the ordinary worker, however, he had little to offer beyond his belief that the highest level of freedom to which humans dare aspire is to recognize what is necessary and accept it.

This definition of freedom is, of course, convenient for those who happen to like the way things are set up in the world. For others, such as real (as distinguished from Hegel's theoretical) slaves, it offers little consolation. During Hegel's own lifetime, for example, the principal experience of slaves in the American South was not one of self-discovery but of self-effacement. In that agricultural setting, before mechanization, they functioned like the moving parts of a carefully designed plant. "Though agriculture was not yet mechanized," says Kenneth M. Stampp, "the large plantations were to a considerable extent 'factories in the fields.' " On the typical small-scale farm in the South, owners tended to work hard right alongside their slaves. But most slaves lived on large plantations on which the master worked rarely, as in an emergency, or not at all, leaving the everyday management of the workforce to one or more overseers. The overseer, in turn, would be assisted by one or more slave drivers; and if he had several he might designate one as head driver. The slaves themselves were commonly divided into household servants and field hands, and each of these groups was usually subdivided according to a variety of specialized functions. And up and down the pyramid of control, careful checks were made to assess both the quantity and the quality of the work done.[13]

Such interest in the efficient use of slaves was becoming an economic Sisyphus early in the nineteenth century. But this changed when the world market for cotton dramatically increased and Eli Whitney came up with a timely invention known as the cotton gin. As a result, the slave population increased from 1.5 million in 1820 to 4 million in 1860.[14] Then the American Civil War changed that forever: the wartime Emancipation Proclamation was strengthened after the war by amendments to the U.S. Constitution that proscribe involuntary servitude; and a century later various civil rights rulings and enactments mandated equal opportunity.

One might conclude from this history that the once-heated debate in this country about whether slavery can be legally espoused is finally over. It is not. The focus of attention has shifted, however, from agriculture to industry. So-called yellow-dog contracts and other antilabor arrangements were prohibited under the National Labor Relations Act (NLRA) in 1935. But when labor unrest boiled over after World War II, Congress responded, over President Harry Truman's veto, with the Taft-Hartley Labor Act. Condemned by United Mine Workers leader John L. Lewis as "the first ugly savage thrust of fascism in America," it was generally branded by labor leaders as "the slave labor act." For, under the mantle of protecting the workforce against communist infiltration, the new law severely limited the organizing efforts of labor.

To what extent the restrictions of the Taft-Hartley Act constitute slave-labor conditions is a matter of considerable debate. But in some respects the outcome of that debate has been rendered moot by another by-product of World War II: automation.

Job loss because of automation is in some respects an alternative solution to the ancient problem of forced labor. Aristotle, in the *Politics*, saw too much to be gained from the possession of slaves not to rationalize at least the ownership of non-Greeks. But in so doing he does suggest that "if . . . the shuttle would weave and the plectrum touch the lyre without a hand to guide them, chief workmen would not want servants, nor masters slaves." [15] This autonomous functioning of tools, only an idea to Aristotle, is now nearing reality as a result of mechanization and automation. And, as Massachusetts Institute of Technology mathematician Norbert Wiener so eloquently warned, this very process adds an entire new dimension to the notion of forced labor.

A pioneer in the development of computers and servo-mechanisms, Wiener foresaw the impact the new automation would have on the workforce and tried to warn leaders of the labor movement about the massive displacement of workers that was becoming technically feasible. In a (largely ignored) letter to Walter Reuther in 1949, Wiener urged labor to take the lead in developing a policy with regard to applications of the new technology, because "any labor which is in competition with slave labor, whether the slaves are human or mechanical, must accept the conditions of work of slave labor." [16] Or, as he put it in a book on the subject, "the automatic machine . . . is the precise economic equivalent of slave labor. Any labor which competes with slave labor must accept the economic consequence of slave labor." [17]

For some, as we will see, the automatic machine is also the political equivalent of slave labor in that it is basically docile, acquiescent, responsive, and, within the limits of the state of the art, reliable. It is these "character traits" that sellers of robots have routinely emphasized in their advertising, thereby implying that merely human workers have contrary tendencies. What they fail to mention are the expanding numbers of people whose skills, however important historically, are now considered obsolete and of only nostalgic value. New skills will be needed; but unless our educational system adjusts dramatically, employers will be faced in the future with an ever more inadequately prepared workforce. The socioeconomic ramifications of this emerging crisis are multifaceted; but a technocratic scenario will undoubtedly appeal to many. After almost ten centuries of trying to persuade one another that our very destiny depends on the work we do, we will turn ever more "paths to destiny" over to machines. And what some will allegedly gain in efficiency others will lose in survivability.

In short, philosophers still raise metaphysical questions about what constitutes forced labor. But the moral debate is essentially over. What stands out clearly through all their views about slavery, however incompatible otherwise, is that freedom has come to be more highly valued than work. With this in mind, a well-informed representative of workers would want to proceed with caution before endorsing a social contract in which work is made obligatory.

Work Ethic and Social Contract

In many, but by no means all, social arrangements throughout history, work has been considered obligatory, at least for some. Why? Because there can be no justice in a society where people are not required to work? Much political rhetoric conveys that impression; so it is tempting to assume that such a commitment might be included in a social contract.

Eschewing originality, one may call this commitment a work ethic. The work ethic is widely praised as a way to get work done: those who work hard do so because they are committed to the work ethic; those who do not lack that commitment. In other words, it is a motivational system internalized by the worker, who responds to its demands by achieving greater productivity. Why the worker should be thus motivated is seldom analyzed. The work ethic is, in other words, a simplistic rationale for extremely complex human behavior. But insofar as it is still taken seriously it might arguably provide a contractarian basis for obligation in a just society. It does not. For not all human beings, be they ever so rational, responsible, and even sufficiently knowledgeable, would agree that they have an obligation to work.

THESIS I. NOT ALL HUMAN BEINGS WOULD RECOGNIZE OR AGREE TO AN OBLIGATION TO WORK. Contrary to the claimed obligatoriness of the work ethic, various peoples, especially at earlier times in human history, seem to have considered play rather than work to be their principal if not exclusive social obligation. This dedication to play has been sometimes preferential, sometimes absolute. The manifestations of an absolute dedication to play in particular have been structured into a broad thesis about culture by Dutch historian of culture Johan Huizinga in his classic study *Homo Ludens: A Study of the Play Element in Culture*.[18]

First, work has not always been considered socially preferable to play, which may be taken to be the opposite of work. Some scholars have in fact concluded that play is the primordial human activity and that work is but a sideline, which, to the detriment of what is aboriginally human, has become predominant in modern times. Lewis Mumford, for example, bases his worries about the excesses of modern technology on the claim that play is the real source of all that is creative in human history. Precursors of this claim, which goes against "mainstream" thinking about work in recent centuries, can be found throughout the history of Western civilization, as will be seen in connection with Thesis II, below.

Second, primitive people do not seem to have distinguished work from other activities. It is difficult to determine at what point in the development of social arrangements such a distinction entered human consciousness. It is commonly accounted for in terms of a group's need to improve performance of different tasks by encouraging the development of various specialized skills—the so-called division of labor. However this may have come about (perhaps by group recognition of the superiority of some individuals' performance of a particular task or simply by decree), the concept of work has not always been front and center in human consciousness. Play, on the other hand, is an important component of the very earliest of social systems—or so, at least, Huizinga has argued.

The principal thrust of Huizinga's pivotal study, written at the apogee of fascist ritual during World War II, is to link ritual and contest as interchangeable manifestations of play and to account, if possible, for their reduction to the cerebral in modern times. According to Huizinga, play was an originary and formative component of ancient cultures, play in the forms of ritual and contest preoccupied peoples in archaic and traditional societies up to the time of the Industrial Revolution, and in technology-driven modern societies play survives only etherally in such endeavors as law, philosophy, and poetry. He defines play as "a voluntary activity or occupation executed within certain fixed limits of time and place, according to rules freely accepted but absolutely binding, having its aim in itself and accompanied by a feeling of tension, joy and the consciousness that it is 'different' from 'ordinary life.' " [19]

This, however, is neither a complete nor a sine qua non definition, because Huizinga identifies as play many behavior patterns or social institutions that clearly violate the terms of his definition and actually adds various further requirements in the course of his discussion. These indications that he is dealing with a concept distinguished by family resemblances rather than, as he seems to believe, with a quasi-Platonic form [20] provide clues to a richer understanding of work.

Huizinga identifies as play activities that violate, respectively, his requirements that play be "fun," or nonserious, that it be in accordance with rules, and that it be done freely. He is adamant on each of these conditions, but his data are uncooperative.

Is play necessarily "nonserious?" He says it must be fun or joy-engendering, but he acknowledges that it can be and often is totally absorbing. He needs this nonseriousness in his definition because he wants to deny moral significance to play. As he puts it, "Play lies outside the antithesis of wisdom and folly, and equally outside those of truth and falsehood, good and evil. Although it is a non-material activity, it has no moral function. The valuations of vice and virtue do not apply here." Seriousness, in other words, is a function of "moral content." So if a combat has an ethical value it ceases to be play, and since "gambling on" or "playing" the stock market borders on seriousness it is not play.[21] Yet he goes out of his way to tell us that virtue and honor were ongoing objectives in archaic competition.

Must a participant in play necessarily follow the rules? Although play is outside the realm of ethics, according to Huizinga, participants are expected to follow the rules in the interest of "fairness." [22] But contest is a basic manifestation of play. So winning, says Huizinga, is crucial—so crucial in archaic societies that violation of rules is an entirely acceptable means to achieving this end.

Is participation in play necessarily voluntary? Huizinga says: "Play to order is no longer play; it could at best be but a forcible imitation of it." Yet he offers as examples of play many social customs the carrying out of which does not appear to be voluntary. These include continuing ceremonies in which competing groups demonstrate their indifference to possessions by destroying them or giving them to others, for example, the potlatch, a series of competitive feasts according to which the guests are required to reciprocate, preferably with a feast more opulent than their hosts have displayed, or the pre-Muslim Arabian custom of *mu' aqara,* which consisted of competing parties cutting the tendons of their camels.[23] (Similarly, males of the Mendi clans in New Guinea play a continuing game of conspicuous consumption by ritually wasting pigs and birds of paradise raised by females.)

How are we to explain these inconsistencies in Huizinga's argument? A number of reasons could be mentioned, but none is more basic than his tacit assumption that play and work must be polar opposites. Why? Because Huizinga thinks the rewards of play are inherent in the doing of it, whereas the rewards of work are derivative. A key element of play, he says, is that "[i]t is an activity connected with no material interest, and no profit can be gained by it." Being outside ordinary life, play interrupts the appetitive process. By contrast, "[w]e do not *play* for wages, we *work* for them." Accordingly, a businessman's claim that " '[n]either my brother nor myself has regarded the business as a task, but always as a game' " "must, of course, be taken with a grain of salt." [24] Not so! Huizinga's radical dichotomy is arbitrary. Were he free of it, he might have identified the Platonic form he sought to isolate as proto-work or, more precisely, as the prototype of "meaningful work" (to be considered in Chapter 5).[25]

Huizinga's first mistake was not to have recognized the functional equivalence between what he considered the "play" of ancient peoples in cashless economies and the "meaningful work" of people today. His second mistake was not to have recognized the applicability to the modern world of his observation about the role of competition in archaic societies: "[V]irtue, honour, nobility and glory fall at the outset within the field of competition, which is that of play." [26] The "field of competition" is, of course, more abstract in a corporate or government setting today than it was on a Mayan pelote field or at a medieval jousting tournament. But both the symbolic meaning and the socioeconomic benefits of success are comparable. All it would take to draw the comparison is a crash course on Abraham Maslow's hierarchy of needs.

Such qualifications notwithstanding, Huizinga's study still supports the claim that not all human beings would acknowledge or agree to a social obligation to work. This support, however, can now be seen to depend not on incontrovertible data but on a suspect dichotomy between work and play. But Huizinga did not invent the dichotomy; he merely repeated an assumption deeply ingrained in his own culture that impinges upon our analyses at many points.

THESIS II. NOT ALL RATIONAL HUMAN BEINGS WOULD RECOGNIZE OR AGREE TO AN OBLIGATION TO WORK. Most of the absolute dedication to play reported by Huizinga can be associated (as he himself did) with the "adolescence" of the human race. If, for the sake of argument, we discount such excessive play-orientation as being "prerational," can we perhaps show that *rational* people (among whom, no doubt, we want to include ourselves) would acknowledge and commit themselves to a social obligation to work?

One bit of evidence for the affirmative will be found in feminist writer Marge Piercy's poem entitled "To Be of Use," which moves from images of useful tasks being accomplished with dedication to the idea that "work that is real" is essential to personal well-being.[27] Many people, of course, share her thinking on this subject. In particular, there is a long history of pro-work sentiment that in Western societies is usually attributed to the values of the Protestant Reformation. Referred to as the work ethic, this sentiment would impose on everyone an obligation to work at least to the extent necessary to provide for oneself and those for whom one is responsible. This work ethic has been closely associated with the rise of capitalism, even to the point of claiming that capitalism would not have been possible without the work ethic. But it has been no less strongly espoused in the Soviet Union, where it is tied to loyalty to the state.

Earlier still, at the time of the Renaissance and the Enlightenment, work was looked upon as having value, even great value, in and of itself. Italians Leonardo da Vinci, Giordano Bruno, and Benvenuto Cellini subscribed to this view. French satirist François Rabelais had Ponocrates train Gargantua not only in the arts and sciences but in the realities of manual work.[28] The characters in Voltaire's *Can-*

dide come to the conclusion at the end of their adventures that willing acceptance of one's work is what makes life bearable.

In the eighteenth and nineteenth centuries some German philosophers, enamored of the idea of progress, looked to work as an especially appropriate means to its attainment. Johann Fichte opposed suicide on the grounds that it represents a wish to stop working.[29] Late eighteenth-century British economists, notably Adam Smith, translated the realities of an agrarian economy into a theory that bases the value of goods on the labor expended in their production. Karl Marx, in turn, drew upon a labor theory of value to condemn capitalist entrepreneurs for being parasites on and exploiters of the labor of others. It was the era of Charles Darwin, in which progress on the level of culture was being explained in terms of evolution, most persistently by Herbert Spencer, whose "social Darwinism" served to justify the expansionism of Victorian England. Meanwhile, Friedrich Engels in Germany, John Dewey in the United States, and Henri Bergson in France, reversing the traditional hierarchy of thought and action, identified toolmaking as the origin of intelligence and a necessary condition of artisan skill. *Homo sapiens* has ever since been viewed (from a paleoanthropological perspective) as very possibly an evolutionary offshoot of *homo faber,* or humans as makers.[30]

Not surprising, then, that the two most disruptive political upheavals of the first half of the twentieth century, those of the Bolsheviks in Russia and the fascists in Italy and Germany, both declared their opposition to lethargy by making work a political obligation. In Italy work was made a social (but not a legal) duty. In the Russian communist charter, work is made obligatory for all "as a means of destroying the parasitic classes of society," and the shirker is warned that "he who works not, eats not." [31]

This harsh but hallowed motto the nineteenth-century French writer Octave Mirbeau reduced to absurdity in a short story entitled "Useless Mouths." An old man is unable to work any more, so his wife stops feeding him, and he dies of starvation. We would be inclined to call this unwifely behavior neglect; but the story is, of course, challenging a social policy. So the claim that the work ethic is a natural obligation does have support; but as Mirbeau's story illustrates, it is open to rational criticism.

In the twentieth century, in fact, there seems to be widespread rejection of the pro-work policy. In the Soviet Union, for example, there is a popular adage among workers that Huizinga would find incomprehensible: "We pretend to work, and you pretend to pay us." Nor, apparently, is people's dedication to work any more assured in the West. According to Canadian philosopher Yves Simon, earnestness about work is characteristic only of American culture; Europeans put more emphasis on pleasure and leisure.[32] As fascism was emerging in his country, Italian Adriano Tilgher, in a book entitled *Homo Faber*, reviewed the traditional attitudes about work and bemoaned the emerging tendency to seek a life of luxury and leisure and avoid work as a means to productivity—except in the play work that is sports, in which new records are ever being sought. This problem, as Tilgher saw it, is with us still; and its origins are lost in antiquity.

Attempts to compare the commitment to working by workers today and that by workers in the past produce mixed results. Some writers conclude, moralistically, that workers today are not as dedicated to their work as people used to be. Work ethic defender David J. Cherrington, for example, chastises Americans on this score, and similar concerns have been expressed with regard to workers in other countries.[33] Michael Rose, on the other hand, insists that lack of dedication to the work ethic among contemporary workers in no way distinguishes them from their forebears.[34] And this applies to earliest times.

Among primitive people (as perhaps among those not so primitive) males are commonly inclined to leave drudge work to females. The ancient Greeks and Romans, or more specifically the ruling classes of these peoples, held work in great disdain, preferring to leave it to slaves whom they acquired as the booty of wars well waged. Such maldistribution of effort they justified, as noted in the preceding section, by appeals to their innate superiority over the losers.

In the early Middle Ages in western Europe there was not even a word for labor (as we know it); but by the twelfth century it had become common to identify workers (*laboratores*) as one important component of society along with prayer-sayers (*oratores*) and warriors (*bellatores*). Throughout the Middle Ages the clergy (the prayer-sayers) monopolized intellectual functions and demeaned other endeavors as "servile" (appropriate for serfs if not slaves), from which they were—all too conveniently, perhaps—banned by law.[35] In that context, it made sense to maintain a list of all the trades and occupations that were "illicit"; and, not surprisingly, almost every activity pursued at the time was "blacklisted" somewhere.

Such dedicated opposition to productive endeavor dissipated rather quickly once the opportunities for economic development were recognized. As the clergy assumed the role of academicians, they looked for ways to justify receiving income in support of their new occupation. It was considered unethical ("sinful") to sell knowledge, so an alternative account was required; and this they found in, of all places, the notion of work (*labor*): it was not for knowledge they were being paid but for their efforts in acquiring and transmitting it to others. Similarly, it came to be recognized that the merchant, once despised as driven by greed, was in fact serving *the common good* by making available to society goods that otherwise would not be available. Thus out of a need to justify ethically what had once been condemned but was now seen as socially advantageous, there appeared the first glimmerings of what eventually came to be called the labor theory of value.[36]

In short, antipathy to work can be traced to attitudes articulated in antiquity, at least from the time people began to recognize work as only a part of their lives. Until the time machines of various kinds began to reduce the number of hours of physical toil that tasks required, work tended to be looked upon as something that needed to be done, but preferably by someone else. Whence the origin of slavery, which some believe first took the form of males "lording it" over females.[37] Whence also the development of fantasies about how it might be, or might have been, to live in a world in which work is not necessary or, if necessary, is either fairly enjoyable or well compensated or equitably distributed or else is done by others. These are the utopian options.[38]

I reject as an unjustified *ad hominem* any suggestion that all who have felt "negative vibrations" about work are irrational; so I consider this thesis to be plausible and worthy of the attention of a well-informed workers' representative.

THESIS III. NOT ALL RATIONAL, RESPONSIBLE PERSONS WOULD RECOGNIZE OR AGREE TO AN OBLIGATION TO WORK. So not all rational persons would endorse a work obligation. The social contract is not necessarily thereby confounded. Perhaps a work obligation could be derived from an agreement entered into only by those who are not only rational but endowed with a sense of responsibility for the broader well-being of society. This would seem promising; but it too falters under careful examination.

Blind, unquestioning dedication to the work ethic! That, says Nathan D. Grundstein, is what a manager may rightfully demand of his workers if he applies Kantian principles "teleologically."[39] His message might seem to have arrived just in the nick of time. For, as some writers have been noting with alarm, commitment to the work ethic is weakening, and the work ethic itself is in danger of disappearing from the face of the earth. But there are signs that Grundstein's defense of managerial austerity is at best anachronistic.

The degree of enthusiasm for the work ethic is in direct proportion to the estimated need for manpower as distinguished from machine power in a given enterprise. This, of course, changes over time as new technology becomes available; so the locus of enthusiasm would be a function not only of the task in question but of the time in history during which that task is considered worth accomplishing. In eighteenth-century America, for example, the work ethic got a good press, so to speak, from people like Cotton Mather and, later, Benjamin Franklin. Their message was perpetuated in success-through-diligence stories in McGuffey's Eclectic Readers, which dominated the public schools well into the twentieth century. But as many industries have turned to more capital-intensive ways of production, the rationale for the work ethic has become confused and the old enthusiasm has waned.

Michael Maccoby, for example, buries the work ethic in the same grave with craftsmanship. As secularized by early Americans such as Benjamin Franklin, says Maccoby, the work ethic amounts to an individualist belief that hard, dedicated work is a precondition if not a veritable formula for success in society. This belief, with or without a religious dimension, makes sense in an economy built on craftsmanship. So he calls the secular version of the work ethic "the craft ethic," which, he says, "fit an experimental, self-improving America of the late eighteenth century, where more than 80 percent of the work force were self-employed farmers, craftsmen, and small businessmen." All this changed, Maccoby believes, when entrepreneurs systematized first unskilled labor and then technology to move beyond dependence upon craftsmanship.[40]

David Cherrington, tracking Maccoby in this regard, diffuses his worries about the demise of the work ethic by noting that improvements in technology and management contribute more to productivity than do "the energy, intelligence, and skill of labor."[41] Such indifference to the input of the workforce is far removed from the attitude that prevailed before unbridled confidence in automation seemed warranted. This earlier attitude was directly tied to the interim strategy of an authoritarian philosophy of work that requires maximizing human productivity in the absence of technological substitutes.

In a world in which at least some human beings need to work so their kind can survive and occasionally even prosper, social planners obviously need to take work into account. But there are at least two ways in which this can be done: by thinking of it (1) as inherently undesirable or (2) as undesirable only circumstantially, as presently organized. This results in two different, but overlapping, traditions with regard to work. Each tradition accepts the idea that much work is unappealing but still socially necessary, at least under present circumstances. Where they differ is in what they think can be done about people's aversion to work. The authoritarian tradition builds on the belief that work is inherently undesirable. The communitarian tradition assumes that work is only circumstantially undesirable.[42]

The communitarian tradition tends to give first priority to people and looks for ways to make the work that needs to be done less painful if not actually enjoyable: the "carrot" approach. The most important "working hypothesis" driving this tradition is the belief that people will work better the more they feel that they share a common bond, and thus have esprit de corps, with their fellow workers. To achieve this state of affairs one might, for example, encourage fellow workers to form a guild, a union, a commune, or even a nation-state, as in the Soviet Union, where all involved are encouraged to think of themselves as co-workers.

The authoritarian tradition is inherently elitist, gives first priority to the work that needs to be done, and looks for ways to get people to do it, notably by appeals to fear or duty: the "stick" approach. The stick in question might be a set of ideas, for example, the work ethic, or, in the extreme, a slave state. Linked together as complementary themes of the authoritarian tradition are the claims of an elite to exemption from some or all work and some rationale to justify imposing the burdens of work on a subservient class or classes of people. The typical reasons given for requiring work of others is that they are being punished or are earning their way to a less demanding life ahead. The typical reason given for excusing oneself from work that one requires of others is that one has more (socially) important things to do.

In recent times the authoritarian view of work has been embodied principally in the doctrines of industrial management. Entrepreneurial strategy with regard to the workforce has long been characterized by an interim rule and an ultimate rule. The interim rule: do what you must to get productivity out of your workers. The ultimate rule: whenever possible, replace people with machines. The replacement rule, the objective of which is production without payrolls, is a kind of technological fix. The chief ideological instrument of the interim rule has been the work ethic.

Many utopian proposals involve an intermingling of these two traditions. In particular, the technophile utopian vision is a hybrid: it looks to technology to satisfy both authoritarian concerns about productivity and the communitarian quest for enjoyment. What matters here is that many managerial, responsible persons espouse this ideal. So we cannot count even on them to insist that a work obligation be part of any social contract. Neither, then, should a representative of workers be too insistent.

THESIS IV. NOT ALL RATIONAL, RESPONSIBLE, KNOWLEDGEABLE PERSONS WOULD RECOGNIZE OR AGREE TO AN OBLIGATION TO WORK. So what if some spokespersons for management would not commit society to a work obligation? Maybe they just lack sufficient knowledge about human needs to handle this part of the contract. Maybe others who are better informed would be less hesitant. There are indications that this is the case, but the weight of evidence is to the contrary.

Largely as a result of the work ethic in its various manifestations, many people do consider themselves totally responsible for their own well-being through work. However desperate their circumstances, they cannot bring themselves to accept any public assistance, which they have been taught to think of as a "handout." As expressed in the slogan "Workfare, not welfare," this attitude encourages people to be alert for abuses of the welfare system and raises suspicions in their minds when a policy of "full employment" is being espoused. For if there really is in the world a "reserve army" of people who are not always needed in the workforce, and if not everyone who wants a job can have one, then not all of them will actually be earning their wages through work. For just this reason the U.S. Congress declined to include the adjective "Full" in the title of an employment bill enacted into law in 1946. In 1978, the Humphrey-Hawkins Full Employment Act was passed and signed into law; but about all this new law asks of Congress is that it go on record each year with a vote for less than full employment. And the situation in the United States is unproblematic compared to that in many less developed countries around the world.

At issue here is the very capability of an economic system to provide employment as a means to subsistence. And underlying this issue is a deep-seated disagreement among policy makers about how subsistence is to be earned. So long as the work ethic is championed, anyone who is unemployed and unable to find employment may be considered not deserving of assistance. "There are always jobs available for anyone who *really* wants to work," the saying goes. So when someone remains unemployed for what is considered too long a time, he or she is thought to be a shirker, unwilling to work. But this, it is argued in opposition, amounts to blaming the victim rather than assuming collective responsibility for the conditions that have led to such unemployment.

This disagreement about the availability of work points to an even more basic confusion, characteristically modern, between work as a status and work as an activity. It is most commonly manifested in the tendency to use *work* and *job* interchangeably. Popular usage notwithstanding, these words are not synonyms. They may even be polar opposites.

On the one hand, a person may work (i.e., be active) long hours for many years without receiving any significant monetary compensation for the work done. Such is the case with millions of people in the Third World. Such is also the case with housewives, especially if they divorce without benefit of a clever attorney. This *activity work,* however inherently valuable and personally satisfying, is *unemployed* and, in economic terms, *unproductive* work.

On the other hand, a job is first and foremost an income-generating *status* (being employed), the activity component of which is secondary if not incidental. To have a job, in other words, is to be employed; and the opportunity for employment depends on the calculated needs and interests of accessible employers. Employment has as one of its consequences receipt of income and, perhaps, other benefits, more or less independently of the amount of one's job-related activity (as distinguished from the amount of revenue generated by that part of the employer's enterprise with which the employee is associated). Work in this sense— call it *status work*—may continue through time regardless of one's personal level of activity. Inversely, this relationship may be discontinued even if one has used it as an opportunity to work very hard, that is, be very active, and even if one's hard work has been productive according to the employer's criteria. In short, there is no necessary connection between having a job (this being a function of, among other things, economic conditions) and being willing and able to work.[43]

The missing link here, it might be asserted, is skill: one who is willing and able to work (an interiorizer of the work ethic, if you will) must in addition have needed skills which presuppose appropriate training. This view, widely articulated these days, in effect looks to education as a technological fix to the problem of unemployment. The demographics of a shrinking labor pool are already under-cutting the urgency of this solution in a number of developed countries, including the United States. Its adequacy is undercut even more, however, by an alternative technological fix that is turning the game of preparing for the job market of the future into a lottery.

Jobs once available are being phased out. Automation is eliminating the need for humans in the manufacture of a wide variety of products, such as automo-biles and refrigerators, through the use of robots and other electronic systems. And the electronic components themselves are likely to be manufactured in plants located offshore in developing countries, mainly in Asia but to some extent in Latin America. Some analysts of the electronics industry believe that the recent development of microelectronics will revolutionize the way many different jobs are done, just as the robot has begun to do in manufacturing. This is already beginning to happen in offices: clerical workers, most of whom are women, are being replaced with electronic devices.

Mention of replacing a workforce with machines, finally, raises a question which some people, notably union leaders in Western Europe, take very seriously indeed. As we will consider in detail in Chapter 8, new technology, especially systems based on microelectronics, will displace vast numbers of workers all over the world, first in manufacturing but eventually in office work and other service occupations. That this will happen is already beyond dispute. All that is disputed now is how serious will be the effects of such a transformation of our working world. One recent study, for example, published by the Business–Higher Educa-tion Foundation, envisions these changes as nothing less than revolutionary, and, accordingly, calls for drastic action. Another study, by the U.S. Congress's Office of Technology Assessment (OTA), is comparatively sanguine about the overall impact, even though it acknowledges that available data do not support any firm conclusions on the subject.[44]

What, then, is to become of work? On this question, opinion is divided. Most people still think that activity work will always be a part of human life. But some believe that status work is on the way out. For the first time in modern history, according to this view, technology has brought it about that there will never again be enough jobs to go around. So, whatever may have been society's need for workers in the past, that need is with us no longer. We have reached one of the goals of technological innovation: to eliminate the need for us to work at a job by inventing machines that will do the work for us. Only so long as technology could not deliver on this promise, according to this view, was there any need to instill in *humans* a sense of duty with regard to work. Now this need is passing from the scene, and we must turn our attention from work, which is no longer a generally attainable goal, to leisure, which we will have in the future whether we are ready for it or not.

Futurist Robert Theobald, for example, envisions a "new society" in which people will work only intermittently, with time off for education and sabbaticals, "because of the impacts of computers and robots, which will limit the amount of human energy needed for industrial-era jobs."[45] This scenario, for all its modern overtones, reiterates the utopian aspirations of working people from earliest times. Over the centuries, working people have dreamed about living in a world in which work would be either nonexistent or at least reasonably enjoyable. Meanwhile, others who exercised control over workers have espoused ideologies that would encourage workers to work all the harder. But now working people tend more and more to associate happiness with having a job, and the managerial class is proclaiming the imminent arrival of a utopia without employees. Unlike its predecessors, this utopia is supposed to come about not through the effort and dedication of participants but as the result of technology.

What the prophets of this new utopia do not ask is whether the end itself, a no-employee world, is desirable; whether technology alone constitutes a sufficient means to its attainment; and, of most immediate concern, whether the end anticipated justifies the social consequences of using the means.

More basic still is the claim that the introduction of technology into the workplace renders obsolete any encomium of a work ethic for the simple reason that there is no longer enough status work to go around. This concern is typically answered by asserting that new technology creates as many jobs as it eliminates. This comforting view is challenged by writers who interpret the data more pessimistically.[46] And the debate goes on. Of philosophical interest in this debate is its impact on the work ethic and on its workfare corollary.

A useful guide to this issue is Israeli social worker David Macarov's *Work and Welfare: The Unholy Alliance*. Macarov notes how we have tied welfare (meaning our personal well-being in society) to status work on the basis of four specific attitudes, which he identifies as believing in the myth of needed work, acquiescing in the "job scramble," viewing work as normalcy, and subsuming work under morality. He calls for clear distinctions among the different meanings of work as a prerequisite to revising our attitudes about work in preparation for increased leisure leading to "an (almost) workless world."[47]

Attention to this very possibility is the hallmark of Hannah Arendt's erudite reconsideration of ancient and medieval thought about work: *The Human Condition* (1958). Arendt traces modern attitudes about work to the views of the ancient Greeks, for whom work, unlike labor, results in a product. Automation renders that distinction obsolete but reestablishes the primacy of contemplation over action.[48]

Absent from Arendt's otherwise brilliant treatise is a recognition of the dialectic of work control. If leisure is a primordial goal, figuring out a way to get necessary tasks accomplished becomes crucially important as a means to the end desired. And in the absence of sufficient self-operating instruments, one is compelled to turn to other human beings for assistance. These others may be forced to do the work. But there are some obvious difficulties with this solution: one may not be powerful enough to implement it; it is not necessary if the others are willing to work without being coerced; and there may well be moral and other objections to coercion.

As we have seen, a society that places a high value on freedom is likely to reject forced labor as a way to achieve goals considered worthwhile. And so it has been for over a century in much of the civilized world, at least with regard to outright slavery. The work ethic, from this point of view, is a motivational substitute for forced labor. Instead of physically coercing people to carry out tasks, one simply appeals to the value of work as a precondition for social acceptance. This approach presupposes, of course, that those to whom one is appealing value being accepted by the society in question. If they do not, they will be persuaded only to the extent that they believe they will benefit at least as much from working as from any alternative means.

In short, not even knowledgeable people (including now our workers' representative) can be counted on to defend an unqualified obligation to work. Work (especially status work) is of value not inherently but only conditionally or circumstantially. The goal or goals to be achieved may well be expressed in abstract or doctrinal form. But, generally speaking, people value work less for its own sake than for the sake of something else. That something else is as varied as human ingenuity can devise and includes quite different and even incompatible goals. Earning one's way to heaven is one such goal (perhaps somewhat more stirring in former times than it is today). Making a better world for one's children still has appeal. And there are many others besides. But the basic reason why people value work still seems to be the most pragmatic of all: to earn a living.

Work in Utopia

Our historical and analytic consideration of views about an obligation to work has called attention to the primacy of freedom and uncertainty about the scope, if any, of such an obligation. So would not a well-informed representative of workers be ill-advised to accept such a commitment in a social contract? Nevertheless, most utopian advice on how to live better lives has (at least until recently) marked out a role for work. Do these documents perhaps prove indirectly that humans think of themselves as being obliged to work? And, more important, do they tell us anything about work and justice in a world that is so different from conditions portrayed in utopian literature? I say no to the first question but a qualified yes to the second. For the role of work in utopias mirrors its role in history: it changes with the "state of the art" of human productivity.

Most utopian scenarios consider, if they do not actually focus on, a model community's arrangements for getting work done. So they could be interpreted as links in a long chain of "soft science" advice about implementing an unchallenged commitment to work. Moreover, a utopian proposal is not meant to be understood as applying only to some particular state of affairs. This would seem to make it a source of ideas for a universally applicable theory that lays down the conditions for just work relationships. But people in utopias are described as working in some particular here and now. For this reason, utopias cannot easily be interpreted as offering a global vision of justice for any workplace in any "here and now." But they do show how the idea of a work obligation has changed as technological substitutes are taken into account.

Why have utopias been created? In a word, to point to a better way of doing things—for reasons that vary with the different authors but generally with a view to maximizing human well-being. And this includes the way humans approach their work. Contemporaneous with the rise and distribution of skills and crafts was a variety of social arrangements in and through which these skills were ordinarily put to use. These arrangements typically subordinated the interests of the individual practitioners to those of a ruling authority. No one who was subject to that ruling authority was likely to state for the record that there was anything inappropriate about such an arrangement. But there is a rich tradition of literature devoted to proposals for better ways to distribute the activity work a society has to accomplish. From the earliest times people expressed a longing for less toil. With the rise of entrepreneurial "manufacturing," however, this longing took the form of works of fiction in which alternative arrangements are described. These alternative arrangements usually provide a communitarian counterpoint to what authoritarians were attempting to accomplish unilaterally but purportedly for the good of all.

In the sixth century A.D., Saint Benedict established a monastic way of life that required in addition to prayer and meditation at least six hours of manual labor a day—a quantity that Thomas More deemed appropriate a thousand years later for his Utopians. When More wrote the book that gave the name *utopia* to the world (1516), he set all the Utopians, men and women alike, to work both at agriculture and at one or another socially advantageous craft—all, that is, except an annually elected group of "syphogrants," about whom More declares: "The chief and almost the only business of the syphogrant is to see that no one sits around in idleness, and that everyone works hard at his trade." [49]

A century later the Dominican monk Tommaso Campanella proposed a *City of the Sun* (1623) as a communitarian alternative to the lazy ways of Naples, "where only 50,000 of 300,000 persons were employed and the rest of the inhabitants were given over either to impoverished idleness or to luxury." Reversing the value system this lifestyle revealed, Campanella says that in the City of the

Sun those who work hardest are deemed most noble (except that the speculative arts are considered more honorific than the mechanical arts). But they work two hours less a day than do More's Utopians.[50]

In the eighteenth century a Huguenot utopia written by Denis Vairasse d'Allais described the happy lot of the Sevarambians (1702), who work eight hours a day without coercion because they like to work.[51] And in 1767 the Edinburgh Calvinist Adam Ferguson warned against wanting to be done with labor because, he said, the activity itself is "the source from which most of our present satisfactions are really drawn."[52]

Communitarian proposals, or experiments, in the nineteenth century differ significantly from all that had gone before in that they are drawn against the background of the Industrial Revolution. For their insightful criticism of capitalist excesses, bourgeois reformers Pierre Saint-Simon, Charles Fourier, and, above all, communitarian industrialist Robert Owen won the praise of Marx and Engels.[53] To overcome the evils of industrialization and urbanism, Saint-Simon encouraged workers to work hard and obey their superiors. Fourier in principle and Owen in practice looked nostalgically to small agrarian-based communities in which the desire for domination would be overcome by rotating workplace roles (Fourier), labor would be seen as ennobling and the source of all value, and all would accordingly participate (Owen).[54] Meanwhile, communitarian experimenters in the United States (other than Owen) looked forward to agrarian settings where congenial intellectuals could enjoy "work without drudgery" (Brook Farm) or where work would just somehow get done (Oneida).[55]

The rules of the game of planning work relationships were irrevocably altered by the dramatic intrusion of Marxism into the debate. As noted, the Marxists did praise the early socialist utopians; but having done so they ruled out small-scale utopian enterprises as ineffective answers to capitalism, thereby adding the very word *utopian* to the list of obsolete ideas. A few writers have, however, consciously taken up this challenge in defense of a communitarian utopia. For example, William Morris in his *News from Nowhere* (1891) looked to aesthetics as a solution. Inhabitants of Nowhere would produce not for a world market but only to provide for themselves what is genuinely necessary. Their labor would be free of drudgery thanks to an artistic imperative according to which humans are to do only work that is pleasurable, leaving the rest to machines. About the same time, Russian geographer Pëtr Kropotkin appealed to the group behavior of wolves and other beasts to defend a kind of anarchist communism that would count on communal sentiment rather than productivity to determine how goods are to be distributed, a tenet espoused a half-century earlier by Pierre Proudhon.[56]

By the time behavioral psychologist B. F. Skinner took up the utopian challenge in 1948 in *Walden Two*, he dared to commit the inhabitants of his ideal community to only four hours of work a day, presumably for only five days a week. Moreover, he has community leader Frazer proclaim that all "unwanted" work has been eliminated. This state of affairs is said to be the result of a system in which the number of exchange credits awarded for a task is inversely proportional to its desirability (high points for undesirable sewer cleaning, low for desirable gardening); opportunities to learn many different jobs and move from one to another are consciously encouraged; and leisure time is culturally stimulating and enriching.[57]

Thus has the utopian value of work declined over the centuries, especially because of the transfer of tasks to machines. But there is still some support for the utopian vision, especially on a small scale. Noteworthy in this regard is the movement that seeks support for "alternative technology" (AT). Robin Clarke, for example, anticipates the possibility of a "soft"-technology society that would replace our present "hard"-technology society; and work in the former he envisions as being quite different from that in the latter. Instead of high specialization, there would be low specialization; instead of being capital-intensive, it would be labor-intensive. Work would be undertaken less for income, as at present, than for satisfaction; and the current strong distinction between work and leisure would be weak or nonexistent. Finally, the concept of unemployment would simply be invalid in this AT future society.[58] Details aside, Clarke calls for a commitment to the value of human-scale work—a commitment that characterizes the alternative technology movement as a whole.

This and other related movements are continuations of the communitarian tradition. And as such they share the concern for cooperation that has played so important a part in the industrial policy of the People's Republic of China. Technology developed in the West is being introduced into that great country but ordinarily only as transformed by "reverse engineering," the purpose of which is to utilize rather than undermine the role of the people in production. By this device, together with a stringent policy of population control, the value of work is being retained in a land inhabited by a fifth of the earth's population.[59] But in most developed countries and in developing countries still unable to resist their power and influence, the authoritarian tradition dominates decisions regarding work and moves inexorably toward an anticipated time of production without payrolls.

Both unions and transnational corporations cite statistics to support their respective claims that plant relocations do or do not increase the total number of workers in the world. The debate, however, may be of only temporary significance, because the agenda of the corporate decision makers is clearly open to the ultimate elimination at least of all private sector jobs. Whence the concerns now being expressed in the United Nations that research and development aimed at application of technology be done in the countries where the technology is to be introduced.[60]

The final stage toward which these forces are tending is anything but the communitarian ideal of all the people working together harmoniously in groups of appropriate size and complexity. Rather would it be, if carried to the logical extreme, a mechano-maniacal technocracy in which people not only no longer work but no longer even exist. Such an end state exceeds the expectations of those who endorse the authoritarian ideal. For this endorsement assumes that the elite whose needs have been served by human workers will continue to be served by the machines that replace the workers. But why should the process of automation come to a respectful halt when it reaches the elite? Or, what is more to the point, who are the elite? Such questions are already occurring to middle management personnel, whose roles, once thought so necessary, are being phased out by computers programmed for that very purpose. Beyond this point lies the science fiction scenario of societies being run entirely by computers and, beyond that, a posthuman era.

The ends if not the means of this mad quest for productivity without payrolls are questionable. For, as noted above, it is not obvious either that humans will be better off without work or that the pursuit of such a goal itself justifies displacement of workers in the present. But to challenge these assumptions one must redefine progress. Difficult though that may be, it is not impossible, as workers in West Germany have in their own way been suggesting. To create jobs for 2.2 million unemployed in that country, the metalworkers' union, IG Metall, demanded a 35-hour workweek in 1984 and eventually accepted 37.5 hours. Spokespersons for management said this might damage the country's economic growth and even cause a depression. But the union insisted that employers could pay for the change out of their double-digit profits.[61] This, however, amounts to a call for redistribution of wealth, and redistribution is one thing the myth of progress is supposed to avoid.

The fly in the ointment, of course, is that progress for some is only incidentally progress for all in an authoritarian context. The opposite is the case if communitarian values are genuinely incorporated into social arrangements. But this requires more than merely reciting slogans or appealing to some mystical togetherness to which no operative policies or practices correspond. Like philosophers, we have come a distance on the subject of forced labor. We will henceforth be reluctant to think of status work as a necessary component of a social contract; but that is in part because the social contract is a time-bound reflection of utopian expectations. This amounts to saying that the work ethic, so called, does not have a definition set down for all time to come. Rather is it a social construct the durability of which is no greater than is that of the social arrangements it is meant to serve.

3

Whose Work? Which Ethic?

GIVEN THE COMPETING values of work and play and the political dynamic of their allocation, a workers' representative should not agree to include in a social contract any unqualified endorsement of an obligation to work. But that is by no means the end of the matter. For the discussion to this point has assumed, or at least not denied, the existence of a uniform, readily identifiable work ethic. This assumption, however, is unfounded. A work ethic, so called, may be associated with several significantly different motives for working, notably to maximize accumulation of wealth or, more narrowly, money; to fulfill one's duty(ies); to actualize one's capabilities, especially in a skill or craft; and to justify one's existence on this planet.

The fourth version of the work ethic is commonly taught to workers, be they slaves, serfs, or factory operatives; and it is taught to one segment of the population by another. So it has been understood not as a universal mandate (applicable to all) but as a statement about the responsibilities of only some of the people. The counterethic, taught to members of a self-styled superior class, asserts that one should avoid work insofar as possible in the interest of maximizing pleasure, retaining self-respect, and fulfilling duties proper to the ruling class.

Now to be considered, then, are the ambiguity of a work ethic and the relationship between work and, respectively, duty, virtue, and pleasure.

"The Work Ethic":
Weber's Managerial Myth

The work ethic was an invention of post-Reformation intellectuals who wanted to pull the world out of its papist doldrums with the help of some tough-minded individualism. Rejecting without apologies any medieval notion of social responsibility for the poor, they took the position that the poor, like everyone else, are responsible for their condition in the world. This is a harsh doctrine as it stands; but its implications were blurred by a theological etiology that traced one's place in the world to God's ineluctable will. Such, however, is the darker side of the presuppositions that are most commonly associated with the work ethic.

German sociologist Max Weber is especially renowned for having sorted out the main characteristics of this heaven-based explanation of wealth and poverty.[1] As he read the historical data, preachers and other agents of attitude formation found motivation for entrepreneurial capitalism in the Puritan version of Calvinism: the theological notion of predestination is tied to the earthly goal of financial success.[2]

Actually, Weber's study identifies at least two versions of a doctrinal work ethic. The narrowest of these is focused on money: the making of money is the single-minded, joyless, and ultimately irrational goal of the work ethic.[3] As Weber describes this ethic, it could be interiorized only by the actual or would-be entrepreneur. There is, however, a Calvinist-based corollary to the entrepreneurial work ethic that attempts to explain poverty not as circumstantial but as a direct result of its victim's failure or refusal to work. This version of the work ethic has been applied even to the unpropertied wage laborer as an incentive to greater productivity, notably by implementing a piecework system. In this derivative form the doctrinal work ethic has served as an interim strategy of the authoritarian philosophy of work. These two versions taken together constitute a reward/punishment account of property and poverty, respectively.

The appeal of this approach clearly transcends ideological or geographical boundaries. A number of recent studies have shown how a work ethic may be founded on the doctrinal heritage of a non-Western culture.[4] It is enough for our purposes, however, to look for the origins of the doctrinal work ethic in Western culture.

For Weber the work ethic is a social phenomenon that he found exemplified by capitalist entrepreneurs and justified historically by Pietist/Puritan interpretations of Calvin. Only in scattered remarks does he suggest the relevance of this work ethic to workers. These remarks, however, provide enough of a bridge to cross the chasm of the social classes.

Insisting that capitalism dominates the worker as well as the entrepreneur, Weber notes that "traditionalist" (Catholic) attitudes with regard to making money limit progress. Fortunately, in his view, there are countermeasures. Motives can be shifted ideologically by recalling that Saint Paul made working the precondition of eating and by emphasizing the link between a fixed calling and one's niche in the hierarchy of labor; and they can be shifted behaviorally by using "piece rates." Less noteworthy is his attempt to map different types of Pietism on to different levels of the workforce. In particular, he says that the Zingendorf branch of Pietism is most conducive to confirming the exploiters and the exploited in the righteousness of their roles. It is at this point that Weber identifies the notion of a calling, or vocation, with fulfillment of duty.[5]

The ambiguities in Weber's account of the work ethic are difficult to understand, given the precision with which the Puritan persuasion was molded into duty-based demands by seventeenth-century leaders. Pulpit and politician combined their efforts to stimulate productivity. But why, one may ask, did this behavioral norm emerge when it did?

During the previous century in England, as elsewhere, public policy with regard to poverty underwent a major transformation. Past reliance on private alms and public punishment had proven to be an ineffective cure for poverty. With people literally dying in the streets and early forms of enterprise emerging, the need for some level of public intervention became apparent. What resulted, especially during the reign of Elizabeth I, were the Poor Laws, which established almshouses and overseers of the poor as the nucleus of poor relief. It is in this context that one needs to read the various published statements of the time on the salubrious efficacy of hard work as a solution for pressing social problems: Richard Morison, for example, in *A Remedy for Sedition* (1536) and King Edward VI in his *Discourse about the Reformation of Many Abuses*. Sir Walter Raleigh in England (like Cardinal Richelieu in France) counted on a combination of hunger and religious goading to instill labor discipline into the populace. The Puritan sermonizers obliged, even to the point of denying heaven to the uncooperative. In this respect, Protestantism was explicitly viewed as an antidote to the sloth-supporting tenets of popery.[6] It affected, however, not the exempt leisure class nor the destitute, but the emerging bourgeoisie, "for whom," notes historian Christopher Hill, "frugality and hard work might make all the difference between prosperity and failure to survive in the world of growing competition." [7]

Such emphasis on labor as a duty could, of course, misfire if tactlessly applied to the indolent rich as well. Some preachers did just that. But others, especially after the restoration of oligarchy in 1660, were more careful to delimit the scope of the duty to those who were capable of nothing better. By the end of the seventeenth century, however, even the aristocracy was prepared for John Locke's protocapitalist doctrine that property rights are based on labor.[8]

Whatever this idea conveys to modern minds, for Locke it was only a way of saying that inherited wealth needed to make room for bourgeois appropriation. In no way did he mean to imply that the "labouring class" had rights to anything more than subsistence. For, as viewed through a secularized Calvinist lens, the poor are exploited because of their own limitations. In other words, blame the victims: if they are unemployed, this is because of their moral depravity; if they are employed, they are too busy laboring to tend to anything that requires the exercise of reasoning power. In either case, they are not citizens but natural resources that must be managed for the good of the nation. Labor, then, is the basis of property—not, however, for the ignorant laborer but for those smart enough to organize labor profitably. In this perspective, poverty is a problem only if the poor are idle, not if the workers are poor.[9] Carrying this convenient logic one step further, David Hume recommended imposing a tax on the poor to goad them into working more.[10]

Comparable attitudes have prevailed ever since among people who favor an individualist account of responsibility that ignores institutional obstacles. The British Old Age Pension Act of 1908 is built on the belief that poverty is the result of weakness of character, so no pension should be provided to one who has habitually failed to work and save on a regular basis; and, as we shall see in the next chapter, similar sentiments underlay recent approaches to "welfare reform" in Great Britain and in the United States. Robert Nozick appeals to just entitlements to make it all sound philosophically obvious. But these paternalistic assessments of the cause of poverty are just too convenient for those who prefer not to impose on the well-to-do any social responsibility for the poor. They are also unrealistic inasmuch as the poor may have limited opportunities to find work, especially during a time of significant job restructuring.[11]

Work and Duty: Is Work Obligatory?

The idea that one might retain social respectability without working is as old as human history and has been carried into practice by such identifiable groups as males in general, warriors, priests, intellectuals, or the superfluous poor. The corresponding social acquiescence in such an attitude requires, however, some sense of being under conditions of more than adequate, rather than of scarce, resources.

The elitism of Greco-Roman attitudes toward work was gradually undermined over time by the comparatively more favorable assessment of work to be found in the Judaeo-Christian tradition. Not that this tradition is uniformly delighted with the idea of working; it is not. Jesus, as presented in the Gospels, was not a strong proponent of work. Saint Paul the tentmaker, on the other hand, told the Thessalonians that only those who worked should be fed (2 Thes. 3:10). The resulting ambivalence about work was perpetuated by many Christian spokespersons down through the Middle Ages. But eventually, as circumstances came to call for more dutiful industry, theologians managed to find in their ancient doctrines more than enough reason for people to get on with the work. The principal reason: work is a way to heaven. The earliest permissive version of this new theology was that certain kinds of work, such as that of the monk, would lead to heaven. A more expansive permissive version, promulgated in the high Middle Ages, was that almost any kind of work (prostitution remained an exception) could get one to heaven. The extreme, or mandatory, version was developed by the Protestant Reformers, who declared straightforwardly that whoever does not work does not go to heaven.

Jesus himself is not an especially good role model for those who are anxious about improving productivity levels. He talked twelve men into dropping the work they were accustomed to doing (commercial fishing, for example) and taking up a gypsylike lifestyle the emphasis of which was more on talking than doing. To be sure, Jesus was not a "do-nothing," and for that reason he did eventually get himself crucified. But he is well known for his Sermon on the Mount, in which he chided people who trouble themselves about their future more than do the lilies of the field that neither sow nor spin nor do they reap, since our heavenly father can be counted on to provide what one needs. He is also reported to have told his friend Mary, who sat and talked to him when he would come to visit, that this more contemplative endeavor was of greater value than was her sister Martha's tending to domestic chores. (Compare in this regard the Old Testament contrast between Rachel and Leah.) In spite of these ambiguous messages about work, followers of Jesus over the centuries did in time come to have a positive attitude toward work, but with varying degrees of emphasis depending on the background socioeconomic situation.

Saint Benedict is interpreted as having made prayer and work (*ora et labora*) the dual objectives of the monastic order he founded in Italy, and for so doing he is credited with having restored to work the dignity that the Aristotelian taint had put on it. This interpretation is, however, somewhat simplistic. If anything, Benedict stands in history as a dutiful perpetuator of the values of authoritarian rule. He has no respect for "sarabites" because they are monks who consider whatever they think good or choice to be holy and whatever they do not wish to be so as unlawful. The lifestyle of "gyratory" monks, who are "always wandering and never stationary" (who, in a word, imitate in this respect Jesus and his apostles) is, in a word, "wretched." Only cenobites, who live together in total and unquestioning obedience to their abbot, are truly worthy monks. In his renowned and influential Rule he spells out just how the hours of the day are to be divided up, in the different seasons, between manual labor and sacred reading. The former is never to be so "violent" as to drive away the more feeble or delicate brothers; but, he also notes, "they are truly monks if they live by the labours of their hands; as did also our fathers and the apostles." [12] By the time of the high Middle Ages this early commitment to manual labor had been reduced to mere symbolism as the monks left hard work to serfs and wage earners and engaged themselves only in more honorific and less tiring endeavors such as baking, gardening, and brewing. [13]

The holy elitism that characterized "reformed" Benedictinism is also found among the (clerical) intellectuals of the high Middle Ages who depended on institutionalized thinking to earn their living. Thomas Aquinas, a thirteenth-century Italian monk with aristocratic origins, repeated Benedict's endorsement of both contemplation and action but was willing to separate one from the other on the basis of one's position in society. He agreed with Aristotle that contemplation is the highest human endeavor, to which the chosen few might devote all their attention. He also agreed with Saint Paul's admonition that only workers ought to eat—but only to the extent that the work is necessary. It was necessary among the common people, who accordingly had a right as well as a duty to work. They were not to question or attempt to rise beyond their "natural" station in life; but in turn they were entitled to a "just price" (*justum pretium*) for their labor, that is, enough to provide a bare livelihood for oneself and one's family. But, Aquinas notes, in cases of necessity everything is owned in common, so one lacking the basics for survival is entitled to enough to remedy this deficiency.[14]

John Locke inspired English owners to eliminate this traditional, socially responsible limitation on property early in the seventeenth century. But in France, it survived up to the time of the Revolution (1789). For example, in a widely used eighteenth-century *Catechism for the Wealthy* the first question asked is, "What are the sins of the wealthy?" and the answer is, inordinate love of things of this world, forgetfulness of God, and contempt for the poor.[15] Abbé Mery, in response to the individualism of the materialist economists known as Physiocrats, urged more attention to employing rather than punishing the poor. Even King Louis XVI echoed this sentiment by declaring that the right to work is the property of every man and that this property is the first, the most sacred, and the most imprescriptible. A comparable commitment to social responsibility was set in a contractarian context by Rousseau and eventually came to underlie postrevolutionary confiscatory policies.[16] It has survived in its essentials into the twentieth century, with the help of various papal encyclicals and of the political stance of the Christian Socialists, for whom work is a right because it is the means to subsistence so that one who is unable to work has for that very reason a right to be cared for.

It was, however, no more obvious in the Middle Ages than it is today just who is sufficiently disabled to merit care without working. At the time of Thomas Aquinas there was apparently a significant surplus pool of labor. As a result, begging was not only an accepted means of gaining one's livelihood, it was a recognized profession—one to which the formerly wealthy Saint Francis of Assisi had already given spiritual dignity by requiring his monks to rely on it (not, however, without having done work) for their daily bread. But this comparatively permissive policy with regard to the work obligation came to an end a century later, when a situation of surplus labor was catastrophically transformed into one of labor scarcity. To this new problem, as noted above, the secular side of society responded by imposing severe civil and even criminal penalties on identified

shirkers. The spiritual side of society, in the meantime, was able to find a duty
to work in their sacred texts.

People in many traditions are familiar with the story of Adam and Eve dis-
obeying Jahweh and being expelled from the Garden of Eden. Adam's punishment involves a need to work hard at agriculture to get enough to eat. Says Jahweh
to him: "Cursed is the ground because of you; in toil you shall eat of it all the
days of your life; . . . In the sweat of your face you shall eat bread till you return
to the ground" (Gen. 3:17, 19). Read in context, this statement says not only
that man must toil in order to eat but that this conditional relationship between
toil and eating represents a divine punishment for wrongdoing. We humans have
to work, in other words, because of our own failings—or at least those of our
protoparents.

This account of the Fall, as it is called, eventually came to provide in the
Middle Ages the basic reason for working: to do penance and thereby make up
for the taint of the "original sin" and its effects, which are, directly, a weakened state of virtue, and, indirectly, one's resulting personal sins. This penitential
motif underlay Benedict's committing his monks to labor and in the high Middle
Ages served as the basis for encouraging other clerics, even bishops, to work
as well.[17] The positive side of this penitential theory of work is that work can
be the means to one's salvation. And as economic growth became an ever more
important social goal, theologians developed an ever larger list of occupations
through which one could get to heaven. The next step would be taken by the
Protestant Reformers, who came to insist that work was not only an appropriate
path to salvation but was indeed a necessary prerequisite to eternal happiness.
And with this subtle shift in the medieval theology of work, the ancient world
came to an end and the modern world began—built initially on the economically
more congenial doctrine of a duty to work.

Martin Luther still drew upon the just price theory to justify telling people to
work at the trade or profession into which they were born. But he attributed equal
value to any kind of work, active or contemplative, and stressed the religious
dignity of one's work as a vocation or calling. Thus in his little book about vaga-
bonds, *Liber Vagatorum*, he linked the Reformation to the growing movement
against beggars by endorsing almsgiving only to duly certified indigents.

John Calvin pushed the significance of one's work even farther by tying it
in some inscrutable way to one's eternal salvation. Although committed to a
rigorous doctrine of divine predestination according to which human choice is irrelevant to the final outcome, Calvin insisted that the faith by which one is saved
is expressed in and through methodical, disciplined, rational, uniform, and hence
specialized, work. Casual work is for this purpose inadequate, and dislike of work
raises serious doubts about one's being among the elect. Puritanism, which was
an offshoot of Calvin's teachings, drew the logical conclusion that wealth-seeking

is a fine way to assure one's salvation; and in this way, according to Max Weber, Calvin's austere theology provided the ideological underpinning for capitalism. According to another interpretation, however, what Calvin provided was a religious justification for the capitalist's hard-nosed approach to discipline on the assembly line.

That interpretation is certainly borne out by the technocratic moralizing of Scottish engineer Andrew Ure. Ure, the Calvinist ideologue of the Industrial Revolution, explained the need for hard work by associating its pain with that of the crucifixion of Christ.[18] But Calvinism was not alone in its endorsement of work at the time of the Industrial Revolution. Pierre Proudhon, for example, developed an anarchist glorification of labor around the idea that the value of work is directly proportional to how hard it is. Karl Marx, by comparison, was open to the possibility of a work-free utopia, as are some of his modern-day followers. Not so long ago, however, André Gorz, a neo-Marxist student of work, asserted that "after the communist revolution we will work more, not less." [19]

The discrepancy here illustrated between Marxist and neo-Marxist views about work is of more than minor interest. It is at the very heart of a fundamental revision of Marx's views by the ideologues of the Soviet revolution. Marx himself rejected the duty-based work ethic as a device of capitalist exploitation of the working class. He distinguished between physical and intellectual labor and looked forward to the day when machines would tend to the former and thereby leave people with an abundance of time for the latter. According to Herbert Marcuse, this utopian state of affairs, in which the level of unemployment rather than full employment would be the measure of social wealth and freedom, can now be envisioned as an entirely feasible "[c]onsummation of technical progress." [20] But the interpreters of Marx in the Soviet Union have taken an entirely different tack. They have reendorsed in a secular frame of reference that very duty-based work ethic that Marx himself repudiated.

Proclaiming the value of Soviet patriotism and love for the motherland, Soviet moralists endorse work as the primordial purpose of one's life. Marx had sought to abolish alienated labor and looked upon socialism as a means to this end. The Soviets, however, emphasizing the need to compete effectively against capitalism, call upon every person to work according to his or her capabilities for the good of the people. This means that there is to be no negative attitude toward one's work, as is characteristic of workers in a capitalist society. Production having been nationalized, there is by definition no alienated labor in Soviet society. Under socialism Soviet style, one is to identify positively with one's work, with whatever work to which one happens to be assigned, whether it is or is not the sort of work that Marx might have endorsed as contributing to the fulfillment of one's human potentialities. Having thus removed the notion of alienation from the approved vocabulary, Soviet moralists thereby eliminate the basis for complaining about one's work: one labors for the state, and all labor for the state is good by definition; so, the intransigent logic concludes, there is no (ideologically acceptable) basis for complaining about one's work. Of course, as available information suggests, one might very well be contributing to the high level of absenteeism as well as to that of drunkenness. But a Weberian work ethic (without religious overtones) continues to be official policy.[21]

Work, in short, can be a burden. And insofar as it is a burden humans avoid it if they can; and if they cannot they need to have a reason for taking it up. Getting to heaven or simply making a contribution to society are long-favored reasons. But such reasons would not be very persuasive in abstraction from concrete social realities. And the social reality that has usually been of preeminent importance is the use of force by a few to assure compliance by the many.

Work and Virtue: Craft Pride

Largely ignored by Weber, although not by the Reformers, is the fact that work for some people is a way of exercising craftsmanship. Work so conceived can be very fulfilling. But, says Michael Maccoby, this way of working, what he calls a "craft ethic," is dead and gone, having given way to the wizardry of the entrepreneur. If so, this may not be an unmixed blessing.[22] In fact, if the mysterious German writer B. Traven is to be believed, it may even be a curse. In his short story entitled "Assembly Line" a Yankee entrepreneur in Mexico offers an Indian basket weaver a higher price per basket if he will increase his productivity for export. The craftsman turns down the entrepreneur's offer because "there would no longer be my soul in each, or my songs." This beautiful attitude, though hard to translate into market strategy, is still appreciated in some circles. It too is a kind of work ethic, one whose roots will be found in ancient ideas about virtue as self-actualization. I call it craft pride. It is indeed on the defensive, largely because it depends on mono-operated technologies that are becoming increasingly tangential to mainstream modes of production.

As technology makes possible less labor-intensive production, the value of work is increasingly called into question. This questioning has not resulted in any uniform or consistent set of answers. But the types of responses are comparatively few in number. Here they may be reduced to two: the synchronist view that technology has changed only the conditions of work (for better or worse) and not the traditional value of work; and the diachronist view that technology makes traditional evaluations of work irrelevant and inappropriate.

Illustrative of the synchronist evaluation of work is the body of literature that endorses craftsmanship even in a technologically transformed environment. This somewhat countercultural appreciation of craftsmanship is especially apparent in Tracy Kidder's factual account of an ultimately disillusioned computer design team: *The Soul of a New Machine*.[23] In his widely read philosophical novel *Zen and the Art of Motorcycle Maintenance* (1974), Robert M. Pirsig popularizes the view of many industrial therapists that proper attitude is the key to satisfaction in a technology-intensive environment. Norman Mailer even links this satisfaction to masculinity in his *Of a Fire on the Moon* (1971). Such views are reminiscent of Mark Twain and other nineteenth-century American writers.[24] The failure of all these writers (except, perhaps, Kidder) to acknowledge that the human factor can be overwhelmed by technology is counterbalanced by Jacques Ellul's well-known warnings and by E. F. Schumacher's reasoned insistence that the human need for work continue to be met by limiting the scale of technology to what is by that very test "appropriate."[25]

The diachronous view that technology supersedes human craftsmanship is more widely defended. As computer experts work out the fine points of "expert systems" that can substitute for and perhaps eventually replace their human models, there is a growing belief in managerial circles that craftsmanship is a thing of the past. Yet in a survey reported by David J. Cherrington 86.6% of respondents identified the most desirable work outcome to be "feeling pride and craftsmanship in your work." This response was even more frequent among older workers, but it was unaffected by such variables as income, seniority, sex, education, and occupational status.[26] The tragedy inherent in this conflict between informed expectations and personal preferences is clear enough. But Cherrington's survey does provide a reason, if any is needed, to retrace the history of this deep-felt human delight in careful craftsmanship.

The origin of most traditional crafts (including arts and trades) is lost in antiquity. But their importance is apparent from earliest times among peoples all over the world. Three things in particular about crafts deserve our attention: (1) they gave practitioners not only a personal sense of accomplishment ("craft pride") but also social status; (2) practitioners of each craft typically sought through organizations known as guilds to exercise control over access to the craft and over the terms and conditions of its practice; and (3) authoritarians long opposed, and at the time of the Industrial Revolution did in fact destroy, the guilds.

An example of primitive craft pride is contained in the autobiography of Quesalid, a Kwakiutl Indian who lived in western Canada early in this century. In a document preserved by anthropologists, Quesalid tells how he entered into a four-year apprenticeship to shamans, or sorcerers, to learn their tricks and expose them as charlatans. Especially important, he learned, was the "bloody worm" technique whereby the Kwakiutl shaman would heal a sick person by appearing to suck the disease out of the body and displaying it, all bloody, for others to see. The trick was to conceal a little tuft of down in the corner of one's mouth, bite one's tongue or lip to draw blood, and bring forth the bloodied down at the proper moment. Neighboring Koskimo shamans, by contrast, would spit saliva into their hands and claim it to be the afflicting disease. Agnostic as he is about his own technique, Quesalid is drawn into competition with the Koskimo shamans. With the bloody worm technique he cures a woman whom they have not helped with their saliva and ends up defending his technique against its rivals and taking pride in his therapeutic skills.[27]

Pride in less exotic crafts is already found in Greek mythology. As described in the myths, the gods and titans and heroes devote most of their time and attention to getting the better of one another, especially with regard to preferred sexual partners. But even there a certain "craftiness" seems highly prized. More to our purpose, however, is the role of the god Hephaestus, the titan Prometheus, and the hero Heracles or, as he is known from the Latin, Hercules.

Hephaestus, unlike the more aristocratic gods, made his mark on the world through craft skills. When Athene was born from the head of Zeus, it was Hephaestus who made the necessary breach in the skull. When his wife, Aphrodite, had children by the war-god Ares, he ensnared the adulterers in an unbreakable bronze hunting net, as fine as gossamer, that he had hammered out on his forge and dropped over them when they were together in his marriage bed. He made weapons for Athene and armor for Apollo; an urn for the ashes of Archilles; a chariot in which the sun-god Helios makes his way across the heavens; wedges to keep Prometheus pinned to the mountain; and a set of golden mechanical women who could talk and do whatever tasks he entrusted to them. On order from Zeus he made out of clay the most beautiful woman of all time, Pandora, in whose infamous box would be stored all manner of plagues on the human race, *including labor*. But it was the four Winds who breathed life into the clay, and it was left to the goddesses of Olympus to tend to her adornment.

Prometheus, best known for stealing fire from the gods, also learned from Athene such arts as architecture, astronomy, mathematics, navigation, metallurgy, and medicine, which make him perhaps the source of science among humans. Hercules, by contrast, is of particular interest for having undertaken under the direction of Eurystheus twelve awesome "labors" after having killed a number of his own children in a fit of madness—a version, if you will, of redemption through work.

Comparable appreciation of the social value of craftsmanship is found in the lore of many other cultures. The Gauls, whose warriors devoted themselves to inactivity, did nonetheless honor Lug, the god of techniques and crafts.[28] And people all over the world viewed the process of mining as intimately tied to, and no less mysterious than, sexuality and reproduction.[29] Even Jahweh, in Genesis, worked so hard at creating as to require a rest; and man, who would subsequently be "punished" with work, was originally responsible for tending and keeping the Garden (Gen. 2:15).

In the early Middle Ages (fifth to ninth centuries), when priests and warriors were prestigiously indolent, they had sense enough to value what creative craftsmen could do for them. So highly esteemed were ironsmiths and especially goldsmiths that their tools were included in the funerary furnishings of their tombs—a practice which is fully appreciated against a background of legal sanctions for losing or damaging such scarce items as tools. Not all crafts were equally valued, to be sure. As has already been noted, workers as a class were at the bottom of the social hierarchy. But within this class there was a gradation of status, as is illustrated in the sixth- to seventh-century law of the Burgundii assigning a kind of wrongful death value (*wergeld*) to various trades or skills, as follows: 30 sous for plowmen, swineherds, shepherds, and other slaves (*alii servi*); 40 sous for carpenters, 50 for ironsmiths, 100 for silversmiths, and 150 for goldsmiths.[30]

Such payments, presumably, went not to the family of the deceased but to the deceased's lord, in keeping with the proprieties of a feudal system. In time, however, new options became available as the mores and structures of capitalism began to develop. And as they did, craftsmanship came to be viewed as a means of achieving wealth and freedom. A living example of the former is Benvenuto Cellini; a theoretical proponent of the latter is Jean-Jacques Rousseau.

Benvenuto Cellini, a sixteenth-century Florentine goldsmith, describes in his autobiography how he rose through the apprenticeship system to become a favorite of popes and princes. A master goldsmith in Rome is impressed with work Cellini shows him, accepts him as his apprentice, and tells him: "Welcome to my workshop; and do as you have promised; let your hands declare what [manner of] man you are." After making a copy of a sarcophagus in silver for a churchman to use as a salt-cellar, he enters the service of another master. After two years under this new master, he returns to Florence to serve a second time, now with added skills, under a former master of his, "with whom I earned a great deal, and took continued pains to improve my art." As his reputation for quality work grows, he befriends some goldsmiths but arouses the jealousy of others. An altercation with the latter results in his being charged with assault. He gets off with just a fine, thanks to the eloquent defense of one of the judges, who says of him: "He is a young man of admirable talents, and supports his family by his labour in great abundance; I would to God that our city had plenty of this sort, instead of the present dearth of them."[31]

Rousseau two centuries later promises freedom through creative craftsmanship. In his book *Emile*, which is a kind of handbook on how to educate youth for the world he foresaw as imminent, Rousseau warns that one ought not count on any favored status in society because all this may change. Everyone, accordingly, even those in the aristocracy, ought to learn a craft with which to earn a living, if need be. In so doing, one "depends only on his work" and thus is "the most

independent of fortune and men." Some trades, such as sewing and "the nee-
dle trades," he would restrict to women. Men are better advised to learn a trade
that requires manual labor, but preferably one that is clean, such as carpentry,
from which "elegance and taste are not excluded." In stark contrast to carpentry
are "those stupid professions in which the workers, without industry and almost
automatons, never exercise their hand at anything but the same work—weavers,
stocking makers, stonecutters. What is the use of employing men of sense in
these trades? It is a case of one machine guiding another." [32]

In anticipation of the French Revolution that will come soon after his death,
Rousseau eschews all titles, so would not have anyone identified as a master.
Each should rather "prove himself a worker not by his title but by his work." The
goal is not just to know how to use a lathe or a hammer or a plane or a file but
to use it "quickly and easily enough to equal in rapidity the good workers who
employ it." To this end, he says, it is necessary to spend an entire day once or
twice a week with a master, all the while balancing the needs of the mind with
those of the body: one must "work like a peasant and think like a philosopher so
as not to be as lazy as a savage." [33]

Both Cellini and Rousseau convey a sense that individuals who excel at a
craft "stand out from the crowd," meaning from others in their society, who, for
whatever reason, have not developed comparable talents. Little did they know
just how difficult it would become to achieve such distinction in the wake of the
Industrial Revolution. The skewed distribution of skills is the basis for job control, as will be seen in Chapter 5, and the target of deskilling, to be discussed
in Chapter 8. An even more basic issue in this connection, however, is the role
that craft pride plays in providing human beings with a sense of dignity and
worth. For both Karl Marx and Jean-Paul Sartre the introduction of machines has
seriously undermined this most humane benefit of work.

Marx, to paraphrase Rousseau, considered work to be the natural means to
human freedom but found workers everywhere in chains. What he called the
labor process involves not only instruments directed to an object but work as a
purposeful activity. Too often, especially in a capitalist system, the purpose as
well as the knowledge needed to formulate that purpose is imposed on the worker
from without. Not so with precapitalist modes of production. Guilds in India
have assiduously preserved the integrity of each craft against being subordinated
to mercantile objectives. A guild in medieval Europe gave status to a team of artisans who practiced a handicraft based on "the more or less sophisticated use of
tools" for the direct benefit of a consumer. Such "team-concept" arrangements
(as one might say today) were disrupted first by capitalist objectives and then by
technology. Skills are transferred from laborers to technology; and technology
determines, from industry to industry, where and how workers are needed. This
process of undermining the value of traditional skills may occur gradually, as

in the case of weavers in Great Britain, or abruptly, as in the case of weavers in India.[34] But the long-term consequence, in one industry after another, is the creation of a reserve army of workers whose undifferentiated labor has no market value except what may be extrinsically and circumstantially acknowledged. Hence the need for a communist society in which such alienated labor would be precluded.

Returning to this theme a century later, French philosopher Jean-Paul Sartre claimed to find openings for individual skills in that very modern world which Marx feared could only extinguish creativity. This he was able to do, he thought, because he reversed the order of Marx's analysis by building up his account of human labor from that of individuals to that of groups.[35]

Sartre found some autonomy among isolated agricultural day laborers in southern Italy. But more important for his case are airline pilots, actors, and athletes, among others, who transcend the sociotechnical limitations of their assigned occupations. Thus "the *common* is transcended in work itself" by individual workers "*doing more* than is expected of everyone at the normal level of organisation." [36] Such bourgeois accomplishments, however, are not available to the undifferentiated worker, whom "freedom of contract" leaves "at the mercy of material constraints." These constraints involve in particular the impact of technology directly on the workplace and indirectly on the citizenry. "Universalized" machines, more common in the nineteenth century, require skilled operators who derive dignity in their work in comparison to the unskilled laborers who serve their needs. That dignity has, however, been undermined in the twentieth century by the introduction of automated and semiautomated "specialized" machines that require no skilled tenders. Thus the elitism defended earlier in this century by anarcho-syndicalists (skilled craft unions) was justified only by the temporarily limited scope of mechanization and in time became moot as machines massified all industrial labor. This in turn led to mass unions whose members can claim little if any craft pride.[37]

Such observations suggest (and the details so manifest) as seemingly ineluctable a process of deskilling as Marx had discerned. But Sartre surely intends otherwise; for his principal thesis is that human actors remain free to transform their world, however complex may be the given set of conditions within which they are required to work. He died, however, before those incalculably more "universalized" machines known as computers changed yet again the rules of the workplace game.

Underlying all these ideas about the importance of craft pride is a recognition that the practice of a skill ordinarily takes place in the context of a social structure that determines for the most part what will be valued and how much. This is typically done not just by a wage scale but by the complex way in which crafts are organized in the society. So yet again, from yet another point of view, must one choose under conditions of uncertainty, if choose one must, some rules of organization whereby craft pride might be maximized in society.

Work and Pleasure: The Quest for Leisure

Perhaps the earliest and still the most basic perspective on work is that it is a burden. Not just a burden, but a burden that has to be taken up. But taken up by whom? Absent any qualifications, one might be inclined to universalize the responsibility and say: By everyone! But the mule and other "beasts of burden" stand as both instances and symbols of exceptions to such a rule—as does the institution of slavery, not to mention the emerging role of robots. In other words, the very idea that everyone is obliged to help carry the burden of work is easier to state than to justify. In particular, the socioeconomic conditions in which one lives may not provide sufficient opportunity for everyone to work. And this may be the case regardless of the level of development that has been achieved.

Nevertheless, a desire for development and progress may play a significant part in determining how strongly the burden of work is likely to be emphasized. In a society that does not have "moving forward" on its agenda, the amount of work to be done is likely to be fairly constant and fairly routinely distributed. But to borrow a corporate slogan, once progress has become a society's most important product, all bets are off as to how burdens will be assigned. In such circumstances, the intensity of appeals to duty will be inversely proportional to the society's level of technological capability.

So it is not always socially necessary to put every nose to the grindstone. And to the extent that it is not, the burden of work will somehow be allocated unequally, to the benefit of some more than others. To address this problem of allocation, many approaches are possible in principle, but historically there have been only three live options. The first, which is completely feasible only under conditions of abundance, is simply to turn a preference for not working into a glorification of leisure. The second is, under conditions of scarcity, a corollary of the first, namely, to persuade others to do the work by appealing to some type of work ethic. The third, which becomes necessary given the attitude of the first and the failure of the second, is simply to force others to do the work. Only the quest for leisure will be considered here.

Human beings have from their origins had many tasks to perform that are necessary but not fulfilling or even pleasurable. And by far the most economically feasible response to this state of affairs is to dream of an altered reality in which there is only leisure or, at worst, no unfulfilling work. This may in part explain why the idea of a life without work seems to appeal to people in direct proportion to the severity of their working conditions. Historically, at any rate, there seems to have been a causal connection between present involvement in work and projection into the past or future of a workless state of affairs.

The idea of a workless future is exemplified by the glorious promises in Jewish Talmudic lore of a World to Come in which everyone will have ample harvest without effort. More broadly stated in apocalyptic literature: "For men there will be inner sincerity and freedom from care, no unwilling engagement with practical things, and no forced labor."[38] One of Vergil's *Eclogues* also envisions a work-free future.[39]

Remembrances of leisure past are found in many cultures. The Hebrew myth of Adam and Eve in the Garden and of hard agricultural labor being imposed on Adam for his disobedience is well known. A comparable story is told on ancient Sumerian tablets.[40] The Greeks also taught one another that work is a curse, due indirectly to the upstart behavior of Prometheus, and that once upon a time it was otherwise. Hesiod, in his *Works and Days* (c. 700 B.C.), describes five races, one being a "golden race" of people who lived before the curse of work in a place where food grew bountifully without cultivation. Later tradition recalled this as a golden *age* and divided into a modified version that some work was required and the no-holds-barred mainstream version that nature did it all without assistance.

Because some readers of a "history" by Diodorus Siculus took his account of the labor-free and fun-filled life of the Hyperboreans at face value, the temporal dream became for some only a problem of geography. But it was Ovid in Book I of his *Metamorphoses* who set down the mainstream myth in the form in which it inspired subsequent utopian visions. An earlier statement of this version will be found in *Life of Greece*, by Dicaearchus of Mersana, a pupil of Aristotle.[41]

Aristotle himself perpetuated the curse theory of work, agreed in principle with Plato that it is necessary for society as a whole, and inserted an elitist wedge in the form of exemption for intellectuals, who are by definition capable of exploiting leisure to attain fully human happiness in the form of wisdom.

Aristotle believed that the highest goal to which humans can aspire is the attainment of wisdom. Wisdom according to Aristotle involves a knowledge of the causes of things on some level of abstraction: with regard to some circumscribed area, such as sculpture, or to more all-encompassing causes up to and including the ultimate causes of anything whatsoever. To attain any sort of wisdom, a fortiori wisdom regarding ultimate causes, one needs time to contemplate; and contemplation requires freedom from concern about the necessities of life. So, as he notes in his *Metaphysics*, leisure is a precondition for the attainment of wisdom. And this in turn suggests that the freer one is of such concerns, the wiser one can become. The master craftsman knows the causes (or principles) of what is done in his particular craft, whereas the manual workers in that craft "are like certain lifeless things which act indeed, but act without knowing what they

do, as fire burns, . . . through habit." Inventors of arts directed to giving pleasure
are wiser than inventors of arts directed to attaining the necessities of life, and
wisest of all are those who invented arts valuable for their own sake. These latter
include mathematics, which, says Aristotle, arose first in Egypt, "for there the
priestly caste was allowed to be at leisure."[42]

This elitist attitude toward work was fairly widespread in antiquity; but not
all work was equally out of favor. Work on the land, for example, was not considered demeaning. What was especially demeaning was to work for someone
else for pay or to be confined to working indoors, thereby subjecting one's body
to deterioration through disuse. This explains in part why the philosopher Socra-
tes was so disgusted with the Sophists, who offered for a price to teach people
how to "beat the system" if they should happen to be brought into court. It also
explains in part the practice of enslaving others to do the work.

Plato, Aristotle's teacher, envisioned a society in which the many would provide for the needs and the wants of the few. According to the master plan set forth
in his *Republic*, everyone born in this society would be assigned for life to the role
for which he or she is best suited "by nature." For most, this would be unskilled
labor or at best a craft or trade. The ruling guardians, however, not only would
practice no manual art or craft, they would not even take notice of such occupations. The philosopher, that rare individual who focuses on eternal ideas, would
be the most "useless" of all citizens. This arrangement, critics have argued, is
most advantageous to those whose natures incline them to the meditative lifestyle
that leisure abetted by the labor of slaves makes possible.

It has been suggested that the Athenian elite disliked not manual labor as such
but only excessive, monotonous, or unhealthy labor.[43] This idea ignores the fact
that their economic system was based on slave labor and disregards such indications to the contrary as the following: Aristophanes' satires of the Athenian dream
of idleness: *The Parliament of Women* (a dystopia), *Plautos* (on the hardships
of the poor), and *Birds* (about a kind of "petit bourgeois" utopia); Xenophon's
warning that the mechanical arts cause deterioration of both body and soul and
accordingly are illegal for citizens in the more warlike cities; and Plutarch's warning that being a sculptor, such as Phidias, has distinct disadvantages in that one
may become both dusty and sweaty.[44]

For all their differences, then, many different peoples in ancient times relished
the idea of a state of affairs in which they would not be required to work. Such
leisure-prone distaste for work as something harmful to one's status in society is,
according to Marx, characteristic of the exploiting class, in his day the bourgeoisie. But not everyone in modern times is equally persuaded that work without
qualification is an unmitigated blessing. Not even Marx would agree to that. And
others, in the tradition of Weber, are more inclined to portray the bourgeoisie
as hardworking. This, for Josef Pieper, is appalling; for Thorstein Veblen it is

simply not true. Pieper and Veblen thus offer alternative guidelines to finding the true contributors to society: for Veblen, leisure-proneness is a disqualification for running society, but for Pieper it is a necessary precondition.

Josef Pieper, a German Catholic philosopher, criticized the bourgeoisie for working not too little but too much. Upset mostly with Marxist efforts to reduce all values to that of work, Pieper sings the praises of leisure as a necessary condition for celebration, worship, and (old-fashioned) philosophical speculation. Leisure, in this view, is not merely a catalyst for better work but an opening to a more profound life-meaning beyond "the dome that encloses the bourgeois workaday world," where "wonder does not occur." [45]

Thorstein Veblen, a Norwegian-American economist, shared Marx's disdain for exploitive loafers, but for reasons having more to do with putting the engineering ethos at the helm. In his *Theory of the Leisure Class* (1899), Veblen argues that social preference for a life of leisure developed out of ancient male chauvinist priorities that are no longer appropriate in a modern industrial society.

Veblen assumes that social arrangements as we know them in the modern world have evolved from arrangements in simpler societies, including even those of anthropoid prototypes of the human race. The first human stage of social organization beyond the anthropoid he calls "savage," which is characterized by its lack of role differentiation. The next stage he calls "barbarian," which in its earliest form is "primitive." There is already a form of "industry" in a barbarian society, but involvement in industry is a mark of dishonor and is typically assigned to women. Men in a barbarian society are more attracted to predatory activities that involve some element of "exploit": hunting, fishing, and, if the opportunity presents itself, warring. As a result, "Virtually the whole range of industrial employments is an outgrowth of what is classed as woman's work in the primitive barbarian community." [46]

This primitive division between men's and women's work, he says, is the origin of the division between a leisure class and a working class. The first form of ownership was ownership of women by men, which in time was expanded to include the products of women's industry, hence ownership of things as well as persons. Gradually, industrial activity displaces predatory activity in importance to a community; and, as a result, "accumulated property more and more replaces trophies of predatory exploit as the conventional exponent of prepotence and success." [47]

Males do not at this stage become more involved in industry; they just take more interest in the productivity of those under their control.[48] In time, the subservience of women and slaves to their masters leads to further role differentiation. Slaves or, in more recent times, servants who attend directly to the comforts of the master are of higher rank than those engaged in productive activities. So also the head wife, or in modern times the only wife, is exempted from industry so she can serve her husband's needs with total dedication. This involves above all the now commonplace "conspicuous consumption": the expenditure of wealth to demonstrate to, and maintain before, others the status of the household.

Not every household, of course, is able to practice conspicuous consumption as readily as do the wealthiest families. In the middle-class household, Veblen says, the male is compelled to work at "occupations which often partake largely of the character of industry" so that the wife and, if available, servants can carry out in his behalf "vicarious leisure and consumption." The working class and even the poverty-stricken do likewise within their means.[49]

These arrangements, defended "[b]y tradition and by the prevalent sense of the proprieties," were already being challenged in Veblen's day by the "New-Woman Movement," led by those who were thought to have benefited most from conspicuous consumption, namely, the wives of the idle rich. Their demand for "emancipation" and "work," he believed, would restore a "proto-anthropoid" type of human nature and a cultural stage that is "possibly sub-human." But, he conceded, it would lead to socially and economically important progress.[50]

Much, of course, has changed in the world since Veblen proclaimed his "open door" policy. In the United States, for example, white males no longer constitute a majority of the workforce. But the changes that have led to this state of affairs are not as uniformly beneficial as Veblen might have anticipated. Women in most developed countries of the world can now be found occupying every sort of occupational slot, but they still do not enjoy the same status or income as their male counterparts. They constitute a majority of the physicians in the Soviet Union, for example, but this is due in part to the comparatively low esteem attributed to health care in that country. Changes in the workforce in the United States in recent decades have been accompanied by heated debate over affirmative action and so-called reverse discrimination and more recently over "comparable worth." In Japan women constitute close to half of the workforce, but they are paid less than 50% as much as their male counterparts; thus they are making it possible for Japan to continue to compete against less developed countries whose wage scales are even lower.[51]

These work policy questions about appropriate compensation were, however, not the focus of Veblen's attack. He just wanted the incompetent loafers of the leisure class to move over and let the talented and industrious members of society see to it that the work gets done properly. But only three decades later, at the time of the Great Depression, Bertrand Russell announced in his essay "In Praise of Idleness" (1932) that Veblen had gotten it all wrong. Leisure, for Russell as for Pieper, is the goal and the precondition of civilization. The benefits of leisure have until recently been available only to a small privileged class that defended its prerogatives with self-serving theories, gave other people orders, and debated among themselves as to what orders to give. Now, says Russell, "[m]odern technique has made it possible for leisure, within limits, to be not the prerogative of small privileged classes, but a right evenly distributed throughout the community." Unfortunately, the old morality of work, which is "the morality of slaves," still prevails. This is temporarily appropriate in a developing economy such as that in the Soviet Union. But in an industrialized economy it results in the insane practice of overworking some while leaving many others unemployed, rather than letting all share the benefits of technology.[52]

Both leisure and unemployment, of course, involve a certain freedom from work responsibility. But the concept of leisure in our culture tends to imply a right not to work, whereas being unemployed has just the opposite connotation and comes complete with a sense of personal blame and its correlative, social stigma. Hence the continuing need for some association with work, even where there is little if any work to be done. Failure to take this problem into account contributes to the kind of antibureaucracy that led California voters to require that their state's budget be balanced (Proposition 13) and, in general, generates numerous related challenges to the role of government as employer of last resort. This attitude is at the heart of C. Northcote Parkinson's maxim, first stated in 1957, that work expands so as to fill the time available to complete it—the well-known Parkinson's Law. What Parkinson and other conservatives bemoan, however, Dennis Gabor views with equanimity as a society's natural defense against the psychological threat posed by technologically created unemployment.[53]

With regard to the claim that there may eventually cease to be a need for work, some scholars, such as Frijthof Bergmann, see at the end of the tunnel a light as bright as the ancient dream of a workless utopia.[54] But science fiction writers typically articulate scenarios in which the realization of such a possibility is destructive of human values. Their worries along these lines are shared by many scholars.

Already in the 1950s Georges Friedmann joined with other analysts of work to worry about a possible world without work. He did not consider it likely but complained that the implications of its happening had not even been studied and noted that if "new technology" should bring it about the profits must be fairly distributed.[55] Melvin Kranzberg and Joseph Gies conclude a history of work and its attendant miseries by speculating that the "oncoming army of robots" might bring it about that in the future as in the distant past man "will have no word for work because he no longer needs to do any."[56] These concessions to the possibility of a workless world, even if expressed without great conviction, show little advancement in thought over the view of William Morris almost a century earlier. In his novel *News from Nowhere* he simply had people do whatever work was enjoyable and left the rest to machines.

A more ominous note is struck in Czech playwright Karel Capek's *R.U.R.*, in which robot armies fight a war for humans but eventually revolt against them, thereby suggesting what our lives might be like if we indiscriminately left the hard work to robots. Engineer Robert Boguslaw also takes the possibility of a workless world very seriously. Writing before microelectronics had made the computer revolution as awesome as it has since become, he portrays electronics-assisted systems designers as being engaged in an authoritarian perversion of utopian planning in that they focus not on people but on "people-substitutes." The problem with their agenda, according to Boguslaw, is that they assign humans only marginal utility in any given "operating unit," tend to exclude them from decision making, and leave it to others to clean up the social mess after the new technology has become an established fact. In a word, the "new utopians" have replaced humanitarianism with efficiency.[57]

What complicates any evaluation of work on the human agenda is that until very recently it has been discussed in the belief that, at least in this life, work is inevitable. So the politics and the ideology of work have centered around the question of who will do the work; and once that question was settled in a particular socioeconomic setting, it was up to those doing the work and those sympathetic with their plight to build dream worlds in which work is, if not eliminated, at least fun or fulfilling.

By contrast, Karl Marx in his youth envisioned a future in which machines would be doing the work and the only question would be who was going to reap the benefits. He did not, to be sure, think of the road to such a state of affairs as one easily traversed. In contrast to utopian-socialist approaches to dignity in a world being transformed by industry, Marx and Engels sought to confront the new monster head-on to salvage a future for the vast majority of human beings who make up the working class. On this view, labor, however valuable in the capitalist setting, has no intrinsic value, and machines are welcome as a means to the eventual liberation of human beings from dehumanizing drudgery. With a view to that end, Lenin welcomed even the pioneer time and motion study methods of American Frederick Taylor as a helpful way to increase productivity.[58] Workers are alienated from their work in the typical factory system; this, however, is caused not by rationalization of work but by capitalist ownership. Scientific socialism promises the surmounting of alienation, first by assuring workers that collectively they own the means of production, and in time perhaps, by freeing them of responsibility for production and handing this over to machines. Classical Marxism, then, did tend to romanticize the liberating role of technology; but its proponents counted on a doctrinal work ethic for the duration of our dependence on human labor for productivity.

As noted above with regard to duty, the version of Marxism that has been espoused in the Soviet Union also romanticizes work by abandoning Marx's notion of alienated labor and justifying all labor insofar as it is done for the state. Such, at least, is the thrust of Soviet Marxism as interpreted by Herbert Marcuse. Marcuse himself expressed a guarded optimism about the benefits that laborsaving technology will bestow upon the working class. Marcuse's hope that technology will ease the worker's burden reiterates that of the early Marx, whose writings Marcuse took seriously.[59] This hope also suggests a way out of a problem posed by another of Marcuse's mentors, Sigmund Freud.

Freud saw himself faced with a dilemma: civilization depends on work but people show little interest in working. Given his commitment to civilization, he saw shirking (along with the resistance of the passions to reason) as sufficient justification for "a certain degree of coercion." At the same time, he considered "all present-day cultures" to be built upon the "suppression" of some members by others and found it entirely understandable "that the suppressed people should develop an intense hostility towards a culture whose existence they make possible by their work, but in whose wealth they have too small a share."[60] Claiming no expertise with regard to the then new experiment in the Soviet Union, he reserved judgment on the possibility of coming to a different conclusion with different data. But within the context of his own well-established culture, Freud found work to be culturally necessary, occasionally fulfilling but usually done begrudgingly. Particularly pertinent in this regard is a much quoted footnote in his *Civilization and Its Discontents*. The good news here is that work is the best means of tying an individual to the community and, if it is work at a profession, an excellent instrument of sublimation. The bad news, however, is that

> as a path to happiness, work is not highly prized by men. They do not strive after it as they do after other possibilities of satisfaction. The great majority of people only work under the stress of necessity, and this natural human aversion to work raises most difficult social problems.[61]

This may indicate nothing more profound than bourgeois disaffection from the aims of the labor movement; but the father of psychoanalysis should not be written off that facilely. For he is suggesting that work, even if eventually unnecessary for economic productivity, is nonetheless an important vehicle of human creativity. This view underlies the concerns of Erich Fromm about the possible demise of work.[62] It is basic to Morris's aesthetic of work and to Proudhon's glorification of work as having intrinsic dignity. And it was important to William Wordsworth and to John Ruskin as they watched cottage industries give way to dehumanizing division of labor in factories.

This endorsement of the human need for work is a key feature of E. F. Schumacher's insistence that we move toward appropriate technology. As he once expressed his prowork assumption, at least for the poor person, "the chance to work is the greatest of all needs, and even poorly paid and relatively unproductive work is better than idleness."[63] Schumacher himself tried to incorporate this prowork view into a "Buddhist economics" that stresses the importance of work to the individual and to the community. Disregarding such communitarian concerns, anarchist Murray Bookchin sees labor as "the personalized work of a man" and a tool as something that "amplifies the powers of the craftsman as a *human*." [64]

There is, in short, a strong lobby for the idea that work, even laborious work, is a valuable instrument of human fulfillment. To the extent that this view has merit, the quest for leisure cannot be endorsed without qualification. Even if work has value only as a means of support for oneself and for one's dependents, praise of leisure, to borrow Russell's title, is idle speculation until public policy recognizes welfare rights not as a recipe for sloth but as an acknowledgment of human progress. I will turn to this issue in the next chapter. But first a note about where we stand with regard to the ethics of the work ethic.

Analysis of the work ethic as consisting of four distinct types, some mutually incompatible, reveals from yet another perspective just how cautious a workers' representative would need to be about a proposal to include a commitment to work in a social contract. Even assuming that the usual divisions of a society into directors and doers could be somehow neutralized, it is still important to know to what extent the resources and arrangements of the society accommodate concerns about pleasure or virtue or duty or wealth through work. Time, place, and circumstances are again crucial determinants. An advanced technology-driven society might stress pleasure instead of work; a basic society might better think of work in terms of duty; a society on the way to development might emphasize the utility of work as a means to wealth. A society such as those that prevail in much of the developed world today might better build its agenda out of a conviction that work makes one virtuous, or, to use familiar jargon on this subject, actualizes one's potentiality. This, as a matter of fact, is what is being emphasized today under the banner of "meaningful work," to which I will turn in Chapter 5 after considering social responsibility for workers' welfare.

Chapter

4

Work and Welfare:
A Crisis of Responsibility

Our search for a light that would lead a workers' representative to endorse some sort of work ethic in a social contract has led us to the notion of meaningful work, to be considered in Chapter 5. It should be noted at once, however, that meaningful work is not a light that shines regardless of time, place, or circumstances. For it too is fueled by an ambiguity that reduces any maxim in which it is mentioned to a merely conditional imperative. The ambiguity arises from our not having specified whether status work would be the principal source of subsistence. If it would be, then the meaningfulness of such work is of only secondary importance. If not, then individuals might choose to find meaning in ways not involving work for compensation. Consideration of this latter alternative has led Canadian philosopher David Braybrooke to suggest, in effect, that social policy might have to be concerned with play rather than work.

Braybrooke stands out among philosophers for his careful attention to the implications of a world in which there are fewer jobs than there are people needing them. This, he believes, is a serious problem because people tend to fulfill themselves in and through their work. But they can do this only insofar as the work they do satisfies four conditions for relatively high esteem (RHE conditions, for short): the work produces truly needed goods; the needed goods would not otherwise be available; to do the work well one must acquire and exercise skills that command respect; and there is no adequate technological substitute for this human input. As Braybrooke looks ahead, he sees a significant decline in the number of available jobs that would yield relatively high esteem, especially because of the introduction of new technology. He therefore suggests a need to use as a basis for social policy the very earliest form of a utilitarian ethic, namely, one whose objective is to maximize pleasure—in short, a hedonism.[1]

If work opportunities should become scarce, people would presumably become more sensitive to the value of work—to worker, to employer, and to society.

Predictions about a coming scarcity of jobs, however, often assume, as does Braybrooke, that this will occur in a context of abundance. But if such is to be the case, why should people continue to focus, as we do, only on how to allocate available work and how to deal with those who are left out? After all, we think of the problem ascetically as one of allocating a scarce resource largely because of management's long-standing search for productivity without payrolls and libertarian hostility to redistribution of wealth. The ascetic perspective itself is defended by a dragon whose principal responsibility is to prevent us from developing a work policy that is visionary enough to meet the full range of challenges that lie ahead. We owe it to workers of the future, then, to look for a way around this dragon.

The dragon in question happens to be two-headed in that it influences both eligibility for employment-related benefits ("workfare") and eligibility for benefits not tied to employment ("welfare"). Because social benefits are tied so closely to one's status as a worker, the workfare/welfare dragon causes these seemingly distinct issues to overlap in many ways. So it is difficult to separate them neatly even for purposes of discussion. I propose instead to identify the ideology that underlies the linkage of welfare to work and then to analyze more closely how this linkage hampers efforts to locate responsibility for the unemployed, especially on a global scale.

Work and Benefits

Benefits that flow from the work relationship extend well beyond immediate compensation to include provision for the worker and the worker's dependents, even when the worker has stopped working, either temporarily (because laid off or on sick leave) or permanently (because disabled, retired, or deceased). Given the expectations with regard to "fringes" that are typical in capitalist countries, this overflow of benefits can be thought of simply as postponed portions of earned compensation. But different workers have very different benefit packages; these benefits are provided for in significantly different ways; and, regardless of how basic any of these benefits might be, working at a paying job might be the only way to qualify for them. These observations suggest three basic questions: Why should involvement in a work relationship be a precondition for receipt of such benefits? Out of whose pocket should these benefits be provided? And what is to be done, and by whom, if the arrangements made to provide these benefits prove inadequate?

Taken together, these questions constitute the framework for work policy with regard to social insurance. Of particular philosophical interest in this regard are questions about the nature of the relationship between work and welfare; the basis, if any, for a claim that workers as such have welfare rights; and the basis, if any, for a claim that society as a whole is responsible for honoring these rights should employers fail to do so.

By welfare rights is meant not just the right to emergency relief—a meaning still fairly common in the United States—but rights to any social benefit that is provided through the instrumentality of government. As thus understood by philosophers and others,[2] the concept of welfare rights is retrogressive according to the libertarian who opposes dependency on government for anything more intrusive than protection of private property. (Exception might be made for agreements to assist the innocent poor, such as children through Aid to Families of Dependent Children.) Because of this minimalist view, favored in some current government administrations, the philosophical basis for more ample provisions needs justification. Far more has been written to this end than can be considered here; but at least the following questions must not go begging for answers.

1. WHY SHOULD STATUS WORK BE CONSIDERED A PRECONDITION FOR RECEIPT OF BENEFITS GENERALLY TAKEN TO BE BASIC? As we have seen with regard to the work ethic, the authoritarian tradition nourishes the claim that benefits, however sparse, should be dependent on work that someone has performed. But there is good reason to wonder if a work relationship as means will generally be available to all who need the benefits as end. Employers come and go, leaving behind deserted mines and empty plants where money once was earned and ghost towns where money once was spent. Efforts to control such socially and economically disruptive closings have to date been much more successful in countries other than the United States, where the relocation of a professional sports team is still the plant closing most likely to activate a constituent-conscious legislator if not his or her elsewhere-oriented colleagues. To the extent, then, that a society relies upon the work relationship for distribution of basic benefits, is it not leaving to chance (or, in theological terms, to divine predestination) the determination of who will receive those benefits? Is this an acceptable public policy?

To the libertarian, this is the only acceptable policy. For to a libertarian, chance is at least implicitly a sine qua non of competition, and competition is the instrument through which all social benefits are generated. As economist Milton Friedman once stated, life itself is a lottery, and any attempt to redistribute income "after the fact" would be equivalent to telling people that they cannot have a lottery. From this point of view, freedom is so basic a value that any intrusion upon it for the sake of effecting a more equitable outcome is counterproductive in the long run because it undermines the only incentive that gets results for all: the opportunity for enterprise to win greater than average gain.

One flaw in this logic is the assumption that everyone in a society at some point did in fact start out on something like equal terms, so that whoever has risen to the top is rightfully there and, by way of corollary, so much the better for the rest who by definition cannot be more than second best. The weakness

of such a self-serving justification of existing economic hegemonies has inspired
Robert Nozick to modify his attempt to establish entitlement "historically" with
the proviso that current claims not be based on a chain of transfers that includes
illegal takings. But since the history of greed is full of conquistadors, Custers,
and Carnegies, Nozick's entitlement theory of justice is built on sand. Nor can
he shore up the foundations merely by raising questions about how far back
one has to go to clear a title.[3] The issue before society, now as always, is not
whether present arrangements were innocently entered into but whether they can
be perpetuated without guilt. Society thus understood is defined not merely by
recognized success but by collective needs and obligations. Circumstances do
change, even drastically, so that what may have made sense before might well be
senseless now, as for example to say in all seriousness that the king can do no
wrong.

Other capitalist-oriented theories of justice, including those of most utilitari-
ans and contractarians, as well as socialist theories, agree that government can
and should distribute some benefits and that eligibility for welfare benefits need
not depend exclusively on the work relationship. Each of these theories would
stop short of severing all connections between work and welfare. But certain
socialist theories, especially as espoused in Western Europe, come close to doing
so, as does the utopian ideal of Marxism ("From each according to ability; to
each according to need"). In spite of such theorizing, however, both capitalist
and socialist welfare policies require at least a prima facie obligation to work.
But in lieu of an all-stop philosophical side trip, a kind of tour guide's generalization may suffice at this point: where these theories differ is in the way they go
about determining the most acceptable social balance between work incentives
and welfare.

This problem of social balance is at the heart of ongoing debate about welfare
reform in most developed countries. On one scale is the benefit to society as a
whole of providing at least minimally for those who are in need but for some
reason are unable to work. On the other scale is the social benefit of retaining
an incentive for "able-bodied" people to work. In the abstract, of course, there
should be no conflict between these two recognized needs, since those given
support are only those who by definition are unable to work. In the concrete,
however, the problem is very real insofar as this group includes not only those
who are constitutionally unable to work but also those who are circumstantially
unable to work, including those laid off and unable to find other employment and
parents with salable skills who must take time off to care for their children. The
concern of a well-structured welfare program is, it is believed, to avoid compensating the unemployed so well that looking for employment is made less attractive
than continuing to accept welfare beyond the period of time that the qualifying
circumstances justify.[4]

Unemployed recipients of welfare benefits are subject to social stigma more or less in inverse proportion to their degree of involvement in the workforce. At the lower (or "freeloader") end of the spectrum is the person with needs but without any workplace affiliation. Such a person will typically be required to pass some sort of needs test to qualify as an appropriate recipient of "charity." At the upper (or "earned vacation") end of the spectrum is the longtime employee who by virtue of seniority has first right of refusal of a more or less fully paid layoff when the employer is experiencing economic downturn. In between are all sorts of persons whose situation has been recognized as closer either to that of the freeloader or to that of the faithful servant who has earned time off. Noteworthy in this regard is the vast number of individuals who have qualified for a "middle layer of protection" between that available through emergency relief and that available through private initiative and by private mechanisms, namely, contributory social insurance benefits to which one is understood to have a strict right by virtue of having participated satisfactorily as a worker in the appropriate public sector program.[5]

The political and economic realities of a given society do, of course, impose limits both on welfare benefits available and on eligibility to receive them. The tendency until quite recently, however, has been to add additional categories in both respects. Thus, for example, self-employed persons were not included under the original Social Security Act in the United States (1935) but were subsequently added when a compromise formula for their contributions (half again as much as those of employees) was worked out. Similarly, benefits under the program did not originally include health care as such; but this was eventually added at least partially (over the strenuous objections of the organized medical profession) by the enactment of Medicare. The onset age of sixty-five, originally set in accordance with the retirement age most commonly expected in business, is presently (subject to some qualifications) down to sixty-two and has no minimum in the event of permanent disability. In 1988 Medicare was amended to require senior citizens to pay into a public sector program that insures them against catastrophic illness. In the United States, however, there is still no public recognition that technological unemployment is comparable in some instances, notably those involving older workers, to permanent disability. However unrealistically, public policy looks to job retraining as society's principal weapon against redundancy, but funding for this purpose is limited to the point of being mere tokenism, and laid-off workers often jump through many legal hoops before they are qualified for benefits under an unemployment compensation (UI) program.[6]

2. WHO SHOULD PAY FOR THE BENEFITS PROVIDED? Leaving aside the extreme libertarian view that the worker alone should pay for those out-of-work benefits that he or she personally wants, say, via private insurance, there is general consensus in Western capitalist societies that the cost of these benefits should be fairly divided, insofar as possible, among those who gain from them either directly or indirectly and are able to pay. Included here in all plans is the employer and the employee and in many plans, especially in Western Europe, society as a whole. The reasons for these choices are of considerable philosophical interest.

That the employer should contribute to the postemployment welfare of employees is an idea that was accepted at least in principle by slaveowners with respect to slaves who were no longer productive. Whatever the value of such an appeal to "noblesse oblige," it is in fact good business practice for a variety of reasons. It helps increase the job satisfaction of good workers who might otherwise be lured into the fold of a competitor. It helps ease out the "superannuated" worker to make way for talented new blood. It may be argued, alternatively, that funds allocated by an employer for employees' retirement benefits are really just a component of wages and hence actually are being paid by the employees themselves. But if all firms competing in an industry do likewise, the cost per employee can be recouped from the consumer without affecting anybody's competitive position. So already at this level the public may be paying the bill, just not through the instrumentality of taxation.

That the employee should contribute directly to his or her postemployment welfare is by no means obvious. After all, a somewhat different set of expectations obtains in more traditional societies where those of working age assume the obligation of caring for elders who in their time have been the family providers. Such expectations are conspicuously absent among primitive people who find ways for useless elders to pass on to a life beyond. But individuals raised in a society that is committed to cross-generational caring for the aged might for that very reason return to it after having worked for years in a more technologically advanced setting, be it one of the nation's urban centers, such as Belgrade in Yugoslavia, or a foreign country that is receptive to "guest workers," like West Germany for several decades after World War II or Sweden today. This informal system of old age insurance is a kind of communitarian precursor of the more formal arrangements of modern societies. And it is just the sort of system that serfs and peasants in the West were relying on when their world was overtaken by the Industrial Revolution and such accompanying practices as enclosure.

Upon finding themselves in the comparatively hostile environment of industry without benefit of communitarian structure, workers tend to recreate such structure at least in a piecemeal way in an effort to establish a comparable level of security. In the process they typically sort out risks for which they hold the employer responsible from other risks for which they acknowledge their own responsibility, at least in part.

Understandable concern about workplace health and safety has over the years been translated into claims against employers for tort liability. These claims are not often as dramatic as the various class action suits filed against Union Carbide in the wake of the gas leak disaster in Bhopal, India. But if all the individual actions against an employer for work-related sickness, injury, and death are added together, the resulting total, especially for a company whose production process is inherently hostile, may well be more staggering than can be conveniently built into the cost of doing business. To some extent an employer may attempt to minimize such claims by offering hazard pay in the hopes of neutralizing the harmed workers' attraction to litigation. A more straightforward way of handling these problems is to circumscribe work-related claims through the establishment of workers' compensation. Statutes of this genre are very congenial to employers (and to their insurers) in at least three ways: they restrict the list of qualifying injuries; they cap amounts recoverable (at initially low rates made lower still by inflation); and they preclude any other remedy at law.

Similarly, workers typically consider their employers (if not society as a whole) responsible for conditions that result in layoffs. One way they deal with this problem is by seeking employment with the more stable companies. Those less stable are thereby pressured into offering some sort of compensating insurance against layoffs. Out of this set of problems has evolved the public programs of unemployment compensation. As operated by the various states in the United States these programs establish rates for insurance based on the stability of the company. In this way a favored company may be enticed away from a "greedier" state with manifestly lower if not subsidized rates.[7] Workers generally do not think of themselves as being responsible for such arrangements.

By comparison, workers seem much more willing to contribute to a fund that will provide for them once they are retired. This may be because, generally speaking, no one else is to blame for one's aging. Anyway, there is a long tradition of workers establishing mutual aid societies to provide a pension for themselves when they are no longer able to work. Since, however, no group of employees can be entirely confident that they will remain with the same employer throughout their working years, there is clearly a need for a system of old age assistance that is independent of any particular employer. Emergency relief may assist the destitute, and powerful unions as well as valued executives are likely to have pensions provided for in the private sector. The great majority of workers, however, at least in the United States, fall into neither category. For them the availability of a government-managed social insurance program to which they contribute through a tax on their paycheck is considered appropriate. J. Douglas Brown, chairman of the first Social Security Advisory Council in the United States, attributes this acquiescence, even in the face of rising tax rates, to a shared sense of social contract.[8] It may be that, but it is also a device through which the employer is relieved of some responsibility for the needs of its former employees. Moreover, limiting the amount of income on which the social security tax is applied has a regressive impact on the lower-paid workers. As will be seen in the next section, this can only get worse in a system arranged as has been that in the United States.

The third possible source of support for a contributory social insurance program is society as a whole. In its role as consumer, society does contribute indirectly by buying the goods and services of employers who contribute to the fund. What is here meant, however, is a direct application of general funds to the pension obligations of retired and qualified workers. This involvement of government is a standard component of programs in Western Europe, where typically the worker, the employer, and the government are each responsible for one-third of the pension obligation. This, it would seem, is a reasonable division, since employer and employee each benefit (for the reasons indicated above) and society also benefits by having in place a program that reduces dependence on a needs-test relief program. The same reasoning is clearly applicable to the program in the United States; yet, incredibly, the U.S. government has avoided assuming any direct liability for our national program of social security (it does participate indirectly, by virtue of its involvement with the basic Medicare health insurance plan). So as far as up-front policy is concerned, the U.S. government leaves this obligation to employers and employees on a fifty-fifty basis.

Political backpeddling is largely responsible for the failure of the U.S. government to assume any general responsibility for pensions on a national level. When the Old Age and Supplemental Income (OASI) program was originally set up during the Great Depression, it took over the accrued liability of the government to people who would otherwise have needed emergency relief. For the same reason, the nation as a whole benefits from OASI on an ongoing basis. But in spite of Advisory Council recommendations to follow the lead of European nations, the federal government had by the late 1950s begun to portray the fifty-fifty arrangement as being somehow inherent in and sacred to the original social contract that established the program. This rationalization was convenient to a government committed to the military priorities of the Cold War. Only employers still heavily dependent on manpower, as in construction, have had reason to oppose the resulting gradual increase in their share of the rates; and construction is becoming less dependent on union-scale labor. Unorganized employees, who tend to be totally dependent on the federal pension plan, have not found a voice to protest either the steadily rising tax or the ever more strident demand for diminished benefits.[9] In fact, the average American probably thinks of the social security assessment not as a tax but as an insurance premium.

Parallel to this ideological squabble on the national level is a very troublesome shift in private sector policy with regard to paying for health care benefits. As health care costs continue to skyrocket in spite of the economizing efforts of government (notably, its use of DRGs [diagnosis-related groups]) and of the insurance industry, and as a third of all retirees are below the minimum age to qualify for Medicare, companies have been moved to lighten the load of their financial commitment to workers' health. Workout equipment is moved in, and health insurance benefits are moved out. Variously referred to as cafeteria plans or flex plans, this new money-saving approach thrives on burdening the insuree with higher copayments, less protection against inflation (the employer pays only a part of any increase in premiums), fewer cross-subsidies (claimants pay more, nonclaimants less), and skewed options (high price tags on items the employer wants to discourage). Perhaps the most insidious aspect of these new plans is the way they require employees to pay as they grow, as they have families and then with age begin to have health problems. Young single workers like having less withheld from their pay; but they too will come to realize the true cost of what they briefly "saved." [10] Even in the short run, as a result of this "copayment" trend, the average employee premium for family coverage under an employer-sponsored medical plan jumped 400% in just eight years, from $97 per year in 1980 to about $484 in 1988.[11] Inversely, workers need to appreciate that when an employer proffers a lump-sum payment, this is not necessarily a sign of special appreciation but a way to avoid the liabilities that go with wage increases.[12]

3. IF EXISTING ARRANGEMENTS PROVE INADEQUATE TO PROVIDE FOR BENEFITS AS PLANNED, WHAT IS TO BE DONE AND BY WHOM? In the past, societies have relied in one way or another upon the direct participants in a work relationship (employers and employees) to provide the means of supporting those who, for whatever reason, were not working. This reliance has extended far beyond a worker's immediate dependents (for whom he or she is the "provider") to include those temporarily unable to work (notably the sick or injured and the young) and those permanently out of the workforce: the disabled and the retired. For a number of reasons, one of which is technological displacement, we need to reconsider this traditional arrangement.

To see just how serious a problem is at issue, consider, for example, the future status of retirees in society. It is commonly thought that a retiree lives on income that he or she has somehow "earned" through direct or indirect involvement in the workforce. But this view of the retiree is for the most part unrealistic. This is the case whether the "pension" in question has been set up in the public or the private sector.

Take first of all public sector pensions. Until recently, Sweden, Canada, and Japan were the only developed countries (the United States is now another) that did not support their qualified retirees on a "pay-as-you-go" basis, out of taxes imposed on current employers and employees. Under this arrangement, the amount of money needed at any given time depends on what benefits are to be provided and to how many individuals. Since the size of the population that is eligible for retirement benefits changes over time, to plan a budget for this purpose it is necessary to know as accurately as possible what will be the size of the retiree cohort of the population over any given period of time. Insofar as these retirees are to be paid out of contemporaneous taxes on both employers and employees, the amount of tax imposed has to be based on information regarding the size and the average income of the workforce. At any given time, then, tradeoffs between taxes imposed and benefits distributed will be more or less difficult to arrive at depending on the ratio between the number of those in the workforce and the number of retirees entitled to pensions.

This ratio, referred to technically as the "dependency ratio," is defined by economists as the number of retired people for each man or woman of working age. So by definition the ratio will be lower the more working-age people there are compared to retirees. Customarily expressed as a percentage, the ratio varies significantly from one country to another and within a country from one time period to another. In Japan, for example, the ratio in 1976 was 8% (1:10). In West Germany in 1984 it was 45%, or, roughly, 1:2; and in the United States, 20%, or 1:5. But the ratio will increase to 63% (2:3) in Japan in 2025 and to 90% (almost 1:1) in West Germany in 2030. In the United States, it is expected to rise as follows:

2000	23%	(1:4)
2020	33%	(1:3)
2030	42%	(2:5)
2055	>50%	(1:2)

These projections have been taken to mean that if future retirees are to receive benefits at least equal to those provided to current retirees and if the pay-as-you-go approach is still used, the level of funding has to be increased substantially. In the United States, this means that (barring an unlikely change in funding allocations) employers and employees would have to be taxed at a higher rate. Improvements in productivity could, in principle, neutralize the expected impact. But on the basis of other considerations, more troublesome conclusions can be drawn. In the first place, employers would, as now, simply include these taxes in the cost of their product or service, which means that the workers' standard of living would be reduced indirectly by a comparable amount. Second, if economic growth should decline and/or inflation rise, either the tax burden or the level of benefits or both would be affected negatively. Third, and most important in light of the goal of profits without payrolls, if fewer than all those of working age actually work, the effective dependency ratio would be just that much greater than the percentages here cited.[13]

These concerns about the viability of public pension programs generate two kinds of proposed solutions, some to reform the government-sponsored program, others to rely more on private pension programs. Reform might focus either on the way the program is funded, on the benefits to be provided, or on the criteria of eligibility for benefits. As the two latter factors are manipulated, the total bill can be increased (as was the case for many years) or decreased (as is now becoming a policy objective). For example, raising the retirement age, as has been done recently both in Japan and in the United States, reduces the total number of eligible retirees; but lowering the retirement age (as in Western Europe, to reduce unemployment) increases the number of retirees.[14]

Attention to the method of funding requires reconsideration of a basic philosophical stance with regard to a pension program. In the United States, as noted, funds needed to pay retiree benefits have been covered, until recently, on a pay-as-you-go basis: the amount of money needed at any given time to cover claims under the program determined the amount of OASI taxes imposed. A more investment-oriented approach, at least in principle, would be to make a retiree's benefits directly dependent on returns to contributions made by that worker and his or her contemporaries during their working years. This approach is demographically sound; but, like any accessible trust fund, the monies being stored up are vulnerable to manipulation for the sake of interim needs. This has happened in Japan and now seems to be happening in the United States as well.

In view of the burgeoning retiree population expected in this country in the early decades of the twenty-first century, Congress in the mid-1980s enacted legislation with the announced purpose of building up a surplus in anticipation of the coming need. This surplus, expected to be about $100 billion by 1993 and $2 trillion by 2020 (in 1988 dollars), is to be created by more than doubling the social security tax on lower- and middle-income salaries (up to $45,000), reducing benefits over time, and increasing the retirement age to sixty-seven in 2003 and thereafter. It would appear to be a perfect example of an actuarially sensitive program in which a currently large workforce pays for its own retirement and thereby lightens the next generation's burden. Previous concerns about underfunding being now moot, members of Congress, economists, and others have turned to debating the wisdom of having so much money stored up.[15]

One problem with this scenario is that it may be a myth, for the supposed surplus exists only on paper, thanks in part to some very creative accounting. As the tax money comes in, it is in effect being spent to help hold the federal government's budget deficit within statutorily mandated limits. In return for this service to the built-in pitfalls of electoral politics, the Social Security Administration (SSA) receives what amounts to ever-mounting IOUs. How will these IOUs be paid when they start coming due a few decades hence? As noted above, the options include more taxes, fewer benefits, and fewer eligible recipients. Sound familiar? In the meanwhile, workers not only are paying more in taxes (not new in itself) but are being misled both as to the purpose and as to the beneficiaries of these taxes.[16]

Such being the drawbacks to a public pension program, some would seek relief in a private sector program. Libertarians strongly favor such a solution. But private pensions have drawbacks of their own. In the first place, some three-fourths of all corporate pension plans are of the "defined contribution" type, based on some market-vulnerable system such as profit sharing or deferred savings. "Defined benefit" plans (available to most salaried and many unionized employees) are more dependable. Those based on one's average career income ("career average") may be inadequate in inflationary times, even if bolstered in some way. More reliable is the "final-pay formula," benefits of which are determined, as the name suggests, by one's pay at the time of retirement. But this type of pension is hardly a cornucopia. One may have to be employed twelve to twenty-four years to qualify and as long as forty years to be eligible for the top rate. A five-year phase-in period will limit benefits to a newly eligible employee. In addition, the value of benefits earned is diminished by inflation, so a plan is unreliable if it is not upgraded periodically, as is required in UAW and United Steel Workers of America (USWA) contracts. But such concerns are often a luxury from the viewpoint of the displaced worker. If a person loses a job before his or her pension rights vest, then typically they will be lost, unless some "portability" provision ties together years of service under successive employers. Vesting now occurs after five years in a fixed plan or during the third to seventh year of employment in a graduated plan (as compared to 50% vesting after ten years before the Employee Retirement Income Security Act [ERISA], discussed below). Even if one's pension rights have vested, inflation may, as in recent years, reduce their value significantly.[17]

Serious as these very practical considerations are, they are secondary to a far more fundamental concern: who in fact is the rightful owner of a private pension fund? In the past decade, a number of companies—first one, then in time many—have acted as if the funds are theirs to do with as they wish, subject only to certain minimum obligations to employees. Some corporate analysts agree, but others assert that shareholders are the ultimate owners of "surplus" pension fund money. Last of all on the list of candidates for ownership are the employees themselves, whose rights in this regard have found amazingly few defenders.[18] However this theoretical question is answered, in actual fact the U.S. government, in behalf of the country's taxpayers, is becoming the insurance underwriter for more and more so-called private pensions. How this has come about is a fascinating illustration of Gunnar Myrdal's thesis that, ideologies notwithstanding, Western democracies have become welfare states not by design but by way of ad hoc responses to otherwise insoluble private sector problems.[19]

The entry of the United States government into the business of underwriting private retirement plans may be said to have begun with ERISA, which was adopted in 1974 to deal especially with the problem of employees' losing their retirement benefits when their employer goes out of business. The stimulus for this complex law was the pension disaster that occurred when Studebaker folded, leaving its employees empty-handed. Its overarching purpose was to establish more rigorously a dissolved employer's liability for its employees' vested pension benefits. Before ERISA, a dissolved company's pension obligation was limited to the amount employees themselves had contributed to the fund. ERISA added to this a requirement that a company pay insurance premiums into a newly created Pension Benefit Guaranty Corporation (PBGC) and that it be liable for unfunded benefits for up to 30% of its net worth. This was an idea whose time had definitely come; but it was not a perfect instrument. There have been problems.

The first problem that came to the fore had to do with multiemployer pension funds, which were especially common in industries like trucking and construction. Under ERISA as originally written, when one employer went out of business, its pension liability would be transferred to the others still in the plan. This threat to the very idea of a multiemployer fund led to the Multi-employer Pension Plan Amendments Act of 1980 (MPPAA). These amendments require most employers who withdraw from a multiemployer plan to pay a share of the plan's unfunded vested benefits as of the end of the plan year prior to the year of the company's withdrawal from the plan. In cases of corporate restructuring, this could mean that stockholders would be responsible for delinquent contributions.[20]

Next came problems involving discriminatory distribution of benefits. Plans that assigned benefits to top executives that were not available to other employees were proscribed by the Tax Equity and Fiscal Responsibility Act of 1982 (TEFRA); but because the 1974 law required that all employees receive the same percentage of benefits, TEFRA has had a negative impact on all. The Retirement Equity Act of 1984, however, does have the salutary effect of preventing employers from canceling the vested benefits of employees who discontinue working —an obvious boon to a parent who takes time out to raise children.

As declining industries continued to flounder, the U.S. government's PBGC has found itself increasingly responsible for the pension obligations of single-employer plans. This problem arose indirectly because of a loophole in ERISA. With a view to giving employers an incentive to improve their plan benefits, lawmakers exempted pension funds from taxation. Investments of these funds (estimated to amount to over $1 trillion) prospered during the 1980s beyond immediate obligations, and companies have been diverting the allegedly "excess assets" to other purposes. According to one estimate, $18 billion have been taken from nineteen hundred employee pension funds in just seven years.[21]

The procedure is relatively simple. A company claims that its pension plan is "overfunded," terminates the fund, provides differentially for old and new employees, and diverts the balance to other business purposes, including the take-over of other companies. This coffer-raiding could possibly work out well at least for the employer and for established employees, but only if the economy cooper-ates. If not, the employees can lose as much as 40 to 50% of their pension, for an annuity is vulnerable to inflation, a stock option plan provides no guaranteed income, and profit sharing is worthless if no distribution is made.[22]

This problem was addressed, albeit inadequately, by the Consolidated Omni-bus Budget Reconciliation Act of 1986 (COBRA). Title IX of the act, known as the Single Employer Pension Plan Amendments Act of 1986 (SEPPAA), restricts an employer's ability to terminate a single-employer pension plan by allowing only two kinds of termination. A standard termination is allowed only if assets of the plan are sufficient to pay "benefit commitments," including all accrued benefits plus any early retirement supplements or subsidies plus any plant closing benefits—in short, a much higher liability than before. A distress termination is allowed only if the company is in bankruptcy or is in reorganization and has court approval to terminate or the PBGC finds that the company could not stay in business or pension costs have become "unreasonably burdensome" solely as a result of a decline in the work force. When a distress termination is allowed, plan participants, beneficiaries, alternate payers, unions, and the PBGC must be given sixty-day notice of the termination, and any person adversely affected, or a union representative, may sue for injunctive or other relief.[23] Such constraints are, to be sure, appropriate, but they do not prevent a company from going out of business and throwing its pension obligations onto the federal government, meaning the PBGC, which insures the pensions of over 40 million Americans.

The PBGC has become especially responsible for pensions in the steel indus-try, which now has twice as many retirees as active workers. Working for ten steel companies are 143,000 vested employees whose pensions are underfunded in the amount of $3,070,000. Unfunded liabilities in steel are projected to be at $15 billion by 1991. Taking into account benefits owed them under their USWA con-tract, unemployed steelworkers were supposed to receive $400 per month until eligible for social security at age sixty-two. But they will probably not receive this much because the PBGC does not assure payment of supplemental benefits when a company is in a stress situation.

Similar problems are being faced in Europe and in Japan, but in these coun-tries funds are used to redevelop steel communities. In the United States, there is a fear that such assistance would encourage shutdowns; besides, relatively healthy competitors such as Inland Steel oppose bailouts in principle. As a result, steel towns in our country are becoming "involuntary retirement communities on the verge of municipal bankruptcy."[24]

One may hope that this is not a microcosm of what lies ahead; but it is sobering to note that as people live longer and longer (there are now one hundred thousand persons in the United States over the age of one hundred, and there will be ten times as many by the year 2000), there may be three generations of retirees at one time.[25]

Responsibility for the Unemployed

We have seen that a society's welfare benefits may be influenced by presumptions about work obligations, but that nonetheless one's involvement in the workforce does not guarantee eligibility for benefits. The time-honored principle that working should be a precondition for welfare presupposes at least the availability of work. So if work is not available, the justice of the precondition is on the defensive. Only in a state of nature of the Hobbesian sort might "devil take the hindmost" stand as an adequate response to the problem. But the unavailability of work might be a merely local phenomenon, in which case worker mobility can be put forward as a convenient antidote.[26] But worker mobility addresses only a part of the problem. In the case of long-standing communities, it weakens the workers' roots, even if they are able to commute to and from their new place of employment. In more extreme cases, immigration becomes necessary, with all the attendant problems of distributing jobs among longtime residents and those newly arrived, whether they have been admitted legally or illegally. The localized problem of allocating jobs among new and old inhabitants has, in turn, been upstaged in recent times by the increasingly common tendency of transnational corporations (TNCs) to leave workers in place but out of work and move workplaces instead—not just to different parts of the same country but all over the world. It is in this global context that we must address the difficult question of responsibility for the unemployed.

In principle, any philosophical study of an employment-related issue, say, with regard to welfare, immigration, or equal employment opportunity, could be relevant. But few such treatises address underlying issues about work.[27] In particular, philosophical writing about justice has taken the availability of work for granted. Notable exceptions in this regard are articles by Lawrence C. Becker and James W. Nickel. Becker argues that work is a social obligation that should be enforced by law if it is "reciprocity for a special benefit." Nickel defends a right to employment, but only when wealth is sufficient to accommodate such a right.[28]

Analyses like these are suggestive insofar as they explore various implications of the employment relationship. Their significance is diminished, however, to the extent that this relationship is changing rapidly and fundamentally, is increasingly ill matched to available skills and interests, and often enough is simply being terminated in favor of alternative means of production. More on target in this regard are studies that take into account the instability of employment in the face of new technology and other related factors. These studies consist primarily of philosophical considerations of corporation and employment law, which are being incorporated into business ethics texts. Texts in this field have not been very attentive to the interests of workers; but this is beginning to change, as witness such recent texts as those by Patricia Werhane (1985) and Thomas Donaldson (1982). Werhane argues somewhat guardedly for recognition of employee rights as well as obligations. Donaldson in particular focuses on the nature and scope of corporate responsibility.[29]

Donaldson's agenda is to get corporations to police themselves internally to preclude the need to police them from without. To this end, he looks for reasonable ways, first, to attribute moral agency to a corporation and then to facilitate a corporation's own ability to exercise moral agency. One attempt to establish corporate moral agency, he finds, exaggerates the similarities between a corporation and a moral person acting intentionally. Another (defended by Werhane, among others), by oversimplifying the way a corporation behaves, is able to conclude that, like a machine, its structural organization prevents it from exercising moral freedom so consequently it must be regulated from without. Other approaches focus, for example, on the rational agency, or "mind," of the corporation or on its operational process. On the basis of his review of these various approaches, Donaldson concludes that a corporation may be considered a moral agent only insofar as it has the capacity to use moral reasons in decision making and its decision-making process has the capacity to control not only overt corporate acts but also the structure of its policies and rules.[30]

The second condition can be read as a plea for the often alleged need to "get government off our backs." This ambiguity aside, responsibility understood in these terms is fairly easy to assign if what Donaldson calls a direct obligation is involved, for example, to fulfill a contract or comply with pollution standards. Not so easy to determine are a corporation's indirect obligations, meaning, I take it, those that are not well established in law but depend rather on moral judgments as to propriety and fundamental decency. This one probusiness distinction commits Donaldson to espousing a legalism ameliorated by good manners and turns his otherwise truly excellent analysis into a tactful plea for superior corporate etiquette. But his definition of corporate responsibility is salvageable, provided only that one append to it a variation on a theme by John Donne: no corporation is an island.

Taking Donaldson's thus qualified definition of corporate responsibility as a convenient point of departure, I now propose to explore whether and in what ways it applies when the employment relationship has been terminated. At issue is employers' responsibility for the unemployed. I shall be seeking to assign such responsibility by means of a series of arguments, each of which points the finger either at or beyond the employer. For the sake of simplicity I assume that participants in the debate are limited to two, namely, labor (symbolized as "L") and capital ("C").

L1. EXPLOITATION OF WORKERS

Management is to blame for the current workplace crisis because of its long history of manipulating people into servile dependence by touting the work ethic on one hand and the doctrine of employment at will (EAW) on the other. The work ethic tells people they should work as hard as they can; EAW tells them that no matter how hard they work their continued employment is entirely up to the employer. The unprincipled ruthlessness that underlies this two-pronged manipulation of workers is evident in management's simultaneous efforts over the years to achieve productivity without payrolls. First, employers defined brains out of jobs as much as possible, then they started looking for and introducing machines to do the brainless jobs. Now, to their surprise, they have at their disposal even brainier machines that will allow them (those who are left) to shrink payrolls even more by eliminating even personnel recognized as having some brains.

C1. ADVANTAGES OF EAW TO EMPLOYEES

In the course of the twentieth century, the alleged severity of EAW has been tempered in a variety of ways, as a result of legislation, regulation, and especially contract bargaining with regard to the terms and conditions of employment. This tempering has improved the status not only of present but of former and future employees. And the other side of the coin is the freedom of the employee to quit the job in question and take skills, often employer-taught, to a better job with another employer. To prohibit such mobility is to endorse involuntary servitude, which is prohibited in all of the civilized world, including the United States since the Civil War.

L2. DISADVANTAGES OF EAW TO EMPLOYEES

There are still employees in the United States, especially in agriculture, who have been maneuvered by their employers into positions of involuntary servitude. Leaving this problem aside, it is unrealistic to equate the freedom of the employee to end a work relationship with that of the employer. Such an equation may apply in the case of the small proprietary business. But another order of magnitude is involved in the case of a large corporation that has located a plant in a particular community under certain terms and conditions over an extended period of time. This large corporate employer may well have become the only ongoing source of income for its employees and for others economically dependent on them. To justify that employer's dismissal of hundreds if not thousands of employees on the basis of EAW is comparable to appealing to self-defense to justify grand larceny.

The basic presupposition of this doctrine, namely, the mutuality (equal bargaining position) of the parties, is repeatedly shown by events to be a myth. Regardless of developments abroad, as in Sweden, not even the most powerful unions in the United States have been able to prevent plant closings and massive layoffs. Even the belated enactment in this country of a mere sixty-day advance notice was strenuously opposed by management spokespersons as being intrusive, anticompetitive, likely to forestall openings rather than closings (and, one suspects, likely to give employees the wrong message about their rights).[31] In short, improved provisions for the time of transition do not change the basic fact that large corporate employers can and do end one-to-many relationships with consequences quite devastating outside the four corners of their ledger sheets.

C2. THE PROFIT MOTIVE

Problems do arise when an employer is required by business necessity to reduce a workforce, discontinue the operation of a plant or production of a product, or even get out of an industry entirely. But when profitability is insufficient, there is no alternative that is or should be acceptable to investors, including, as often as not, the pension funds of many, even millions, of workers.

Besides, management can hardly be blamed for a philosophy of work with which even unions have agreed to a great extent, at least with regard to the idea that the work relationship depends on the availability of work as determined by management. In any event, in a free enterprise system it is essential that employers not be required to retain employees regardless of bottom-line considerations. Cost-cutting, including plant relocation and workforce reduction, must always be available as options if we are to attract the capital that makes employment possible.

L3. BAD MANAGEMENT

An employer should in principle have the right to be free of an unproductive worker (or machine or plant or division), but only on condition that the employer is in no way *responsible* for that worker's lack of productivity. In particular, persons (employees) have rights not granted to mere equipment. Even if the failure of my watch to "work" any more is due entirely to my own negligence (say, because I wore it in the swimming pool knowing it was not waterproof), I still retain the right to dispose of it without pausing to contemplate its future. I do not, however, *own* another person as I might own a watch by virtue of my being that person's employer. So to the extent that I am responsible for that person's becoming less productive or unproductive, I continue to have obligations to that person. If I failed to provide tools and equipment in a timely way, if I failed to seek customers (say, as a contractor), if I failed to modernize to stay competitive in my business environment (as in the case of West German watchmaking or U.S. steel production), if I failed to manage prudently,[32] then am I not for any of these reasons responsible for the financial and social misfortune of the person who has come to work for me? The other side of management rights is management responsibility. Claim the one and you must accept the other.

C3. RISK CONTROL

A negligent employer may indeed be held responsible for *some* misfortunes of an employee, for example, those involving the employee's health and safety on the job. Hence the need for appropriate insurance and, at least for the sake of argument, some form of government oversight. Such responsibility must be circumscribed, however, or the employer will remain forever uncertain of its financial status, as would have been the case with Johns Manville absent the availability of bankruptcy. Take away these limits on an employer's responsibility, expose the employer to open-ended liability, and you create a monster that will devour management and labor in one big bite. As is often demonstrated in competitive industries, management is no less at risk in the face of technological change than are workers. So if business is to be encouraged to the benefit of all concerned it ought not to be exposed unduly to interference on the part of courts with regard to terms of employment. Leave that to the parties immediately involved, either one-on-one or by means of collective bargaining to terms understood and acceptable on both sides.

L4. UNEQUAL PARTIES

Contrary to the traditional mythology still canonized by most courts, contracting parties in the employment situation are seldom bargaining at arm's length. The typical work relationship today is between comparatively vulnerable workers and a large corporation. So it is appropriate for society, through its courts and otherwise, to base its work policies on the realities of the working world today rather than on the alleged need for entrepreneurial autonomy that characterized the pioneering days of the nineteenth century.[33]

C4. UNION POWER

The heavily one-sided employment relationship just described is more typical of the previous century than of today. In the interim the labor movement has organized much of the workplace, thereby giving workers power coequal to that of management. And even if the majority of workers, at least in the United States, are not organized, the legal structures are there to make such organization available to them if they feel a need to bargain with their employer collectively, especially with regard to job security.

L5. CONSTRAINTS ON UNIONS

The previous argument must be tongue-in-cheek in view of management's dedicated efforts over the years to see to it that as small a percentage of workers organize as possible. In particular, it conveniently disregards all the legal constraints that have been imposed on union organizing since the end of World War II. Antiunion statutes, and antiunion interpretations of statutes (notably in the area of antitrust and, more recently, bankruptcy laws) severely hamper the growth of unions in the United States.[34] Labor movement efforts to have the ninety-fifth Congress put teeth into the statutory prohibition of employer obstruction of organizing (HR 8410) met with heavy and ultimately successful opposition from business interests. So even an umbrella organization such as the American Federation of Labor–Congress of Industrial Organizations (AFL-CIO) can do little in the face of plant closings, outsourcing, and change of product or production process. These law-embodied constraints on the labor movement represent as much as anything else our society's de facto policy with regard to the rights of workers in the face of corporate changes that cost jobs and, in many instances, undermine the economies of entire communities.

C5. DEMOCRATIC PROCESS

The position of unions in the United States has deteriorated in recent years because of the competition-engendered decline of the most highly organized industries. But this deterioration is neither inevitable nor irremediable. If we as a society so choose, we can still change our public policy with regard to job security, as has been done in Sweden, or our approach to industrial policy below the level of government, as has been done in Japan, West Germany, and the United Kingdom. We as a people need only be persuaded that it is in our long-term best interest to be more solicitous of workers necessarily left by the wayside as we move on to new technologies.

L6. POWER OF TNCS

Nation-states, even one as powerful as the United States of America, are inadequate instruments of effective industrial policy in this age of massive TNCs, some of which have annual budgets larger than those of most national governments combined. Chilean President Salvador Allende learned this harsh lesson at the hands of U.S.-based corporate enterprise.[35] Others, such as Simon Nora in his report to French President Valéry Giscard d'Estaing, see that the TNC can shift its assets and liabilities around by paper (or, rather, electronic) transfers that effectively immunize the company's proceeds. So how is our government or any other going to formulate a policy that will effectively solve the problem of technological unemployment?

C6. INTERNATIONAL LAW

Pessimism is not a justification for inactivity. Even granting the alleged impotence of nation-states in the age of the TNC, one is reminded all the more forcefully of the need for a world government that is capable of rising beyond the provincial limits of the past. Such a supranational structure already exists in limited form in such agencies as the United Nations and its subsidiaries (such as the World Health Organization and the Food and Agriculture Organization) and such international entities as the International Monetary Fund, the European Economic Community, and the General Agreement on Tariffs and Trade (GATT). These international arrangements may be inadequate; but by their very existence they attest to the possibility of building broader-based agencies to see to the survival and advancement of the human family.

L7. CORPORATE RESPONSIBILITY

World government, even if possible, may not be desirable. But the question is moot because no world government presently exists. Even if there were a world government, empowered to determine somehow the rights of workers around the world, it would need some basis on which to make such an important determination. The establishment of this basis for determination of rights should precede any actual set of laws in any particular governmental unit, however advanced. What is needed for this purpose, however, is an emerging sense of *human* rights with regard to work prior to and independent of any particular politico-economic arrangements, be they in a developed or a developing country. But merely globalizing some sort of work ethic is not an adequate way to deal with a problem that is brought on precisely by the diminishing availability of compensated work. So leave world building to a future generation. There are issues enough before us with regard to the legal environment of work in particular locales, including many in the United States. Here, as already noted, there are good reasons for laying responsibility for technological unemployment at management's door.

C7. SOCIAL RESPONSIBILITY

You say the employer should be responsible for technological unemployment. What you mean is that the public, via higher prices for the employer's products, should pay for the employee's historically inevitable misfortune. To every action there is an equal and opposite reaction. In the language of systems thinking, this comes down to saying that you cannot do just one thing. A system by definition is a set of components so interrelated that a change in one effects changes in all. With this in mind, there may be a need to develop a global system the components of which are known, anticipated, and taken into account in planning for the future so as to keep the shifting TNC under control. So be it. But this cannot be achieved overnight. In the meantime, employers, wherever based, must compete in the world marketplace.

In the case of American-based companies, however responsible they may have been historically for the policies that worked well enough within our national borders, they did not formulate those policies in a vacuum. Government (whether responsibly or not is beside the point) went along with, even canonized, those policies which even in retrospect served us all well enough through the years of nation building. If a new social contract is in fact required for the coming era of world building, then let us get on with it. But not in an adversarial relationship of "the people" against "business." Let us rather recognize the universal myopia that characterized our past as we build a base for our future. And having acknowledged this myopia for what it was, let us now, *as a society,* take *collective* responsibility for the victims of our shortsightedness. And for this project we might well accept as a basic maxim that no group or institution should be held responsible, or liable, for displaced workers except to the extent that it has participated in the displacement-causing decisions.

L8. CORPORATE BIAS

This plea for diffusing responsibility beyond corporate headquarters under the guise of collective responsibility has ample historical precedent. Corporate decision making has over the years enjoyed benign neglect at the hands of government in the United States, notably with regard to plant closings. It has also enjoyed taxpayer insurance against costly blunders, with notable examples in steel, airplane, and auto manufacturing. Requiring taxpayers to cover some $100 billion that savings and loan institutions lost because of irresponsible and even fraudulent management is the latest case in point. But in spite of this willingness to let government rescue management, no comparable willingness is displayed with regard to workers and their communities. In particular, it is now being contended that so-called foreign competition requires leaving business even more unhampered than before so that it can find new and better ways of competing, for example, by the introduction of robots. What is left off this agenda is any consideration of the scope of interests that will in fact be served by such flexibility and that will not. Management left to itself will consider at best only the interests of its investors, not those of its workers. But if workers (like managers) cannot protect themselves on their own, say, by negotiating job security arrangements, then why should government not help them too? If great benefits really are derived from displacing workers, then why shouldn't some of those benefits go to the workers who are being sacrificed to that end?

C8. WORKER CONTROL

If the basic concern here is that management cannot represent workers fairly and objectively in these crisis situations, this can be remedied by expanding the role of workers in decision making, not only on the shop floor but on executive boards as well. To the shared responsibility of management and workers on a board of directors can also be added appropriate government input. The broader the representation, the better the input and the better the resulting output in the form of policy. In this way, management would retain responsibility but would share it with representatives of both workers and government. Quality circles, profit-sharing plans, worker ownership, and various other arrangements, as appropriate, can be implemented to increase workers' involvement in and appreciation of challenges to the survival and growth of the company that employs them. With some modification of the legal constraints on unions, unions could even take responsibility for some of these new approaches to management, so long as they would not thereby enter into unfair competition in the very industry one is trying to salvage.[36]

L9. ECONOMIC POLICY PLANNING

Even management can sound prolabor if the situation is desperate enough. Worker ownership is a good example. How often do you hear of employees being offered ownership of a thriving business? Employees are turned to as a convenient way to bail out of a plant or business with minimum damage to the corporate image before community and customers. Even the Reagan administration, which boasted impeccable antilabor credentials, seriously considered selling Conrail to its employees to get it off the public ledger.[37] As this example illustrates, deregulation is about as close as the U.S. government has come to any coordinated, consistent industrial plan. But not even an economy as large as that of the United States can function effectively in the face of world competition without serious broad-based planning combined with research and development (R&D). Nor can we rely any more on incidental civilian applications of military R&D.[38] The Japanese study world markets on a national level, locate areas of business decline, stagnation, and growth, then focus R&D accordingly. Companies *collaborate* on R&D (no need for domestic industrial spying) and do their competing with products in the marketplace.[39] Similarly, the West German government controls industrial plant relocation by assessing the total cost of any proposed move, including the cost to workers, on the infrastructure.

These examples from abroad would seem to invite election-conscious political parties to compete with one another for proposals after years of relying in vain on fiscal manipulation.[40] Instead, Washington politicians have focused on deregulation, protectionism in the form of import restrictions, "local content" requirements for products to be consumed domestically, and (in the wake of stock market woes in the late 1980s) modest reform of trading technology. Such reactive measures constitute little more than a band-aid approach to curing unemployment.

Band-aids are needed, as are tourniquets and even transfusions. But we need to go beyond concern just for the transition of the worker (adequate, if at all, only for cyclical, or frictional, unemployment) to concern about moving from an obsolete industrial base to one with a very different mix of skill requirements and resulting employment needs.[41] Just because it will be difficult is no reason not to take seriously the titular goal of the Humphrey-Hawkins Full Employment Act of 1978.

C9. GROWTH THROUGH AUTONOMY

This appeal to government to solve the problem of unemployment is understandable in its historical context, but it is misguided in two important respects. It is understandable because it grows out of a period in our history when the labor pool, especially as it swelled with the baby boom generation, did for a time exceed employers' hiring needs. It is misguided because it assumes government has powers it does not have and it is rendered moot by an emerging scenario of too few workers for the jobs that will need to be filled.

First, it is naive to assume that government can solve any problem through the magic of its burdensome bureaucracy. Anyone who believes this needs to explain why welfare programs developed in West European countries in decades past are being cut back by survival-bent governments at both ends of the political spectrum.[42] As countries all over the world are learning, deregulation of an industry allows once badly structured companies to economize in various ways that help preserve jobs for people. Granted there is need for better planning. Any business that has to meet the competition knows very well that profitability, not to mention survival, depends upon a well-laid-out plan of attack. So why ask government to do at great cost what competition does for free?

Second, the employment problem for the foreseeable future will be one of too great a demand for too small a supply of workers. Population growth in the United States has been declining significantly and as a result anyone wanting to work and willing to learn will not only find employment but will be in a better bargaining position for wages and benefits than are those presently in the workforce.[43] Under these circumstances, competition will diminish among workers even as it intensifies among potential employers. So the marketplace will solve very well a problem that government was hardly even able to define.

A response on behalf of labor to this encomium for independence from government might begin with a rejoinder about the pot calling the kettle black, then point to the implications of automation, and, finally, show how neatly capital's scenario disregards the availability of Third World workers, both by virtue of minimally effective efforts to keep them from immigrating to the United States (and to Canada as well) and by virtue of the growing tendency of employers to locate their plants and facilities in Third World countries. To these observations, in turn, yet other responses could be formulated on behalf of capital. But that way lies a dialogue ad infinitum. So let us call a halt at this point to arguments and counterarguments regarding responsibility for displaced workers and assess the results.

A clear winner has not emerged. But labor certainly has a prima facie claim that it is being treated badly in the United States; and occasional judicial findings of unjust dismissal will not suffice to balance the scales of justice. On the other hand, random expansion of workers' defenses against EAW would unquestionably hamper management's ability to meet serious competition. But we are all losers if we continue to acquiesce in a public policy that for all practical purposes abandons displaced workers like tools no longer needed. We do not cut off benefits to veterans of yesterday's wars just because they served with now obsolete means of destruction. Still less should workers be forgotten simply because they served with now obsolete means of production. Yet rosy predictions notwithstanding, full employment however defined is probably an unattainable goal at least for the foreseeable future. What, then, is to be done and how?

For a start, there is an urgent need to undertake a broad-based dialogue toward the development of a humane work policy that accords people at least as much respect as profits. Out of such dialogue might come employee rights legislation to counterbalance the more brutalizing aspects of employer autonomy. In the United States, such legislation should systematize and democratize protections against the excesses of EAW that are presently available only to those able to bring their complaints to court. Second, the long-term social impact of allowing employers to engage in "defensive hiring" practices needs to be scrutinized with the utmost care and concern. For at the very time we are being told to expect an increasingly inelastic labor supply, more and more employers are trying to squeeze more productivity out of a "downsized" workforce. Regular employees are often required to put in many overtime hours; but instead of increasing their benefit-laden numbers, employers prefer to maximize their "flexibility" by means of part-time, or independent contractor, employees.[44] Yet warnings about an imminent labor shortage should not be allowed to rationalize an unprincipled commitment to automation when improved education, better day care facilities, and more liberal immigration policies might prove no less effective. Public sector planning must increasingly complement and if need be constrain the untrammeled marketplace as we seek to distribute available work more rationally and equitably.

What is especially problematic about predictions of a domestic labor shortage is their potential to become self-fulfilling prophecies. For, when read by executives already persuaded of the merits of automation, globalization, and every other species of workforce restructuring, they constitute a convenient counterpoint to voices that tell instead of a coming age of leisure. What seems clear is that one prediction can be compared with another only if each presupposes a more or less equivalent (transnational) workforce and makes more or less equivalent assumptions about the mobility of both employers and employees. Only in this sort of context does it make much sense to talk either about too few jobs or too few workers in the years ahead. For example, to defend current restrictive immigration policies while at the same time expressing concern about a coming shortage of workers seems both racist and, in view of the reasons why many people wish to enter the United States, irresponsible.[45]

Thus have we come full circle in our attempt to articulate basic policies with regard to work that a workers' representative might endorse without qualification. The global mobility of major employers suggested a need to establish appropriate community standards for work relationships. But tradition-based proposals to make work obligatory were undermined by the problem of unequal distribution of any such obligation and by uncertainty about employment opportunities for workers. Concern about people's need for fulfillment, however, suggested that society might be obligated to provide work to that end. Doubts about being able to provide such work to all in the form of jobs suggested as an alternative that more attention be given to play, or pleasure, as a social objective. But that could be a cruel and indiscriminate hoax if made available, as now, only on the basis of one's involvement in status work, and even then unevenly. Predictions about a coming workforce diminution offer no panacea, because employers look increasingly beyond national borders to fill their employment needs, and they show every sign of preferring to hire those who make the fewest demands. This leaves us with a problem of considerable scope. But before returning to it in earnest, let us consider what kinds of relationships there ought to be between employers and employees.

PART II

Worker and Corporation

5

"Meaningful Work": A Two-Edged Sword

SHOULD A WORKERS' representative
agree that, as long as there is work to be done, it ought to be as meaningful as
possible to the worker? Or might the quest for meaning lead to another dragon's
lair? There is something quite seductive about the notion of "meaningful work"
(MW). It is thought to be something that workers want and even need; so, not
surprisingly, there are philosophers who defend it as a worker's right.[1] Less clear
is who or what is obliged to bring this about. For in the history of the human
race there has been no shortage of drudgery, peonage, slavery, and just plain
unpleasant endeavors, many enduring throughout those short, nasty, and brutish
lives Thomas Hobbes associated with the state of nature. Nonetheless, appeals
for MW commonly assume that it was the rule until capitalism came along to
upset the good old ways, deskill self-actualizing craftspersons, and reduce the
workforce to cogs in the wheels of corporate progress. But if this is the case, then
perhaps the corporations themselves should be required to build meaning back
into jobs. Or should they?

Proponents of MW have not been altogether clear on this point. They seem
to assume that the meaningfulness of one's work is inversely proportional to the
dividedness of labor—what libertarian philosopher Robert Nozick calls "fragmentation of tasks." But if fragmentation is the culprit, MW might be systematically unattainable. Arguments in support of a claim to MW presuppose the
ability of some institution—in the last resort, of some unit of government—to
make this happen. But according to available records, once Humpty Dumpty
went to pieces, neither the king's horses nor the king's men could put that poor
egg together again. This suggests (aside from its political implications) that the
effects of decomposing a whole may be irreversible—at least in the case of jobs
the quality of which must somehow be assured by government ukase.

In view of how difficult it would surely be to achieve MW by government fiat,
might a corporation be thought to have an obligation in this regard? For Nozick,
the answer is comparatively simple. As he sees it, only a corporation could be

obligated to make work meaningful—but the imposition of such an obligation would be either superfluous or violative of an individual worker's right to choose a good other than MW.

Taking MW to involve subjectively fulfilling and worthwhile activity that is understood to contribute to "some overall goal" in a "larger process," Nozick thinks a company would maximize MW if doing so increased productivity and profit or if, without diminishing profit, it gave the company a hiring edge over its competition. So for him, "the only interesting case" involves achieving a level of MW that diminishes profit. This, he says, a worker could choose in exchange for lower wages, or a consumer could choose by paying more for MW-produced goods or services, or government might mandate by prohibiting non-MW work or products. But this latter, even if implementable, would unjustifiably limit workers' alternatives.[2]

Nozick's assumption that income is a function of productivity or profit falters before the facts. In a capitalist economy, wages may rise when labor is scarce, but they do not ordinarily rise in direct proportion to what employers gain. Nor is there any direct correlation between the annual compensation of corporate executives and their companies' productivity or profits. A far more challenging problem arises out of Nozick's assumption, common to all who discuss MW, that MW depends somehow on job classification, which is a function of the division of labor. To examine this assumption, I will consider more carefully the context of MW and the reasons for classifications. It will then become clear that Nozick's dismissal of more profitable MW as uninteresting is at best naive—for the same reason that an unqualified demand for MW as a "right" is woefully ill-considered. Having shown why this is so, I will suggest that a workers' representative should endorse not MW but opportunity to exercise human creativity.

Meaning or Manipulation?
A Question of Control

For a long time and for many reasons (not all of them consistent) it was considered "rational" to divide a complex work process into minuscule components, each of which could be tended by a minimally skilled and comparably paid operative. This division of labor has generated all sorts of learned ruminations both pro and con, about which more in the next section. Atomistically viewed, it results in jobs that, as one worker put it, are "too small for our spirit, not big enough for people."[3] In other words, people's jobs are no longer (if they ever were) totally satisfying. Indeed, many a job may be so "small" (lacking in challenge) as to be perceived as meaningless.

This, to Ralph Helstein, president emeritus of the United Packinghouse Workers of America, is not a problem but an opportunity: "Learning is work. Caring for children is work. Community action is work. Once we accept the concept of work as something meaningful—not just as the source of a buck—you don't have to worry about finding enough jobs."[4] This idea is certainly worth exploring. But what businesses pay "bucks" to have accomplished is not "something meaningful" but something that can contribute to profitability. Whether those employed as means to that end find meaning in what they do is incidental to considerations that determine the size and configuration of a workforce. So the more people expect their work to be meaningful, the more they seem to challenge employers' claims to control over the work relationship. There are, however, four serious objections to this expectation, namely, that it is of only secondary importance to a worker's need for income; no more assured in high-skill than in low-skill jobs; no substitute for job security; and manipulable by employers for purposes hostile to employees' interests.

FIRST OBJECTION: JOB SATISFACTION IS NOT A SUFFICIENT REASON FOR KEEP-ING, AND THE ABSENCE OF JOB SATISFACTION IS NOT A SUFFICIENT REASON FOR LEAVING, A JOB. People often choose to continue in unsatisfying jobs, notably for economic reasons; and, inversely, people often leave satisfying jobs, for example, to take a less satisfying but better-paying job or to exercise other options made possible by an inheritance. The controlling consideration is that people hold jobs to earn their livelihood. This being the case, even the unsatisfying job is better than none at all; and the satisfying job, being conditioned on a need, is not necessarily more satisfying than not working at any job in the absence of that need. So liking or not liking a *job* is subordinate to the need to earn a living. What is not so clear is whether liking or not liking one's work is subject to the same financial constraints or rather depends on a more basic human need to ac-complish something, to become "somebody" in one's lifetime. Such a question is difficult enough to answer in the abstract. So one can only be in awe of those who include answering it as a part of their own job description—namely, those peculiarly modern experts, the workplace therapists.

Workplace therapy thrives on such ideas as quality of work life (QWL), inte-grative holism (Theory Z), employee involvement (EI), New Age training pro-grams (spawned by "humanistic psychology"), and other inventions of social and behavioral scientists. These inventions are sold to management (and, if possible, to workers) as organizational innovations that will make workers more satisfied with their jobs. This is ironic, since for well over a century it was received doc-trine that the way to manage workers was to make sure they did not find too much satisfaction in their jobs. But deliberately engendered dissatisfaction is ex-perienced by workers as dissatisfaction, and this has had some counterproductive consequences. So management policy toward workers has gradually shifted from a concerted effort to drain the meaning out of jobs to trying to put meaning back in—all in the name of productivity.

The "dehumanizing" consequences of authoritarian pyramids in the workplace was recognized long ago by industrial psychologists and other consultants to management, notably by Abraham Maslow in his *Motivation and Personality* (1954) and by Frederick Herzberg in *The Motivation to Work* (1959). A number of ways to improve job satisfaction were proposed, both in the United States and abroad, and some were actually implemented, for example, by Robert N. Ford at AT&T. Reflecting on the AT&T Work Itself Program, Ford endorsed job enrichment as a way of undoing "job denuding" brought about by almost automating jobs out of existence, simplifying and partitioning them to save on training costs, or "tightening up" a job by moving its assigned responsibilities to a higher level.

Dedicated as their proponents often were, many of these workplace changes were essentially cosmetic, in no way affecting the underlying relationships between controllers and those controlled. This is illustrated all too well by the extensive and now even government-endorsed worker displacement that characterizes more recent employee relations at AT&T. There have, however, been some noteworthy exceptions. In the United States such companies as American Velvet (in Stonington, Connecticut), Donnelly Mirrors (Holland, Michigan), and Lincoln Electric (Cleveland) showed the world how to conduct a profitable business that is at the same time congenial to workers' needs. The French champagne company Moet & Chandon did the same, especially by rewarding workers' efficiency at each distinct stage of production. The most dramatic changes, however, were taking place in Scandinavian countries, especially Norway and Sweden. Well known in this regard is the shift of automotive manufacturers Volvo and Saab from assembly line production to a team-based process eventually implemented in an expensive new plant. Less known about these revolutionary changes is that these companies were, so to speak, driven to make them. Young Swedes were staying away from mind-numbing assembly line work in droves, with the result that these companies already depended on such countries as Finland and Turkey for close to half of their workforce.[5]

In spite of this ferment in the world's manufacturing sector, it was widely assumed in the United States at the end of the 1960s that most working people liked their jobs. Then in 1971 Studs Terkel published *Working*, in which some 133 different individuals, from all over the United States, talk "from the heart" about their jobs. Most of those interviewed are working class, but all levels of society are represented, as are all ages and just about any type of jobholder one could imagine; and what they say calls into question the received wisdom of the workplace therapy industry. Before the year was out, President Richard M. Nixon appointed a task force to study "work in America." A year later, he received a report that challenged his reliance on the work ethic by stressing the importance of satisfying work. At that point, work therapy became a growth industry.[6]

SECOND OBJECTION: IT IS COMMONLY BELIEVED THAT MEANINGLESSNESS IS A PROBLEM PECULIAR TO LOW-SKILL JOBS THAT ARE DISAPPEARING WHILE SATISFACTION IS BUILT INTO JOBS ON THE INCREASE THAT REQUIRE SKILLS MORE HIGHLY RESPECTED AND REWARDED. BUT THIS IS NOT NECESSARILY THE CASE, FOR TWO REASONS. On the one hand, employers are deliberately creating new jobs that are and are intended to be meaningless. This is the direct result of a process that might be called Planned Alienation.

Ties between technology and alienation are spelled out in some detail in Marxist analysis of the so-called labor process (see Chapter 8). In recent times this analysis has been stimulated by the work of sociologist Harry Braverman, who blames management for conspiring to deskill jobs in order to reduce if not eliminate dependence on human workers. But what Braverman and others consider detrimental both to the worker and to productivity is seen by others as a means to greater productivity. In a book entitled *Silicon Valley Fever*, for example, deskilling is defined as a process of job simplification by means of computer technology so that less-skilled, lower-paid workers can be substituted for more educated, higher-paid employees. Deskilling thus understood is made for the intrusive phone call approach to sales called telemarketing. One company involved in this business claims it can increase a minimum wage "communicator's" sales per hour by as much as 20 percent by providing this person with a computer-accessed script containing all anticipated questions and answers. Case in point: thanks to "a powerful script that focused on overcoming objections," a Maryland bank generated a 15% positive response to its offer of an 8% savings account at a cost of a mere $2.77 per completed call.[7] Jobs in which thought and action are so rigidly compartmentalized in the name of efficiency "are not at all natural," in the words of one observer; "they are a method of social control."[8] But the key point here, Horatio, is that there are more reasons in the world for meaningless work than the secluded philosopher is likely to have dreamed of.

On the other hand, all sorts of jobs thought to be MW-rich do not necessarily come through as expected for those who hold them. And this problem is indifferent to position in the presumed hierarchy of MW.

Consider first of all an area singled out by Ralph Helstein as a locus of MW. "Worker burnout" has been identified as a genuine health problem that affects not only the worker but the company as well because of reduced efficiency, absenteeism, and turnover. These problems, according to one analyst, are especially acute in service professions (social work, teaching, health care, and even law).[9] For example, interns and residents in hospitals have for years been expected to be on duty for several days in a row; but as their exhaustion is found to contribute to lawsuits more than to professional growth, this curious rite of passage is being modified.[10] More generally, stress is indigenous to any workplace where

long hours of regular attendance, without regard to productivity, are made a prerequisite to advancement—or where the technology-driven demands of the job
are inherently stressful. Thus, as workers years ago went on strike to protest de-
bilitating machinery, so in recent times have air traffic controllers done the same,
with comparably futile results.[11]

Consider second an area often pointed to as a paradigmatic source of MW:
electronics engineering. The computer-designing team chronicled by Tracy Kidder in *The Soul of a New Machine* is a case in point.[12] Digital Equipment (DEC)
management lured them into the project with a carrot of awesome job satisfaction. Yet most of the "young Turks" who worked twice forty hours a week
for the sake of a new computer subsequently left the company, and many were
disillusioned by their experience.

A third purportedly MW-rich area of employment that many find disappoint-
ing is none other than management, especially middle management. Constituting
about 10% of the U.S. industrial workforce in 1980 (as compared to 4.4% in
Japan), middle managers have been well represented among the victims of corporate downsizing and restructuring in the past decade. Experts advised that
this would leave the survivors with lots of MW to thrive on, but instead it has
left many overworked and underappreciated. They may find their responsibilities doubled (this not necessarily being reflected in additional income) and their
free time at a premium. Or they may find themselves bypassed by a new chain
of command. Especially vulnerable are staff people who advise, consult, or coordinate: their responsibilities are being transferred to computer data bases and
"expert systems." The resulting corporate structure, according to one analyst,
will be not the classical pyramid but an hourglass—with few managers in the
middle. To some extent wishful thinking on the part of bloodless bottom-liners,
this scenario envisions a generation of middle managers who cannot help but feel
used, discarded, isolated, unimportant, and unfulfilled. And, by the way, most
women brought into management in recent years are to be found in these sectors
under siege.[13]

As a result of these and other related experiences, unbounded dedication to
one's job, once taken for granted, is now likely to be thought of not as a virtue but
as a disease called workaholism. So workaholic excess is becoming more difficult
to require of people.[14] There are, however, two exceptions to this generalization.
One of these is the carrot-driven job, as in law or electronics, in which unstinting
performance is a prerequisite to upward mobility. Another is the fast-growing,
stick-driven job involving the "transitory employee," who is by definition and
design quite at the mercy of the employer (see below, next section).

Many workers, in any event, are becoming less committed to their jobs—for
reasons, however, that do not justify blaming them. Nonetheless, interested observers worry that the correlate of declining commitment is lower productivity.[15]

Causes aside, this is not obviously so. In the 1970s some countries, notably Japan, West Germany, and France, increased their productivity at a faster rate than did the United States. But U.S. productivity levels are still among the highest in the world. And both management and labor have been looking for ways to bring about a "productivity takeoff" through changes in both the means and the relations of production.[16]

Changes in the means of production range from better product design to total automation of process. Changes in the relations of production are aimed especially at improving performance, for example, by establishing what are purported to be quasi-managerial teams, by expanding worker participation in decision making, and by introducing bonus or stock ownership plans, including even outright worker ownership. Whatever the approach, benefits to workers are not thereby assured. Even discounting the possibility of plant relocation, neither ownership nor participation alone is a sufficient condition for high motivation. But a worker ownership arrangement that is highly participatory, as is true of the cooperatives in Mondragon, Spain, may be very successful for all involved.

THIRD OBJECTION: WHETHER A JOB IS "TOO SMALL" OR IS "BIG ENOUGH FOR PEOPLE," IT REMAINS SUBJECT TO TERMINATION. This termination may be direct or indirect ("constructive," in legalese) and, as noted above, may affect salaried as well as hourly personnel. This being the case, in the words of a former TWA flight attendant, "one might have to search further than the workplace to find his/her fulfillment." The example she has lived: the TWA flight attendant strike of 1986.

> 6500 flight attendants were asked to take a 44% pay cut or be replaced. The entire workforce went on strike. They were replaced by a younger workforce who received minimal training. After two years five thousand of the original staff are still on the street and have their pride and dignity, which you can't take to the bank. This case . . . shows that everyone is replaceable and that there are many waiting to take someone's job even if it is for minimum wages.[17]

To this problem a government worker offers a wise but elusive solution: "[W]e should have a basic security—a decent place to live, decent food, decent clothing, and all that. . . . They get what they want out of people by threatening them economically." [18]

This sense of being expendable has been methodically exploited in recent years by companies faced with excess plant capacity. Workers in each plant are made to feel they must outproduce those elsewhere if the plant in which they work is to remain open. The level of productivity thus engendered, through lower wages or poorer working conditions, seldom becomes the determining factor in plant closing decisions. But in the meantime management has at its disposal an effective instrument of control that is only minimally defused by a requirement of short-term advance notification.

Precisely because of workers' insecurity in their jobs, a "workplace democracy" movement that seeks expanded participation only within the workplace is too narrowly conceived to overcome job dissatisfaction.[19] Yet the concept of workplace democracy does presuppose that democratic processes are operative in society beyond the workplace. But how significantly does a sociocultural milieu affect on-the-job relations and attitudes?

Political scientist Alfred Diamant suggests a way to answer this question by distinguishing three different sociocultural models, any one of which might be adopted as an "organizational culture," that is, a set of norms, values, and behaviors characteristic of a particular workplace: democratic pluralism, corporatism, and any of a number of versions of Marxism. The first, though subject to varying interpretations, may be considered familiar to readers of this book. The second Diamant traces to the communitarian guilds and estates of medieval times as perpetuated and distorted by modern fascist governments. The third is perhaps best illustrated by the ideas of Antonio Gramsci, who insisted that workers must create their own hegemonic areas at work and in society, especially by forming works councils.[20] Gramsci, in other words, agrees with other Marxists that only broad-based political transformation can overcome the economic roots of what Marx learned from Hegel to call alienation.[21]

FOURTH OBJECTION: HOWEVER WELL-MEANING THE MOVEMENT FOR MW, ITS OBJECTIVE IS PECULIARLY VULNERABLE TO CO-OPTATION BY EMPLOYERS. Marxists more than most have been systematically suspicious of capitalist employers' motives. This may help to explain why, after years of neglect, some Marxists are now returning to the old theme of alienation. For employers now present themselves not as causing but as having a cure for alienation. Under such labels as job enrichment, QWL, and cooperation, they are luring even unionized employees out of deskilled niches inherited from the past into purportedly more complex and challenging assignments. Workers in their turn are expected to respond to this recognition of their potential with deepest gratitude. But gratitude is not the most common response. As these experiments in MW are carried out at the workplace (rather than in scholars' skulls) they frequently involve more stress and less compensation.

To these changes—touted as everything from "bold" to "radical" and even "revolutionary" in business publications—union response was at first sceptical, then reluctantly tentative, and now more and more disillusioned as plants close regardless of productivity improvements. Reports of union acquiescence neglected to mention how the background conditions left them with only a Hobson's choice; but to some extent the true picture is slowly emerging. For example, the UAW's change in attitude is neatly chronicled in three articles in *Business Week* published at three-year intervals. "The New Industrial Relations" (11 May 1981) gave the impression that management's revolution had been tidily accomplished. An article about Ford Motor Company's daring to let hourly workers stop the assembly line to repair defects (30 July 1984) was subtitled: "Despite years of tensions, employee involvement is boosting quality and morale." "Detroit vs. the UAW: At Odds over Teamwork" (24 August 1987) presented a one-sided company account, but at least acknowledged that the changes are controversial.[22]

It is against this background that renewed scholarly interest in the concept of alienation is of some importance. For many years Marxists dismissed Marx's theory of alienation as the work of the youthful ("humanist") Marx.[23] But some sociologists and philosophers are again taking it seriously. One philosopher finds *positive* meanings of alienation in the history of philosophy; another distinguishes between a descriptive and an evaluative concept of alienation. One sociologist prefers a structural sociological theory detached from "alienation"; another calls for "self-determination" beyond workers' participation, control, or even self-management; and a third argues that "pre-occupational socialization prepares the individual for a normative acceptance of the conditions of alienated work."[24] Continuing an old debate about the revolutionary potential of job dissatisfaction, Joachim Israel insists, in disagreement with André Gorz, that in the absence of class consciousness, job dissatisfaction will never lead to revolution.[25] But the development of class consciousness is inhibited in the United States, in the anomalous opinion of social historians and others, by the "homogenizing" effect of various new technologies.[26] As for technology, some theorists see it as the cause and others as the cure for workers' alienation; others, like Marx before them, prefer a socioeconomic etiology.[27]

This learned analysis of alienation tends to be meticulously positivist in its approach. But it is sensitive to a normative question that underlies the issue of meaningful work: what, after all, constitutes a just relationship between employer and employees? And so long as answers to this question are not forthcoming, no informed workers' representative can espouse meaningful work as a surefire way to ennoble the worker. This note of caution becomes even more understandable when one takes into consideration how both job classifications and opposition to them are used to put workers in their place.

The Politics of Job Classification

People have long had a penchant for sorting out the different kinds of work they do. At first glance, this would seem to be a fairly straightforward, noncontroversial endeavor. But it is not and never has been. Classification may indeed provide a handy list of the different work roles (the butcher/baker/candlestick maker routine). But it also establishes boundaries, hierarchizes function, and thereby provides a basis for political and economic distinctions. Task classification, in other words, might in the abstract be value-neutral; but as different tasks are mapped onto different jobs the holders of those jobs are subject to second-level classification with regard to social status and power. Job classification, then, is a kind of technology of work that is adopted in principle to assure accomplishment of necessary tasks. But because this technology has important social consequences, it is as subject to controversy as is any other technology with social impact.

The controversy in this instance arises because the kinds of jobs there are in the world depends only in part on the nature of the tasks performed. No less important are political considerations that sometimes take the form of austere metaphysical pronouncements. These, in turn, are often inspired by economic realities that are themselves a function of available technology. Job classification is inescapably political in its effects and, as often as not, in the intention of the classifiers as well. To make this point I will consider three forms of political control of work, each of which presupposes a job classification: organization of work, work rules, and job control. What I hope to show is that work classifications are value-laden and that, accordingly, control over or changes in these classifications is no less value-laden.

Organization of Work

In many ancient societies the most basic distinction was between those who were required to work and those who were required not to work. This tidy distinction, however, was ever subject to more subtle differentiations, notably that between the work of a slave and that of a freeman. In some cities, such as Carthage, this distinction may have been somewhat less harsh in its consequences than in other cities, such as Athens, and eventually in the Roman Empire. But no lengthy historical review is required to support the claim that the distinction between those who were slaves and those who were (relatively) free had profound political implications. At issue, as Abraham Lincoln once pointed out when debating Stephen Douglas, was simply who would make the bread and who would eat it; and the slave/free dichotomy provided a very simple answer to that question. Whether the technology of such an arrangement was the most appropriate even for those times is debatable, especially if one has doubts about the importance of having great stone pyramids and temples on the face of this earth. But the more complex became the mix of tasks to be performed, the less responsive any such dichotomous arrangement could be. It all broke down in the later stages of the Roman Empire as the few masters had to devise all sorts of subcategories of slaves to take into account the great variety of assignments the slaves carried out. But these developments support rather than challenge the claim that the classification of work is political.

Plato's job classification in his *Republic* is another case in point. On the basis of tasks to be performed, there would be three classes in his ideal society: artisans and merchants, warriors, and guardians. Guardians, or rulers, would be selected from among the offspring of all citizens and would be educated on a level appropriate to their respective responsibilities. Each artisan or merchant would be required to stick to his or her assigned craft or trade for life. The assignment itself would in principle be determined not by birth but by merit; however, better breeders would be expected ordinarily to breed better offspring. The state would see to it that artisans earn enough to purchase and maintain the tools of their trade. But they would not participate in government in any way, nor would they be permitted to aspire to higher responsibility (although one or another might become philosophical). Thus would Plato cure the ills of an unmanaged democracy.

Comparable classifications prevailed among different peoples of both East and West throughout the classical era down to the time of the Industrial Revolution. In feudal times, work in rural areas was typically organized around the manorial court, which meted out justice on the basis of "the custom of the manor." With all aspects of life so regulated, correlative duties determined one's debts independent of money. Far more important was the sense of shared community that these feudal arrangements provided. Consider in this regard first an example of a local organization and then some arrangements for larger-scale organization.

At the Abbey of St. Germain des Près near Paris both general labor and specialized craft work were required. In the men's workshop were a blacksmith, a shoemaker, a carpenter, and two silversmiths; and in a separate area, working under a steward, about a dozen women spun and dyed cloth and sewed garments. Legally free workers (*coloni*), who were bought and sold with the estate, had to perform a certain amount of field work and such manual labor as repairing buildings, cutting down trees, picking fruit, making ale, or carrying loads, not only out of a duty of service but as a means of paying rent. Any farmer who happened to be an artisan was further obliged to pay a portion of the product of his craft: lances from the smith; barrels, hoops, and vine props from the carpenter; a cart from the wheelwright; cloth or garments from the serf women. It was up to the steward to see to it that all these services were rendered and rents paid, sometimes with the help of subordinate officials known as deans.

One such set of obligations is laid down in the records of the Abbey of St. Germain des Près from 811 to 826 A.D. as follows:

> Bodo . . . and his wife . . . Ermentrude have one free manse. . . . He pays
> 2 silver shillings to the army, 2 hogsheads of wine for the right to pasture

his pigs in the woods. Every third year he pays 100 planks and 3 poles for
fences. He ploughs at the winter sowing 4 perches and at the spring sowing
2 perches. Every week he owes 2 labor services . . . and 1 handwork. He
pays 3 fowls and 15 eggs and carrying work . . . when it is required of him.
And he holds half of a windmill, for which he pays 2 silver shillings.

In other words, Bodo and Ermentrude earned their subsistence by serving an
estate holder, which in this instance happened to be a monastery. Work arrangements in this monastic setting are described in the estate book drawn up by
Irmion, the abbot of St. Germain des Près. According to Irmion, the abbey's
lands are divided up into a number of estates. Each estate is divided into seignorial lands, occupied by the monks and administered by a steward, and tributary
lands, which are possessed by various tenants and divided into little farms called
manses, each of which is occupied by one or more families. These latter, the
serfs, do a certain amount of both "field work" and "handwork" every year for
the seignorial manse and use the uncommitted time to cultivate their own little
farms.[28]

Medieval crafts were organized not only locally but regionally, depending on
the extent of a ruling power's empire. The Emperor Charlemagne, for example,
insisted that each of his stewards have available in the district assigned to him
such craftsmen as blacksmiths, goldsmiths, silversmiths, cobblers, turners, carpenters, sword makers, fishermen, brewers, bakers, and net makers.[29] What this
suggests, of course, is that a powerful ruler exercised control over crafts as widely
as his military might made possible. And in this respect each particular manor
remained subject in one degree or another to a central authority greater than that
of the lord of the manor. As Jacques Le Goff notes, the category of workers
(*operatores*) did not refer broadly to all agricultural workers but to a special class
of agricultural contractors the product of whose labor brought them some benefit. As organized under the tutelage of a governmental "elite," they operated on
the basis of contracts for the use of the land that tied the level of their social
status and legal rights to the efficiency of their labor: contracts to plant different
crops jointly, long-term leases, and contracts that made land tenure dependent on
expansion and improvement of the land being cultivated.[30]

Organization of crafts under a central authority was, in short, already being
practiced during the Middle Ages. And in the time of Cellini, some types of
"manufactured" work were already organized into mass production enterprises.
What remained to be achieved was a systematic linking of the tasks of different
workers toward the achievement of a collective product, along lines that would
come to be so admired by Adam Smith. Advantageous though such developments
may have been for entrepreneurs and their investors, they tended to undermine
the dignity of traditional crafts—or so, at least, believed Smith's contemporary

Jean-Jacques Rousseau. Such disillusionment was not shared, however, by one Thomas Deloney, a contemporary of Cellini.

In 1626, poet Deloney praised a textile entrepreneur for the high level of MW that practitioners of all sorts of crafts and trades enjoyed in his employ:

> Within one roome being large and long
> There stood two hundred Loomes full strong.
> Two hundred men, the truth is so,
> Wrought in these Loomes all in a row.
> By every one a pretty boy
> Sate making quil[t]s with mickle joy,
> And in another place hard by
> An hundred women merily
> Were carding hard with joyfull cheere
> Who singing sate with voices cleere
> And in a chamber close beside
> Two hundred maidens did abide,
>
> . . . .
>
> These pretty maids did never lin
> But in that place all day did spin,
> And spinning so with voices meet
> Like Nightingales they sung full sweet.
> Then to another roome came they,
> Where children were in poore ar[r]ay;
> And every one sate picking wool,
> The finest from the course to cull;
> The number was seven score and ten,
> The children of poore silly men;
> And these their labours to requite
> Had every one a penny at night,
> Beside their meat and drinke all day,
> Which was to them a wondrous stay.
> Within another place likewise
> Full fifty proper men he spies
> And these were Shearemen every one,
> Whose skill and cunning there was showne;
>
> . . . .
>
> A Dye-house likewise had he then,
> Wherein he kept full forty men;
> And likewise in his fulling Mill
> Full twenty persons kept he still.
>
> . . . .

He kept a Butcher all the yeere,
A Brewer eke for Ale and Beere;
A Baker for to bake his Bread,
Which stood his hushold in good stead.
Five Cookes within his kitchin great
Were all the yeare to dress his meat.
Sixe scullion boyes unto their hands,
To make cleane dishes, pots, and pans,
Beside poore children that did stay
To turne the broaches every day.

.   .   .   .

This was a gallant Cloathier sure,
Whose fame for ever shall endure.[31]

That workers' bliss was a consequence, intended or not, of the gallant Cloathier's centralized organization of crafts and trades is as questionable as are the motives of the poet who makes the claim. For more than poetry is needed to justify such total organizational control. Michael Maccoby appeals instead to productivity. In his opinion, the "craft ethic" got America going but had to give way to the incomparably superior productivity that entrepreneurial ingenuity engenders.[32] With this the U.S. Supreme Court is not likely to quarrel; for the justices still think of business as though it were being conducted by isolated individuals who outdo one another in ingenuity by coming up with ever better mousetraps. Apparently absent from their repertoire of realities are the countless colonial systems, literal and figurative, whereby meagerly paid workers produce valuable cash crops or other raw materials for export by ingenious multinationals exercising near total control over the market they serve.[33]

The kinds of jobs available in a complex modern economy are, of course, in the thousands, as can be seen, for example, in the directory published annually by the U.S. Department of Labor. One must look behind the surface descriptions, however, to detect political aspects. Especially notorious are the number of jobs that involve comparable tasks but whose titles vary depending on whether the jobholders are typically male or female. The only difference between an administrative assistant and a secretary, for example, might be the gender of the jobholder—and salary varies accordingly. Such terminological gerrymandering complicates but will not forever blunt the campaign for "comparable worth."

To this end, feminist theorists are systematically demythologizing received doctrines regarding the appropriate allocation and evaluation of work. Feminist studies of work typically involve some sort of comparative evaluation of the work process. What is compared, typically, is the assigned value of work commonly done by males and that commonly done by females. Analysis of the politics of patriarchy and reproduction reveals indefensible discrepancies between discriminatory practices and the reasons given for them.[34] Of similar import are reconsiderations of other aspects of our heritage, including in particular the ideology of creativity and innovation, which some scholars find to have male supremacist implications.[35]

More than feminist critique will be required, however, to sidetrack the growing tendency of corporations to cut their labor costs by creating all sorts of multilayer workforce arrangements that include jobs which may be just as demanding as "regular" jobs but are less rewarding financially. These include both in-house and "rented" employees.

Employers save money on in-house employees who in their own name or through the employee union agree to work for less than what other experienced employees earn. Introduced during a time of high unemployment, these inherently discriminatory wage systems—whether applied to airline pilots or to grocery clerks—are defended by noting that a low-paying job is better than none at all. But, needless to say, such appeals do little to maintain employee morale.[36]

Much more widespread is the practice of converting from a regular to a contingent workforce. Variously classified as part-time, contingent, or temporary, what most workers so employed have in common is a lack of either job security or employment benefits. They are, according to one usage, "disposable," meaning dismissable without fear of legal ramifications. Including so-called homeworkers, employees of subcontractors, involuntary part-timers, temporary workers, and leased employees, these workers now make up well over one-fourth of the workforce in Sweden and the United States and about half that much in West Germany.[37] This industry was once thought of as providing primarily unskilled or semiskilled workers, but the range of skills now being marketed in this way includes those of lawyers, chief financial officers, high-tech specialists, and even physicians.

Perhaps not surprising, a very high percentage of these ancillary jobs are held by—and often created for—women.[38] The stated reason for "renting" employees, however, is not to discriminate against women but to reduce company expenses. This objective was encouraged in the United States by the so-called Safe Harbor provision of TEFRA, which excuses employers from paying ERISA-required employee benefit taxes on their employed nonemployees. But the 1986 Tax Reform Act made Safe Harbor available only to employers who lease no more than 20% of their employees; and courts have denied the exclusion to an employer (a so-called joint employer) that shares or codetermines matters governing the essential terms and conditions of employment along with the so-called broker employer.[39]

Job classification, in short, is seldom if ever politically—not to mention economically—neutral. What one does and how much one is paid for doing it depends in all sorts of ways on what such doing is called and what calling it that implies. So a workers' representative should not agree to include any system of job classification in a social contract without having carefully assessed its likely political implications.

Work Rules and the Division of Labor

For much the same reasons, a workers' representative should be slow either to endorse or to disavow any generic idea of work rules. Work rules delimit the scope of tasks that any one type of worker is permitted to perform, thereby pressuring an employer to maintain a workforce of a certain size. By means of work rules, unions, especially in the manufacturing sector, have been able to exercise some control over the numbers of jobs to be filled, the rates of pay, and the status of workers. But recent strategies of workforce restructuring, including automation, are changing this situation dramatically.

The machinery needed to automate a plant is often so expensive that a company can introduce it and remain competitive only by reducing costs of some other component of its enterprise. The component deemed easiest to manipulate is likely to be labor costs. The automating company increases production by operating the new equipment twenty-four hours a day, reduces significantly both the number of job classifications and the size of the workforce, and requires the smaller workforce to work longer shifts (with overtime). With the likelihood of no work at all as their alternative, skilled workers accept these machine-centered arrangements, which often require them to perform tasks formerly assigned to the unskilled.[40]

Aimed at cost-cutting (and, incidentally, union-busting), these changes in work rules can have very negative effects on job satisfaction and perhaps ultimately on productivity. For example, skilled maintenance and construction tasks formerly divided among craft jobs such as millwright, welder, rigger, and boilermaker may all be handled now by a "helper," who might in fact be a journeyman. In the name of "flexibility," rigid distinctions between groups of die makers might be eliminated or miscellaneous machine operators might be combined with light machine operators into one category. In Lynn, Massachusetts, GM made continued operation of its older plants conditional on union endorsement of a new plant in which one hundred workers with only three different categories would do jobs elsewhere distributed among up to twelve job categories. Such changes, along with others affecting everything from break time to cleanup, result in significantly lower wage scales and worker morale. Many union leaders, seeing little alternative, have been adaptable and conciliatory. But rank-and-file workers are not always willing to go along, especially if automation will pare the workforce no matter what the workers decide, as was the case at GM's Detroit Diesel Allison Division in Indianapolis.[41] Another reason for resisting is to avoid multiplant whipsawing, a process in which an employer uses concessions won at one plant to pressure workers elsewhere to concede the same if not more.[42]

Management's interest in doing away with job-circumscribing work rules is ironic, since these rules were originally created not by workers but by management. Especially influential in this regard was the movement known as scientific management, a time-study approach usually associated with Frederick Taylor, who was active in the first quarter of the twentieth century. Taylor gave management greater control over manufacturing processes by breaking down each complex job assignment to its basic components and rearranging the production process accordingly. This engineering approach to productivity is a somewhat extreme application of the hallowed principle of the division of labor, which antedates Taylor by more than a century.

Adam Smith, the eighteenth-century English economist, offered the first reasoned defense of the division of labor. His now classical description of pinmaking at the beginning of *The Wealth of Nations* is the point of departure for an argument that comparatively unskilled workers can do more and better work than skilled specialists provided that they are assigned only one discrete and easily understandable portion of the overall process. That more and better work is possible when done in this atomistic way Smith attributes

> first, to the increase of dexterity in every particular workman; secondly, to the saving of the time which is commonly lost in passing from one species of work to another; and lastly, to the invention of a great number of machines which facilitate and abridge labour, and enable one man to do the work of many.

According to Smith, then, the introduction of machinery into a work process upgrades the quantity and quality of work done by each worker, thereby reducing the size of the workforce needed for that process. But production of the machinery itself requires the labor of many workers with many different skills, so worker displacement is only a matter of lateral transfer. The division of labor arises out of the "trucking disposition" of human beings to trade goods and services among one another and as such enables each individual to concentrate on a limited number of tasks. So Smith's final assessment of the division of labor is that it enhances individual capabilities by facilitating specialization.[43]

Karl Marx is often interpreted as having opposed the division of labor. But this interpretation is not incontrovertible. Few writers have been more sensitive to the value implications of work categorization. In *Capital*, a later work, he presents a bleak picture of how mechanization causes workforce deskilling directly and impoverishment indirectly. In the *Grundrisse*, he displays a certain nostalgia for precapitalist work arrangements that maximize individual skills. But Marx did not conclude from these observations that mechanization is inappropriate or that the old ways were better. His historical materialism calls for continual transformation of the means of production; what concerned him were the relations of production, by which he meant the organizational arrangements by means of which a social system distributes jobs and job opportunities. His distinction between the means of production and the relations of production serves as a device for distinguishing socioeconomic classes. But, as he well understood, this distinction ultimately consumes its own tail, because the relations of production are themselves a means, or technology, of production. He had not faced this eventuality in his early writings, in which he looked forward to a day when a person might carry out all sorts of functions without concern about walking on another's turf.

Herbert Spencer, for all his individualist predilections, saw some evolutionary advantages to a division of labor in society, but he warned that it would be successful only by "proportioning of benefits received to services rendered," in a manner analogous to that of different organs in the body. In other words, each component member must "severally benefit in due degrees by one another's activities."[44]

French sociologist Emile Durkheim agreed with Spencer that the division of labor is an instrument of progress; but he based his conclusion on entirely different premises. Rejecting Spencer's rationale as an egoistic defense of competition that only pays lip service to social values, Durkheim endorses the division of labor on the grounds that it can enhance group solidarity. It arises within a social context (rather than among isolated individuals) as one possible solution to the struggle for existence (other options being emigration, colonization, subservience of some to others, and suicide). It *increases* the complexity of each occupation by engendering the in-depth concentration of the specialist. The "decomposition" of workers to the level of machines that Auguste Comte had worried about will not be a problem if workers maintain a sense of collaboration. For this wholesome state of affairs to be achieved, however, the state must make it possible for individuals to select tasks for which they are suited and in which they are sufficiently occupied.[45]

Durkheim's *The Division of Labor in Society* tried in effect to base a system of ethics on an analysis of work relationships. In particular, he claimed that the division of labor requires us to excel at our own specialized work both as individuals and as members of a professional group. Reviewing Durkheim's theory some fifty years later, Georges Friedmann declared his optimism to have been little more than futile speculation, because the industrial worker typically has no special skill but only "a dexterity due to neuro-motor co-ordination, which in the long run causes automatism and routine." For such jobs to be meaningful, notes Friedmann, workers must be recognized as full members of their community, with a sense of being fairly remunerated rather than of being exploited—conditions Durkheim failed to take into account. Still less did Durkheim take into account the impact of technology, whereby engineers enable management to create a "technical interdependence" of workers that does not result in any "moral interdependence." The latter requires a common state of mind which, contrary to Durkheim's expectations, is more likely to arise not in the context of the workplace but beyond the workplace in the structure of society, in particular, in the "class solidarity" of workers as wage earners.[46]

Friedmann's emphasis on the social context of job definition is still timely, as management continues to seek, however inconsistently, for new narrow job descriptions even as it tries to do away with the old ones. The result? According to one expert, "[W]e are caught up in a treadmill of retraining, reskilling, retooling . . . for job descriptions that are as narrow and as shortsighted as the ones [the workers] have come from."[47]

With such important considerations in the background, it would be difficult for a workers' representative to approve a set of work rules without considering carefully the broader, long-term interests of workers and their communities. Nor would concern for the community make it any easier for a workers' representative to propose that those who know jobs best should take charge of the jobs. For this, after all, is the no less controversial arrangement known as job control.

Job Control

Job control means control over access to employment and employment-related income opportunities. It has long been high on the agenda of labor unions that more recently have been stressing job security. In industries such as construction a union might effectuate job control through a hiring hall arrangement (making job seekers dependent on the union for job referral). Other ways of controlling jobs involve preference for graduates of certain schools, or for members of a certain race, gender, ethnic group, political party, or even social club. Having such preferences routinely realized typically requires some sort of "old boy network": an unofficial but carefully articulated system of selecting preferred individuals for jobs.[48]

Defenders of job control are on the defensive these days because job control has become a scapegoat for whatever is wrong with business, especially in the United States. Rather than blame the shortsightedness of management or the indifference of government or the self-interest of the investment community, it is easier to point a finger at the power of organized labor. The fireman on a diesel locomotive stands as a symbol of how unreasonable are the controls that labor exercises over productivity and progress. Managers appeal to competition from abroad, especially from the Pacific Rim, as reason enough to do away with work rules and, if possible, with unions. Politicians backed by a business constituency cautiously cite the very existence of unions in their bailiwick for their failure to attract more of that very foreign competition. Flexibility, all say, is what is needed in troubled times like these; and thus do they offer a newly phrased version of the original authoritarian insistence that job control should be the prerogative of employers.

It is understandable that employers might oppose worker control of jobs and do everything possible to prevent it. Antiunion sentiment is strong enough in some jurisdictions to enable a politician to use unions as a scapegoat. But it is somewhat surprising that few intellectuals have been particularly supportive of job-controlling organization. This may be because intellectuals come from or at least identify their interests with the decision-making class. Marxists value unions, but mainly as vehicles for revolutionary goals better perceived by the avant-garde, which includes intellectuals whose own backgrounds are often not in the working class. Liberals tolerate and even endorse unions so long as they fit fairly neatly into organizational structures that are allegedly far better understood by management. Conservative pundits are more likely to tell workers that isolation from one another enhances their dignity as individual human beings. Such confusing signals notwithstanding, many workers still elect to unite in their common interest. This basic fact gives occasion for intellectuals (not to mention government agencies) to debate whether such efforts at autonomy are in the public interest. Arguments about the desirability of unions as such will be considered at length in Chapter 6. To be considered here is the preliminary question as to whether workers should exercise control over their jobs.

A job-control system, arguably, reduces the likelihood that the persons employed are, by objective standards, the best qualified. But it is not obvious that employment selections made in this way are any less job-related than those made by an employer. Moreover, not all criteria applied in job-control arrangements are equally irrelevant to employment qualifications. Except in a family business, the hiring of only Smiths or Joneses is ordinarily unjustifiable on any objective grounds. But there is much to be said for encouraging groups of professionals to tend to the placement of their peers. For who, this argument asks, is better qualified to pick an expert than another similarly specialized expert? This *expertise rationale* for job control is commonly practiced by lawyers, health care professionals, and university professors, among others.

Another rationale is found in attempts to explain the historical development of workers' job control by appealing to communitarian principles. Employers have traditionally preferred that their workers remain organizationally isolated from one another and dependent upon the employer for their survival. But workers, who might otherwise live out their lives as individualists, have often been driven by the excesses of an authoritarian employer to recognize their common plight, develop a strong sense of a shared fate if not of community, and form a protective association to look after their common interests. From this point of view, workers are entitled to exercise job control not so much because of their own virtues as because of the vices of the employer. This account, then, though focused on the benefits of organization, presupposes hostility in the employer and as such is perhaps better characterized as *the self-help rationale*.

Considerations such as these obviously do not settle one way or another the multifaceted question as to who should control jobs. As we will see in Chapter 6, this question has a history that goes back in antiquity at least to the origins of the craft guilds. And it continues to this day in the efforts of professional organizations to regulate their own affairs while government becomes more and more insistent on setting the terms and conditions of employment of professionals of all kinds, including professional government employees. What is clear under the circumstances is that not even job control can be depended upon as a guarantor of MW.

Work and Creativity

Disagreements and disputes over workers' classifications make it abundantly clear that MW cannot be assured by a job description. Yet it seems plausible that what philosophers want guaranteed by asserting a right to MW is essential to human well-being. But in what way it is essential is not usually spelled out. Take, for example, David Braybrooke's account of the demise of status work that can provide "reasonably high esteem." His RHE conditions depend on external factors over which the individual agent has no control. His nomination of hedonism as a possible remedy is similarly flawed in that it focuses on social conditions rather than on personal accomplishment and it fails to clarify what kinds of pleasure are to be facilitated. Taking a cue from John Stuart Mill's cerebralization of the utilitarian calculus, I suggest that the essential human need which defenders of MW want guaranteed is an opportunity to exercise creativity.

This need to be creative has long been defended by humanistic psychologists. Philosophers, in turn, have attempted to show that it is a basic need by tying it to such ontological priorities as autonomy, self-respect, and self-fulfillment. It is generally assumed—and Adina Schwartz explicitly claims—that these basic human objectives cannot be achieved only outside of the workplace but must be facilitated on the job as well. The opportunity to exercise human creativity, however, cannot always be provided by jobs. Depending on the state of technology in any line of endeavor, jobs that do need to be done may not require much, if any, creativity. Yet creativity remains a human need. What, then, is to be done? What general policy on this subject might a workers' representative espouse? To address this question I will reformulate the problem of MW by drawing upon an unlikely source: a theological distinction in the Catholic tradition between sacraments and sacramentals.

A sacrament, according to an old catechism definition, is an outward sign of inward grace—that is, an assurance to observers that God is here and now bestowing grace on a suitably disposed human subject. Theologians justify this assurance by saying that a sacrament is agent-independent for its efficacy: it works automatically (*ex opere operato*) if the prescribed actions are performed, regardless of the qualities of the performer. A sacramental, by contrast, is agent-dependent, meaning that its efficacy depends on the qualities of the performer (*ex opere operandi*).

This old distinction can be used to formulate the difference between meaning-less work and work that is meaningful if we secularize it and invert its priorities. Work is meaningful to the extent that the qualities of the performer are not irrele-vant but crucial. Work that can be carried out efficaciously without any agent-originated input may be meaningful to whichever individual or group defines that work. It may also be meaningful derivatively to individual workers who, to some degree at least, depend for their identity upon the definer. But such work is per-sonally meaningless inasmuch as it does not owe its efficacy to the worker—as is increasingly the case in enterprises that rely as much as possible on organiza-tion and automation for success. Whence the importance of work the efficacy of which depends on the worker's input.

The limitations of automatically efficacious work might not be so troublesome were it not that such work is intentionally designed as a desirable objective. The quest for ever greater productivity through technology tends to deprive human work of all but an instrumental value, which itself is considered to be only tem-porary. Work is thought of as a necessary evil to be endured until the coming work-free utopia is established. Thus is set up a dichotomy between work and play, with work being viewed as an interim necessity and play as an ultimate objective. Play, ironically, is encouraged in our own time primarily because it provides yet other opportunities (at least indirectly) for inherently meaningless work. In this context it is hard not to recommend that work include play as an essential component.

The concept of playful work is not only not self-contradictory but is well exemplified in the attitudes and practices of human beings with regard to a num-ber of their activities. These activities have in common a recognition of work as "opus." The word *opus* comes from the Latin, in which it means work with about the same broad range of meanings as does the Anglo-Saxon term. (Italian does the same with *lavoro* and French with *l'oeuvre*.) In English, however, *opus* is limited to the work product of a creative artist.[49] To refer to one's work product as an opus, then, is to give it a certain importance, a certain durability if not immortality. This same sense of importance is also conveyed by other modern terms that are based on derivatives of the Latin *opus*. The verb *to operate*, for example, implies being engaged in an endeavor considerably more significant than mere "doing." [50] An "operation" points to an accomplishment of more than ordinary import, be it mathematical, military, medical, mechanical, or whatever. Similar significance is attached to the term *operator*, in both canonical and colloquial senses. Efficacy and effectiveness mark the meaning of *operative*, especially when it is used as an adjective. [51]

Nothing is proven by word usage, of course. But the usage of *opus*-words does help make us aware of the creative dimension of activity work, as distinguished from a job, and that is enough to suggest an alternative to the problematic claim that a worker, qua worker, has a right to MW. Human beings, qua human, it might better be argued, have a right to exercise their creative potential. But this in no way precludes an employer from luring workers with creative opportunities and workers from seeking such, either in their jobs or elsewhere.

As for job-related creative opportunities, employers would be well advised not to identify their future needs just with better training narrowly conceived. [52] More insightful in this respect was American folksinger Harry Chapin, who in his song "Flowers Are Red" decried the creativity-crushing sort of education that reduces learning to the learning of rules. Comparing work to the game of golf, organizational researcher William H. Mobley makes much the same observation about jobs. [53] Lewis Mumford, a major scholar in search of the ultimate impact of technology, expands these insights by tracing the evolution of the human mind not to labor, as some would, but to the dreaming whence comes creativity. Others, expanding on science historian Thomas S. Kuhn's concern about rule-based limitations on scientific progress, urge leaders of developing countries to base their priorities for scientific research not on the marketing needs of TNCs but on creative application of technology to their peoples' real needs. [54]

What, in conclusion, should a workers' representative espouse with regard to meaningful work? Maybe nothing at all—or (so as not to appear unmindful of what is at stake) maybe something like the following. People need to find meaning and satisfaction in their lives, and to this end they must be free to exercise their creative potential. Employers are to be encouraged to provide opportunities for the exercise of creative potential. But people must remain free to decide for themselves how they personally want to go about exercising their own creativity, and so should not be coerced into any job change on the grounds that such change will enhance their creativity. Truly self-fulfilling activities are necessarily agent-dependent. One's status work may be automatically efficacious.

Worker Organizations

So MEANINGFUL WORK may be a dragon and as such not the sort of thing a workers' representative should endorse absent an abundance of additional information. Never mind. Laying down minimum standards for job content is not the only way to promote fair employer-employee relations. One might, for example, follow John Rawls's lead and call for *procedures* that would satisfy people's sense of justice. This idea gets a strong boost toward "reflective equilibrium" [1] because it has already been put into practice and institutionalized. The practice in question is called collective bargaining. But collective bargaining by definition involves collective activity on the part of workers—in other words, a union. Yet, if one may be permitted an understatement, reasonable people disagree about the social desirability of unions. So if anything like procedural justice in the workplace is to be included in the social contract, it seems incumbent upon us to examine arguments in support of workers' rights to organize and bargain collectively with their employer the terms and conditions of their employment.

There is certainly no shortage of material examining every imaginable aspect of the labor movement; but philosophical consideration has not been abundant. In the United States, unionists themselves have preferred a more pragmatic approach and philosophers have for the most part remained aloof. But there is a legacy of philosophical reflection about unionism, especially in Europe, and it lends prima facie support to Rawls's intuitions about priorities for a just society. For its basic assumption has been that liberty, or freedom, is of primordial concern. But there are three clouds over this clue to fairness in the workplace: (1) there is sharp disagreement about the meaning of liberty as applied to the workplace; (2) the history of some worker organizations suggests that they want power more than liberty; and (3) present realities are too complex to articulate solely in terms of liberty.

During the first century of the industrial era, both entrepreneurs and workers appealed to the Enlightenment concept of liberty to articulate their claims to control of the workplace. Both understood liberty to involve self-help; but they arrived at alternatively individualist and collectivist interpretations of this idea.[2] From the outset, employers have been seeking profits without payrolls. More recently, as they become increasingly reliant on workforce restructuring, their workers are pushed to the metaphysical limit as they seek to defend somehow their very right of survival as workers. Traditional arguments, to be examined in this chapter, barely address the issues that these new management strategies are generating. Hence the need to consider more carefully both worker displacement (Chapter 7) and automation (Chapter 8) and to explore community-oriented responses to the human problems these strategies bring about (Chapters 9 to 11). In this chapter I will focus on workplace organization as a source of liberty or power.

Worker Organization and Liberty

Some people are convinced that workers give up much of their freedom if they come together to form a labor union. Sufficiently widespread is this antiunion attitude that twenty states (mainly rural or southern), about half before and half after passage of an enabling provision (s. 14(b)) of the Taft-Hartley Act (1947), have enacted statutes to protect a worker's "right to work," meaning his or her freedom to continue working without joining a union even if that union has been duly established under applicable law by a majority of the workers.

That such an antiunion attitude can thrive in the United States is somewhat ironic. After all, our founding fathers did include freedom of assembly in the First Amendment. But strictly speaking, this right pertains only to political association free from intrusion by the federal government and, by virtue of the more recent Fourteenth Amendment, by the governments of the various states. These constitutional protections have been applied to corporations but not to people in their role as workers.

It took half a century just to establish the right of workers to organize and another half-century to build collective action into this right. The French constitution as interpreted by the Law Le Chapelier (1791) placed a Rousseauist ban on every kind of association among citizens of the same status or profession, including trade unions.[3] Associations of workers were considered criminal conspiracies in England until permitted under laws passed in 1824–25 and in the United States until *Commonwealth v. Hunt* in 1842. Only a half-century later were unions legally empowered to take any collective action in behalf of workers.[4] In the United States, union leader Samuel Gompers advised unionists to back off from efforts at political reform and concentrate on "business unionism," the chief instrument of which is collective bargaining. But as employers in bad times disregarded agreements made in better times, workers had to resort to strikes and boycotts. The courts, however, saw only employers' interests in the hallowed doctrine of freedom of contract.[5] And in defending this interpretation in the twentieth century they enforced so-called yellow-dog contracts whereby employees promised their employers that they would not join a union and applied an "ends-means" test to determine if workers were in fact being "coercive," say, by picketing, and if so by enjoining such activity. These antiunion rulings were repeatedly bolstered by applying the Sherman Antitrust Act (1890), without benefit of any legislative history to this effect, to labor unions.

Such favoring of employers over employees only exacerbated industrial turmoil in the United States until at last a series of legislative enactments that culminated in the Norris–La Guardia Act in 1932 and, in response to judicial restraints, the National Labor Relations Act (Wagner Act) in 1935, established the right of employees to organize and bargain collectively in their own interest as an essential condition for industrial peace. After World War II various laws were enacted which taken together have the effect of restraining the power of unions by increasing the oversight role of the federal government. One enactment in particular, the Labor-Management Reporting and Disclosure Act (Landrum-Griffin Act, 1959), imposed upon union executives many reporting regulations, notably with regard to use of funds and conduct of elections, for the alleged purpose of giving union members a "bill of rights."

Even assuming good intentions, Landrum-Griffin is yet another manifestation of a long-standing antiunion denial of any identity between individual workers who join a union and the union they join. In other words, rather than acknowledge that the whole, or local union, is a sum of its parts (its members), the antiunion analysis insists that the whole, understood to be primarily the international union, is entirely other than the parts. Relying on this metaphysical assumption, the antiunion analysis raises two principal objections to workers forming a union, each of which has a libertarian cast: first, that the union, being something other than the workers who join it, is an undesirable *tertium quid,* an "outside agitator," whom the employer has never hired but with whom the employer is constrained to deal; and second, that the employees, who enjoyed perfect liberty before the union arrived on the scene, are deprived of their liberty when they join that union.

This emphasis on individual liberty is apparently uppermost in people's minds when they question the right of workers to organize. But a case can surely be made that organization is in the interest of workers. So there is reason to believe that this libertarian opposition to organizing originates not with workers but with their employers. And in view of the well-known linkage between dividing and conquering, it would seem to be self-serving for an employer to sing the praises of individual liberty in personnel matters. So there is need to examine more carefully the relationship between unions and liberty.

Basically, three questions have been debated about unions and liberty:

(1) whether unions unduly constrain an employer's liberty; (2) whether they unduly constrain the liberty of workers; and (3) whether they unduly constrain the liberty of society as a whole. Each of these questions involves allocation of power. But, partly for historical reasons, the first two questions will be taken as put as questions of liberty; the third, having stayed more in the background of the debate, can and will be considered in connection with power.

Whether Unions Unduly Restrain the Liberty of Employers

It is often assumed that unions unduly restrain the liberty of employers. But unions offer many benefits to employers, including, for example, a mechanism for preserving peace in the workplace, an instrument through which stability can be assured for an agreed-upon period of time, a reliable source of skilled workers, and at times a buffer of responsibility should it become necessary to take some action that has a negative effect on the workforce. These and other such benefits notwithstanding, it is widely assumed that unions do unduly constrain employers. This assumption may be based on a belief that unions are not cost-effective because they cause wages to go up more than would otherwise be the case, or they undermine productivity, or they diminish the employer's power and control over the workers.

The claim that unions cause wage inflation needs to be evaluated in light of what workers were paid when there were no unions. Also, many nonunion workers are paid enough to discourage their interest in organizing.[6] As a result, nonunion workers have at times had the greatest *rate* of wage increase, as did U.S. agricultural workers in the 1960s (who, however, remained the lowest-paid group of workers).[7] Besides, if wage increases can be passed on to the consumer, as is often done, the employer is not directly harmed (but society as a whole may be).

The claim that unions undermine productivity is usually based on the assertion that a union's insistence on work rules and other limitations on conditions of employment prevents the employer from getting maximum "mileage" out of the workers per unit of pay (not, as Marx rightly observed, per unit of work). This monolithic view of productivity is too inflexible to be taken seriously.[8] But even if workers could be driven to produce more and the more produced would be sold rather than warehoused, the gain would be of only short-term significance as compared to the long-term disadvantage of a debilitated workforce (absent a strategy of deliberate workforce turnover, advantageous only if skill and experience are not factors). But some people still posit a causal connection between workers forming a union and productivity declining, as if workers are more interested in "loafing" than in helping to maintain the source of their livelihood. This, in turn, implies that productivity can be increased by keeping the workforce non-union. Such has been the attitude of many companies in the South of the United States and in many Third World countries, to which employers are increasingly attracted. But there is reason to reject the negative correlation between unions and productivity.

One comparative study concludes that "union and nonunion establishments (in U.S. manufacturing) can compete in the same product market despite the fact that the former pay their workers more because unionized workers (establishments) are more productive by a roughly offsetting amount."[9]

Another widely respected study agrees that unionism improves productivity because it fosters better workers and workforce stability and better managerial practices but finds that higher wages result in lower profits.[10] Corroborating the connection between unionization and productivity are reports that employers in the construction industry who have turned to nonunion workers have difficulty locating skilled workers that a union apprenticeship program routinely provides.[11] So there is evidence for a positive correlation between unionization and productivity.

There are various reasons for this correlation, including the role of union apprenticeship programs in developing skilled workers and the labor stability that a union under contract can provide. But there is obviously an upper limit on how much productivity this one factor, the presence of a union, can generate. In the case of deep-pit mining in the United States, that upper limit is thought to have been reached; so presumably some concessions will have to be made in the future if this industry is not to go the way of the government-subsidized mines in the United Kingdom.[12]

More generally, it may be conceded that an autonomous union may diminish *management's* power and control over the workforce. But it does not follow that a union necessarily constrains the liberty of the employer. A company under pressure from a government regulator or from consumers may find it helps the bottom line to work with and not against a union.[13] In some instances, management left to itself may actually hinder rather than help the employer achieve productivity and profitability. Some companies have come to recognize this and have, accordingly, shortened their chain of command, eliminated middle managers, and moved toward worker participation and even worker ownership—at times with the assistance and cooperation of one or more unions—certainly not just to be nice to the workers but because such changes are thought to be in the interest of the employer.

"The interest of the employer," in other words, is a superficially simple notion behind which lurks substantial controversy, because of the ambiguity both of *interest* (long term or quarter by quarter?) and of *employer*. Who, after all, is the employer in the case of a large, possibly transnational, corporation whose performance is the basis for important decisions by investors, including those interested in acquiring the company or merging it with another? Efforts to sort out these and other related questions in law are complex and transitional as the buying and selling of companies, especially by a complementary company, becomes an institutionalized process.[14]

In summary, it need not be conceded that unions unduly constrain the liberty of employers. A union may diminish *management's* control over its employees, but by facilitating competitiveness it may actually provide the difference between profitability and its opposite. So unionization may actually improve the liberty of employers, who, by the way, retain all sorts of "management rights," including control of hiring and firing, even under the most astutely bargained contracts. But these considerations are seldom addressed in the debate about unions. For this debate has focused not so much on the liberty of the employer as on that of the employee and, indirectly, of society at large.

Whether Unions Unduly Constrain the Liberty of Employees

With some notable exceptions throughout history, learning and even literacy tend to be more at the disposal of the employing than the employed, so it is easy to find arguments in print that warn workers about the harm that unions will do them. But not every institution has been antiworker, and more recently the prose has begun to balance out. In particular, arguments intended to show that unions destroy the liberty of workers are countered by no less impressive arguments that they have just the opposite effect; and some of these arguments start from libertarian assumptions.[15]

Arguments based on liberty in opposition to unions assume that individual autonomy is the primordial if not the only absolute value in the world of commerce. The basic structure of such an argument is simple: anything that interferes with individual autonomy is unjust. X interferes with individual autonomy, so X is unjust. In place of X one might insert "government regulation"; but more pertinent here is *joining or organizing a union.*

This reliance on individual autonomy for maintaining workplace justice is crucial to libertarian antiunionism, which goes beyond speculating about the basis of rights to making ontological claims about reality. Central to this approach is the hallowed libertarian principle known as "the law of equal freedom," according to which each individual is free to compete for the best deal available in the "open" labor market. The general formula for this system of "voluntary [as distinguished from union-coerced] cooperation," according to nineteenth-century British philosopher Herbert Spencer, is not "Do this, or I will make you" (presumably the formula for slavery) but "Do this, or leave your place and take the consequences." This wonderful freedom of contract unionists destroy when they make workers join and thereby not only trample on the liberties of people in their own class but with total disrespect give "peremptory dictation to the employing class." [16]

A union, on this view, undercuts what is most sacred to the libertarian: personal choice. In lieu of a primordial right to strike his or her own deal with management, the unionized worker must abide by whatever agreement is reached on behalf of all members of the union; and in lieu of a fundamental "right to work," the unionized worker may work only when and as the union directs.

But the administrative center of the company by which the worker is employed may also be abstract and remote from the on-site personnel who actually do the hiring. So management obviously would not want to claim that just any exogenous intrusion on a working person's pristine liberty is inherently undesirable. Or is an individual worker's agreement with the employer somehow less destructive of liberty than is that worker's agreement with his or her fellow workers to join with them in a union?

Pro-union arguments start with the extremely dependent status of the typical working person in an industrial society, that is, with the worker's basic lack of liberty; so they portray the union as a mutually advantageous instrumentality whereby separately powerless individuals create collectively a basis for shared liberty. They challenge the libertarian position in one of two ways: (1) by attempting to show that organizing is a sine qua non for liberty in a workplace; or (2) by defending the ethical and/or political propriety of organizing.

In the early 1900s, John R. Commons argued that organization is a precondition for workers' liberty. What antiunion libertarians were missing, noted Commons, is the new fact in history that workers are dependent on employment for their livelihood, and hence liberty for the wage earner derives not from being free to work or not as one chooses but from being employed. So a union, according to Commons, plays a liberating role by providing security against arbitrary discharge.

Another liberty-based defense of unions was articulated a few decades later by Selig Perlman. Consciously avoiding what he called intellectualist (de facto, European) philosophies of labor that treated labor as an abstract entity, Perlman concentrated empirically on rank-and-file workers, who (he claimed) think in terms of scarcity of opportunity and the resulting need for "rules of occupancy and tenure." In other words, liberty for the wage earner is a function of job control:

> "[S]hop rights" . . . to the workingman at the bench are identical with "liberty" itself, since thanks to them, he has no need to kowtow to foreman or boss as the price of holding his job. . . . [I]s not this . . . the only sort [of

liberty] which reaches the workman directly and with certainty and that can never get lost *en route* like the "broader" liberty promised by socialism?[17]

This job-control theory of liberty does not preclude but may be the basis for broad-based identification of self-interest with the success of the labor movement as a whole, for example, through a sympathy strike or a joint political action.

These reactive interpretations of workers' liberty are consistent with the more politically oriented recommendations of Alexis de Tocqueville early in the nineteenth century. In his prognostications about democratic government in the United States, Tocqueville noted that the "influence of democracy on wages" was essentially to create an undesirable imbalance between entrepreneurs and industrial workers. The latter, unlike small farmers, have no means of survival other than their employment; so if they choose to "withhold their work," the master (to use Tocqueville's word) is usually wealthy enough to wait them out. Moreover, when his profits are down, "he can lower their wages at his pleasure and easily recover at their expense that of which fortune has deprived him." Legislators, notes Tocqueville, need to be attentive to this special problem. For, as he argues at length throughout his analysis of American institutions, "the art of association," the "knowledge of how to combine," is a precondition to progress in a democratic society.[18]

Buttressing this equilibrium argument for unions is a related argument that finds moral worth in the very process of organizing to achieve collective goals and accordingly views collective action not only as permissible in certain circumstances but as inherently desirable. This argument comes in both religious and secular packaging.

Included among religious defenders of unionism are both Protestants and Catholics. Some Methodist ministers in England, for example, and the Catholic hierarchy in various countries, notably the Irish in the United States, identified very closely with the problems and concerns of working people, who were the mainstay of their churches.

Early in the twentieth century Walter Rauschenbusch articulated his version of the so-called Social Gospel of militant Protestantism by characterizing unions (in spite of some admitted excesses) as training grounds in altruism. Similar sentiments have been expressed in official statements of the Federal Council of Churches of Christ in America.

Catholic social teaching about unions has supported the right to organize on the grounds that coming together into groups is in accordance with natural law (Pope Pius XI's *Quadragesimo Anno*, 1931); that unions are continuations of medieval guilds and the guilds benefited workers, their industry, and society at large (Pope Leo XIII's *Rerum Novarum*, 1891); and even that organization is necessary to ameliorate oppression by employers. Accentuating this third reason, the

Polish Pope John Paul II, in *Laborem Exercens* (1981), draws on a distinction between direct and indirect employers to criticize the way transnational corporations exploit the dependency of Third World countries.[19]

With a view to achieving perfect democracy, socialists and communists alike see the development of democracy in the workplace as an important step in the right direction. Where they differ, in particular, is in their assessment of the degree of social change required to attain full democracy. Communists have considered any level of workplace democracy achieved by workers in a capitalist society to be only transitional, since to them the full attainment of democratic rights is dependent on a transformation of the entire society. Socialists, generally more willing to assume that the society as a whole is already more or less democratic, focus on extending that democracy into the workplace.[20]

This task of extending democracy to the workplace justifies the existence of unions, according to British Fabian socialists Beatrice and Sidney Webb. Individuals have lost control over their own lives because of industrialization, but they can "regain collectively what has become individually impossible." Uncontrolled managerial power causes great "loss of liberty" for the worker, who will have no genuine "freedom of contract" until individual bargaining gives way to collective bargaining between comparable parties. This is what the Webbs called the device of the "common rule," which simply means that all terms of employment are applied uniformly to all workers. In this way individual liberty will be enhanced, because liberty or freedom is constituted by "such conditions of existence in the community as do, in practice, result in the utmost possible development of faculty in the individual human being." This "development of faculty" is the decisive factor for the Webbs, who trace the origins of unionism to recognition on the part of the journeyman that under the changed circumstances arising out of capitalism his chances of ever becoming a master are "infinitesimal."[21]

During the Great Depression, the American philosopher John Dewey expanded such pleas for workplace democracy to include worker participation in ownership. As he put it, "the only form of enduring social organization that is now possible is one in which the new forces of productivity are cooperatively controlled and used in the interest of the effective liberty and the cultural development of the individuals that constitute society."[22] This position Dewey thought of as American-style "collectivistic liberalism" in contrast to British-style "individualistic liberalism." Without mentioning the Webbs, whose views are not very different from his own, he attributes the development of collectivist liberalism to the influence of such British literary figures as Coleridge, Wordsworth, Carlyle, and Ruskin and to the "organic idealism" of such nineteenth-century German philosophers as Hegel. Conspicuously absent from his rationale was any reference to ideologies then prevalent in the Soviet Union, where the issue was not whether trade unions should exist but whether they should participate in plant management at the plant level or at the national level.[23]

Needless to say, not everyone is persuaded by these ethico-political arguments in support of unions. As with any argument that is built on value judgments, these also can be turned upside down. In other words, one can construct an argument either for or against unions on the grounds that unions foster, respectively, virtuous or vicious traits in its members. Just be careful to emphasize only those aspects most supportive of one's own bias on the subject. This inherent weakness in the value-based arguments once led labor relations experts Clark Kerr and Abraham Siegel to assert that all traditional arguments in defense of unions are defective because they take a moral or normative stance. For each pro-union theory sought a villain in some aspect of the capitalist system. Eliminate the ethical concepts of good and evil, or moral right and wrong, of justice and injustice, they said, and these traditional prounion arguments lose their bearings. Instead, they proposed, one should study objectively each work environment, whether capitalist or not, to determine the appropriate role, if any, of a union in that environment's "web of rule." [24] What Kerr and Siegel failed to take into account is that antiunion arguments also appeal to a conception, albeit a different one, of ethics, morality, and justice, especially with regard to the meaning and purpose of liberty.

In short, whether or not unions are thought to constrain workers' liberty unduly depends on what problems workers are perceived to have and what is considered to count as a solution to the problems identified. In particular, arguments on either side of the question take the liberty of the worker to be a basic value the protection of which is a given. They differ in their totally divergent views about the nature and conditions of individual liberty, from which follow their respective assessments of the impact of a union.

One side views individual liberty as a metaphysical given and a union as an intrusion on the labor-management relationship. The other side views individual liberty as empirically vacuous until rendered meaningful through group solidarity.[25]

The antiunion argument starts with a theoretical assumption that the working person is an inherently free agent and that accordingly any unilateral (as distinguished from contractual) intrusion on that aboriginal state (by an "outside force" such as a union) can only diminish liberty. Its proponents do not explain why an individual worker's agreement with an employer is any less destructive of liberty than is that worker's agreement with his or her fellow workers to join with them in a union. The prounion argument starts instead with a more realistic assessment of the extremely dependent status of the typical working person in an industrial society, that is, of the worker's basic lack of liberty, and accordingly sees the union as a mutually advantageous instrumentality whereby separately powerless individuals create collectively a basis for shared liberty.

Union leaders may, of course, become so powerful that they themselves suppress the freedom of the individual members of the union. This very possibility inspired the 1959 Landrum-Griffin Act. But with comparatively few exceptions it is not union leaders but corporations and their management personnel who exercise final control over both workplace and workforce. Nevertheless, one hears more and more in recent years about the advantages of worker participation, worker control, even worker ownership. The meaning of these terms is subject to considerable variation from one context to another; but participation suggests involvement in the making of company *policy,* perhaps as a member of a corporate board of directors; control implies involvement in the actual *management* of a company; and *ownership* means just that, through any number of different arrangements, including majority ownership of a company's stock.

Do these options, or any combination of them, eliminate the need for unions? The answer may be an unqualified maybe: it depends on the circumstances of each arrangement, in particular, on whether the participation or ownership or control is real or in name only. And this, in turn, might depend on how the union itself relates to management. For example, what if the union is merely "a tool of the Establishment" and functions with regard to the workers like a puppet government set up by a colonizing power? This, says British philosopher Anthony Skillen, is the typical situation in Great Britain. Accordingly, he tends to be very sceptical about the value of job enrichment programs, at least as they are being implemented in his country.[26] But questions of this kind, however serious, are bland in comparison to those with regard to commerce and survival.

Worker Organization and Power

The history of labor relations has left a lot of scars, some of them intellectual. In particular, it has branded into the consciousness of both management and labor that each side is, or at least must perform as being, the adversary of the other. Thus is it sacrosanct in the lore of labor relations, at least in the United States, that with ownership comes an identifiable set of prerogatives known collectively as "management rights." As built into negotiated contracts, management rights tend to draw the line beyond which workers may not go in pressing their demands. In particular, they may not ask for a voice in management, since by definition they are not management but labor. This neat dichotomy broke down decades ago in western Europe and is being called into question in the United States by arrangements involving worker participation in management and even worker ownership. These latter, as noted in Chapter 5, are viewed very cautiously by union leaders; but unions have begun to show an interest in corporate ownership. The resulting blurring of the canonical divisions of responsibility is a challenge to well-established expectations. It also recalls a long-forgotten battle before the Industrial Revolution over the appropriate role of craft guilds in society. Today's concerns about workers' power will, accordingly, be better understood if preceded by a brief consideration of their historical predecessors.

The Economic Power of Guilds

A craft guild may be thought of as a type of job control that was common before the Industrial Revolution and survives in traditional forms in some countries and in newer forms as professional interest groups. In simplest terms, a craft guild is an interest-group association the purpose of which is to maximize over time the common welfare of practitioners of a particular craft. The ways this might be done include controlling entry into the craft and the quality of work done by its practitioners and protecting (expanding, if possible) the scope of tasks reserved to them. A state bar association for attorneys or a medical association for physicians is a contemporary analogue of what a craft guild is all about, provided that one takes into account the political environment within which such professional organizations operate.

The social utility of craft guilds is historically controversial, in part because of the diverse ways in which these organizations have been interpreted and in part because of the diverse ideologies of the interpreters. The definition of a guild offered above abstracts from these controversial considerations. But before attempting to evaluate the guilds' economic power, we should have before us at least an overview of the controversy.

In the first place, the organization and purpose of the craft guild varied considerably over time and from place to place. With origins in and even before feudal times, they underwent profound changes in response to changing technologies, expanding commerce and trade, and turbulent transformations of government structure. As the pace of these changes varied in different countries, so did the role of the guilds. Intended as instruments of power, they have left as records of their doings mainly what they generated at the interface with government, the unrecorded remainder having gone the way of all well-kept secrets. In the face of this challenge to the inquiring mind, equally competent historians have viewed the guilds as free craftsmen organized in opposition to city government; agents of government to police particular industries for the benefit of consumers; or self-governing bodies of craftsmen whose decisions were subject to government sanction or veto.[27]

Second, because social arrangements in times preceding the Industrial Revolution varied from one century to the next and from one country to another, it is difficult even for the most specialized historian to avoid imposing something of our own world upon them. So it is that the guilds have been viewed as early versions both of labor unions and of modern corporations. They were neither, and yet they were in a sense both, but not at the same time or at the same level of complexity. This seeming anomaly can be explained (as intimated by the differences in historians' interpretations) by taking into account who controlled a given craft and how over the course of time. The image of the autonomous craftsperson is just that, an image. In reality, the practice of a craft was subject to control— in different degrees at different times and in different places—by other craftspersons, by merchants who marketed the products of the craft, by trading companies (proto-corporations) that controlled the merchants, and by city or national governments that monitored, competed against, derived benefits from, but primarily served these emerging enterprises.

Finally, because of these historical complexities, one should avoid appealing to some aspect or other of a guild to bolster one's case for or against either modern labor unions or modern corporations. Many otherwise meticulous scholars have yielded to this temptation. Take just two examples, at opposite ends of the ideological spectrum. Fabian socialists Sidney and Beatrice Webb started with the assumption that owners and workers are inherently adversarial by virtue of their respective interest in or indifference to profits; whence their conclusion that craft guilds were not proto-unions.[28] Howard Dickman, a libertarian who considers American labor law to be a fascist intrusion upon free enterprise, paints the guilds not as probusiness, which they unfailingly (but in time inadequately) were, but as incontrovertible evidence of the mischief that results when unions run amuck.[29]

With these cautions duly noted, we are in a better position to try to assess the social benefits of the sort of job control exercised by craft guilds. For, while there are various arguments for and against guild control of jobs, these cautions suggest that proponents of the different arguments are not always talking about the same thing. Throwing caution to the wind, I will attempt to cover the issue by way of a stylized debate.

ARGUMENTS IN SUPPORT OF CRAFT GUILDS

CRAFT GUILDS HAVE EXISTED IN MANY DIFFERENT CULTURES. Organizations of the practitioners of a particular trade or craft are known to have existed in both Europe and Asia from fairly early times: from 600 B.C. in India; in Rome under the emperors; in China and in western Europe from the early Middle Ages. They still exist today, in more traditional forms in Asia, and in modern variations in the West. At one time or another, they have been endorsed in just about every country on any and all levels of government. This in and of itself is certainly not a persuasive consideration; but, for better or worse, craft guilds have over time been widely perceived to be needed.

CRAFT GUILDS FOSTER WORKER SELF-ESTEEM. The sense of shared participation in a common enterprise of social worth—a kind of esprit de corps—helps give a person pride in what one does and in who one is. This was a most important consequence of practicing a skill or trade under the aegis of a guild. Guilds in the Middle Ages expressed and solidified their social status primarily by means of various rituals and pageants. Thus, for example, did practitioners of an otherwise low-esteem occupation like fish-mongering win the respect of the community. In later centuries, they achieved that and more by erecting impressive halls, many of which are still standing today. In the eyes of the church (before the Reformation) they were respected as fraternities. In the eyes of government they were officially recognized as crafts or even misteries, that is, agencies of government.[30] There was, to be sure, a great deal of political controversy surrounding the guilds; but this very controversy is a sign of their importance as instruments of social prominence for their members.

CRAFT GUILDS HELP TO MAINTAIN QUALITY CONTROL. One of the principal purposes of a guild was to maintain the quality of the product (or, in more recent times, the service) for which its members were responsible. It is with this objective in mind that governments, municipal or national, empowered guilds to regulate the performance of their members. For example, even surgeons (from the fifteenth century on) policed fellow practitioners within the structure of a guild. Under the terms of this social contract, then, they were tolerated (in the long run) only so long as they did in fact perform this quality-control function for society as a whole. As is true of modern professional organizations, this approach to quality control is based on the well-supported assumption that skilled practitioners are best able to determine for any time and place an appropriate standard of performance.

CRAFT GUILDS HELP PROTECT SOCIALLY VALUABLE SKILLS FROM DOMINATION BY INTRUSIVE FORCES WHICH PRACTITIONERS AS INDIVIDUALS COULD NOT WITHSTAND. The entire history of craft guilds could be written as one long saga of competing and conflicting interests seeking to control use of the skills around which the guilds were organized. Charlemagne, who, as we have seen, wanted all valued skills well represented in his domain, issued a ban on any organization of skill practitioners. Once these skill-based organizations emerged in the West, municipal governments sought in various ways if not to control at least to profit from their power; and they in time found themselves competing with national rulers for this right to a share of their profit. As more guilds were established, interguild turf disputes became common, and governments were called upon more often to settle them. (Comparable disputes occur in our day between professional organizations, for example, between physicians and nurses or between attorneys and real estate agents.) Still more challenging to the integrity of skill performance were the increasingly common and frequently successful efforts of merchants and traders to control the terms and conditions under which these skills could be exercised. This aspect of turf control continues as the problem of professionalism within more or less dictatorial corporations. The point of all this, however, is not to determine how well guilds have functioned as skill protectors but how important it is to society at large that they do so.

ARGUMENTS AGAINST CRAFT GUILDS

CRAFT GUILDS UNFAIRLY EXCLUDE PEOPLE FROM JOBS WHICH THEY WOULD OTHERWISE BE ABLE TO LEARN AND CARRY OUT. One of the principal functions of a traditional craft guild was to limit access to the occupation to which its members owed their living. To this end they both appealed to and exercised the power of government. From their typically municipal base they sought to extend their exclusive territory into the countryside and even into nearby towns. They excluded poorer people from membership by charging burdensome entry fees and annual dues and requiring for admission to the guild a "masterpiece" which they would evaluate on the very highest of standards. To prevent what today would be called "practicing without a license," they routinely entered people's homes on the basis of government-granted search and seizure powers. Poorer skilled people unable to become masters under these repressive conditions would, if possible, become small masters in their own right, as they did under the system of "yeomanry" in England. As some guilds became wealthier and hence more powerful than others, they either persuaded government to legislate in minute detail what specific tasks the others could carry out or, when possible, simply brought these other crafts completely under their control.[31]

Comparisons with the behavior of what later emerged as corporations are both obvious and appropriate. But one is perhaps better advised to consider the behavior of professional groups, say, of physicians, attorneys, and engineers, as they strive to limit admission to their ranks and to expand their hegemony. It is by no means coincidental that their emphasis on the "mystery" of their craft usually has consequences favorable to profitability.

A CRAFT GUILD IS JUST A MEANS WHEREBY ITS MEMBER PRACTITIONERS CAN MONOPOLIZE THEIR PRODUCT OR SERVICE AT THE EXPENSE OF THEIR CONSUMERS. This, from all indications, is a well-justified criticism, in spite of the focus of their rhetoric and pageantry on what today we would call "social responsibility." What is debatable is what significance to attach to this finding; for though there are some similarities between earlier guilds and modern-day labor unions, there are even more similarities between the guilds, especially in their later, more complex forms, and modern corporations. Still more on target, as noted above, is a comparison with modern professional groups.

Traditional guilds did control access not only to participation in their chosen endeavor but also to the product or service which resulted from that endeavor.

The standard justification for this hegemony was, as noted above in support of guilds, that it safeguarded quality and that this benefited the community as a whole. Quality may have been a consideration, but price served as a convenient measure of quality. As is evident from the existence of antitrust laws, we still have problems with such arrangements. But concern about monopolies has not precluded our tolerance of vast enterprises that are both horizontally and vertically integrated. By contrast, a traditional guild was typically able to exercise hegemony over one or more crafts only in a particular locality.

Often this control came to be hereditary and even established by law. After 1314 in Ghent, for example, only members of the controlling guild were permitted to make cloth within three miles of the city walls. The principal guilds in a particular area sometimes exercised total control of the municipal government, as was the case in Liege, Utrecht, and Cologne. (Similar power was exercised by guilds in China and India.) The basis of the power gradually shifted, however, from municipal to national government; but even that level of support was rendered obsolete by the Industrial Revolution. By the middle of the nineteenth century every country in Europe had abolished the guilds in the interest of the more expansive requirements of global trade under capitalism.[32]

CRAFT GUILDS HINDER THE DEVELOPMENT OF CAPITALISM. Craft guilds presupposed a cottage industry mode of production. When more collective modes of production were introduced in Europe, the constraints that guilds imposed became intolerable to the very same entrepreneurial instincts that had dominated the guilds until then. The opportunities for capitalist expansion brought to an end any pretense of cooperation between merchant and maker such as had characterized at least the public image of companies dedicated to bringing the wares of master craftspersons to the public at prices both reasonable and fair. Machines were becoming the makers, and devil take the hindmost. This conflict between wealthy capitalists who controlled the markets and poor craftspeople who were subservient to them was already widespread in Great Britain in the seventeenth century; by the middle of the eighteenth century the cleavage was complete; and out of that cleavage came labor unions as we have come to know them since.[33]

It is important, finally, to update the history of the traditional guilds, here only sketched, by considering the fate of professions that have survived into our times. Perceived as individualist or at most cottage industries less than half a century ago, each has been undergoing both technological and structural transformation. In place of the sole practitioner of days gone by, the delivery of legal services is increasingly in the control of massive, highly technology-based firms. Replacing the private practitioner of medicine are various complex organizations which are themselves increasingly dependent on health care technologies that are controlled by corporate enterprise. The co-optation of engineers into one or another niche in the military-industrial complex is almost total. And similar transformations may be cited with regard to just about any other profession that comes to mind, be it in food service, real estate, accounting, retail trade, sports, travel, or recreation. In short, it would be a mistake to look upon the history of the guilds as something over and done with a century or so ago. It continues apace, toward levels of complexity that we can barely envision.

The Economic Power of Unions

Whether one thinks of guilds as having been abolished outright or as having been superseded by corporations, one is left with a vacuum where once there had been organizations attentive to the interests of at least some skilled workers. Into that vacuum came the labor movement. It did not emerge at the very outset of the Industrial Revolution in Great Britain; for family ties were for a time a component of factory hiring policies, and at one point employers took to presenting themselves as quasi-patriarchal leaders and models of everybody's "self-help" efforts to succeed.[34] But the dynamism of production led for the most part to increasingly formalized relationships, with the roles of owners and workers clearly demarcated. In contrast to the ambiguities of old, a dialectic of opposites was in place, and at one pole were labor unions. Precisely because of this dichotomous birthing, their role was from the outset carefully circumscribed.

The problem at issue here was neatly stated as early as 1776 by Adam Smith, who noted the difference in the following words:

> The masters, being fewer in number, can combine much more easily; and the law, besides, authorises, or at least does not prohibit their combinations, while it prohibits those of the workmen. We have no acts of parliament against combining to lower the price of work; but many against combining to raise it.[35]

Nothing substantial has happened in two centuries to change the contrast that Adam Smith describes. Of course, a whole body of law has evolved, admittedly out of great turmoil along the way, to establish the ground rules for rational labor relations as we know them today. But this only means that the locus of the battle has shifted, as has the immensity of the stakes at issue. For example, the U.S. National Labor Relations Board has for some time been so antilabor that many unions use its "services" only when it is absolutely unavoidable to do so. The conservative account in this regard is that there has indeed been a shift, but the shift merely corrects a long-standing imbalance on the part of these agencies in favor of labor. To this defense there is a more fundamental rebuttal.

There are many statutes in the United States, as elsewhere, the express purpose of which is to keep unions within certain bounds deemed socially appropriate. In addition, as James B. Atleson has shown, common law endorsement of management rights in the United States is being perpetuated in judicial interpretations of statutory law that on its face clearly grants certain rights to employee unions.[36] In the spirit of Atleson's analysis, accordingly, it will be useful to identify socially assigned constraints on organized labor in the United States by considering the state of the law with regard to the right of unions to conduct business.

Increasingly over the years, unions in the United States have showed signs of wanting to function as businesses. And certain investment plans of fairly recent origin allow employees to invest in the company that employs them. These plans go beyond traditional stock-purchasing arrangements. Most discussed in this regard is the Employee Stock Ownership Plan (ESOP) authorized in 1978 and subsequently expanded by the U.S. Congress, especially through advantageous amendments adopted in 1984. Since the intended purpose of the ESOP idea was to give *management* a new way to raise capital at a time of economic distress, it was not anticipated that somehow the workers themselves, operating collectively through their union, might choose to be the management. That they are interested in doing so has given new life to a bevy of traditional shibboleths, the most noteworthy of which is the hallowed dichotomy between management and labor. What the new legislation, passed in the interest of management, has shown all too clearly is the extent to which laws based on the adversarial model of labor relations encapsulate labor in a role bereft of an owner's rights.

Some who consider it their responsibility and prerogative to protect business consider a union-run business to be somehow detrimental to the liberty of society as a whole, by which they usually mean the business community. They still think of and reason about unions on the basis of a prejudicial straitjacket of legalities that owes more to the antiworker hostility of nineteenth-century British ideology than to economic reality. Depression-era ameliorations that were justified on the basis of a need for industrial order and peace have since been all but overwhelmed by a resurgence of the hostile gene, requiring pro- as well as antilabor advocates to perpetuate the myth that the law of labor relations is irrevocably the law of a jungle.

No wonder, then, that legal scholars have found it difficult to build into their accustomed patterns of thought the emerging world of ESOPs, union representation on corporate boards, and worker ownership. So circumscribed are they by the old biases about the role of labor that, even when totally sympathetic to the concerns of unions, they still cast the present in a mold from the past. Thus Deborah Groban Olson, author of a favorable legal analysis of worker ownership, concedes too much in trying to reconcile new realities with an NLRA prohibition of union interference with the employer. "[A] court," she writes, "should distinguish between a union *qua* union, using its typical weapons such as strikes or job actions to obtain a change in employer bargaining representatives, and a group of stockholders or directors using their corporate powers to seek a change in management personnel or policy." [37] Everything else that Olson has to say in her article belies this characterization of "a union *qua* union" as resorting to strikes or job actions as "its typical weapons." That she falls back on this stereotype is symptomatic of the problem she so artfully addresses. Far better for her case would have been a recognition that that very stereotype of a union ought to give way in light of current realities to a considerably more rounded characterization. Unions may respond to a wide range of challenges only some of which are manifestly within the purview of labor law. In particular and with ever greater frequency, unions may be actively engaged in (and not merely negotiating with) business.

By the latter part of the 1980s, workers in the United States owned a majority of stock in some 1,000 to 1,500 companies, and union and nonunion employee representatives held seats on about 250 (mainly small) companies. Union buyouts of companies had occurred at several hundred companies. Most of these were management-initiated, but not all. Through investments involving a variety of mixtures of cash, loans, concessions, and stock options, unions have acquired partial or total ownership of such companies as the Vermont Asbestos Group, Saratoga Knitting Mill, Western Airlines, Weirton Steel and Atlas Chain in Pennsylvania, Northwestern Steel and Wire, Unimar (a northwestern shipbuilding and tugboat company, 73% union-owned), and the Copper Range Company in northern Michigan (70% owned by its 930 employees). Purchase prices are no longer a limiting factor, as witness the following: Chase Brass ($23 million), Oregon Metallurgical ($35 million), Southern Pacific Railroad ($1 billion), and United Airlines ($4.5 billion).[38] Only the hesitance of the federal government has prevented the employees of Conrail from buying their federally owned employer.[39]

Unions in other countries have also been involved in buying, owning, and participating in the management of companies. Best known the world over in this respect are the worker-owned companies in Mondragon, in northern Spain. Tembec Forest Products in Quebec, Canada, kitchen equipment manufacturer Manuest, in northeastern France, and watchmaker Lip in the Ardennes are other cases in point, especially interesting because of the role of community activism in effecting the respective transitions.[40]

In short, only by the most technical of subterfuges could one still deny that there are unions "in business." It is, however, a bit more of an uphill climb to the claim that a union may *be* a business. The common-sense answer might well be in the affirmative; but courts of law are not so easily persuaded, as can be seen from certain interpretations of U.S. labor law and antitrust law.

U.S. labor law presupposes a dichotomy between management and labor, and the courts see it as their responsibility to keep the dichotomy sharp and clear—in spite of some blurry issues "in the middle of the road." Under the NLRA a union may be an employer whose employees may organize under a different union. But as is already apparent, this role as employer of in-house staff is only a small part of the picture. Also to be considered—and this is where it becomes complicated —is the possibility of a conflict of interest between a union as owner of a company and that same union as representative of the (same or competing) company's workers. Such conflict, if any, would seem to violate the NLRA's absolutely basic prohibition against an employer interfering, dominating, or financing a "labor organization": NLRA, Section 8(a)(2).

As defined in Section 2(5) of the NLRA, a labor organization is "any organization of any kind, or any agency or employee representation committee or plan, in which employees participate and which exists for the purpose, in whole or in part, of dealing with employers concerning grievances, labor disputes, wages, rates of pay, hours of employment, or conditions of work." Because there are various types of labor-management "cooperative" arrangements, some commentators favor interpreting this language so as to facilitate more of these cooperative arrangements in the nonunionized setting. And, as a matter of fact, there is a line of cases that provides some legal basis for such a preference, including in particular some NLRB rulings in the 1970s. But the impact of these rulings has since been called into question by the decision of the U.S. Supreme Court in *NLRB v. Yeshiva University* (1980).[41]

Two 1977 NLRB decisions allow for some form of cooperation, as distinguished from isolation, between labor and management: *Mercy-Memorial Hospital Corp.* and *General Foods Corp.* [42] In the hospital case the board ruled that a five-member elected grievance committee lacking final authority is not a labor organization under NLRA section 2(5), hence the employer is not in violation of section 8(a)(2). In *General Foods* the board found, against a defeated union complainant, that 8(a)(2) was not violated by employer's establishment of a job evaluation plan, a wage incentive system, and a team plan whereby employees carry out a variety of management functions cooperatively.

Two similar board rulings have been upheld by the Ninth Circuit. In one case, this court held that establishment of five employee committees after a union lost a decertification election is not a violation of 8(a)(2) because cooperation is not against but is rather a goal of the NLRA.[43] In another,[44] the court enforced and modified an NLRB ruling[45] that had found a three-member impartial adjudicatory body of employees set up by the employer not to be a Section 2(5) labor organization, hence no violation by employer of 8(a)(2). All of these decisions— and they are comparatively few in number—are in the spirit of *Chicago Rawhide Manufacturing Co. v. NLRB* (1955), in which the Seventh Circuit had reversed the board and held that an "employee committee" that works cooperatively with management can be recognized as a bargaining agent.[46]

What importance, if any, can still be given to *Chicago Rawhide* and its progeny is uncertain in the wake of the *Yeshiva University* decision. In *Yeshiva* the court found that this university's faculty exercise managerial functions and hence are not entitled under the NLRA to union representation for purposes of collective bargaining. In arriving at this decision the court resolves a conflict in the act in favor of management and against the board's interpretation, substitutes its own judgment for that of the board with regard to the power structure of an institution of higher learning, and thereby sets up yet another legal obstacle to employee ownership of a business.

The conflict in the act results from its definitions of two categories of individuals, one of which is and one of which is not entitled to form a union that can be recognized under the act. "Professional employees" may organize and bargain collectively;[47] but "supervisors" may not.[48] To oversimplify somewhat, the board had been ruling in a number of cases, including *Yeshiva,* that various types of skilled personnel were entitled to unionize in their capacity as "professional employees." The Supreme Court takes the other horn of the dilemma and excludes university faculty and others similarly situated on the basis of their being "supervisors."

Writing for the five-judge majority in *Yeshiva,* Justice Lewis Powell complains that the question before it is "a mixed one of fact and law" but "the Board's opinion may be searched in vain for relevant findings of fact." This lacuna does not prevent him from setting forth an imaginary, or at best medieval, description of faculty authority as being "absolute" in academic matters and of faculty interests as being inseparable from those of the institution.[49] Writing for the four dissenting judges, Justice William Brennan challenges the majority's statement of the facts, asserting that "the Court's vision is clouded by its failure fully to discern and comprehend the nature of the faculty's role in university governance." [50]

This decision constitutes a kind of Catch-22 for just about any employee ownership of a business. For, whereas *Chicago Rawhide* recognized the possibility under appropriate circumstances of combining unionization and cooperation, *Yeshiva* represents a warning that any such involvement by employees in managerial functions may have the effect of denying them the right to have their interests defended by a union through collective bargaining under the act.

Yeshiva-type concern about the intermingling of legally established adversaries is, however, only part of the problem faced by a union that would in some fashion become actively involved in business. Not only would it face serious challenge under antitrust and, if stock is issued, under securities regulation, but it would have problems enough defending its role as employer beyond the limited provisions of Section 2(2) of the same act. It is here that a union is recognized in a most convoluted way as being an employer *only* for the purpose of allowing its in-house personnel to organize. "The term 'employer,' " according to this subsection, "includes any person acting as an agent of an employer, directly or indirectly, but shall not . . . include any labor organization (other than when acting as an employer), or anyone acting in the capacity of officer or agent of such labor organization."

Because of various obligations imposed on a "labor organization" under other sections of the NLRA, a union local is less likely to become involved in arrangements open to charges of conflict of interest when its own employees are organized by a different union. The interesting cases, however, in these days of worker ownership arise in precisely those situations in which the union is both the employer and the representative of workers who are both employed by and members of that union. To avoid just such conflicts of interest, unions that are entitled to one or more seats on a company's board of directors commonly appoint to this position an outsider who is sympathetic to their interests.

In short, the adversarial interpretation of U.S. labor law is based less on historical realities than on ideological assumptions about the proper place of "the working class" in business affairs. With appropriate translations, the same can be said about antitrust law. Even as use of antitrust law to restrict corporate mergers is falling out of favor, courts continue to find these century-old statutes useful devices for controlling "anticompetitive" activity on the part of unions. But they have not often seen their way clear to allow unions to use antitrust law for the same purpose. As a result, unions have in recent years been subjected to a great deal of litigation and legal expense, growing out of charges under antitrust law that they are hindering competition—which comes down to saying, in another curious way, that they do not qualify as businesses.

The Clayton Antitrust Act is so written as to be available to "[a]ny person who shall be injured in his business or property by reason of anything forbidden in the antitrust laws."[51] Most—but, as we shall see, not all—courts have denied unions standing to maintain an antitrust action. Their inconsistency in this respect is a tribute to the versatility of an institution that remembers its priorities well.

Courts commonly think of a union as a business when presented with a complaint alleging that a union is engaged in anticompetitive activity. What exactly constitutes the business of the union is, however, seldom addressed directly, no doubt because the assumption is ordinarily being made only to justify the applicability of the business-related law in question. Sometimes this assumption as to a union's business is indicated only tacitly as the proper alternative to an allegedly improper alternative. In one case, for example, an employer was exempted from bargaining with a union local because it had set up an optical business in direct competition with it.[52] In another case a decade later, the status of the *international* as creditor of, with controlling interest in, a competitor of plaintiff employer was held not to excuse the employer from bargaining with a local of the international because the alleged conflict of interest was "too remote."[53]

In 1975, the U.S. Supreme Court applied the Clayton Antitrust Act against a union that had pressured a building contractor not to deal with nonunion subcontractors.[54] Unions have tried to reverse the impact of that decision by challenging comparable employer activities under antitrust law, but with mixed results, depending in part on how the court chose to characterize the union's business. In one case a federal appellate court refused to apply antitrust law to a union's complaint that "they were restrained *in their business and enterprise of earning wages*" because it discerned "no anticompetitive effect unrelated to collective bargaining negotiations."[55] In another case, a different federal appellate court granted standing to a carpenters' association to argue its claim that it was being injured *in its business* by a conspiracy on the part of certain contractors which, it claimed, was illegal under the Clayton Act.[56] This ruling was vacated on appeal.

The appellate court agreed that the California State Council of Carpenters had been anticompetitively injured *in its business* by a conspiracy on the part of certain contractors to boycott union-signatory contractors, maintain nonunion shops and divisions, and induce other contractors to breach collective bargaining agreements with unions. To arrive at this decision, the court characterizes the business of the carpenters' State Council as consisting of organizing of the carpentry industry employers; negotiating and policing collective bargaining agreements; and securing jobs for its members.[57] Three years later the U.S. Supreme Court reversed the appellate court and declared that the carpenters' union does not constitute a person under the Clayton Act.[58]

Viewed as an assessment of the status of unions, primarily in the United States, this account is more selective than systematic. But it reflects well enough for our purposes the sorts of issues that a workers' representative would need to consider before agreeing on the role unions should be assigned in a social contract. For one thing, this representative should avoid making any unqualified endorsement of the priority of liberty. For no amount of explanatory gloss—of which this chapter is a sampling—would neutralize class biases well enough to arrive at a reliably worker-friendly formulation that could not be undone by constraining judicial interpretations. So the question of power has to be addressed. In particular, how much power should unions be allowed? A case has been made at least for people's right to organize in their own interest. (Never mind that Rousseau's dream of an institutionalized general will untrammeled by special appeals is indistinguishable in principle from Lenin's populist autocracy. Dreams aside, corporations are, if nothing else, well-organized interest groups. And as Rousseau warned, if there are any of these, there had better be many.) This may not be reason enough to endorse worker ownership or union commercialization; but in a world of freely practiced workforce restructuring, workers' liberty is vacuous without some basis for workers' power.

7

Equal Opportunity Employment?

A WORKERS' REPRESENTATIVE would have a hard time coming to terms with other social contractors about justice in the workplace. What principles should govern the distribution of meaning, or of liberty, or of power in the workplace? Such questions, we have seen, are difficult to resolve. But at least they take for granted that people are working, that is, that they have jobs. But if for some reason there are not or are not likely to be enough jobs to go around, the representative may have to endorse some morally acceptable way to allocate available openings.

Here, one might think, John Rawls's theory is especially apropos, because he would allow inequalities only if they benefit the least advantaged group (unskilled workers, for example), and he would assign the more desirable positions only by means of fair procedures open to all. But these admirable principles are to be implemented according to a set of temporizing priorities. To begin with, Rawls gives satisfaction of the basic needs of the less well-off (his so-called difference principle) a higher priority than attainment of equal opportunity. And he makes satisfaction of basic needs dependent upon (hence a lower priority than) attainment of maximum basic liberty, especially for entrepreneurs. But, as we have seen, liberty is an ambiguous guide to workplace justice. So Rawls may be irrelevant in this regard. For what is actually the case, not only in the United States and other developed countries but in those less developed as well, is far removed from Rawlsian equality of opportunity, in large measure because liberty has been maximized—for the employer. This situation, Rawls might say, violates his difference principle; but, having rigorously prioritized liberty, he cannot easily raise this objection. Anyway, job allocation is concerned less with liberty than with survival, and this suggests a need for creative social contracting.

As already noted, having the opportunity to work is for all but the independently wealthy an amenity that has a considerable bearing on the quality and even the possibility of life. Whence the idea of a claim to a job and a corresponding obligation on the part of others, including both employers and, if need be, society as a whole, to provide jobs insofar as possible and to do so in a fair and impartial way: equal employment opportunity. But getting there is only half a right. The other half is being treated fairly once on the job, and this includes in particular not being fired unfairly: employment rights.

Concern about fair procedures for hiring and advancement has been concretized in various programs the purpose of which is either to neutralize favoritism in current hiring and advancement practices or to remedy the results of past practices now considered to have been unjust. The latter kinds of programs are vulnerable to the complaint that they cause "inverse discrimination" by penalizing in the present some persons who are in no way responsible for the past injustices being remedied. To defuse this objection somewhat, supporters of the preferential remedy will typically qualify it as a temporary expedient to be continued only until "protected groups" have achieved proportionate representation in the workforce.

These issues have been thoroughly debated for several decades.[1] For present purposes it is enough to note that the debate assumes some sort of meritocracy as the objective and that it has not produced a consensus as to proper criteria for just hiring and promotion. This being the case, a workers' representative concerned about being fair to workers is hamstrung from the outset; but this in itself is an incentive to examine rather carefully the obstacles to developing a reasonably fair approach to equal employment opportunity. With this limited task in mind, I propose to show that workforce restructuring together with job scarcity poses a basic challenge to a meritocratic ideal. First I will consider the purpose and the limitations of four efforts to answer this challenge: preemployment testing, seniority rights, employment rights, and union internationalization. Then I will suggest that all such efforts are inadequate in the absence of a community-oriented public policy with regard to workforce restructuring.

Toward Getting a Job and Keeping It

Two hundred years after its establishment, the American version of democracy still does not speak of an equal right to employment but only of equal employment *opportunity*. Leaving the former to the socialist world, we in the United States are committed only to the latter, more limited, goal, on the assumption that through reasonably fair competition we will each find our appropriate level and niche and that as we do, society as a whole will reap the benefits of well-distributed talents. To approach this rational allocation of opportunities, of course, the effects of any factors that tend to obstruct the potential of an individual or group need to be neutralized insofar as is humanly possible (the objective of civil rights legislation in general). Once it is assumed that an adequate mechanism for neutralizing disadvantage is in place and operating, any subsequent indications of disadvantage can be attributed not to the system but to the inadequacies of the individual or group in question. This is especially the case with regard to job entry selection.

Preemployment Testing

Is anyone in the United States entitled to a job? If so, on the basis of what considerations? Certainly not on the basis of some constitutional protection. About all the Constitution has been found to require in this regard is that a public sector firing that threatens an individual's right to "liberty" or "property" must be preceded by a hearing.[2] And from pretermination hearing to job entitlement is a leap of seven leagues. Civil rights legislation has gone part of the distance at least for protected groups (those subject to discrimination on the basis of such usually irrelevant traits as race, sex, or religion and, more recently, handicap or age). This has come about in part by building into public policy a requirement that employment screening tests be sufficiently objective and unbiased to exclude systematic prejudice and that they match applicants to jobs with as much rigor and precision as the young science of psychometrics can muster. This, at least, was the hope of the Equal Employment Opportunity Commission (EEOC) and its onetime patron, the U.S. Supreme Court.

Title VII of the Civil Rights Act of 1964 endorsed an employer's right to screen applicants in the following words (known as the Tower Amendment, after its sponsor, Senator John Tower of Texas):

> Nor shall it be an unlawful employment practice for an employer to give and to act upon the result of any professionally developed ability test provided that such test, its administration or action upon the results is not designed, intended or used to discriminate because of race, color, religion, sex, or national origin.[3]

In the years following, the EEOC, created by the same legislation to carry out "technical studies" and provide "technical assistance," gradually assumed a regulatory function. In 1966 it published brief *Guidelines on Employment Testing Procedures*, the main thrust of which is a recommendation by a panel of psychologists that the EEOC advocate use of "a total objective personnel assessment system fairly administered and professionally implemented" that would compare individual employees' scores with their criterion performance and neutralize cultural differences by either comparing minority scores to culture-specific norms or evaluating the minority applicant on the basis of job performance rather than test scores.[4]

Drawing on the panel's report, the fledgling EEOC recommended, among other things, administering tests objectively, using tests selected on the basis of specific job-related criteria; comparing test performance against job performance; retesting failures with subsequent experience or training; and validating separately for minorities. The term *test*, though not explicitly defined, is clearly understood in this document to mean a psychological test of general intelligence or special ability. Such test, says the EEOC, should be job-related (related not to supposedly job-related traits or qualities but to job performance), part of a comprehensive personnel assessment system, and unbiased with respect to minorities.

Four years later, in 1970, the EEOC issued a more detailed set of *Guidelines on Employment Selection Procedures*[5]—this time not as recommendations but as federal regulations, which, the agency claimed, were not subject to the usual requirement of notice and delay for response. The Supreme Court would subsequently deny the regulatory status of these guidelines, disagree internally about just how much deference they deserve, but endorse the EEOC's position on minimum test validation methods.

The 1970 *Guidelines* identify as a test any measured or scored evaluative assessment of job suitability on the basis of any recorded information from or about the applicant and, by extension, any technique or procedure, whether scored or not, that functions as a test. Aside from any question of intent, if such applicant assessment has a discriminatory impact on a protected group, its use is permissible only if it satisfies a two-tier test: it must be both valid and useful to a high degree, and there must be no available alternative.

The favored method of validation is said to be on-site empirical or criterion validation: statistical evidence showing that among a "normal or typical" group of hired job applicants there is a greater-than-chance correlation between test scores and job performance (statistical significance) and that this correlation is of sufficient utility (practical significance) to justify use of the test in view of the particular circumstances of the employer's hiring and employment needs. Similarly, an employer's test may be validated on the basis of the job performance of off-site workers (synthetic validation) provided that there are no significant differences between the work and workers of the criterion and the employer's work and tested applicants. Thus neither synthetic nor concurrent validation would be in full compliance so long as an available protected minority upon whom a given test has a discriminatory impact is not fairly represented in the sample group studied for purposes of validating that test. Whence the controversial requirement in the 1970 *Guidelines* that an employer with an unrepresentative workforce may come into full compliance only when its test has been *differentially* validated: shown to be separately valid for each subgroup of applicants and the respective cutoff scores adjusted accordingly.

The empirically and differentially validated test being adjudged singularly acceptable, mere professional supervision of one's testing program or mere un-verified assertions are, without more, not evidence of a test's validity. Only if criterion-related validity is not feasible may evidence of validity be based on content (an actual sample of the job to be performed) or on a construct (the measurement of one or more traits that can be shown to be job-related). And even if criterion validation is claimed, the "subjective evaluation" involved in supervisory rating scales is suspect, so these scales "need to be examined to in-sure freedom from factors which would unfairly depress the scores of minority groups." [6] In this way the *Guidelines* tend to support only criterion validation that is based on "objective" measurement of productivity.

Without adopting the EEOC's complete package on validation, the Supreme Court did soon after decide that job-relatedness is the controlling question with regard to preemployment test validation. In a unanimous 8–0 decision the Court held in *Griggs v. Duke Power Co.* (1971) that irrespective of intent an employer whose test has a demonstrably significant discriminatory impact on a group pro-tected under Title VII must show that such test is "a reasonable measure of job performance," especially if the results of that test are given "controlling force" in selection for a transfer that amounts to a promotion.[7]

Drawing on procedures promulgated by the Court in 1973, lower courts called on to apply the *Griggs* decision would find that the discriminatory impact of a challenged test was justified after all by "business necessity." [8] But when the U.S. Supreme Court looked again at employment testing, in *Albemarle Paper Co. v. Moody* (1975), it explicitly limited its concern to job-relatedness.

In *Albemarle* the Court looked at how transfers were effected from relatively unskilled to relatively skilled jobs, given that blacks were employed almost ex-clusively, and locked, in the former. The company, having been enjoined by a federal district court from requiring a high school diploma for certain skilled jobs, began to use the Revised Beta, purportedly a test of nonverbal intelligence, and the Bennett Mechanical Comprehension Test to screen transfer applicants. The Bennett was soon dropped; and in 1963 Wonderlic A and B tests, which purportedly discern verbal intelligence, were added. To qualify for transfer to a skilled line of progression, an applicant in the unskilled department had to score 100 on the Beta and 18, which is the national "norm," on one or the other of the Wonderlic exams—standards few of the blacks were able to meet. Incumbents in the skilled lines, almost all of whom (101 out of 105) were white, were not required to pass these tests to hold their jobs; and when tested as part of the validation study, many scored below the stated minimums.

Once the process of litigation got under way on a Title VII class action charge of discrimination, the employer hired an industrial psychologist, who devoted a day to designing a concurrent validation study of various job groups near the top of the skilled lines of progression. The actual study was conducted by plant officials, who relied for local criteria on supervisors' ratings, which were based on "a 'standard' that was extremely vague and fatally open to divergent interpretations."[9] It having been established that Albemarle was using a testing system with a racially discriminatory impact, the Court found that the company had not satisfied the EEOC's requirement of proving job-relatedness for the group discriminated against and only for jobs immediately or proximately being applied for. Thus did the Court endorse the EEOC's 1970 *Guidelines* with regard to differential validation and promotion potential, and, indirectly, the testing standards of the American Psychological Association.

The *Griggs* and *Albemarle* standard is indifferent to discriminatory intent. If de facto discrimination is shown, it would be applied unless the employer could show "business necessity" and complainant could not show a nondiscriminatory alternative. This is surely a rational way to neutralize discriminatory employment practices. But it may now be of only historical interest. In 1989, the U.S. Supreme Court in effect overturned *Griggs* by requiring employees to prove that policies they challenge cannot be justified by business necessity: *Wards Cove Packing v. Antonio* (No. 87-1387). This retrenchment was already under way a year earlier in *Watson v. Fort Worth Bank and Trust*.

The fact situations of *Griggs* and *Albemarle* are narrowly focused on unskilled minority employees locked in at entry level. Federal appellate courts were ruling inconsistently as to the applicability of these cases to candidates for skilled and professional jobs, whom employers select on the basis of qualitative, or "subjective," criteria. In *Watson*, the Court decided that the policy does apply to such cases. But the justices were very divided over what would count as an adequate defense, with a plurality favoring just "job relatedness" or "legitimate business reasons" over the harsher standard of "business necessity."

The openness of *Watson* to "flexibility" in filling higher-echelon jobs is consistent with the Supreme Court's acquiescent scrutiny of professional school admissions standards, which leaves schools relatively free to determine how they will select a mix of students from among a pool of applicants.[10] The tendency under a laissez-faire U.S. president to downplay enforcement even of established law has further demoralized efforts to institutionalize equal employment opportunity. Meanwhile, labor unions have argued in vain (for example, in amicus briefs submitted in connection with relevant cases) that EEOC standards should be applied across the board on all skill levels. Policy is to the contrary, partly on the grounds that persons hired to do jobs requiring higher skills may be presumed to have those skills. Meanwhile, where testing is required, unions oppose managerially controlled testing programs; and some arbitrators have even allowed unions to participate in the testing program.

In sum, the use of standardized tests in employment screening has been limited for the most part to lower-echelon jobs. Professional employment screening is much more complex, with testing in the strict sense only one small component. But testing is a factor in sorting out who gains admission to which schools; and the fortuitous circumstance of birth still determines to a great extent how well one's schooling will prepare one for these tests and thus, along with other advantages, open doors to better positions.[11] So testing has not turned out to be, as some dreamed, a technological star that can guide us to meritocracy.

Seniority Rights

At least among "nonexempt" employees, seniority status provides some protection against massive layoffs. But for that very reason seniority is also an obstacle to achieving meritocracy, at least when combined with workforce reductions. For if worker layoffs are based not on lack of merit but only on a comparatively shorter period of time on the job, then unemployment will inevitably delay meritocracy. Or is it reasonable to claim, at least with regard to the U.S. labor pool, that white males are by definition more meritorious as workers than are nonwhite males and females of whatever color? Some would answer this question in the affirmative, on the grounds that the white male has better job skills precisely because he has been on the job longer. But layoff policies commonly look to factors no more subtle than total years on the job; so this circumstantial justification is beside the point.

In the past, the seniority system was defended well enough on the basis of patriarchal assumptions about the role of the male (especially if white) as head of family and elder in society. To the extent that this model is no longer related to facts, defenders of the system need to come up with a different rationale. And just such a rationale is available, in practice if not in principle, in the way business and government have been dealing with unemployment.

Governments try to avoid making welfare so attractive that it discourages people from looking for work. But when business is slow, as in the early 1980s, employers would rather not have any more people on their payrolls than they can profitably use. So one obvious solution to unemployment is to find ways business can employ more people profitably. Direct assistance to a business sometimes keeps it afloat, as in the case of U.S. government loans to the Chrysler Corporation; but in other cases, such as the Italian government's expenditure of $18.5 billion in support of various industries since World War II, even subsidies may be in vain.[12] So in one way or another businesses look for ways to reduce their costs, in particular their payrolls. Short of such extremes as closing a plant or declaring bankruptcy, this means paying out less money in salaries and wages. This can be achieved by paying the same workforce less or by having a smaller workforce to pay.

Less pay for the same workforce can be achieved in several different ways. The same number of individual workers might agree to work the same number of hours for a lower hourly wage ("concessions") in return for some alternative benefit, such as job security or profit sharing. Or the same number of individuals might agree to divide a reduced number of total hours among themselves in such a way that each works less and earns less, usually on the assumption that this arrangement is only temporary until business "picks up" again. (What distinguishes the 1984 IG Metall strike in West Germany is that the union wanted, and in part won, a reduction in the forty-hour week with no reduction in pay.) The less imaginative but more typical approach to payroll reduction is, however, to lay off some part of the workforce. And it is here that the notion of seniority provides a comparatively easy criterion for selecting survivors, whether the workforce is unionized or not.

This process of selection is experienced as "bumping" as those with more seniority take over the jobs of those with less, either at the same or even at a different workplace. Seniority-based bumping has been challenged in court on the basis of affirmative action law. And affirmative action would seem to offer good grounds for challenging seniority, because in many sectors of the economy women and minorities do have the least seniority. But in spite of EEOC support, challenges to seniority *as a basis for layoffs* have generally fallen on deaf ears, even before the U.S. Supreme Court. Seniority alone, however, is no defense against an employer committed to deep cuts in the workforce. Take the case of a certain meat-packing plant which management wanted to automate. As the workers with less seniority were laid off, women with fifteen to twenty years in the plant would be reassigned to entry-level jobs they could no longer handle, with the result that they too would end up on layoff.[13]

Although seniority may keep senior workers on the job, those newer to the workforce who are laid off must be satisfied with hoping for reemployment. Any hope they might have, however, is clouded by two considerations. First, so long as there is uncertainty in the marketplace, as in the case of a mature or declining industry, the employer (commonly with the support of its continuing workforce) is better advised to assign overtime to those employed than to bring back former employees. Why? Because if these latter have to be laid off again, they will in the meantime have qualified for more (employer-contributed) unemployment compensation. The second consideration, far more serious, is that the company might have already decided to discontinue a particular product or line, to get out of an industry entirely, or to replace most if not all of its workforce with machines, or to move to a lower-cost environment. In any of these instances it will interpret its interests as being better served by never seeing those displaced workers again.[14]

Employment Rights

According to a wry Haitian proverb, "If work were a good thing, the rich would have found a way of keeping it to themselves." In an ironic way, they have done just that. The rich themselves are exempt, almost by definition, from the obligation to work. Others may also be excused if they are in some way disabled, by virtue of age (either too young or too old) or physical condition. In the absence, however, of some socially acceptable excuse, one's entitlement to income is largely a function of one's perceived utility as a worker. This utility is based primarily on market conditions, but as mediated by complex social and political structures. In a socialist economy employment tends to be a given, even if absenteeism reduces the amount of work actually performed to a minimum. (Recent policy shifts in the Soviet Union may, however, undermine the basis for the adage, noted above, about pretended pay for pretended work.) In a capitalist system, the basic determinant of employment, even in an organized plant, is the needs of the employer, as defined by the employer.

In Anglo-American law, the employer's prerogative in this regard is expressed in the doctrine of "employment at will" (EAW), a nineteenth-century juridical device that infers from a mythical mutuality of contract to the right of either party to end the relationship without cause. What this has meant in effect is that an employee has rights qua employee only so long as the employer sees fit to continue that relationship. Unilateral dismissal is subject to modifications in various ways, however, notably either by agreement between the parties or by government intervention. Government intervention may be statutory or judicial.

Under a bargained agreement in the United States, a worker's dismissal is sometimes obviated through a grievance procedure. But the grievance mechanism does not save jobs; at best, it may help determine whether one individual rather than another will have an existing job. If the employer determines that there is not enough work to go around or enough money to pay for the work, layoffs are taken to be inevitable, with only their terms and conditions subject to negotiation. And if the employer, say, a transnational corporation, determines that all the work done in a particular plant can be done more cheaply elsewhere (outsourcing) or otherwise (automation), then the entire local workforce may be terminated.

Western European countries have more expansive programs in place to smooth the transitions made necessary by industrial transformation. At least in principle, they have more adequate unemployment benefits than is the case in North America. The percentage of the labor force covered by such benefits is significantly higher in the United States than in Europe, where smaller firms and agriculture tend to be exempted from coverage. Nonetheless, there is substantial evidence that European societies assume greater responsibility for workers displaced by technology, especially in Sweden and other Scandinavian countries. Various job-securing agreements, now fairly common in Europe, are not unknown to American unions; but American workers are for the most part less protected in this regard.[15]

Many unions in Europe and some in Japan and in the United States have negotiated "data agreements" and "new technology agreements" as ways of mitigating the impact of robots, word processors, and such on the jobs of those presently doing what these devices are designed to do better. These agreements may provide substantial benefits to workers displaced by new technology. But these workers are just as likely to settle for some tangential benefit such as a limitation on the number of hours a day an employee can be required to work in front of a visual display unit (VDU). Moreover, the vast majority of these agreements affect primarily white-collar workers, such as the members of APEX in the United Kingdom. There is as yet no such agreement at any national, not to mention international, level. Agreements are usually at plant or, on occasion, company level; and they are seldom arrived at without considerable resistance on the part of management.

A common concern that is often the subject of agreement is the health risk associated with use of visual display units. In Norway and Sweden in particular, both statutes and negotiated agreements assure workers a significant voice in determining how computer-based technologies are to be introduced. Especially important to these programs are the establishment of worker representation in the decision-making process and a program to develop computer literacy among the rank and file with the cooperation of academics. Similar but less progressive developments have taken place in West Germany and in the United Kingdom.

Building on a checklist of issues published by the Trades Union Congress (TUC) in 1979, British unions have negotiated over one hundred new technology agreements, mainly at company level or below and mainly for the benefit of white-collar (clerical and managerial) workers. About half of the West German workforce is now covered by collective agreements that give special protection in the event of rationalization, for example, in chemicals, leather and footwear, paper, textiles, metalworking, and especially (a recent focus of controversy) printing. As a matter of fact, it was primarily at the initiative of the metalworkers' union in West Germany (IG Metall) that that nation's watchmaking industry was finally prodded out of its complacency to switch from mechanical to quartz technology.[16]

By contrast, only a comparatively small segment of the workforce in North America has been able to protect itself against obsolescence in the face of new technology. Agreements entered into in the past by coal miners and by longshoremen are illustrative of strategies that focus on salvaging job security for those already employed without regard to the future. Somewhat more advanced in this regard are the more recent agreements negotiated by auto and communications workers respectively. Canadian workers, it should be mentioned, were among the first to recognize and attempt to deal with microelectronically created unemployment.

In addition to bargained agreements that ameliorate somewhat the impact of new technology on workers, some progress has been made through legislation and, to a lesser extent, through litigation. At issue here is the emerging claim of unfair dismissal or, as it is sometimes called, abusive discharge. Some workers have a statutory cause of action if dismissed in retaliation for having exercised rights granted under the statute in question. Others, mostly managerial or professional, have achieved comparable results through judicial rethinking of traditional concepts of law, especially with regard to contracts. The overall effect to date has been a narrowing of the scope of EAW.[17]

Generally speaking, statutory limitations on EAW in the United States are not directly concerned with new technology. Federal courts, however, have tried to think of the introduction of new technology as a kind of subcontracting, and in that way they can require effects-bargaining under the National Labor Relations Act. In addition, there are a number of other statutory grounds for limiting EAW, on both the federal and state levels. Under federal law there are prohibitions against discharge of an employee for union organizing activity (NLRA); for claiming rights under Title VII of the Civil Rights Act of 1964 or the Fair Labor Standards Act of 1976 or the Occupational Safety and Health Act of 1970 or the Age Discrimination in Employment Act of 1967; or for having one's wages garnished (the Consumer Credit Protection Act of 1976). Various state legislatures have protected employees against discharge for political activity, because of physical handicaps, for serving on a jury, for refusing to take a lie detector test, or, quite commonly, for filing a workers' compensation claim.[18] In cases involving layoff of a significant number of workers, advance notice is appropriate. But if notice is not explicitly required by statute, our courts are unlikely to read it into an employment contract. Few states have statutes requiring more than one week advance notice. After a long and heated debate, the U.S. federal government in 1988 passed legislation that requires large businesses to give employees sixty days advance notice of the intention to lay off a substantial portion of the workforce or close a plant.

Statutory limitations on employers' freedom to discharge employees are considerably broader in some foreign countries, especially because they are highly conscious of the social ramifications of such actions. Sweden and other Scandinavian countries are exemplary in this regard. But so in its own way is West Germany.

West Germany is committed, as a nation, to a policy of full employment. This policy was severely tested by the economic crisis of the 1970s. But the commitment is there, in statutes and in practice: in West Germany keeping people employed is a top priority. Proposals to move a plant are subjected to serious scrutiny by the government. If work slacks off, employees are put on "short-time working" and the government pays the difference to keep them at full wages.

Under the Protection Against Dismissal Act, an employer who has dismissed a significant number of employees (as defined in the law) has the burden of proving that none of these was the victim of a "socially unwarranted dismissal." This is defined as a dismissal "not based on reasons connected with the person or conduct of the worker or on urgent operating requirements precluding his continued employment in the undertaking." Courts have held that a fall in profits is not per se an "urgent operating requirement." Advance notice up to three months must be given to the employee and to the works council, with the result that 20% of the layoffs are averted and more than half of another 10% win compensation before a labor court.

Specifically, an employer in West Germany is required by statute to consult with the works council about every proposed "organizational change." This includes any rationalization of production operations, working methods, technology, communication and decision making, management and leadership, or control methods. Over 50% of the country's workers over the age of forty are protected under this statute with a good mix of transitional assistance; and under an Employment Promotion Act any costs incurred in moving to take a different job are reimbursed.[19]

Workers in Great Britain who are laid off also have recourse through statutory arrangements. Under provisions of The Employment Protection (Consolidation) Act 1978, many employees may seek monetary damages for wrongful dismissal in a court or for unfair dismissal before an industrial tribunal. Similar statutory protections are available in New Zealand, where a claim must be processed through the appropriate union of which one must be a member.[20]

Except for the plant closing notice requirement enacted in 1988, there is nothing in the United States to compare to these now well-established statutory protections abroad. But the protections made available to workers abroad are to some extent available in this country by virtue of the expansion of tort and contract law into the new field of employment law. In courts in various jurisdictions attorneys for dismissed employees are convincing juries that their clients have endured "unfair dismissal" or "abusive discharge." These verdicts typically result in damage awards in the $200,000 to $300,000 range; but they have gone as high as $4 million. The complaints assert breach of express or implied contract (in the employee handbook), breach of implied covenant of good faith and fair dealing, or public policy (as in the case of a "whistle blower").[21] This area of law has burgeoned in recent years, requiring management to pay more attention to detail when dismissing employees. Mishaps in this regard, however, will be challenged mainly by those with more than average means at their disposal.

The most far-reaching judicial modifications of EAW have been based on some public policy consideration. Public policy exceptions to EAW have been recognized to penalize and even undo discharges for refusing to violate a criminal statute, fulfilling a statutory duty, exercising a statutory right, or acting in accord with a general public policy. The United States Supreme Court has tended to favor job security for *public* employees, found that workers have rights to liberty and property under the Fourteenth Amendment, and even authorized a tort of wrongful discharge in cases in which filing for workers' compensation triggers the discharge. Traditional contract law with regard to terms of an express or implied contract has persuaded courts in some states. But the real engines of change are the emerging doctrines of reliance, estoppel and additional consideration (involving, for example, an employee's sacrifice of a tangible or intangible right), promissory estoppel, or equitable estoppel on the basis of considerations analogous to the equitable theory of *quantum meruit.*[22]

Although only a minority of state courts has either adopted or considered adopting such a contract law modification of EAW, commentators in the law journals wax eloquent on the long-term implications. For a few, nothing less than the downfall of capitalism is at stake. For others, this judicial trend provides some long overdue protection to the great bulk of American workers who are not unionized—a consideration, by the way, that has not gone unnoticed by the unions themselves. Still others anticipate nothing more dramatic than a need to word a discharge notice as carefully as one words a divorce action in a jurisdiction that still requires a finding of fault.[23]

Careful wording is being given no less attention at the front end of an employee relationship: general disclaimers of any contractual import in the employee handbook and special disclaimer forms with comparable intent that new employees are asked to sign. But these efforts at avoiding liability are themselves being challenged in the courts as employees fired after refusing to sign a disclaimer of employment rights are suing their hard-nosed employers. The costs of litigation can be staggering, so employers are becoming motivated to establish dispute-resolution mechanisms and, in addition, encourage legislation that would put a ceiling on awards.[24]

That the modifications being introduced into the century-old doctrine of EAW necessitate some employer protections is perhaps true. That a slippery-slope argument is applicable to the kinds of modifications being introduced is, however, highly questionable. Organized labor surely has more serious problems to be concerned about in this age of technological unemployment than whether judge-made rights for some workers are an obstacle to organizing. And the percentage of the workforce that is likely to avail itself of such rights is and will probably remain small, for reasons both financial and social; so predictions about the demise of free enterprise are at best premature.

Taking on the World

It is no doubt inevitable that we think about issues like employment security in the context of our own culture and values. But employment is most assuredly not a provincial problem. As these words were being written, during a U.S. presidential election year, the Department of Labor had just published figures showing, conveniently, the lowest unemployment rates in years. Even if reasonably accurate, however, those figures did not reflect reality on a global scale. And our species is, or at least ought to be, grown up enough to think about work and justice on no smaller a scale. After all, the world's principal employers certainly do. But workers and their unions have dealt with globalization about as effectively as Archimedes moved the planet without a fulcrum.

Already in 1847, in *The Communist Manifesto*, Karl Marx and Friedrich Engels called attention to the globalizing tendencies of capitalism, as follows:

> The need of a constantly expanding market for its products chases the bourgeoisie over the whole surface of the globe. . . . The bourgeoisie has, through its exploitation of the world market, given a cosmopolitan character to production and consumption in every country. . . . In place of the old local and national seclusion and self-sufficiency, we have intercourse in every direction, universal interdependence of nations.

With a view to countering this global strategy, they called for communists everywhere to encourage workers to transcend merely local and national interests and strive for common action based on a comparably "international" perspective. This internationalist talk came to worse than naught as the proletariat of the world put on the uniforms of their respective nation-states to kill and be killed as a way of sorting out which branches of capitalism would control which markets. Revisionists in the twentieth century have defended a strategy of independently advancing the interests of workers in each country. But objections to this approach are not hard to find, as Leon Trotsky noted in 1937. For Trotsky, "[t]he Bonapartist degeneration of the Soviet state" is "an overwhelming illustration" of the correctness of Marx and Engels's original global doctrine. Indeed, he says, it is no longer enough for just workers in the "leading civilized countries" to think and act globally. For, he notes, "[t]he subsequent development of capitalism [i.e., since 1847] has so closely knit all sections of our planet, both 'civilized' and 'uncivilized,' that the problem of the socialist revolution has completely and decisively assumed a world character."[25]

In the half-century since Trotsky's defense of proletarian internationalism, history has witnessed countless other developments that exacerbate the imbalance between global corporate power and local workers' interests. Yet union movements in most countries focus on affairs within their own national borders. Many unions in the United States refer to themselves as being "international," of course, but this means only that they have members in at least one other country, most commonly in Canada. Any suggestion that their leadership has communist sympathies is belied by their history and their conservative political stance.

How, then, are even unionized workers going to be able to defend their interests locally when the decisions that affect those interests are often global in scope? Some union leaders see the seriousness of this question. But union attempts to answer it have been comparatively limited in scope.

In 1919 conferees deliberating the Peace Treaty of Versailles, concerned about social revolutions like the one under way in Russia, set up a commission for international labor legislation, headed by Samuel Gompers, then president of the American Federation of Labor. Urged to establish an international body consisting of representatives from governments (one-half) and from employers and labor (one-fourth each) that would recommend labor legislation to national governments, the commission proposed bones without much flesh. The peace conference, though concentrating on what were to be Germany's economically impossible punitive reparations, did insert the proposal in the treaty, and thus was born the International Labor Organization (ILO). Now an official agency of the United Nations, the ILO has, for the most part, focused its efforts on research and education, the former out of its institute in Geneva, the latter through vocational training for different types of enterprises, including cooperatives in Third World nations.[26]

Immediately after World War II, in September 1945, the World Federation of Trade Unions (WFTU) was founded at a convention in Paris attended by 350 delegates representing 67 million union members from 56 countries, including the United States (the CIO but not the AFL), the Soviet Union, and many developing nations. Now, three decades later, it is by far the largest international labor organization, representing over 206 million trade unionists in 70 countries, including France, Japan, and the Soviet Union. But neither the United States nor the United Kingdom is represented. In 1949, as the Cold War intensified, the British trade unions and the CIO split from the WFTU to form the International Confederation of Free Trade Unions (ICFTU), which represents only 85 million workers in 92 countries. Its origins notwithstanding, even this organization was for over a decade considered too leftist for U.S. participation: in 1969, when it dared express reservations about U.S. policy in Vietnam, George Meany, president of the now combined AFL-CIO, withdrew his organization from membership, and it stayed out until 1982.

Cold War politics also affected the ILO, which inevitably became a microcosm of the East/West and North/South global divisions. As large numbers of Third World countries became members of the United Nations, the ILO became ever more concerned about problems in developing countries, and unionists from socialist countries encouraged this concern. U.S. government and labor leaders demanded that the ILO be "depoliticized" and return to its traditional concerns about labor standards, union rights, and workplace health and safety. In 1977, just when it seemed that this was being done, George Meany withdrew the U.S.

union movement, and its 25% of the budget, from the ILO. Having already withdrawn the AFL-CIO from the ICFTU a decade earlier, Meany thereby effected
a total isolation of the U.S. labor movement from contact with socialist-oriented
unionists in other developed countries.[27]

Meany's hostility toward these international labor organizations was based
primarily on his vehement anticommunism. This political posture, shared by most
of the AFL-CIO leadership during his years as president, proved so useful to the
U.S. government that it practically underwrote AFL-CIO foreign affairs activity.
In 1985, long after Meany's death, his legacy was still intact: the AFL-CIO allocated $43 million to foreign affairs—almost as much as its domestic budget. Of
that amount only $5 million came from union dues; the rest came from the U.S.
Agency for International Development (AID) and the National Endowment for
Democracy (NED), the latter a congressionally funded foundation the purpose
of which is to "sell the principles of democracy abroad." This selling of democracy caused the AFL-CIO to be involved in some eighty-three countries through
various affiliate institutes the principal concern of which has been to support
anticommunist unions and governments, especially in developing countries.[28] In
addition, some seventy global companies have funded the AFL-CIO's American Institute of Free Labor Development (AIFLD), which has worked closely
with the Central Intelligence Agency (CIA) to contain communist influence over
European unions and keep Latin American unions docile.[29]

This close ("tripartite") identification of U.S. unionists' interests with those
of government and business has effectively alienated unionists in other countries,
as well as some in the United States, who take the realities of class conflict more
seriously. But their hopes for a globalized union movement comparable to that
of transnational corporations did not seem to be so urgent during the decades
of growth and relative prosperity in First and Second World countries. Then in
the 1980s the urgency became apparent; but it was even more apparent that the
necessary institutional structure simply does not exist.

The ability of newly inaugurated President Ronald Reagan to fire striking U.S.
air traffic controllers and abolish their union (PATCO) in 1981 showed how loose
were union ties across national boundaries.[30] A year later, 40 million European
unionists from thirty-one nations, affiliated through the European Trade Union
Confederation, were taught a similar lesson when the manufacturers' Union of Industries of the European Community squelched efforts to pass the Vredeling proposal in the European Parliament. As a means of giving workers some leverage
over plant closings, this proposal would have required transnational corporations
with European subsidiaries to disclose their global operations to labor unions
twice a year and consult with them on any major decision affecting workers.
Corporation representatives objected that existing national laws are adequate to
protect workers' interests and that their right to confidential data would be jeop-

ardized; but their underlying concern was that the Vredeling proposal would open the door to the internationalization of collective bargaining.[31]

Reflecting on this history in 1983, Canadian labor leader Dick Barry observed that "the labor movement has had a badly fragmented structure and has been dominated by ideologies that ignore or downplay the fact that our fundamental difficulties arise out of the nature of capitalism; and that any real solution requires the replacement of capitalism with socialism."[32] Not all labor leaders in the Western world would agree with Barry's political solution; but they can no longer deny the problem. As transnational corporations move capital in and out of countries, transferring jobs as they go, union responses that are, in every sense, only local will be ineffectual. Some unions in Europe, recognizing this, have achieved a degree of corporationwide bargaining with transnational companies. The World Michelin Council, for example, covers 80% of Michelin's unionized employees in twelve countries.[33] By means of coordinated strikes across national boundaries other unions have persuaded transnational corporations (such as AKSO, N.V.; Caterpillar; Hoechst Chemicals; and Ford) to reconsider plant moving plans.[34] The International Union of Food and Allied Workers' Associations (IUF), an umbrella organization for 176 affiliated unions with 2 million members, has proposed a global boycott to prevent Coca-Cola Company from closing a bottling plant in Guatemala City. (The IUF is one of seventeen secretariats that promote unionism across national boundaries.)[35]

In the United States, by contrast, the AFL-CIO still lobbies for protectionist legislation rather than recognize that most government officials are more responsive to the concerns of those who benefit most from freely moving capital. This sort of tunnel vision leads some analysts to speak of "the obsolescence of American labor." But there are indications that this judgment is premature, even with regard to the AFL-CIO. And the UAW has, in some respects, set an example by working closely with international secretariats in Geneva to raise auto workers' wages around the world and achieve common worldwide contract-termination dates.[36]

Wage differentials are, of course, only one factor in plant location decisions; but among global manufacturers salary gaps from country to country are narrowing. Japanese workers now earn more than their U.S. counterparts ($12 per hour as compared to $10 for Americans) but five times more than workers earn in South Korea.[37] But South Korean workers have recently begun to establish independent unions and are winning increases that lead local economists to encourage more automation at home and relocation of labor-intensive manufacturing offshore to Bangladesh and Sri Lanka.[38]

It bears mentioning that one of the South Korean auto plants, Daewoo Motor Company, is co-owned by General Motors. GM, meanwhile, is expected to close six more plants in as many states in the United States, and nine of fourteen new plants scheduled to open in North America by 1990 will be located in Canada and Mexico. As this game of musical plants intensifies around the globe, Japanese auto makers are beginning to move into the very heart of the rust belt from which U.S. manufacturers are still busily escaping. About half of that nation's $10 billion invested in 450 U.S. plants is invested in six auto plants of which one each is located in a midwestern state (Honda in Ohio, Mazda in Michigan, Mitsubishi in Illinois, Nissan in Tennessee, Subaru-Isuzu in Indiana, and Toyota in Kentucky). With investments ranging from Mitsubishi's $350 million (matched by joint venturer Chrysler) in Illinois to Honda's $1.7 billion in Ohio, the Japanese reduce their trade surplus, gain political support against unfavorable trade legislation, build a base for exports to places (such as Europe and South Korea) that exclude Japanese-made products, and on occasion even accept a union whose members are still smarting from unemployment (Mazda in Michigan).[39]

A hundred years from now, this denationalization of production may be just as intelligible as we now like to think the era of colonization is to us today. But in the meantime one of the few common ingredients of all these moves appears to be a concerted effort on the part of major transnational corporations to dominate the markets in which they are active. As they move around the globe, however, the needs and interests of workers in any particular locale are of much less importance than their inability to demand competitive wages. In a sense, globalization does benefit the least advantaged. But *exploit* is just as appropriate as *benefit* in this context—indeed, it is more appropriate if one considers only the instability of this supposed benefit. Stability is a sine qua non to justice in the world. But it cannot be guaranteed by any one corporation, however extensive its holdings. (Some of the players, notably the Japanese, do seem sensitive to the importance of benefiting not only their investors but the communities where they locate.)

This topic remains to be addressed in its own right. But it is relevant here insofar as it affects one's analysis of equal employment opportunity. For in the absence of counterforces sufficient to rein in the liberty of employers to come and go "at will," employment rights are but transitory tickets to a movable trough. Accordingly, a workers' representative would favor neither national interests nor workers' expectations by agreeing that employment rights be subordinated without qualification to liberty. Workplaces subject to nothing but liberty are but pieces in a game of chess. No one has devised a plan that will lead to capture of the king, so checkmate is never achieved; but in the course of the game the pawns are sacrificed to that end. This is how it goes, of course, in chess; but a well-informed workers' representative knows that the world of work should not be treated as a game and, in particular, that people are not just pawns whose survival is secondary to the well-being of some corporate king. This knowledge might, in turn, suggest a need for the workers of the world to transcend divisive ideologies, unite (at long last) on the basis of their common interest, and bring the so-called game to no worse than a draw.

What Ever Happened to Meritocracy?

These efforts to institutionalize job security are of considerable importance, at least as statements of principle. But taken as they stand they cannot counterbalance the social and economic problems that worker displacement imposes on our essentially laissez-faire public policy with regard to status work. Considering the scope of technological unemployment that we face in many occupations up and down the hierarchy of the workforce, mere "*sauve qui peut*" stopgap measures are inadequate. Jobs are not merely being moved from one place to another, as has historically been the case; they are being taken from humans and given to supposedly more efficient, reliable, and productive machines. Workers thus replaced may be provided with a "transitional" cushion.[40] But a new job is not always forthcoming.

There are certainly plenty of important tasks to perform. But performance that is remunerated in a capitalist economy occurs ordinarily on jobs; and companies do not unilaterally create jobs on the basis of society's employment needs. A veritable revolution in the processes of performance is diminishing the need, once thought insatiable, for people willing to work. This is not equally true everywhere or for all sectors of the economy, and several decades of low birth rates are beginning to lower supply and increase demand for workers. But microelectronic devices, such as robots and word processors, are picking up where scientific management left off.

Workers in the past were no less vulnerable to workforce restructuring. But there was usually more than enough to be done that could only be done by "hands," however much or little aided by "brains." Occasional periods of severe unemployment, however upsetting to the unemployed and those dependent on them, seldom caused anyone seriously to doubt that it is indeed by the sweat of one's brow that one should earn one's bread. Mechanization and Taylorization of one industry after another never seriously challenged the received mythology, for the simple reason that the technological best was not good enough to render human workers superfluous.

Any claim that the technology of our day now changes all that would be premature. But the corporate dream of profits without payrolls is no longer idle fantasy. Workers of all kinds, with all kinds of skills, including those of managers, are being rendered obsolete by the influx of new devices. In some countries, workers whose livelihood is thereby jeopardized have ways to minimize the impact of new technology on their own careers. And in the United States some former managers have persuaded juries that they (the managers) were unfairly dismissed. But generally speaking the termination of one's employment in this country is followed soon after by the termination of one's rights as a (former) employee. In a matter of months at most, compensation comes to an end, and if one is still unemployed at this juncture, people tend to assume that one is "lazy and shiftless."

This game that society plays is but another version of blaming the victim. The only thing that is particularly curious about it is that it is still taken seriously. It certainly was in the past, of course. Even as Depression-mindful parents frightened their baby boom offspring into succeeding, so did meritocratic appeals for "excellence" provide assurance that the high achiever would find a comfortable niche in the economic system of the future.[41] This promise needed special attention to make believers out of minorities and women; whence the social agenda of the 1960s and 1970s. But in the 1980s the rules changed again. Frederick Taylor lives, in the unlikely form of a microchip that not merely organizes human labor in accordance with mechanical principles but increasingly replaces them with better-performing machines. The result is technological unemployment. And the longer this unemployment continues, the more difficult it becomes to believe that we are on the way to meritocracy—unless, perhaps, we consider rationalization a suitable substitute for creativity. But clearly it is not.

Given a commitment to meritocracy, a society should presumably arrange things, for the greater benefit of all, so that the most competent workers perform their way to the most important positions. The more a society is convinced of the efficacy of this approach, the more rigorous is likely to be its system of testing candidates for advancement along the way. Such has been the case in western European countries since they became parliamentary democracies some one hundred or more years ago. And such has been the case more recently in both the United States and Japan. But all of these countries have come to recognize to one degree or another that societally instituted hoop-jumping cannot of itself produce genius or even creativity; so modifications of various sorts are being introduced to accommodate this wholesome insight.[42]

Worry about loss of markets because of less fruitful research and development is a factor in the search for better ways to encourage creativity; and in the long run this is of economic significance to all members of the society in question. There is, however, a more down-to-earth reason for current disenchantment with the theory and practice of meritocracy: it has not been evidenced in people's pocketbooks. Those who are supposed to benefit most from a meritocracy, namely, the hardworking middle class, have cause to wonder. In the United States, middle management people complained about inadequate compensation in the late 1970s; but in the 1980s at least half a million of them could complain about having been fired.[43] Altogether, almost 10 million U.S. workers who had been employed for at least three years lost their jobs to plant closings and layoffs within a five-year period (1983–88). Many were reemployed, but barely half of them at no less than the same level of income and 30% of them at a rate at least 20% lower. As blue-collar workers in particular are being shunted from well-paying manufacturing jobs into much lower-paying service jobs, many are losing whatever claim they once had to being middle class.[44]

In view of these persistent threats to the employment relationship and to the benefits derivable only from that relationship, the question of whether technology is value-neutral has serious practical implications. Philosophers have tried to answer this question on a theoretical level. Trade unions also deal with it, at least implicitly. In Europe they do so explicitly; and for reasons ideological as well as tactical, they tend to favor the neutralist position, saving their energy to do battle against a coterie of unintended consequences. This is the case, for example, in France, where Marxism is the ideology of preference within the union hierarchy.[45] In the United Kingdom, Marxist laborites are on the fringes of power and tend to the position that those in control of the unions are at fault precisely because they do accept technology as neutral and hence do not fight with sufficient vigor against it.[46]

That workers should lose their jobs is, of course, nothing new. Nor is it unprecedented that the installation of a new technology is the immediate cause of worker displacement. It is not even new that the impact of a technology is localized in one sector of the economy. (The mechanization of agriculture beginning a century ago is a case in point.) What is new is the wide range of specialized skills that new technology is rendering economically unattractive. But these skills have served companies well, in some cases for many generations. They have been acquired as a result, directly or indirectly, of business priorities and programs. It would seem, then, that only the ungrateful or perhaps the amnesiac company would simply abandon these victims of its own devices.[47]

What a company chooses to do, however, is not likely to exceed what society believes ought to be done. And in the United States individuals are not considered entitled to the kind of support received, for example, by the now resurgent Chrysler Corporation. Economists, resigned to the demise of the balanced budget, debate whether there is such a thing as a Phillips curve to account for unemployment and on occasion wonder if perhaps technological revolution is a factor after all, as economists K. Y. Kondratieff and Joseph Schumpeter after him maintained early in this century.[48] But as we enter an age of revolutionary transformations of production, we seldom look to anything like communitarian values to help us deal humanely with the unemployment that it engenders. Instead, we cling to the obsolescent maxim that each individual must earn his or her own subsistence and that this is best done through work.

One overarching message comes through this maze of uncertainty about the availability of jobs in the future: the dynamics of employment are so volatile that a workers' representative would be hard-pressed to come up with worker-appreciative rules on the subject. But a compassionate representative might think about including the unemployed among what Rawls refers to as the least advantaged.

Chapter

8

Automation:
Laborsaving or Dehumanization?

OUR REFLECTIONS ON various aspects of the work relationship have shown how difficult it would be to formulate principles that protect the rights of workers. Meaningful work, though widely endorsed, is a dragon insofar as it can so easily be co-opted and transformed into an instrument of exploitation. Liberty, even maximum mutual liberty, is no less attractive in the abstract; but when applied in a world of unequal bargainers, it too is suspect as a guide to fair terms and conditions of employment. Equal opportunity also seems to deserve inclusion in a social contract. But should it be understood in an egalitarian or in a meritocratic sense? Even if equality is adopted as a goal, through what mechanisms should this goal be approached? And given the instability of plant locations, can the list of job applicants be only local or must it in fairness be nothing less than global? Answers in the abstract are but fair-weather friends; for in the world of employment relations the meaning of any policy adopted is a function of the way it is applied.

Here again John Rawls seems at first glance to have some helpful suggestions. Knowing full well that earthlings are not going to implement the ideal overnight, Rawls offers them a "nonideal theory" by means of which they can adjudicate the drag of circumstantial delay. In the interim between unjust and just social arrangements (in the world as we know it), they are to advance toward justice as fairness "with all deliberate speed." The U.S. Supreme Court has chosen to interpret this expression, after *Brown v. Board of Education* (1954), in terms of juridical remedies; Rawls, being a true child of his profession, talks in terms of rationality. He prioritizes equal basic liberty in principle, but he allows its achievement in practice to be a function of reasonable expectations "under favorable circumstances." [1]

Applying this concept of just postponement of justice to our particular concerns, one might say that for now and for the foreseeable future, the outside pressures of competition prevent even the well-intentioned employer from providing employees with meaningful work, worker ownership, or even continued employment. Working conditions in one location cannot be any better than those that are acceptable somewhere else. Workplace liberty must take a back seat to concessions in a context of obsolescence and restructuring, mergers and acquisitions, and a global labor pool. So honoring workers' rights, though unquestionably a worthy objective, must wait while globally oriented business strategy assesses the short-term preferability of plant closings and relocations.

A globally neutral workers' representative might be tempted to go along with this, so long as some people somewhere in the world have jobs. After all, as viewed from nowhere (à la Thomas Nagel's curious concept), only chauvinism and xenophobia could make one say that when choices must be made one's own people should be employed. However low or even exploitive the wages elsewhere, these too will no doubt rise eventually, and in the long run all will be either dead or comparably compensated.

But after giving the matter some thought, the workers' representative would reject the application of nonideal theory to the workplace—in part because of the suspect ideology of automation. However accepting of present inequities not ripe for removal, our representative cannot be indifferent to bad intentions. Institutions may be temporarily unjust, but only so long as those responsible for them intend to make them fair as soon as conditions permit. If what they intend is not eventually to satisfy workers' just demands but rather to do away with the workers, what patience is due their interim acquiescence in imperfection? This, in the absence of a commitment to community welfare, is precisely the problem with a goal of profits without payrolls.

To bring this point home, I will first review the known (negative) impact of microelectronics on employment (with an initial focus on the robot revolution); then I will assess commonly announced motives for enduring such negative impact (what I call engineering unemployment), including the ultimate objective of total dehumanization of the workplace—an objective that should be viewed with some suspicion.

The Robot Revolution

Much more is involved in the process of automation than just the introduction of robots to do work done until now by or at least with the help of humans. But the introduction of robots on to the factory floor is a kind of microcosm of the electronics revolution. So some observations about robots can serve as an appropriate introduction to the broader issues.

It is difficult to determine just how many robots there are in a plant or industry, or in a particular country, or in the world, because there are different definitions of the word *robot*. Three should be noted here. The most common in popular usage as well as in science fiction is a manufactured apparatus that has a humanoid appearance and exercises humanlike functions well enough to be considered human in a given context. Such were the original *"robota"* in Karel Capek's play *R.U.R.* (Rossums's Universal Robots); and there are robots of this type in use in Japan to direct pedestrian or vehicular traffic.[2] But robots do not need humanlike features to take over the jobs of humans.

Research and development people think of a robot as an artificial intelligence (AI) machine that can perform humanlike functions. Programmable automation manipulators have been around for decades. AI machines are only now beginning to make their appearance, but they are expected to mushroom in the next several decades. A still broader definition of the word *robot* is a programmable manipulator of versatile automation components. This usage, although perhaps more biased than necessary toward imitating human performance, was for years generally accepted in the U.S. robotics industry. I will use *robot* in this sense, subject later to an important qualification.

From the human-matching perspective, robots differ in their degrees of freedom, method of articulation, control of motion, or method of actuation.[3] Three degrees of freedom are required to position an object in space, three more to orient the object in any direction (a minimum for a "general-purpose manipulator"). Robot joints may swivel ("polar"), slide ("cartesian"), or combine these two methods ("cylindrical"). Only a terminal point is specified in point-to-point control; the precise path and the velocity of the entire movement are determined by continuous-path control. Pneumatic actuation, cheap and simple but adequate only for point-to-point operations, and hydraulic systems, which yield better dynamic performance and power-to-weight but tend to leak, are both obsolescent. Electric actuation, which is simple to install and easy to maintain, is now becoming standard.

Typifying the human-matching perspective, Jasia Reichardt has identified nine levels of automation (she calls them "stages" or "degrees"), with robots on or above the fifth level. If the task to be performed is bending a pipe and some tool is employed in the process, the prerobotic tool might be (1) a hand tool, (2) a power tool, (3) power machinery under human control, or (4) powered machinery executing a programmed sequence of operations without variation. A robotic tool bending a pipe might be (5) preprogrammed only for that task as to sequence of, and length of time between, operations; (6) provided with several programs stored and selected automatically (a variable-sequence robot), (7) controlled by means of programs stored in a large memory device and subject to change automatically (continuous-path robots with servomechanisms), (8) a computer-aided manufacturing system (CAM) that activates the motors of numerically controlled robots by means of programs stored on punched paper tape, or (9) "smart" or "intelligent" robots with tactile and visual capabilities.[4]

According to one estimate, in the early 1980s there were fifteen thousand robots installed around the world, about half of them in Japan and a fourth in the United States.[5] In second place was the Soviet Union, where there are some six to seven thousand units (most of which U.S. writers have tended to downplay as technologically retarded, having only three to four axes of movement).

Estimates vary widely as to how rapidly robot usage will grow in the decades ahead.[6] Some project only modest expansion. Others anticipate awesome growth rates. For example, the Russians were expected to have added forty thousand units by the mid-1980s and then in the second half of the decade be installing sensory robots. In Japan 150 companies produced robots at a level of $400 million in 1980, and they were expected to be producing at a level of $2.2 billion by 1985, $4.5 billion in 1990. In the United States a year later, an equal number of robot manufacturers had sprung up to produce at a level of only $50 million per year in 1981, as the projected market was being estimated as high as $250 billion by the turn of the century.[7] Actual U.S. expenditures as of 1986 were at a level just under $2 billion a year.[8]

One key factor in the expansion of robot production and use is a fundamental disagreement about the capabilities that robots need to have. Reichardt expressed the earlier belief that cost-effectiveness will come only when "quality" can be built into robots so they are "capable of working in moderate disorder, with some ability to recognize colors, shadows, markings, and textures." This is the goal of artificial intelligence, which uses increasingly sophisticated microelectronic technology to solve problems heuristically. In this way sensory capability with regard to both "touch" and "vision" are becoming technologically and economically feasible. A Mitsubishi robot, for example, "knows" when it has reached the correct object on a workbench by comparing images of it in two television cameras, one mounted on the robot's hand and the other overlooking the workbench. A Hitachi robot is so touch-sensitive that it can insert a piston into a cylinder with a clearance of twenty microns in three seconds. And three major Japanese companies are working on a robot that will be able to position a component within 4/100,000th of an inch. Selective choice and evaluation of parts may be available before too long; and farther into the future is a "thinking" robot that when shown what to do will establish the most efficient way of doing it.[9]

Underlying these projections, however, is a strategic question which most U.S. robot manufacturers answered incorrectly, at least in the short run. Enamored of the human-imitating six degrees of freedom, they produced robots whose versatility came at the price of slowness and imprecision. The Japanese, meanwhile, have concentrated on robotic machines with fewer joints that may move in only one direction (usually vertically) but do it faster and more precisely, with less vibration, and in a row with others, each of which is designed to fit into a preplanned and easily reprogrammed process of production. Thus are produced such continually improved consumer products as videocassette recorders, portable stereos, and television receivers.[10]

The world's largest producer of robots is yet another Japanese manufacturer, Fujitsu Fanuc, Ltd. In the early 1980s, Fanuc opened a $38 million plant to produce other robots and computerized tools automatically, using robots, numerically controlled machine tools, and only one shift of one hundred human workers to assemble robot-made parts (until, that is, robots become skilled enough for that task as well). MITI, the quasi-governmental research arm of Japanese industry, had committed $140 million over a seven-year period to develop smart robots to assemble an entire product, such as an automobile, beginning as early as 1983. With this new system one could effect changeover simply by changing the system's software. Even more advanced is a flexible manufacturing complex (FMC), a $60 million prototype of which is now in place: five fully automatic manufacturing operations all of which are interconnected and controlled by a hierarchy of computers, with humans on hand only as safety overseers of lasers used for treating and machining.[11] By virtue of this advanced know-how, Fanuc has come to dominate the U.S. market for robots and other automation devices. Its onetime U.S. competitors now market its products.

Among U.S. auto makers, General Motors has been a devotee of automation. The PUMA (programmable universal machine for assembly), a $20,000 robot arm developed by GM and Unimation, is a case in point. GM had planned by 1990 to be using five thousand of these arms in assembly work and four thousand to load and unload machines, thereby displacing 50% of its assembly line workers.[12] In addition, GM once planned to spend $200 million by 1983 to install eight hundred robots on fourteen assembly lines in seven of its plants in Italy. (Fiat's Robogate system boosted production 15% in 1978 without replacing many workers, but since then the Italian auto maker has become a leader in highly automated, low-labor production.) By 1990, GM once claimed, it would have $1 billion invested in thirteen thousand robots to paint, load, and unload machines and assemble components, with the help of Robogate, thereby cutting labor costs by an estimated 70% and the labor force by 50%. From a total of some five hundred robots in the early 1980s (when the Japanese already had some seven thousand in place), GM hoped to expand to five thousand by 1985 and to thirteen thousand by 1990.[13] Instead, GM has cut back significantly on robot orders, most of which would have gone to GMF Robotics, GM's 1981 joint venture with Fanuc.

The PUMA program was designed to interface with humans and as such was intended to be transitional. On a larger scale, GM has counted very heavily on automation as the answer to global competition. In addition to its joint venture with Fanuc, it spent $2.5 billion to buy Electronic Data Systems Corporation to help develop a computer network. It spent $400 million to automate the Buick

City complex in Flint, Michigan. Unfortunately, the system did not work out as planned. Robots were dropping windshields on cars' front seats. An entire robotized welding line had to be pulled to let people do the work, and GM had to endure a costly delay in the introduction of new models. As its profits continued to fall, GM came to realize that "new technology pays off only when coupled with changes in the way work is organized on the factory floor." This lesson the company learned most forcefully from its NUMMI (New United Motor Manufacturing, Inc.) plant, a joint venture with Toyota. At this plant, in Fremont, California, it is being demonstrated that "organizing work more efficiently and giving workers more say can produce more impressive results than millions of dollars worth of robots." [14]

Another industry targeted for transformation by robotics is consumer appliances, which in the United States is dominated by General Electric. [15] GE had two robots in 1978, added twenty-six more in 1979, and hoped to be using a thousand by the end of the 1980s. The company spent over $15 million in 1980 for forty-seven new robots and expected to save $2.6 million per year in labor and materials. At first, displaced assembly workers were transferred, for instance, to robot maintenance, with workforce reduction limited to attrition. GE's dishwasher plant in Louisville, Kentucky, is 60% automated, but workers are free to stop the line at key points to prevent defects from being built in. But the technology for full-scale automation, including a robotic "eye" and a CAD/CAM (computer-aided design and manufacture) system, has been under development. And once this is in place reduction in workforce will undoubtedly follow. In fact, GE plans to robotize as many as half of its thirty-seven thousand assembly line jobs to achieve 6% per year improvement in productivity—largely in response to competition from Japanese manufacturers, such as Sanyo, which has an automated refrigerator plant on the West Coast and others in Tennessee, Arkansas, and other states. To this end, however, GE will not be relying on its own ingenuity.

Not that GE did not try; it just did not succeed on its own. As the market for robots began to burgeon in the mid-1980s, GE decided it would supply robots and other automation equipment to other manufacturers. So it acquired licenses to use the robotics technology of Italy's Digital Electronic Automation, Japan's Hitachi, and Germany's Volkswagenwerk (VW). According to reports, the arrangement with VW authorized GE to build five of that company's robot models and sell them worldwide. These additions were to give GE a total of twelve models, including one capable of handling components weighing more than two hundred pounds and targeted for the automotive, aerospace, and heavy equipment industries. In 1987 GE closed its robot-making department in Orlando, Florida, and began marketing Japanese-made robots in Charlottesville, Virginia —through a joint venture with Fanuc called GEF Automation.

Several other large U.S. companies, such as IBM and the emerging Adept Technology, which concentrates on handling and assembly robots, are likely to find a stable market for themselves. But others have proven to be no more prepared for this new technology than was General Motors. Westinghouse is a case in point. In the early 1980s, when customers for robots were waiting in line for delivery, Westinghouse set up a Robotics Division and gave it a mandate to robotize "any and all manufacturing areas." Toward this end the company, like others around the country, did a feasibility study (on National Science Foundation money) of automated batch-assembly of 450 different versions of eight different fractional-horsepower motors at a rate of 1 million units per year. In 1983, it bought Unimation, a pioneer robotics company that was turning out $30 to $40 million worth of robots a year. But it treated the creative people at Unimation so indifferently that all its key technical personnel left. Besides, Unimation was locked into the obsolete hydraulic robot (in contrast to its closest competitor, Cincinnati Milacron, which makes electric robots). At this writing Westinghouse has consolidated Unimation into its factory-automation division, keeping only fifty of its two hundred employees, and has turned to another company, Prab Robots, to make, service, and replace Unimation hydraulic robots (thirty-six hundred now in use).[16]

In summary, the robot revolution is not as sweeping as some early prognosticators expected. But with the help of compact and versatile microprocessors that can drive so-called smart robots and other components of automated assembly systems, the "automation revolution," prophesied from the outset of the Industrial Revolution[17] and prematurely announced following development of the computer after World War II,[18] may now be on the verge of realization. If so, by the twenty-first century the configuration of human work may well have been radically transformed, along with the technology that supports and replaces it. David Cherrington presumably anticipates this development with considerable relief. According to him, it will be recalled, today's workers are less committed to the work ethic than were workers in the past; but well-managed technology, he believes, will fill the gap.[19]

The Impact of Microelectronics on Employment

Cherrington's devaluation of labor in comparison to management and machines is symptomatic of a long-standing and pervasive commitment to Project Dehumanization: the systematic elimination of human beings from production processes. To appreciate the import of this effort, however, let us first look beneath broad-brush figures about the growth of robotics in industry to assess the impact of this growth on the workforce, in this country and in others as well. To be considered in turn are some concrete examples of Project Dehumanization, some estimates of their long-term impact, and an indication of the ambivalence of experts about all of this.

At racetracks, window betting has been taken over by an automated "sell-pay" system that shortens lines, saves 10 to 50% on costs of operation, and eliminates jobs.[20] Robotic milking and harvesting of crops (everything from artichokes to grapes) is the objective of "agrimation" researchers in the United States and France.[21] Similarly, when U.S. air traffic controllers went on strike in 1981, their complaint about job stress (now being repeated by their successors) was badly timed. For the U.S. government was then engaged in a ten-year, $8.5 billion project aimed at reducing the need for technicians and controllers by one-third with an automated air traffic control system that would require only one rather than three humans per display screen and allegedly save $6.7 billion in the 1980s and over $17 billion in the 1990s.[22]

Microelectronic technology might render entire industries obsolete. It has already transformed a number of work processes, including tool and die manufacturing, printing and publishing, retail sales, banking, insurance, and clerical work, to a point at which in these sectors comparatively few jobs need to be done by humans. Many traditionally valued skills are being rendered obsolete, and fewer new skills are likely to be needed in the sectors affected.[23]

This trauma of transition has been carefully documented in Western Europe. Between 1969 and 1978 eight manufacturers of business equipment, as surveyed by Olivetti, reduced their employment by 20%. In three years, from 1975 to 1978, Ericsson, a Swedish manufacturer of telecommunications equipment, reduced its production workforce from fifteen thousand to ten thousand. Between 1972 and 1979 in West Germany thirty-five thousand employees in the printing industry lost their jobs, usually to a visual display unit. Similar workforce reductions have occurred elsewhere in manufacturing of computers, farm implements, and small- to medium-sized engines.[24]

In the production of machine tools, once requiring high-grade human skills, humans now do little more than monitor and feed information. Skills still needed are based more on analytic and logical ability than on workplace-acquired experience. Clerical skills, which often include a range of administrative responsibilities, are now being dissipated by the word processor, a development that disproportionately affects women in the workforce.[25] Electronic components of an earlier generation were produced by a workforce made up mainly (70 to 80%) of semiskilled workers. New electronic components (large-scale integrated circuits) are produced by a workforce almost equally divided into thirds among trained engineers and technicians, semiskilled workers, and unskilled workers.

As a result of this transformation of the means of production, even *sushin koyo,* the vaunted job security system of Japanese factory workers, has become vulnerable. The manufacturing workforce in Japan dropped from 14.4 million in 1973 to 13.7 million in 1980. The conclusion of a government study that the impact of microelectronics on employment would not be serious was heavily criticized, and the once acquiescent unions have begun to worry. One result: the Federation of Japan Automobile Workers' Unions has entered into an agreement with Nissan that protects the jobs of those presently employed against layoff or downgrading due to the introduction of robots and microelectronics.

Thanks, then, to the creative efforts of some engineers, many blue-collar workers, especially in manufacturing, are losing their jobs to "iron-collar" substitutes. Estimates vary as to the long-term impact of this trend. According to one analysis, there will be a 36% reduction in the auto industry globally by the year 2000, including a 39% decline in the United States from 982,000 employed in the peak year 1979 to just 596,000 in the year 2000: a loss of 386,000 jobs in one U.S. industry alone.[26] Even the more conservative projections give reason for concern. Hunt and Hunt, for example, in a recent private sector study, conclude that some one to two hundred thousand jobs will be eliminated in the United States by 1990, one-fourth of them in the auto industry, affecting 6 to 11% of auto workers.[27]

Hunt and Hunt foresee a concurrent increase in jobs for engineers, not enough of whom are likely to be available. Engineering is the dominant occupation in robot manufacturing: about 23.7%, mainly mechanical and electrical, but also electronic and computer specialists. Moreover, a large number of the managers, officials, and proprietors are trained engineers, and so are some "proposal sales engineers" and some R&D people. Engineering technicians account for an additional 15.7% of the workforce as "robotics technicians" and the like, who do testing, programming, installing, and troubleshooting. Taken together, then, engineers and engineering technicians constitute 40% of the robotics workforce. This, however, involves only a hundred thousand jobs nationwide, resulting in a "skill-twist" to two-thirds white collar compared to only one-third in all manufacturing combined. In short, unskilled or semiskilled jobs are being eliminated, and the jobs created require substantial technical background. This, say Hunt and Hunt, is "the true meaning of the so-called robotics revolution." [28]

Larry Hirschhorn expands this "skill-twist" notion into a full-blown encomium of the wholesome consequences to be gained from automation. Contrary to the Taylorist quest for perfectly rationalized production, production in the new electronic era, he says, calls for "flexibility," which requires ever more intelligent workers who draw upon tacit knowledge, holistic thinking, heuristics, and even engineering expertise to catch "second-order errors" beyond the ken of even smart machines. Since human workers will continue to have these august responsibilities, "[w]e can no longer think of the worker as simply redundant." [29]

Missing from Hirschhorn's description of these upgraded workers of the future is a credible description of who they are, how many of them there will be, and how they will have been trained. Likely to be absent, for example, are numerical control (NC) programmers, who are currently identified with management (in spite of machinists' efforts to include this function in their job description).[30] Unions will emphasize seniority, but this is no substitute for appropriate skills. So unless workers and management are very sensitive to the trauma of transition, older workers are not likely to be the ones who are comfortable with computers and robot technology.[31] Moreover, others who study the same data have concluded that "smarter" people (semiskilled and skilled workers, lower and middle managers) are especially vulnerable to automation.[32]

The divergence of opinion manifested in these projections about the long-term impact of automation is mirrored in their evaluative assessment by academicians past and present.

Today few responsible analysts of this process deny that worker displacement is an inevitable *short-term* consequence of introducing laborsaving technology.[33] But in general, social scientists other than those with Marxist leanings have been rather blasé about the *long-term* impact of technology on work. Typical in this respect are computer problem-solving experts Herbert A. Simon and John Diebold. Sociologist Daniel Bell practically eliminates industrial work in his vision of a society run by science-sensitive professionals; but he ignores the worker displacement that scenario implies. Stephen Hill, by contrast, carefully evaluates this problem against the background of sociological theories about work. And political sociologist Claus Offe says work is "the key sociological category." [34]

Historian H. J. Habakkuk found that Americans adopted laborsaving inventions much more readily than did the British during the nineteenth century, which he attributed to the fact that at the time the Americans, unlike the British, had to deal with a labor shortage.[35] During the decades around the turn of the century, vast numbers of immigrants took their places on ever more numerous assembly lines that were the wonder of the world for half a century. But with the invention of the computer during World War II, the possibilities of automation loomed ever larger in industrial planning. At the time many writers foresaw only the benefits of the coming automation, or, like George Terborgh, chastised those who expected a more negative impact. The Hunt and Hunt study (1983) holds automation blameless for any future unemployment, and a 1981 Carnegie-Mellon University study finds the problem to be only mildly worrisome.[36]

More alert to negative consequences are defenders of the labor movement, among whom must be included such humane geniuses as Norbert Wiener, who joined a long tradition of writers who had seen clouds on the horizon because of the unregulated introduction of new technology into the workplace.[37] Unions, too, have challenged the wisdom of Project Dehumanization.[38] And the impact of laborsaving technology on women in particular is a concern today as it was for Marx and others more than a century ago.[39] There is a burgeoning literature about the role of women workers in patriarchal societies which are incorporated into an increasingly globalized economy. The resulting feminization of poverty, especially in the Third World, is the focus of a field of study called Women in Development (WID).

Men profiteer from the informal labor of their carpet-making wives in Iran; the prostitution and sex tourism industry exploits hundreds of thousands of women in Bangkok and Tazmania; agribusiness enterprises in Nigeria and Malaysia deprive women of traditional skills and rights to land; and transnational electronics and textile corporations in increasingly ubiquitous Free Trade Zones thrive on paying bare subsistence wages to some 2 million women. There is reason, then, to challenge "the interrelated global structures of capitalism, patriarchy and white supremacy." [40]

This challenge is being taken up by many scholars, who counter libertarian claims about the benefits of TNC-provided employment by documenting the extent to which TNCs exploit patriarchal structures and values to maximize their own profits. Male workers are still preferred in capital-intensive import-substitution plants, which cater primarily to local elites. But the opposite is the case in the more recently established export-processing enterprises. In return for jobs with nontransferable skills, especially in the garment and electronics industries (90% female employees), TNCs persuade host governments to disregard protective legislation and counter any attempts at unionization, thereby actually destroying local female-intensive cottage industries. Meanwhile, women lose comparable jobs in developed countries, where wage levels and workplace health and safety are more advanced.[41]

Women, then, may be the principal victims of corporate dominance in the world. Nonetheless, this is but one aspect of the negative impact of TNCs on human beings and their communities around the world. This is not a subject to examine in a few words, however; for the ongoing phenomenon of technological displacement of workers is raised to a higher order of magnitude in a global context. Not just one society but many are being disrupted and transformed to serve the needs of TNCs, only to be discarded when those needs change—as when European Economic Community countries decided in the 1970s that they had hosted migrant workers long enough. With regard to automation in particular, what can be automated once can very well be automated many times, in every corner of the globe.[42]

Engineering Unemployment:
Motives in the Madness

Project Dehumanization has been planned and publicly proclaimed for at least two hundred years with comparatively little opposition from anyone except those most immediately affected at any given time. This is truly remarkable. Considering the costs in human terms, this high degree of public acquiescence must be a manifestation of deeply held values—values related perhaps to a love of leisure. However this may be, we are on somewhat surer grounds in uncovering the motives of the project participants themselves.

The plan to replace humans with machines involves four distinct but interdependent goals: the financial goal of cutting the costs of production; the managerial goal of controlling production by deskilling workers; the strategic goal of remaining competitive in the market; and the ontological goal of totally dehumanizing production. All four goals have been consciously and seriously pursued from the earliest moments of the Industrial Revolution, but they have been differentially emphasized over time. The fourth, ontological, goal is teleologically preeminent. Not only does it represent the highest aspiration of the engineering community, it also constitutes the objective correlate of the Frankensteinian hubris that has been the real driving force from the beginning.

It is easy enough to distinguish in theory between cutting the cost of production and maintaining control over the workforce as motives for introducing laborsaving devices. In the literature, however, these motives are inextricably intertwined, explicitly in earlier, less cautious times, but perhaps no less so in this current era of technical writing expertise.

Who knows when human beings first entertained the idea that they might get as much productivity out of machines as they had been accustomed to sweating out of other humans? What is clear is that organization was the recognized instrument of profit until the Industrial Revolution put mechanization in high gear. Between farmer Adam Smith and engineer Andrew Ure, for example, lies a great chasm that separates the age of "manpower" from the age of machine power. For Smith, who lived in what was still predominantly an agrarian society, organizing workers according to function was still the best way to maximize productivity. A mere half-century later, Ure was telling entrepreneurs how much they stood to gain from factories run by machines. Realizing full well that workers would thereby be displaced, Ure was ecstatic about this eventuality. For he considered all human workers to be potential troublemakers—males more than females and adults more than children, but, to some degree, all. "It is," he said, "the constant aim and tendency of every improvement in machinery to supersede human labor altogether, or to diminish its cost, by substituting the industry of women and children for that of men; or that of ordinary labourers for trained artisans." The ultimate objective: total dehumanization. But management's ability to achieve this objective is limited by the replacement capabilities of available machinery. So what he called "the automatic plan" still includes a role for humans: "[S]killed labour gets progressively superseded, and will, eventually, be replaced by mere overlookers of machines." But even this partial control of the labor process benefits management: "[W]herever a process requires peculiar dexterity and steadiness of hand, it is withdrawn as soon as possible from the *cunning* workman, who is prone to irregularities of many kinds, and it is placed in charge of a peculiar mechanism, so self-regulating that a child might superintend it." In this way, "when capital enlists science in her service, the refractory kind of labour will always be taught docility." [43]

A decision to replace human workers with some laborsaving device is seldom made, of course, just to achieve docility. For one thing, science is not always prepared to provide industry with a quick technological fix, nor is laborsaving the only motive for introducing new technology. A substantial part of management strategy regarding the means of production is to estimate accurately what will be feasible in a given period of time and at what cost, and what course of action is most likely to be profitable in light of all calculable variables, including the likely moves of competitors. Having determined all of this to the best of one's ability, one might in a given situation choose not to introduce an available device —at least not until there is a significant change in one of the variables under consideration.

Classical economists believed that a rise in the cost of labor would precede a decision to mechanize.[44] Karl Marx was able to illustrate this view prolifically. He notes, for example, how manufacturers in England turned to mechanization only after the Factory Laws limited child labor to four- to six-hour shifts and parents refused to let their children work as "half-timers" for less than full-timers. He also points to the practice of producing machines in one country to be used in another country where high wages motivate such substitution. But, he argued, the process of displacing workers ("variable capital") by technology ("constant capital") is inherently contradictory, because it results in underconsumption (on the part of those displaced) and thereby negates the supposed advantage of introducing the technology. But he also notes that when machines are introduced into a country the labor pool there is expanded, creating a buyers' market, so other industries are spared the need to mechanize. For, as he notes, the capitalist's "profit comes . . . not from a diminution of the labour employed but of the labour paid for." [45] So even where displacing workers by machines is prohibitively expensive, if not still technically unfeasible, the very threat of doing so can contain costs by dissuading workers from demanding higher compensation.[46]

Neoclassical economists such as J. B. Clark emphasized this disequilibrating function of technology to argue against Marx that new technology does not eliminate but only lowers the value of human labor. Each technological advance, according to the "marginalists," lowers the wage an employer can profitably pay in view of the marginal productivity made possible by the new technology.[47] This effort to save a place for wage labor as machines take over may be of some comfort to the few who are willing to work for less. But it is a Pyrrhic victory in view of management's continuing desire to cut the cost of production.

The cost-cutting techniques of turn-of-the-century engineer Frederick Taylor, usually associated with systematic organization of work, also accommodate Ure's agenda. A "Taylorized" manufacturing system would fulfill its economizing potential, according to Taylor, only when machines in the shop are run by men who are of smaller caliber and attainments and therefore cheaper than those required under the old system.[48]

Even today industrial engineers and robot suppliers hawk their wares with worker displacement as the bait.[49] As expressed straightforwardly by pioneer robot engineer Joseph Engelberger, "The basic production problem to which robots are addressed is the reduction of cost by eliminating human labor."[50] Such blunt talk naturally reinforces workers' concerns about being dispensable. But workers will derive no more comfort from the more technical language of chemical engineer Lawrence B. Evans:

> The cost of complex electronic circuitry continues to decrease exponentially.
> . . . The real cost of a system is in the hardware for communication between
> man and that system (displays, keys, typewriters) and this cost is a function
> of the way the system is packaged. Thus, automation functions and data pro-
> cessing become economic if they can be done blindly, without the need for
> human communication.[51]

It should further be noted that the target is no longer limited, as it was in the past, to the less prestigious members of the workforce. The target of laborsaving now includes not only the comparatively insignificant direct, or "touch," labor costs (10 to 15% in the United States) but additional factors that account for three times as much of the cost of production: indirect labor, middle management, and other overhead.[52] And beyond this doubtfully rational depopulation is the often irrational disposal of top managers whose companies have been bought out from under them. But however much these observations may sound like criticisms, they generally fall on deaf ears in American corporate headquarters and, with some notable exceptions, in our courts as well. Under American labor law, in particular, corporate cost-cutting is just good business, unless (in some situations) it is demonstrably motivated by antiunion animus.

Saving labor, however, is not always equivalent to saving money. Machinist-turned-researcher Harley Shaiken has identified all sorts of social, technical, and financial problems in connection with Project Dehumanization. For example, because of heavy downtime, the so-called flexible manufacturing system (FMS) at the Messerschmitt-Bolkow-Blohm factory in Augsburg, West Germany, has not been nearly as effective as its advertisers claimed. As noted by Melvin Blumberg and Donald Gerwin, "System designers, in their haste to develop smoothly functioning systems free of human variability, [ignore] the simple fact that humans are also critically important sources of control for human variability."[53]

These lessons may be getting through to guardians of the bottom line. Once true believers in the doctrine of cures by gadgetry, they are becoming increasingly wary in the wake of promises unfulfilled. Take the case of robots, for example.

Providers, of course, like to emphasize the cost savings that an innovative management can expect from the installation of robots and the more complex automation into which they might be integrated. But buyers no longer accept sellers' figures uncritically. In the early days of robot marketing, providers claimed that the cost of robots would be recouped within a three-year payback period from savings in direct labor alone. As one writer put it, very simplistically, a Japanese robot in automotive production can do at $5.50 per hour what a UAW worker does for $18.10 (wages and fringes).[54] In fact, providers suggested, as more units are produced, the initial cost of producing a robot could drop from, say, $50,000 in 1980 to $10,000 in 1990. This way of estimating assumes that one can compare known labor costs to the relatively unknown costs of procuring and maintaining a robot. Such estimates have not proven to be very reliable. So providers have been shifting their emphasis to the worst-case scenario, that of a business ceasing to be competitive because it did not automate.[55] But scare tactics have not protected the robot industry from a very sobering slump. "One reason for the slump," according to one observer,

> is the growing sophistication of manufacturers regarding factory automation.
> Contrary to the early hype, it rarely makes business sense simply to replace a
> human worker with a robot and expect the machine to pay for itself in saved
> labor costs. The benefits of automation have proven to be more subtle.[56]

This is a tactful way of saying that corporate purchasers of automation equipment have, on not a few occasions, been had. The sobering experiences of General Motors and General Electric have already been noted. The experience of Deere & Co. may, however, be the paradigm example of what can happen to a company that buys too much of a (purportedly) good thing.

One thing executives of (and investors in) the largest U.S. agricultural equipment manufacturer have learned is that a combination of workforce downsizing and massive automation limits a company's ability to respond to shifts in the market. Since 1981 Deere, which depends on farm equipment sales for 60% of its $4 billion annual revenues, has cut its workforce almost in half to thirty-eight thousand and supplied tractors to U.S. farmers solely from a $1 billion automated plant in Waterloo, Iowa, that can produce forty thousand units a year. But in dealing with everything from a weak farm economy to a strike and then a drought, annual sales have not exceeded twenty thousand units. The heavily robotized production process at its Waterloo plant was originally "so closely integrated that it is virtually impossible to shut down one part of the operation without shutting everything down." Faced with yearly losses and then a strike in 1986, company executives, who had already resorted to layoffs and inventory reductions to compensate for what one analyst called "a failed corporate strategy," began thinking about rearranging the plant into smaller, more flexible "islands." According to *Business Week*,

> Deere can slow down the assembly lines or run them fewer days—which it did before the strike. But running such a huge factory at only an estimated 10% of capacity means Deere is absorbing heavy overhead costs from capital, labor, and such basics as lighting and heating. Little wonder that Deere's manufacturing operations have lost money every year since 1982, a year after Waterloo began production.[57]

Deere has since introduced more versatile machinery and claims that the plant can now break even at 35% of capacity. In the first half of 1988 the company returned to profitability. But as crops withered away over the summer, retail sales of tractors plummeted.[58]

More generally, business offices all over the world are purchasing personal computers to improve their productivity, but without any clear idea of how much such electronic support is going to cost. The cost is likely, however, to be six times the up-front price of the product over a three-year period. For example, each of one hundred PCs acquired for $5,000 to be shared by three hundred users will actually cost $7,500 a year, including supplies, support, and maintenance, and another $8,000 if it is used on a network.[59] Similarly, a study commissioned by the National Tooling and Machining Association suggests that buying parts and components from cheap-labor foreign suppliers costs much more than ordinarily supposed; for when shipping, paperwork and communications, added inventory, and design changes are factored in, the actual cost is 30 to 50% higher.[60]

Not mentioned in such calculations are costs in human terms which eventually appear as health and safety expenditures that accountants and risk containers cannot ignore forever. Consider, for example, a worker's account of what happened when a meat-packing company automated its plant in Austin, Minnesota:

> In the old plant they had two chains to kill hogs; in the new plant they have one that goes three or four times faster. They are doing almost 900 hogs an hour. The number of injuries is incredible at that speed. People were stabbing each other, plus 75% of the workers have carpal tunnel syndrome. . . .
>
> They brought in a new machine from Holland called "Protocon." It sits on four legs like some giant in a horror movie. It's got this gigantic piston in the middle of it, which comes down and de-bones the ham—squeezes the bone out of the meat. Each machine costs $375,000 and replaces 30 workers. And the workers who are left each operate two machines.
>
> About once a month one of these machines would blow this giant piston

with incredible force. You have oil hitting a ceiling that's two stories high. A guy comes from Holland to fix the machine and tells them: "This machine isn't designed to operate that fast." It was deboning a ham every 15 seconds. They are wrecking the machine. If they feel that way about the machine, how do they feel about the workers?[61]

Some readers would take this account as yet another indication of the need for total rather than only partial dehumanization of production. But few automation experts still view this as a short-term objective. In the meantime, "transitions" have a way of constituting the way things are. These worrisome considerations restore some credibility to the nineteenth-century Luddites and Samuel Butler's fictional Erewhonians, each of whom decided to destroy machines before humans became obsolete, and to Karel Capek, whose characters in *R.U.R.* had to deal with many social problems that automation might engender. But the need for such defensive measures seldom occurs to managements that simply prefer machines to people. So there must be other motives at work.

Why is cost-cutting so closely linked with eliminating human labor? Labor-saving is not the only way to cut costs; other ways are through lowering overhead, streamlining production and distribution, and so on. Besides, as Ure's rhetoric already made clear, there are factors other than profit or revenue maximization that management might consider more important. One in particular that stands out is the desire to control others. But as Hegel noted in his famous analysis of the relation between master and slave, one's desire to be superior to others is frustrated if there are no underlings around to acknowledge that superiority. This suggests that phasing out workers must create psychological conflict in those whose decisions help bring it about. For on this view, their sense of self-worth depends to some extent on retaining those whom they seek to dispatch. Thus, it is reported, a landowner in India will resist profit maximization of his agricultural business if by increasing his tenants' share he risks having his tenants pay off their debts to him and get out from under his control.[62]

In workplaces in the developed world, control over who does what has long been controverted. The way this controversy generates work rules and job descriptions has already been considered. Relevant here is a question of management's preference as measured against a threshold of pain. In other words, at what point do efforts to retain control over a workforce yield less pleasure than not having the workforce around at all? Something of this sort must have been in the minds of British textile manufacturers in the 1830s when they deliberately designed new machinery with the use of children as operatives in mind.[63] Analogous to that old strategy is the practice of some companies today of threatening a plant relocation if the workers do not show themselves more receptive to management's idea of "cooperation."[64]

Control over a workforce is theoretically easier to maintain if workers are paid a piece rate rather than according to time. But in practice piece rates are based on time studies and are set with maximum exploitation of the workforce in mind. Miklòs Haraszti, a Hungarian poet who ran two milling machines in the Red Star Tractor Factory in the early 1970s, figured this out in exquisite detail. "How do you earn money?" he asked himself.

> They give me money in exchange for my work, but . . . I have to go through all the sums they have done to arrive at my pay. . . . I have to add up the value of months, days and hours on the basis of what minutes are worth, and I can hardly afford to be generous. They have already calculated each minute into so much for so much. . . . They have converted my minutes into jobs done, and my output into piece-rates.

And how are these rates determined? "The rate-fixers . . . set a production time which demands a superhuman effort . . . to hold wages down to a level fixed in advance." [65]

Haraszti was tried for trying to share such thoughts with others, but he got off with a suspended sentence and a fine equivalent to four months' work because the court could not think of a way to be harsher without claiming that piece rates are essential to socialism.[66] Of course, they are not, any more than they are essential to capitalism; but they are no less common in capitalist settings, where, however, they are subject to what some call "effort bargaining," which is an ongoing debate between management and labor over the amount of effort that will be expended on a job.

The resulting agreement grows out of a complex of factors ranging from available technology to everyone's interest in appearing fair, and its implementation is subject to such subtle sabotage as "unnecessarily" shutting down a line, booking the same work twice, or booking more down time than actually occurred. But if a study of British workers can be taken as typical, the fundamental claim that normal or average production on a job can be measured is challenged not in principle but with respect to workers' ability to master the job. In one plant with a relatively well-organized work force, management includes an "off-standard allowance" (OSA) for "piece-work drift" and calculates a "bonus index" on the basis of the time set by work study, including OSA.[67] Some, including no doubt John Rawls, would want to interpret such effort bargaining as an ongoing attempt to concretize fairness in the workplace. Others, however, see in it a situational manifestation of socially omnipresent class conflict. More generally, the idea that control over the workforce can even take precedence over profit maximization is central to the Marxist analysis of mechanization under capitalism.

In Harry Braverman's view, for example, control of the labor process is the overarching reason for mechanization. The "deskilling" of production that mechanization causes is not inevitable, according to Braverman, but is deliberate. Management decisions to introduce new technology deskill the workforce, and this result is intentional on the part of management. Capitalism, in the words of the Marxist slogan, is striving for "domination of dead labor [machinery] over living labor [workers]." But the closest Braverman comes to a "smoking gun" is a statement attributed to a French engineer that by installing numerical control Renault can increase its profits—a goal to which control of workers is only incidental.[68]

Braverman's historical evidence for his thesis is largely circumstantial and anecdotal, such as the fact that supervisor-operated numerical control became the automation of choice rather than the equally efficient record-playback system (RP) that leaves programming in the control of skilled machinists.[69] Harley Shaiken has since added to the argument the curious history of the feed rate override switch, which enables a worker tending a numerical control metalworking machine to correct for such problems as a sudden change in the density of the metal being cut. This capability significantly reduces the risk of damage to this expensive equipment. But managers, seeking greater control of the workplace for themselves, seldom want machinists to learn how to use these machines, so they have the machine locked on shifts when programmers are off duty. Besides, a machinist might also use the switch to limit output (hence its nickname: the "job security" switch). Whence the attractiveness of the General Numeric System P-Model F programming computer, which is able to compare a theoretical job performance time against its actual performance, thereby providing management with a high-tech instrument for worker surveillance.[70] On an even larger scale, the U.S. Congress's Office of Technology Assessment sees development of programmable automation as an important means of achieving "the push for so-called 'top-down control,' " because "the integration of databases and anticipated shifts in decisionmaking toward higher staff levels will increase the role of upper management in the production process."[71] This sort of open-ended projection can, in turn, become a self-fulfilling prophecy in the hands of a government bureaucracy with ample money to spend. For example, according to the five-volume final report of the Pentagon's Machine Tool Task Force study of the U.S. metalworking industry, the industry should "reduce the skill levels required to operate or maintain certain machine tools (or to plan the manufacture of a part), . . . by using more automation and substituting computers for people in executing certain decisions or operations."[72]

Additional support for Braverman's thesis will be found in the extensive literature concerning the labor process. In Marxist parlance this has to do with the thesis that the ruling class introduces technology for the explicit purpose of controlling and, when possible, dispensing with workers.[73] Stephen Wood, on the other hand, thinks Braverman's argument is built on sand because it erroneously presupposes managerial omniscience.[74] This objection, however, fails to distinguish between actual omniscience, which is admittedly rare, and managerial behavior that manifests an assumption of omniscience, which is somewhat less rare. Moreover, it fails to account for the underlying commitment to management control given that in some societies such control is not considered essential, in Norway and Sweden, for example, where computer systems are being installed not to replace but to improve the efficiency and creativity of experts.[75]

Counterexamples notwithstanding, the most common motive for introducing a laborsaving device is to save labor, that is, some of the costs associated with paying labor. This motive is inherently antilabor in that the installation of such a device, even if not management's intention, is hostile to anyone whose labor is thereby going to be "saved." Marx and many who have followed him would argue that there is a definite and deliberate antilabor bias on the part of management that tilts cost-cutting decisions whenever possible in the direction of cutting payrolls. But a generalized claim to this effect is impossible to prove.[76] Besides which there are reasons to claim to the contrary that managers "would rather fight than switch," that is, control the workers they know rather than turn to robots they know not. So there has to be a more deep-seated motive for displacing workers —and that motive is to meet the competition.

Given a commitment to laborsaving, worker displacement is inevitable and unemployment is likely. This is so, however, not by virtue of any law of nature or because there are no alternatives but because robots and other microelectronic devices are perceived as being cost-effective in the long run and hence a necessary condition for staying competitive in the industries affected.[77] Peter Drucker, a widely read adviser to management, has recently expressed a contemporary version of this common wisdom. "If a company, an industry or country," he says, "does not in the next quarter century sharply increase manufacturing production and at the same time sharply reduce the blue collar workforce, it can not hope to remain competitive—or even to remain 'developed.' . . . The attempt to preserve . . . blue collar jobs is actually a prescription for unemployment." [78]

Disregarding the twentieth-century idiom, Drucker's recipe for competitiveness is a restatement of a very old idea. As old, for example, as Andrew Ure. Ure is often quoted, as above, for his views on deskilling. But the bulk of his work in *The Philosophy of Manufactures* is comparative analysis of various industries, especially cotton and textiles, in different countries. For, as he well knew, the need to remain competitive was especially important to British entrepreneurs. During a strike in the Coventry textile industry, for example, management blamed its refusal to elevate wages on foreign competition from such Continental rascals as France, Switzerland, and Germany.[79]

For the record, however, such concerns were not first articulated after 1830. In 1517, authorities in London resorted to violence to suppress rioters protesting the influx of foreign skilled traders. And well before that, in the Middle Ages, native weavers in London complained about competition from Flemings and Brabantes, and British traders sought to exclude their foreign competitors.[80]

Today, of course, a company's competition may be not merely regional but global; and "global competition" serves today's technocrats as an alternative rationale for more technology. This new competitiveness rationale Richard M. Cyert, president of Carnegie Mellon University (a major provider of robotics research and development), articulates as follows:

> The major technological development that will be key to our regaining manu-
> facturing competitiveness involves the microprocessor, on the one hand, and
> artificial intelligence on the other. . . . We call these machines robots. . . .
> The development of intelligent robots can give us back our comparative
> advantage in the production process. . . . New methods of production are
> already being installed that are moving American manufacturing closer to
> unmanned plants. As of 1982, 22 percent of the labor force was in manu-
> facturing. By the year 2000, this percentage will be closer to 5 percent.
> American manufacturing will automate or evaporate.[81]

Cyert's dichotomy between "automate or evaporate" is false at least in the short run because unequal exchange can be achieved by producing manufactured goods in low-wage areas and the automated factory does not exist. But his position will endure as a long-term agenda because of two mutually reinforcing attitudes in the business community: doubts about the durability of cheap labor and continued hopes for dehumanized production. Both attitudes are exemplified in a 1987 *Business Week* cover story about "the hollow corporation," meaning a corporate enterprise that depends on domestic employment mainly for planning and marketing functions. "[T]he new technology," says this article,

> would bring a crashing halt to the madcap chase after cheap foreign labor.
> Because labor costs would be virtually zero and other offshore savings—
> cheaper materials and lower overhead—would be overwhelmed by the bene-
> fits of quick turnarounds and low inventories, the computerized factory could
> produce things in Indiana for less than they cost to import from India.[82]

This rationale for bringing production "back home again" reads well in a nation that has had some form of protective legislation under consideration for over a decade. But it takes more than technology to pull off a homecoming, especially under an administration for whom free trade is almost an object of worship. Textiles are a case in point: as occurred earlier in Europe, this industry is now disappearing in the United States, regardless of how technologically up-to-date its remaining plants. Between 1980 and 1985, 250 textile mills in the United

States were closed, eliminating 17% of the industry's workforce, 110,000 jobs. Suppliers of synthetic fibers were also closing, even though they were technologically competitive. In the mid-1980s, remaining plants were operating at near top capacity, plants were being modernized, and profits rose significantly. Yet imports are expected to control 80% of the U.S. market by 1990, with the result that textile/apparel employment in this country will fall by half to 915,000, and another 943,000 jobs will be lost in related industries.[83] Industry leaders have sought protective legislation, but a trade bill passed in 1988 was too little, too late. A similar account applies to other industries, such as footwear, primary metals, and steel.

One flaw in the homecoming theory is that it underestimates the expansiveness of the engineering élan. One meta-level beyond bargain-basement homecoming is the dream of globalized automation: automatic factories producing without people wherever in the world there is a market. The Ford Motor Company is heavily committed to such global dreaming. Its transatlantic production of the Escort, though financially successful, never achieved the desired commonality of a "world car," largely because of insurmountable cultural differences.[84] But top management considers this setback only a learning phase. Having closed fifteen plants worldwide at the cost of some fifty thousand blue-collar jobs, Ford is now focusing on transcontinental "Centers of Excellence," at each of which a downsized management and globally computer-linked engineers are expected to maximize production of common components for automobiles only the final styling of which will vary for particular markets.

In view of this complex corporate ambivalence about the comparative advantages of cheaper labor and higher technology, it seems that not even competition can account for the undaunted commitment of true believers to Project Dehumanization.

Cost-cutting, controlling workers, and competitiveness are clearly identifiable motives for putting machines in place of people. But they are in the final analysis rather pedestrian motives. The underlying motive is ontological, if not theological: to push the creative élan to the absolute limit of engineering expertise. To show, in other words, that it can be done—without any regard whatsoever to any untoward consequences.

This engineering ethos is typically articulated in the most mundane sort of way. For example, in response to the embarrassing fact that human beings still interface computer-controlled machine tools, an industrial engineering researcher at Purdue University recommends the next logical step:

> Analysis of the activities involved in keeping an NC machine tool cutting metal for its entire running time shows that human involvement in the actual production process is the primary slowing down factor. The solution . . .

is to automate as many as possible of the production functions in the same manner as the NC cutting process.[85]

This dream of machines producing without hindrance from humans is the goal of AI experts such as Marvin Minsky, who is one of the founding fathers of the movement. "As progress continues," he claims,

> we'll reap the fruits of our research and start to see machines that display more genuine signs of having minds. We'll start to give them learning skills to organize their little minds, so that they can learn from us, and from each other, as we do. We'll show them how to make copies of themselves. Most of them won't even have to learn such things, because they will be manufactured already knowing them. We'll give them limbs even more dexterous than our own and new kinds of senses that will seem to us uncannily observant. Gradually, they'll begin to slip across that edgeless line of doing only what we programmed them to do and begin to move themselves into the zone of things that WE are programmed to do. Then, of course, mere telepresence will be seen as having been only a passing stage, until the brainy AI machines became smart enough to do the jobs themselves.[86]

Minsky's expectation that "smart machines" will eventually become autonomous, rational agents in their own right is not shared by all observers. Some experts have attacked even the quest for a literally dehumanized workforce as wrongheaded. Especially noteworthy in this respect: the great cybernetics pioneer Norbert Wiener never allowed his electronics expertise to blind him to the human implications of the new technology. He repeatedly warned labor union leaders to defend their constituents' interests in the face of the coming revolution.[87] And he also warned engineers and "organizers of engineering" not to become so caught up in "gadget worship" for its own sake that they forget to determine what human purposes their gadgets might serve.[88] In a similar vein, Robert Boguslaw, a leading systems engineer, warns us about "the new utopians" who replace the humanitarianism of their predecessors with efficiency and focus not on people but on people-substitutes.[89]

Not surprisingly, these humanistic objections to Project Dehumanization have no bottom-line impact on corporate decision making. Faced with global competition and fickle investors, corporate managers are ever on the lookout for better ways to save their company some of the costs associated with paying labor. For all their dedication to the cause, however, this narrow concentration on reducing direct labor costs may be misguided. For it is becoming apparent that direct labor represents a comparatively small part of a transnational corporation's costs and that even greater than the need to get rid of workers is the need to include in the shop-floor mix workers who understand what needs to be done.

Workforce reduction, first of all, does not assure long-term productivity growth, so it may not enhance competitiveness. That is why new approaches to accounting focus more on the entire life cycle of a product from materials to market and try to calculate not just return on investment but increase in business, not just cost-cutting but reduced lead times and inventories, better quality, and greater flexibility.[90] These new ways of calculating costs would place more emphasis on literally calculated risks, with future but undocumentable gains as justification.

In the short run, at least, this new approach to accounting might encourage not automation but any of a wide variety of other less dramatic ways to save money. With Volvo leading the way, manufacturers have introduced automated guided vehicles (AGVs) as flexible and adaptable complements to human labor. By installing an automated etching tool Rockwell International saved only $4,000 in direct labor costs, but it saved $200,000 in inventory-holding costs. By contrast, a company that makes graphics plotters in Anaheim, California, cut its costs by "deautomating" and moving work around on carts. What matters most, according to proponents of this new approach, is that a company move toward "life-cycle accounting," in which all the costs associated with a product, from development to marketing (not just factory floor costs) are calculated. This being done, the company might find out for the very first time how much it really costs to move a production facility offshore![91]

In the second place, an increasing number of employers are beginning to recognize the extreme importance of developing and maintaining an educated workforce capable of assuming responsibility for the workplace tasks that will need to be done: reading and writing for starters, but beyond that the ability to use computers and to understand computer-based technologies. Thanks in part, however, to Project Dehumanization (sometimes justified by the very absence of relevantly skilled workers), this educated workforce simply does not now exist in the numbers already in demand.[92]

Thus at least to a degree meaningful work is becoming indistinguishable from the kind of work that more and more companies will need if they are to prosper. It is therefore time to consider replacing Project Dehumanization with Project Education. As the concerns of this chapter have made clear, of course, merely addressing the need for headier workers is not in and of itself going to bring justice to the workplace. But if such an objective were to become really central to our educational policies it could transform preconceptions about the role of workers that go back before the dawn of the Industrial Revolution. This would be nothing less than another revolution—one the outcome of which would be full citizenship in the workplace for all who contribute to productivity. So should it not somehow be built into our social contract?

These thoughts about employer-employee relations, along with those of the preceding three chapters, are a lot to entrust to a workers' representative. But if the interests of workers are to be adequately recognized in the social contract, all must be taken into account. It has been implicit throughout these considerations, however, that workers alone, even if organized as workers, do not have the power to protect the rights they claim. Such power is perhaps ultimately unattainable. But it can be approximated if workers come to see their interests, and those interests are perceived by others, as being intertwined with those of their local community.

PART III

Corporation and Community

Chapter

9

Corporation and Community
In American Law

For most people, survival is a function of their opportunity to work. This is nothing new. What is new is that this opportunity is no longer assured by a community in and through which their talents are exercised, fulfilled, and appreciated. Work opportunities in a community depend increasingly on decisions made not only without a community's involvement but even without its knowledge. Such decisions, however complex the process by which they are arrived at, are made by a comparatively small number of persons who effectively control one or another major corporation. In view of the inability of workers to counterbalance corporate power by themselves and the importance of a community as the validating context of work, it is clearly not in the interest of workers for the rights of corporations to be routinely favored over those of local communities in which corporations do business. What, then, might a workers' representative endorse in this regard?

Attention should be given to communities all over the world, because each and all are likely to be affected. But as has already been intimated in Chapter 1, the issues faced by workers in any given community may be idiosyncratic. What can be said that would apply equally well to all of them? Surely, it would not be enough just to put in a good word for, say, "the least advantaged." For it is not obvious on the global scale just who would, or should, be thought to constitute this group or, the group being somehow definable, whether any social contractor could plan so expansively as to establish responsibility for its well-being. Nor is it obvious how one might establish fair equal opportunity for each community that competes with others for the jobs, direct and indirect, which a particular corporate decision generates. The availability of appropriate skills would be a factor, as would background considerations of why certain skills are available in one community but not in another, and also whether alternative skills might not achieve comparable results.

Such conceptual difficulties notwithstanding, the well-being of workers clearly

209

requires recognition of the needs of communities as well as those of corporations. "Recognition," however, is not nearly strong enough. What is called for is community constraints on the corporate preference for "flexibility." For without such constraints, corporations may become the only politically significant "communities" in the world; and such communities literally know no bounds. In such a world questions about the rights of workers and their communities would be academic in the most jejune sense of this word. This, admittedly, is a worst-case scenario; the good news is that an alternative outcome is possible. With the latter in mind, a workers' representative might offset the undesirable effects of corporate hegemony by insisting that the social contract impose social constraints on private property and thereby uphold the rights of communities vis-à-vis corporations.

This position, if adopted, would require a social contract to acknowledge that a community has an interest in any property on which it depends for its collective survival and well-being. Moreover, it needs to be adopted everywhere (if it has not been already); but the adoption needs to begin somewhere. So why not on what might at first glance seem most unfertile soil: the United States? What follows is, accordingly, a brief for the claim that the primacy of a community's interest in property is supportable philosophically and is at least inchoatively founded in American law. It is not as yet well distinguished in practice from corporate interests. But the basic issue is beginning to attract attention in both business and juridical circles. So even if many judicial appointees are not well disposed to understand law in anything but economic terms, the time is surely ripe at least for preparing the theoretical underpinnings of reform.

To this end, I shall here consider the difference between private property and corporate property; the problem of controlling corporate property; and some possible grounds for community control of corporate property.

Private Property and Corporate Property

As a way of counteracting the omnivorous tendencies of government, classical social contract theorists claimed to find in or in response to the (pregovernmental) "state of nature" a basic right to private property. For Thomas Hobbes, writing in the seventeenth century, government is established to legitimate and defend private property. A century later, John Locke and Jean-Jacques Rousseau introduced a dichotomy into social contract theory that is with us to this day. Both agreed that private property can exist independently of government authorization and that the latter does strengthen one's claim; but they parted company in their interpretation of government's prerogatives with regard to private property. For the libertarian Locke, people in the state of nature become full-fledged owners of property by improving what nature provided, so government's only role is to protect what people come to own without benefit of its determination. Communitarian Rousseau says government strengthens private ownership—by legitimizing what in the state of nature could be claimed at best by a right of first occupancy. Deviating slightly at the outset, they end up as irreconcilable opposites. Locke leaves his labor theory of ownership in the state of nature and leaves it to money to decide who owns what in a governed state. Rousseau, on the other hand, recognizes modern owners as "trustees for the commonwealth" of property, which "must always be subordinated to the overriding claim of the Community as such."[1]

Many scholars, in at least tacit agreement with Rousseau, support the view that property rights should not be so extensive that they undermine the legitimate interests of communities.[2] This view, it should at once be noted, is not that of a new ideological fringe. Rather is it the outgrowth of a long history of serious thinking on the subject—by philosophers and others, including jurists.

The long history of absolute property rights can be summarized by comparing on this subject John Locke and Herbert Spencer. As noted above, Locke argued that property rights in the state of nature are based entirely on labor, without regard to their origins. He modified this view, however, by requiring that the laborer leave "enough and as good . . . in common" for others. This so-called Lockean proviso, which in the state of nature prevents the greedy from running roughshod over those in need, Spencer two centuries later rejected as an unnecessary complication on the primordial source of progress, laissez-faire.[3]

Spencer's absolutist view of property was in accord with the mainstream attitude of apologists for the status quo in the nineteenth century. While legislators and jurists in France and Germany were busy defending private property, justices such as Roger Taney in the United States were able to base a slaveholder's "rights" on the due process clause and his "liberty" on a doctrine of substantive due process (the *Dred Scott* decision); and what justifications James Kent and Joseph Story could not find in natural law Thomas M. Cooley found in prescriptive law theory.[4] These rationalizations of exploitation, as well as Spencer's pseudo-naturalist defense of untrammeled enterprise, were the dying gasp of absolutist theories of property, marking the end rather than the beginning of an era.

Even as Spencer was writing, others were preparing the way for the twentieth century by redefining property not as an absolute but as a historical concept, subject to restriction for the public good. First came polemical writing.[5] Then came scholarly legal commentaries. German jurists provided the tools for Otto von Gierke to put "a drop of socialist oil" into private property. French theorist Leon Duguit developed a systematic case for "realistic" (social) as opposed to the old "metaphysical" (individualistic) system of law. According to him, an individual owner has rights over property only insofar as he fulfills his duties "to employ his goods for the maintenance and improvement of social coherence." And in the United States, economists such as Richard T. Ely and Simon Patten applied to the American scene what they had learned especially from the Germans, and Justices Oliver Wendell Holmes and Louis Brandeis introduced into legal rulings the new approach of sociological jurisprudence.[6] In 1919 the Constitution of Weimar became the first to sanction a social concept of property, especially in Article 153, which was adopted thirty years later as Article 14 of the Basic Law of Bonn.

In short, the initial enthusiasm for unrestrained use of private property has been significantly modified in response to manifest excesses. Most pronounced in this regard are the centrist approaches of socialist governments. The challenge of socialist tenets to private property is generally recognized, even to the point of paranoia, in the United States. Realities are, nonetheless, far more complex. In Poland, for example, most agricultural land continues to be privately owned by small farmers, and in China some capitalist enterprise is being encouraged. But in the most devoutly free enterprise society, restrictions on owners of private property can be far-reaching, as exemplified by the condemnatory process that lays the legal groundwork for transportation routes. However differently such developments are rationalized in different societies, they affect some property owners less than others. And this is especially true of property owners whose very existence is a legal fiction, namely, corporations.

Given the widespread disenchantment with absolute property rights, one might expect that even corporate property rights have been delimited in various ways in the public interest. This (at least on paper) is the case. Corporate interests are constrained not only on the basis of such common law concepts as nuisance but through legislation regulating terms and conditions of employment, hiring practices, environmental degradation, taxation, product liability, antitrust, securities, pensions, patents, and more. Especially controversial in recent years is the application of the concept of eminent domain to corporate enterprise, as will be seen. But on balance these artificial "persons" seem remarkably immune from any of the social responsibilities that reformist theoreticians defend.[7]

Exemplifying this immunity is the fact that corporate restructuring often undercuts the NLRB's distinction between partial and total closings, thereby exempting the "restructuring" employer from notifying and negotiating with its "lame duck" employees.[8] The impact of this official indifference to corporate relocation is well illustrated by the demise of steelmaking in the area of Youngstown, Ohio.

In 1979 U.S. Steel (now a division of USX) announced that it would become the third company in as many years to shut down a mill in Youngstown, Ohio. This time people not only protested and sought to negotiate a buyout but in addition went to court over the matter. The judge sympathized with the plaintiffs' cause but was unable to translate his sympathy into a legally respectable ruling. As he put it:

> United States Steel should not be permitted to leave the Youngstown area devastated after drawing from the life blood of the community for so many years. Unfortunately, the mechanism to reach this ideal settlement, to *recognize this new property right,* is not now in existence in the code of laws of our nation.[9]

This "new property right" that Judge Thomas Lambros failed to find in his books is in some respects a very old right, namely, the preeminence of the common good over private interests when these conflict. But the predominant legal tradition in the United States supports a more individualist conception of ownership and control, which, however inconsistently, is routinely taken to apply to corporate entities.[10] As a result, we avoid the Scylla of fascism by crashing into the Charybdis of corporate autonomy.

We live in a nation of the corporation, by the corporation, and for the corporation. The nation praised by Lincoln "of the people, by the people, and for the people," if once it was, has for the most part perished from the earth. Rhetoric aside, very little that was said above about a social concept of property can be considered applicable to *corporate-controlled property.* Older notions of absolute control over property have given way to a more refined appreciation of the need for social constraints. But these constraints are not easily imposed on the mightiest property owners of all time, the corporations.

Revelations about communities subjected to radioactive leaks from nuclear weapons plants make headlines, as spokespersons for the U.S. Department of Defense remind us of the need to keep our arsenal up-to-date. The appropriately named town of Phillips, Texas, has had to be abandoned because the oil company that created it needs the land for additional refining capacity.[11] The people in Jay, Maine, have suddenly come to realize that the century-old paper mill there truly belongs to International Paper Company. To break an eighteen-month strike, the company hired permanent replacements, turning relative against relative, neighbor against neighbor. "It's not Jay's paper mill anymore," one former worker observes. "We used to think it was, but it's not. Its workers aren't Jay citizens. It fires Jay citizens."[12]

Though exceptionally dramatic, such extreme examples of corporate abuse of communities are only more obviously reprehensible than most. The more subtle impact of development is often no less negative. In a county outside Indianapolis, people look to their zoning commission to protect their bedroom community from a rock concert amphitheater as the commissioners debate whether they have the power. In a county outside Denver, voters pressured by all levels of state government approve a second airport in their midst for the sake of promised jobs. The federal courts nullify community control over cable companies by characterizing the laying of a cable as an exercise of First Amendment protected free speech; and President Reagan appeals to the same probusiness analogy to pocket veto a bill that would regulate how many commercials can be shown on children's television programs.[13] Unregulated computerized telemarketing is undermining the very idea of a *private,* even if unlisted, telephone number.

It should not be concluded, however, that such favorable treatment of corporate interests is simply an application of libertarian ideology. Companies expect government bodies to channel public funds in their direction for all sorts of reasons. And when it serves their interests, they reject others' claims to private property. For example, developers of special genetic strains, such as Monsanto, consider these to be proprietary and want them patented; but they argue that primitive varieties developed over centuries in now developing countries should be common property.[14]

Who Controls Corporate Property?

Basic, it seems, to all this practice of and preaching about corporate autonomy is a metaphysical assumption that a corporation exists in a fourth dimension that is totally isolated from any community where it happens to have located a facility. This self-serving abstraction is readily abandoned, however, if it is more advantageous to clothe a corporation in the finery of a full-fledged person, as is done in First Amendment sophistry. The impenetrability of such postures by elementary logic seems patent. But more attention-grabbing counterindications will be found in an ongoing debate about ownership and control of corporate property. This debate involves at least five competing sets of claimants whose respective roles are ever subject to change.

The first set of claimants, no doubt the most ancient, is *management and labor.* Before the time of massive corporations, it was easier to assume that the owner was the entrepreneur and that labor's only leverage was the withholding of labor. Few things, however, stay simple forever. Codetermination is a common practice in some West European countries; and worker ownership, though still established in only a small minority of companies, is as common in the United States as it is abroad. Some 8 million workers belong to ESOPs in the United States, and the number of plans grows at a 7 to 8% annual rate.[15] Still more significant, however, is the increasing interest of unions in what are called "corporate campaigns."

A corporate campaign may involve a secondary boycott, now recognized as a First Amendment right.[16] Potentially more effective, however, are efforts to influence the corporate decision-making apparatus directly. Armed with a sophisticated understanding of a company's "linkage" to other companies via institutional shareholders, creditors, and interlocking directorates, unions have made significant gains (notably with the notoriously antiunion J. P. Stevens Company) by attacking the public image of the linked companies. In the future, but already being contemplated, are efforts to have a voice in the investment of pension funds, which are expected to grow by the end of this century from a quarter to a half of all corporate equity in the United States.[17] In view, however, of the games being played by other contenders for control, the interests of unions could get lost in the shuffle.

Compare, for example, the second set of opposing claimants: *stockholders and management*. It is a truism of capitalist beliefs, of course, that the stockholders are the true owners of the companies whose stock they own. But according to managerialist theory, first promulgated by Adolf Berle and Gardiner Means in the 1930s, in large publicly owned companies management exercises such effective control, especially because stock is so widely dispersed, that it can even prefer its own interests over profit maximization.[18]

It is apparent, however, as is emphasized in Paul Baran and Paul Sweezy's class cohesion theory, that management is constrained by the interests of other companies and accordingly by government in its role as agent of intercorporate coordination. Resource dependency theory gives additional weight to the constraining influence of other companies by stressing how companies enter into various cooperative arrangements in an effort to ameliorate their respective dependencies on one another.[19]

The increasingly common phenomenon of a company being bought out by a group of investors points to the inadequacy of the foregoing analyses, especially as the monetary requirements for such takeovers reach into tens of billions of dollars. Institutional investors have come to exercise more influence than the stereotypic single investor. Pension funds, as noted, already control a quarter of U.S. corporate equity, and many of them are now combining their power as the Council of Institutional Investors to facilitate takeovers.[20] But the high-visibility factor is more likely to be a takeover specialist or firm, representing certain financial interests.[21] In light of these increasingly common news events, even the unsophisticated observer can appreciate the merits of what is called bank control theory, which stresses the overarching influence of banks and other lending agencies over the policy and direction of companies that need these institutions to finance their ventures, as did Howard Hughes when the financial industry forced him to relinquish control of TWA.[22] According to this theory, corporate debt (and not corporate equity) determines the path that a corporation must take—a truly important thesis in an age in which companies are becoming increasingly dependent on debt rather than equity to generate income. This suggests a third set of conflicting claimants: *corporate equityholders and corporate creditors*.

A modified version of bank control theory sees financial institutions exercising not strategic control but only "financial hegemony" over companies dependent on them for funds. The financial hegemony theory calls attention to the way a few major banks in the United States influence corporate policy through their dominance of regional banks, of reorganization (Chapter 11) bankruptcy proceedings, and of funding for projects in developing countries. From this point of view, "The biography of American capitalism can, in a sense, be written as a chronicle of the flow of capital into certain sectors and away from others." [23]

A corollary to this recognition of outside influences on the behavior of corporate executives is that a corporation can be identified with its management, if at all, only diachronically. As one long-trusted company after another is raided and restructured, subjected to "downsizing" and corporate flight, the loyalty of their employees, even those on the management level, is being irremediably shattered.[24] As noted particularly with regard to bankruptcy, this process "institutionalizes bank control, [and] also institutionalizes lender discretion over decisions that condition and constrain the lives and prospects of workers, customers, and other citizens affected by the fate of corporations in crisis." [25]

These observations point to a fourth set of conflicting claimants to control over a corporation: *the corporation (however defined) and the community*—specifically, any community that has come to think of some enterprise or other as a permanent fixture in its midst. But only inertia could explain a community's unquestioning confidence in a corporate presence. For it is usually the community that is controlled by the corporation, and not the other way around. The rubber companies controlled Akron, Ohio; the steel mills controlled Gary, Indiana; and transnational corporations, like colonizers of old, control the communities in developing countries where they locate a plant or operation.[26] Such corporation/community relationships are common; a relationship characterized by truly cooperative attention to mutual interests is still rare.

A fifth set of claimants, overlapping but not identical to the preceding, is *a corporation and a host government*. The latter, whose domain may be as small as a village or as vast as a nation, may but in some instances does not represent the interests of the community as it contemplates arrangements ranging from bribery to expropriation. In this regard, as leaders in developing countries have learned, not even a controlling interest in a company is of much value if one does not also control the political and economic environment, often global, in which that company's business is conducted.[27] But this problem is not in principle any more insoluble than was, say, that of emancipation when slavery was widely presumed to be an appropriate application of the received doctrine regarding ownership of property.[28] And, as we shall see, state governments in the United States are a case in point.

Considered only in the abstract, these conflicting competitors for corporate control might be supposed to be all "upstairs" as distinguished from "downstairs," so that the only question before the public is who will be in charge when the employees report for work. These battles for corporate control are not, however, just games for the rich. They have often irreparable consequences for workers and their communities, in large part because the purchase of a business empire must somehow be paid for; and in one way or another it is the people who pay. For example, even when not dismissed outright for the sake of cutting costs, employees of an acquired company may help pay the bill by taking substantial cuts in pay, as has occurred in the deregulated world of airline transportation.[29] Sorting out the results of a series of recent takeovers, Judith H. Dobrzynski notes that, along with such winners as the leveraged buyout specialists,

> [t]here are plenty of losers, too, including executives who lost their jobs in raids and employees who lost theirs in consolidations. Also, more often than not, the shareholders of companies who did the acquiring lost—not only because of the premiums their companies paid to make the acquisition but also because Wall Street regularly marks down the value of their shares after a transaction.[30]

These concerns about negative impact, be it noted, assume a thriving economy. What might be the fallout if the economy falters? What if a company cannot meet its obligation on indebtedness that was the price of a takeover? To such questions some analysts offer the maximin response that equity financing (by issuing stock) is an even more expensive way to raise capital.[31] Echoing the concerns of many, however, even arch-libertarian columnist R. Emmett Tyrell (fearing government regulation) paints a gloomy picture for workers on the bubble: "When a business downturn comes for one of those corporations it will go under, leaving people unemployed and security holders devastated. In a nationwide downturn affecting all industries, the resultant unemployment and bankruptcy will make that downturn deeper than need be." [32]

Buyout artists, and the financial institutions they represent (including ever more foreign banks), are presumably aware of these risks; so they must consider the risks worth taking. Or, as has been suggested, they may expect, in spite of prevailing ideologies, that the federal government, specifically, the Federal Reserve Board, will rescue them from inordinate embarrassment.[33] But, according to Christopher Farrell, "[t]he driving force behind most increases in leverage [corporate debt] . . . is management's desire to stay in charge." [34] Wherever causality is located, few mainstream money-movers show any particular interest in the impact on workers and their communities of this frantic process of "taking America." [35]

It is, regrettably, against this background that one must try to understand the debate over plant-closing legislation (concluded long ago in other developed countries but not until 1988 at the federal level in the United States). For what to workers and their communities may seem to be substantive components of their reality is to corporate buyers and sellers just one commodity among others included in the purchase price. And from the latter perspective all that needs be said is that plant-closing legislation interferes with the mobility of capital and thus undermines the "business climate" of the legislating locality. The negative economic impact on a community that loses a plant is turned aside with assertions that (undifferentiated) job creation generally balances the scales.[36]

Community Control over Corporate Property

One possible antidote to the commodity model of a corporation is to reject the claim that a corporation is nothing but a commodity. So Judith Lichtenberg is certainly correct in saying that "the company's ownership of the factory cannot settle the issue of its responsibility in plant closings."[37] But, as we have seen, ownership is not necessarily coextensive with control, and either may change about as quickly as the price of a stock on the trading board. So a narrowly focused insistence on advance notice and transitional benefits already concedes the characterization of a corporation as a commodity and leaves communities in the position of beggars who, as has oft been noted, cannot be choosers.[38] But it is essential that communities (as well as distant arbitrageurs) be in a position to be choosers. A community being, by my definition, a geographically localized complex of legitimate interests (abstractly) and (concretely) human beings who assign these interests moral priority, the task before us is to tie the community thus understood to a plant or facility which a corporation owns and controls. It is to this challenging task that I now turn, first with regard to (infranational) states and then to infrastate communities.

Consider first why states need to be involved in corporate decision making. In addition to the recent availability of necessary technology, especially computers, a precondition for the recent spate of turbulent turnovers in U.S. corporate ownership is the inadequacy of federal oversight in the area of antitrust law. Earlier indifference to vertical mergers (involving, say, a producer and its supplier) has more recently been compounded by the Reagan administration's indifference even to horizontal mergers of directly competitive companies. Federal legislation passed in the late 1960s (the Williams Act, as amended) does require disclosure of a 5% accumulation of stock; but other tactics, such as greenmail (accepting cash in lieu of a takeover), more than compensate for such inconveniences. In this context, companies are merely commodities, to be bought and controlled by the highest bidder.

Given the laissez-faire attitude at the federal level, it has fallen to the states to protect interests at risk in takeovers. In particular, as takeover expert Robert

Todd Lang has observed, the states "have very serious reasons for seeking to regulate takeovers," especially in view of the impact of mergers on employment at local companies.[39] In the early 1980s they had attempted to do just that, for example, by requiring, as did the Illinois Business Takeover Act, that bidders give management twenty days to comment to stockholders on their offer before they make it public. In 1982 the U.S. Supreme Court struck down such laws as being in conflict with the Williams Act and with the Commerce Clause of the U.S. Constitution.[40] The states went back to the drawing board, and in 1987 the U.S. Supreme Court approved their "second-generation" efforts. Discounting federal securities law standards of management neutrality, the Court looked to a state's right to define shareholder voting rights and upheld the Indiana Control Share Acquisition Act of 1986 that prevents the holder of 20% or more of the stock of a widely held, in-state company (defined in the statute) to vote those shares until a majority of shareholders agree at a meeting, at the acquirer's expense, that management can delay for up to fifty days.[41]

State attorneys general were surely pleased by the decision; for only two months before they had unanimously adopted a set of merger guidelines to combat the federal government's laissez-faire attitude to takeovers.[42] Financial wizards, however, were generally stunned.[43] *Business Week* registered its disapproval but did recognize that "[f]rom the standpoint of managers, unions concerned about layoffs, and communities hurt by the shop-and-chop tactics of some raiders, the decision must seem heaven-sent." [44]

Fourteen other states had enacted Indiana-type protective legislation before its Supreme Court endorsement, and in the year following thirteen more added versions of their own. Some of these latter (North Carolina, Minnesota, Massachusetts, and Arizona), faced with the likelihood of an imminent takeover, even went beyond Indiana's approach by applying protective rules to companies that do significant business in-state but are incorporated out of state. In direct response to the urging of Boeing Company, the Washington legislature enacted a statute so designed as to apply only to the twenty-thousand-employee aircraft manufacturer. Especially noteworthy is the adoption in Arizona, Ohio, and Minnesota laws of a special standard of care for corporate directors in a takeover situation, requiring them to consider the long-term effects of any offer on the company, its shareholders, the affected community, and other corporate constituencies.[45] But important as these laws are to the states that enacted them, the takeover players were not seriously troubled until a comparable law was enacted by a twenty-eighth state: Delaware.

Nearly half the companies listed among the Fortune 500, nearly 46% of those on the New York Stock Exchange, are incorporated in Delaware, which derives 15% of its revenue from incorporation fees (not counting income to corporation law attorneys). So in spite of some initial hesitation, the state legislature began to hold hearings when a number of companies warned that they would move their incorporation elsewhere if Delaware did not pass an antitakeover bill. But both before and after passage of the bill on 2 February 1988, the response was predictable. Before, the chairman of the Securities and Exchange Commission threatened to push for a uniform federal law that would preempt all such state laws; and takeover specialist T. Boone Pickens bombarded legislators with an army of lobbyists called United Shareholders. After, lawsuits were filed within hours challenging the law's compatibility with federal standards. The law requires the acquirer of 15% of a company's stock to wait three years before completing a takeover; but it makes exceptions, for instance, if the acquirer gets prior approval from the target company's board of directors or begins tender offers with less than 15% of the shares and ends up with at least 85% of stock not controlled by management.[46]

As suggested by the list of conflicting claimants to control over corporations, it is no easy task to protect each asserted interest without undermining others. Thus, for example, by disenfranchising "interested" shareholders in a takeover situation, Minnesota's new antitakeover law could facilitate the takeover of a company much of whose stock is controlled by one family.[47] Troublesome as such a result might be, it is no more troublesome than would be government indifference to the interests of communities. The interests of the community in a local plant or other enterprise can, of course, be understood to include those of stockholders, as is emphasized in antitakeover legislation. Also to be taken into account, however, is the investment of the workers, as the then labor-sensitive NLRB asserted in 1966.[48] Similarly, the relevant government units must find ways to accommodate business while at the same time remaining accountable to the people of the community, who are also investors through "industrial development" arrangements made in their name. Meanwhile, the people themselves need to be active participants in the decision-making process.

Changes of this sort are especially difficult to effectuate in the United States, because of the seldom challenged individualist bias that underlies our (tacit) industrial policy. But they would not be unprecedented. In particular, companies like Scott Bader in the United Kingdom show by example that corporate interests can be made to harmonize with the interests of the community. E. F. Schumacher defends this approach as a use of economics "as if people mattered." [49] As he himself acknowledges, his "Buddhist economics" was anticipated by R. H. Tawney, who stressed the interests of community in opposition to what he considered the individualist bias of Max Weber's portrayal of capitalism.[50] It is repeated, in modern garb, by Robert Kuttner:

> A better alternative to the takeover casino would be a more accountable corporation. . . . Boards of directors should be resuscitated and given real power

to hold management accountable. Independent outside directors representing small shareholders and the general public should hold key positions on corporate boards. And employees of the corporation should get formal representation in corporate governance, since they, far more than shareholders, have a long-term stake in the viability of the enterprise.[51]

Less sophisticated concern for the primacy of the community was the hallmark of the British textile industrialist Robert Owen in the first half of the nineteenth century. Owen, however, believed that community could be established independently of government through common ownership of property and a system of general cooperation. His father-in-law, having located the mill in a rural area close to waterpower, was faced with a labor shortage and a need to maintain labor discipline; so, translating his technological imperative into a paternalistic social ethic, he saw community as an instrument of industrial relations. Owen, seeking always to maximize utility, employed mainly women and children and advocated both divorce and birth control. Rejecting competitive capitalism, he and his followers preached the right to the whole product of labor and equality of exchanges. These, according to Owenite John Francis Bray, were to be achieved initially through joint-stock communities and in time in full community of possessions. No substitute for unionism, as American labor historian John R. Commons noted, this ill-fated movement deserves to be remembered as a sincere if misguided effort to realize communitarian ideals.[52]

In the United States Owenism struck a chord with a number of entrepreneurs. But nowhere was it applied more zealously, in all its paternalistic splendor, than in Pullman, Illinois. Founded in the late nineteenth century by train builder George M. Pullman, this factory-centered community (whose buildings still stand on the outskirts of Chicago) expressed in its overall and meticulous detail the prevailing concept of workers' total dependence for well-being on their employers. This market-sustained benevolence was a step in the right direction, according to John Gibbons, because its benefits were labor-generated whereas the alternatives, as he saw it, were government ownership of land on the one hand or government surrender of land to unscrupulous businesses on the other. The one extreme was "Georgism" (Henry George's proposal that government take over unproductive property), which he considered fatally flawed because in an urban setting the value of realty is primarily a function of improvements whereas for agricultural land it is the opposite. The other extreme is government abuse of eminent domain to facilitate the greed of Jay Gould, Cornelius Vanderbilt, and other robber barons. What was needed to fulfill the promise of a place like Pullman, thought Gibbons, would be to allow workers to buy their homes, grow their own food, and share in profits, as was the case in the Swiss canton of Glaris. By comparison, the willingness of government to put huge tracts of land in the hands of private corporations was "despoil[ing] the people of their patrimony." This, he contended, is against reason and against nature, because

> [c]orporations should be the servants of the people, established for their convenience or necessity. When they cease to fill their true functions and seek to exercise a mastery, as they are doing, of those who created them, then the power that gave them their existence should assert its prerogative of control over its own creation.[53]

This communitarian response to corporate power the American philosopher John Dewey articulated throughout his long career, from Gibbons's day well into the twentieth century, most eloquently perhaps in his pre-Depression work entitled *The Public and Its Problems*.

Ever concerned about improving democratic institutions, Dewey saw as a sine qua non for this objective an educational process that would enable workers to function as citizens, both in the public arena and in their workplaces, by means of industrial democracy.[54] As the economy weakened both domestically and globally after World War I, however, it became apparent to him that a democracy of citizen workers would be ineffective in the modern world without the existence of supportive institutions that would function like the community of earlier times. Crucial to such institutions, in Dewey's view, is the fundamental process of face-to-face human interaction and collaboration. But the old town-meeting approach, he felt, is no match for the massive intrusions of widely dispersed modern commerce and industry. So he looked sometimes to modern means of communication as a way to reinstate community on a large enough scale and sometimes to the federal government for more activist involvement in the search for solutions.

The problem, as Dewey saw it, is that "remote and invisible organizations" were undermining the interpersonal relations of communities and, in the process, their control over events:

> The Great Society created by steam and electricity may be a society, but it is no community. The invasion of the community by the new and relatively impersonal and mechanical modes of combined human behavior is the outstanding fact of modern life. In these ways of aggregate activity the community, in its strict sense, is not a conscious partner, and over them it has no direct control.

Rather than blame either democracy or industrialism as such, he identified unregulated corporate-community relations as the cause of social disruption:

> The invasion and partial destruction of the life of [local associations] by outside uncontrolled agencies is the immediate source of the instability, disin-

tegration and restlessness which characterize the present epoch. Evils which are uncritically and indiscriminately laid at the door of industrialism and democracy might, with greater intelligence, be referred to the dislocation and unsettlement of local communities.[55]

By shifting attention from cause to effect, Dewey might be understood to be blaming the victim. But it is clear from other of his writings that he recognizes corporate autonomy as the basic problem and for precisely that reason, ideological scruples aside, would call upon government to regulate corporate activities in the public interest.[56] For basic to his political stance is his conviction that "[t]he local is the ultimate universal, and as near an absolute as exists," and that, accordingly, "[u]nless local communal life can be restored, the public cannot adequately resolve its most urgent problem: to find and identify itself." His proposed solution: "The Great Community," which "can never possess all the qualities which mark a local community . . . [but] will do its final work in ordering the relations and enriching the experience of local associations." [57]

The communitarian focus so important to these earlier writers is advanced in various ways by a number of more recently articulated views, including Paul and Percival Goodman's appeal for human-scale "communitas" in architectural design and Robert Nisbet's studies of the search for community throughout history.[58] Especially relevant to the purpose at hand, however, is Kirkpatrick Sale's extended argument for limiting all our endeavors, including production, to a "human scale."

Seeking to determine sufficient conditions for workplace democracy, Sale concludes that this necessarily presupposes "responsibility of the enterprise to the community in which it is located and in which its workers live." In this connection he distinguishes between two sorts of community in terms of the number of members. In anthropological usage, a face-to-face community cannot get much larger than about five hundred. This Sale calls a neighborhood. In politico-economic terms, which Sale adopts, a community is a system involving as many as five to ten thousand persons. (One may also speak of a community of nations, of course, but Sale bypasses this usage.) On the basis of his size-based definition of community, Sale distinguishes various ways in which a community might be involved in a firm to assure that it remains responsible to the community. This involvement in a company might take the form of (1) community representation through contractual obligation on the part of the company to return some of its profits to the community, for example, the 10% rule in Mondragon, Spain; (2) community representation on a workplace board (Schumacher's idea of a social council); (3) Henry George's worker usufruct principle, to assure a community's financial interest in a company, abetted by community ownership (say, by means of a community land trust), to assure its social and environmental interest; and (4) community ownership and direction, as in Shaker communities and Israeli kibbutzim.[59]

Effectuating such a community-oriented constraint on corporate property rights would require, of course, both procedural and substantive reforms. With this in view, the following considerations are intended to be suggestive and exploratory rather than programmatic.

One approach to procedural reform would be to acknowledge that each facility, regardless of who "owns" it, has rights of its own which may be defended in court by any group of people who can show that they are likely to be harmed by a proposed significant change in that facility (as is now possible in the name of historical preservation). Or, alternatively, empower specially designated members of the community to serve as legal guardians of the facility.[60]

An approach to substantive reform would be to give the needs of the community priority over autonomous corporate ownership as we know it today. For example, why not make the "Oakland" (now "Los Angeles") Raiders football enterprise subject to community interests and impose on its legal owners a fiduciary responsibility to the people of Oakland?[61] As we shall see, there are precedents for such a move in U.S. constitutional law with regard to eminent domain. But these precedents are ambiguous at best because the cases tend to favor the interests of corporations over communities. First, however, let us note for the record several other examples of a procommunity orientation in law: the approach (except in the West) to water rights and the development in real estate of a number of quasi-communal arrangements.

The importance of communitarian rights is illustrated by the legal principles developed to effect a just allocation of the use of water. As a general rule, the avoidance of greater harm is an objective in all cases involving surface water. Where water is plentiful, riparian doctrine respects the principle of equal rights, either on the basis of natural flow or on the basis of reasonable use. Where water is scarce and hence not likely to be adequate for all who want to use it, prior appropriation is respected.[62] To the extent that our economy can be viewed in terms of "cash flow," the riparian model of respecting equal rights is more appropriate than the western rule, so called, that has turned great rivers like the Colorado into private enclaves.

Certain communitarian arrangements in real estate reestablish for specialized purposes something like the generalized proprietary communities that are usual among primitive peoples. As defined by Spencer H. MacCallum, a (real estate) community is "divided into private and common areas according to a system of relations which defines and allocates responsibility for the performance of all activities that might be required for its continuity."[63] Typically based on contract, these "communities" are of various types, including hotels, subsidized districts, industrial parks, mobile home parks, a shopping center, a merchants' association, condominium buildings, and interval ownership arrangements. What they have in common is that they are all bounded, functional artifacts, unlike natural things, like beaches, to which users (like corporations) want unhampered access but which local communities want to protect against overuse.[64]

Legal principles with regard to public intrusions on private property could also provide a basis for a broader view of community interest. These intrusions can be categorized as eminent domain, which effects a social preemption of private property, and inverse condemnation, which effects a social limitation on private property. Each involves what is technically known as a taking, because of the relevant language in the Fifth Amendment to the U.S. Constitution: "[N]or shall private property be taken for public use, without just compensation." [65]

The Fifth Amendment requires that the federal government and, via the Fourteenth Amendment, state governments (or subsidiaries thereof) take private property only for "public use." As applied to eminent domain, there was concern from earliest times that public use might be interpreted to mean nothing more than public benefit. There was good reason for such concern; but in retrospect even that standard would be immeasurably superior to what has been the de facto standard, namely, benefit to corporations.

This abdication of public responsibility commonly takes the form of appellate deference to the decisions of local courts. Such deference would be constructive if local courts were forums in which a community's true interests are deliberated. But these courts are usually under pressure to approve the pet project of one or more corporations cloaked in the mantle of "public use." The practical significance of the following analysis, therefore, depends on the extent to which a truly participatory community can have its real interests impartially adjudicated. The letter of the law is fairly straightforward; what is crucial is how "public use" is interpreted.

A concurring opinion in an 1837 New York State case[66] worried about the implications of identifying public use with public benefit because this would diminish the property rights of the individual against whomever the government represents. This equation, however, prevailed both in the East[67] and in the West.[68] But in the Midwest, courts tended to favor a more conservative approach to taking, limiting public use to what is absolutely necessary.[69] (This, as we shall see, has changed.)

In 1936 New York courts found that urban renewal constitutes a public use even if some structures affected are not substandard and some private firms are involved in the project: *New York City Housing Authority v. Muller*.[70] The *Muller* reasoning became a national standard in 1954, when the U.S. Supreme Court endorsed it in *Berman v. Parker*.[71] Since then public benefit has, to a considerable extent, become virtually indistinguishable from private, that is, dominant corporate, benefit. For example, a New York court saw nothing improper in the condemnation of thirteen city blocks and all the businesses, however thriving, on those blocks: *Courtesy Sandwich Shop, Inc. v. Port of New York Authority* (1963);[72] and a Michigan court blithely upheld the condemnation of an even more extensive urban neighborhood so that General Motors could allegedly provide jobs and taxes by constructing a new plant: *Poletown Neighborhood Council v. City of Detroit* (1981).[73]

The *Poletown* case is an extreme example of corporate interests dictating the meaning of public use. In legal shorthand, this case stands for the proposition that, in Michigan, potential jobs and taxes are enough to meet the public benefit test. But the realities are quite different. In this instance, a private corporation defined the terms and conditions of the project, an automobile assembly plant, and gave the City of Detroit a deadline for compliance. The City agreed, with the result that 465 developed acres in Detroit and neighboring Hamtramck were condemned at a cost to taxpayers of $200 million. Some 3,400 people lost their homes; and 1,176 structures, including housing and business property, three schools, sixteen churches, and a hospital, were destroyed. Jobs? Most of these have gone to robots, since the new plant is heavily automated. Taxes? These will come to $10 to $20 million per year after twelve years of 50% tax abatement, meaning that in economic terms alone it will take a quarter of a century to recoup the unadjusted dollars spent.

Happily, not all eminent domain cases follow the path of least resistance to corporate fiat. For example, in *Hawaii Housing Authority v. Midkiff* (1984),[74] the United States Supreme Court upheld Hawaii's use of eminent domain to redistribute land that had been monopolized by a small minority of owners, resulting in artificially high prices on what little land was available for purchase.

The problem faced in Hawaii was that a very small number of families controlled most of the land in the state, owning as much as 50% of it and leasing even more from state and federal governments, leaving only some 20% in the hands of small private owners. Other homeowners in Hawaii had to content themselves with long-term leases of the land under their houses. To remedy this maldistribution of land, the state legislature passed the Hawaii Land Reform Act of 1967,[75] which authorized the state to condemn land being leased, hold a public hearing, and upon a favorable determination sell the heretofore leased land to the lessee. The Ninth Circuit branded this statute as "a naked attempt . . . to take the private property of A and transfer it to B solely for B's private use and benefit."[76]

Deferring as usual to the state government's prerogatives in these matters, the Supreme Court found the Hawaii legislation to be a "comprehensive and rational approach to correcting market failure."[77] And "where the exercise of the eminent domain power is rationally related to a conceivable public purpose, the Court has never held a compensated taking to be proscribed by the Public Use Clause."[78]

Decisions such as these are encouraging to those who favor recognition of the interests of the community in law. But they do not represent a trend. In 1987 the U.S. Supreme Court held that even a temporary restraint on use of property constitutes a taking and hence requires just compensation.[79] Intended, presumably, to limit excessive government constraint on the private sector, this ruling blurs the distinction between eminent domain and inverse condemnation and, by putting limited budgets at risk, it chills a government unit's desire to regulate property owners.[80]

A year later, the court chose not to apply this reasoning to a rent control ordinance that was never applied.[81] But shortly thereafter President Reagan issued an executive order to bring federal agencies and departments into compliance.[82] And a suitable issue could emerge in Cross Creek, Florida, a literally backwater town made famous by a movie of that name about author Marjorie Rawlings. Because of this movie, Cross Creek has been attracting many visitors, and this has inspired some residents to try to develop the area. The local government has been blocking most development proposals by means of unfavorable zoning decisions. In response, the would-be developers contend that, under the taking clause of the Fifth Amendment, the government should pay them the difference between the potential and the actual value of their undeveloped land. The only question, it would appear, is how long environmental aesthetics can hold out against unbridled commerce.

Regardless of the outcome of cases such as this, the key point here is that the law of eminent domain could *in principle* provide a mechanism by means of which a community organized in its own interest can maintain its integrity. But the U.S. Supreme Court as presently constituted is not likely to be a strong supporter of any such tendency. Not even the more "liberal" blend of justices in decades past showed any interest in modifying the Court's long-standing refusal to consider property other than real estate in the same way. This refusal was renewed recently when the Court denied certiorari to the "plant-closing" case of the (now) Los Angeles Raiders, who moved their franchise but not their stadium from Oakland.[83]

In spite of this pattern of constraint on local government's use of eminent domain, one does find in cases like *Midkiff* some reason for asserting that the law of public use constitutes at least a theoretical basis for a more communitarian assessment of plant closings. This theoretical basis becomes, in turn, a potent legal tool in any context in which legislation and the interpretive judiciary are sensitive to the problem. It can be argued, for example, that under Massachusetts law a municipal agency, known as an Economic Development and Industrial Corporation (EDIC), may for the express public purpose of reducing unemployment take over a plant scheduled for closing, at least if the plant belongs to an in-state corporation. In making this argument, proponents of such government intervention for the common good draw upon both Massachusetts legislation aimed at industrial development and Massachusetts cases involving eminent domain, which typically require only that the taking (and not necessarily the subsequent use of the property) is for a public use and fairly compensated. But this position is consistent with federal rulings in *Berman* and *Midkiff* and derives from the Michigan *Poletown* case the principle (the actual results aside) that providing employment is a public purpose.[84]

For all of the reasons that make some entities more powerful than others, it will not be easy to tilt legal priorities away from corporations and toward communities. This is partly because corporations, especially transnationals, enjoy mobility and flexibility not available to individual communities. Accordingly, one cannot effectively defend the interests of local communities without calling upon more encompassing political entities for help. Say, for example, one wanted to turn the law of eminent domain into a mighty instrument whereby the public good is pursued. This worthy aspiration would be frustrated so long as the corporations, especially the transnationals, could continue to play one community against another as they continued to seek the most for the least. There is, accordingly, a need to change the background conditions that intensify competition between communities, which the corporations are now able to exploit to their advantage.

Global reduction of intercommunity competition is a long-term project, even on a theoretical level (for reasons to be considered in Chapter 11). How it might be facilitated on a provincial (in the United States, state) level is illustrated by the adoption of statutes that enhance the ability of domestic (state-incorporated) companies to contest corporate takeovers. Community-sensitive interpretation of the law of eminent domain would facilitate this development. Because of the preemptive power of the federal government, however, changes in federal law would also be necessary. With no claim to originality, I will simply list for the sake of illustration some changes on this level that would help improve the background conditions for community-centered justice:

1. End the ultimately self-defeating competition among states and localities for businesses that disavow any responsibility for their coming or going.

As steps in this direction, federal standards should be established and enforced with regard to incorporation; plant-closing justification; minimum wage; workplace health and safety; income maintenance, food stamps, and welfare, AFDC (now a 4:1 difference between the highest- and the lowest-paying state) and general assistance (now a 12:1 difference); unemployment compensation (now 2:1) and rates (now a 50% difference).

2. Eliminate tax incentives for exporting capital (which amounts to a tax on people).

Instead of using tax reform as an excuse for cutting what is left of public-supported quality of life, require that companies contribute a fair proportion of their wealth to help maintain the social fabric of communities in which they have facilities. As it is now, these companies are given every advantage imaginable for choosing to turn their back on the people in this country. Our labor law is not interpreted as applying to corporate moves that end outside our borders. The Internal Revenue Code is a handy compendium of incentives for making such moves, including a dollar-for-dollar credit for foreign taxes against domestic taxes; indifference to "transfer pricing," whereby a company sets an arbitrarily high price for an item or service sold by the parent company to an overseas subsidiary to keep foreign profits artificially low; and "political insurance" against the pitfalls of investing abroad, even as support for U.S. exports is undermined.

3. Increase public ownership or at least public-private arrangements with regard to utilities, fuels, and especially "sunrise" industries that government subsidizes.
4. Support demonstrably feasible proposals for worker control, including proposals that call for conversion from military to domestic products.
5. Limit the ability of corporate raiders to take over businesses and run them into the ground, and prohibit parent companies from "milking" subsidiaries.
6. Severely limit any form of absentee ownership.[85]
7. In general, stop regarding resources put at the disposal of enterprise as if they are "giveaways" (*res nullius*) and recognize them for what they truly are: common property (*res communis*).

In short, there may be a place for corporate property in one's set of requirements for social justice. But social justice cannot be assured by always giving first place to corporate property. Also of concern must be what was traditionally called the common weal—or, as some of our older states would have it, the common wealth. This means that we must find a socially less harmful way to accommodate the legitimate needs of corporations. This may be done narrowly by softening the cushion for displaced workers or broadly by giving communities legal standing to challenge corporate decisions that are detrimental to community interests. This much commitment to social responsibility is common in many countries and was espoused a century ago by one of business's staunchest defenders, James Bryce, who explained then rampant strikes as follows:

> The agitation of the last few years has been directed, not against the richer sort generally, but against incorporated companies and a few wealthy capitalists, who are deemed to have abused the powers which the privilege of incorporation conferred upon them, or employed their wealth to procure legislation unfair to the public.[86]

There is perhaps a bit of unwarranted optimism in these pleas for increased community hegemony over corporate property, given not only the power of the corporations but especially that of the financial institutions that, in some circumstances, control them. This variation on a theme by realpolitik is not, however, determinative in a quest for justice with regard to work. Besides, financial institutions are no more capable of functioning indefinitely in the realm of nowhere than are product-oriented corporations. Even the major players in international finance must depend on local institutions to advise them about investment targets in a given local area.[87] The input of community representatives should be no less important with regard to other "imported" decision makers. Such, at least, should be the thinking of a workers' representative; for, if anything at all is clear in this regard, it is that each of us is destined to live, at any given time, not nowhere but somewhere uniquely identifiable.

Chapter

10

The Ideology of
Corporate Autonomy

As WE HAVE seen, there are good reasons why communities should have more "say" over what corporations do or fail to do in their regard and in their presence. The kind of say that is needed has, in fact, been assured in many West European countries for years. But in the United States comparable proposals are still very controversial, as they would, to some, be a violation of the liberty and democracy which are considered prerequisites to corporate autonomy. In this value-laden context, then, we need to look beyond the immediate, or apparent, level of controversy to an examination of the values that some wish to protect at almost any cost.

In the United States, the idea that communities might turn to law to defend themselves against corporate autonomy faces a hostile environment in which live four ideological dragons of great power and intensity. Each dragon guards one of four gates to community-conscious justice. They are virtually invulnerable to attack by merely rational argument, for their stability is based on the magic that sacred myths provide.

Each of these dragons is exceptionally difficult to slay because its very existence is likely to be denied or, if admitted, is defended as being something quite undragonlike. The first dragon is *development,* which is most likely to be defended as a value-free expression of fact or, if value-ladenness is admitted, as a straightforward application of essentially utilitarian principles. The second dragon is *progress,* a battle-scarred old beast that has died many deaths but always manages to revive when people call development's bluff. If one is able to put progress in its place, a more subtle dragon known as *liberal justice* will stand in the way. If even that dragon can be outsmarted, *global justice* will appear on the horizon. This final dragon is the subtlest of them all, for it seems to offer everything a workers' representative should favor, including a check on the excesses of globalization. So it too must be faced—in the next, and final, chapter. Even to reach its lair, however, we must first deal with unilateral justifications of development, the mythology of progress, the idea of social welfare, and a liberal (Rawlsian) approach to justice.

Unilateral Justifications of Development

Change has been around for a very long time, especially since the advent of human beings on this planet. The planet had already done a lot of changing without us; but our emergence added an entirely new agent of change to the mix. This agent that is us has been acting at an ever faster pace, especially as it masters the intricacies of science and the capabilities of technology. These instruments of change effect changes not only in our environment but in us, their makers and users, as well.[1] Both individually and as groups, human beings are changed by the very instruments they have devised to effect change. This well-known phenomenon has been the subject of much debate, especially among scholars concerned about the overall impact of technology on human beings and their world. The conclusions arrived at are many and varied, but they come down to two: that technology is value-neutral, or that it is value-laden.

Extreme versions of the value-ladenness view hold that technology is on the whole bad for people or, alternatively, that it is on the whole good for people. Both the former view (technophilia) and the latter view (technophobia) have renowned advocates, especially in philosophical circles. But mainstream technology assessment is done by people who insist that technology is value-neutral. If they make any concession in this regard, it is to the effect that technology might be incidentally good or bad in its effects, depending on how it is used.

Unmitigated technophobia is rare. But French sociologist Jacques Ellul comes close (if one disregards his more theological writings). His first major work on the subject, *The Technological Society* (1954), is probably the best known, and most often criticized, presentation of this view of technology. Basically, what Ellul claims is that technology, understood as the totality of organizing instruments, is no longer subject to human control but has a life of its own independent of human choice or preference. This technology-out-of-control the American political scientist Langdon Winner refers to as "autonomous technology."[2]

Many writers have expressed similar, if not quite as extreme, concerns, typically with regard to some particular technology or type of technology. Lewis Mumford, for example, lost his enthusiasm for technology during World War II, after which he began warning the world about the "pentagon of power" and the harm it could cause in the world. Norbert Wiener was concerned about how self-regulating electronic systems might eventually automate people right out of their means of subsistence. Similarly, some scientists involved in gene technology have expressed concern about the dangers we face if we do not exercise reasonable control over genetic engineering projects.

Unqualified technophilia is also seldom articulated as a deliberate view about technology. But it does exist in the form of a blanket approval of "development" or "progress." According to this view, any new technology contributes to development or progress and for this reason alone is commendable, whether the technology in question is a new bottling process or a torture instrument or a four-speed baby buggy. A slightly more reasoned technophilia is the view that organized efforts to control technology will cause more harm than good.[3]

Technology-specific technophilia can also be found among devotees of photography, cinema, the computer, and just about any other "breakthrough" consumer-oriented technology. More complex technologies, such as those involved with automated manufacturing, also attract fans and followers. But anyone professing an unreflective support for one technology or another may also oppose some other technology or, inconsistently, all technology. This latter position may be ascribed to Jacques Ellul; for, though he worries about technology-as-a-whole, he is quite impressed with computers.[4]

Generic views about technology and values are replicated in views about the propriety of technology transfer, in particular, the transfer of a technology from one country to another.

The advantages of technology transfer to less developed countries (LDCs) in particular are well advertised by the corporate guests as well as by the government leaders of the host countries. They include anything that is a means to development or modernization, and these expressions might include employment as well as appropriately supportive educational opportunities. Thus lumped together as indications of desirable progress are facilities as varied as a soft drink bottling company in Beijing, a toy manufacturing plant in Taipei, a consumer electronics assembly plant in Seoul, a large-scale cash crop enterprise in Ghana, a publishing house in Malaysia, a major power's military base in Central America, and a military regime's instruments of torture in the repressive dictatorship of your choice. But on balance, it is contended, the people of these countries are better off than they would be if progress had simply passed them by.

The disadvantages of technology transfer to LDCs are noted less frequently, in part because those most directly affected typically lack access to media. These disadvantages may be summarized under the heading of diminution of autonomy —of the nation, of its institutions, and of its people. Such "side effects" are not unprecedented (the Aztecs apparently had a comparable effect on Indian tribes all around them), but they are on a much more massive scale than ever before. They may even be unintended, as were many consequences of High Aswan Dam constructed by the Russians for President Gamaliel Nasser on the Lower Nile. It brought electricity to a large area of Egypt, as planned; but it also caused inundation of irreplaceable ancient monuments; and, primarily because of the disruption of flood patterns and nutrient transport, an alarming increase in the incidence of snail-hosted schistosomiasis and severe negative impacts on both agriculture and mariculture.

Comparable to the modified value-neutralist position with regard to technology in general is a view that technology transfer is good or bad depending on how the transferred technology is used. This view is common with regard to transfer of military technology, which is especially likely to be evaluated against a background of political or ideological considerations. Thus, someone who opposes the use of a technology in one country might approve its use in another country that would use it properly (however defined). For example, someone who supports the stockpiling of nuclear weapons by a major power such as the United States or the Soviet Union might oppose the building of even one nuclear weapon by a comparatively minor power such as India or Israel. A curious inversion of this sort of discrimination is the policy of the U.S. government with regard to communications satellites in the 1960s: though approved for international systems, they were not approved for domestic use over the United States (because such use, it was thought, would jeopardize the American mass media industry).[5] Anyway, a technology transfer is rarely approved or disapproved regardless of the circumstances of its use.

With these brief notes on technology assessment and technology transfer as background, let us turn to the question of justifying development. Of course, development involves more than just the transfer of technology; but the other aspects of development, such as international finance, global communications, and transfer of management structures, are also types of technology—social technology, if you will—and these are now being included in some analyses of technology transfer.[6] The question before us, then, in its simplest form, is this: is development on balance good for the people whose country is being developed?

It is easy to find positive things to say about development as a global phenomenon. The benefits of development, especially in terms of material well-being, have been recognized at least since the earliest days of colonial expansion.[7] So defenders of corporate autonomy tend to dismiss complaints about the negative impact of development as Neanderthalic reluctance to move out of the cave. Whether the project at hand is one of using taxpayers' money to transform an urban center into a corporate headquarters or of installing an electronic assembly line at the city's perimeter, the magic word that justifies resulting harm to some human beings is likely to be *growth,* or *improvement,* or *development,* or *modernization*—in short, any of a number of words each of which conveys a sense of some sort of betterment, or amelioration, at least of a quantitative sort. This end state, though positive by definition, is seldom achieved without negative side effects. But apologists for growth can deaden almost any pain by appealing to a surplus of utility, or to the principle of double effect, or to some lifeboat-ethics-cum-global-triage, or even to future benefits for all. They are unmoved (at least on the level of theory) by the unpleasant realities of which "value-neutral" terminology is but a distant icon.[8]

On these views, then, if development is not entirely for the better, the people who are negatively affected will just have to adapt. Traditional economies and the work relationships dependent upon them might collapse in the process; but such consequences, the defenders of development insist, are a small price to pay for progress. In other words, development is a good thing because it is the instrument of progress. Change is the price of progress; and progress in the long run benefits everyone, notably by making consumer goods available at affordable prices. Of still greater import are the benefits that befall humanity at large as a result of plant location decisions that bring the Industrial Revolution and the Age of Automation to heretofore backward peoples.[9] Although difficult to articulate in the context of domestic politics, this broad endorsement of development takes the form of a cosmopolitan call to transcend petty chauvinism for the sake of global interdependence. It also asks people to believe that pleasurable ends can justify regrettable means.

Knowledgeable people who thus accentuate the positive side of development are not for that reason unethical; they are only (quite often) inconsistent. For the people most likely to endorse corporate endeavors by keeping their eye on the prize are just as likely to favor an ethic that is suspicious of weighing consequences. As articulated, for example, by John Rawls, this view would stress the moral superiority of doing what is right over maximizing the good. But determining what is right is a real challenge when it comes to globalized development. Both rhetoric and technical terminology flow in the direction of weighing consequences in the balance. So, as is the case with technology and technology transfer, there is ample support for the claim that development is, on balance, good for people whose countries are being developed. But this is certainly a case in which it is unwise to leave "well enough" alone.

Even if we disregard the negative impact of workforce restructuring on workers in a point-of-departure country, we still need to ask whether the correlative development in a country that plays host to a transnational corporation is really good for the people of that country. Anecdotal information of the sort cited in Chapter 1 obviously serves only to introduce the question we are now addressing. Nor would the multiplication of anecdotes settle the question in principle, one way or the other. But patterns of results can be discerned from the reports of numerous field studies[10] and the recommendations of distinguished international bodies such as the various agencies of the United Nations Organization.[11] And if we take these more detailed considerations and recommendations into account, especially with regard to the impact of development on traditional societies and their economies, the evidence tilts to the negative.

The effects of development on the workforce of an LDC can be devastating. Some commonly reported examples are the following.

1. Transforming quasi-autonomous peasant societies into the equivalent of a feudal system in which one or more transnational corporations exercises the role of suzerain.[12]

2. Reinforcing traditional gender bias, with consequent disruption of nuclear family arrangements, by favoring the employment of (lower-paid) women.[13]
3. Exploiting the openness of traditional societies to child labor by employing (still lower-paid) children.[14]
4. Undermining the ability of people in the host country to provide for their own basic needs, in particular, food, by shifting the agricultural base of the country from food crops to predominantly cash crops for export.[15]
5. Rendering the people of the host country extremely vulnerable to famine in the event of crop failures, especially in situations, such as that in Sudan, in which one political faction is able to intercept emergency shipments intended for another.[16]
6. Exacerbating the already sharp division between the few rich and the many poor in the host country by making land ownership prohibitively expensive and limiting the availability of even the most basic goods to those who are able to purchase imports.[17]
7. Strengthening the military power of a local dictatorship against the interests of the indigenous population in order to safeguard the interests of transnational corporations that do business in the country.[18]
8. Holding the economy of the host country hostage to the international banking system by lending large sums of money for investments the benefits of which are enjoyed primarily by foreign corporations and secondarily by local officials who use their positions to sell what often amount to licenses to exploit.[19]

The gravity of these arguably unintended consequences notwithstanding, few Western analysts doubt the inevitability or even the desirability of development. Nations of the world are characterized in terms of the extent to which they have been "modernized" to some level of technology-driven productivity. Those that fall short are "underdeveloped" or "on the way to development" or, as is more current today, just "less developed."

Even more insidiously, people are graded according to how well they adjust attitudinally to the disruptions of development. A society is "modern" or "primitive" depending on how well it adapts to the effects of new technology. The primitive society by definition clings to and hence endorses the status quo; the modern society is open to change.[20] This dichotomy inspires Western analysts of "social change" to examine the symbols and myths of people in a changing society to see how their own traditions might lend themselves to a favorable view of this change.[21]

Another approach reserves the term *society* for people who accept development. Openness to new technology thus serves to distinguish a society from a (primitive) community. From this perspective, a society might be defined as a supracommunitarian, hierarchically differentiated set of positions or roles controlled by a government or state that responds appropriately to the demands of technological power. This way of defining society is not obviously biased in favor of "modernization"; but scholars who write in these terms seem persuaded that modernization is at least inevitable if not inherently progressive.[22]

This preference for the society that is open to change ignores the fact that raw intrusive power may be the single most important cause of a society's changing, apart from any internal preferences whatsoever. Take the case of the Native Americans in the nineteenth century. They were forced by events to think beyond intratribal or even intertribal struggles for power and take into account white expansionism and "Manifest Destiny." This external pressure eventually undermined their internal societal maintenance, reducing once proud people to mere appendages of a society that barely acknowledges their existence.[23]

This same process has been occurring all over the world. Numerous pockets of "decentralized" peoples are in the unenviable role of desperate rebels struggling, often enough, for bare survival. Hence the various attempts by leaders of Third World countries to unite scattered forces of opposition against further encroachments by the Great Powers.[24] In the process, neither the supranational haves nor the local have-nots behave as though traditional social systems are insurmountably stable.

This does not mean that people are indifferent to their heritage. Traditional preferences and priorities continue to play a role in societal decision making, and may even be determinative, as was the case in Iran under the Ayatollah Khomeini. So we would seriously distort the complexity of things if we tried to account for development solely in terms of technocrats and their tools. Just as there is a subgroup of Americans involved in high-technology R&D, so also are there Americans suffering the effects of malnutrition; and the success of the former owes something to the ability of the latter to endure deprivation. Similarly, there are large subgroups of people in other countries who are starving while corporate interests exploit the natural resources and the availability of cheap labor.[25]

Reference here is to what Marxists call "marginalization." Many human beings in the world today are not "developing" to a higher level of existence but are retrogressing to a lower one. Many who once had at least some control over their fate are now (classified as) "self-employed": the outcast slag of a technocracy that has no need of their traditional skills. They may be found by the hundreds of thousands in refugee camps or in or around major cities that barely acknowledge their existence.

Less extreme is the plight of developed countries that have not quite kept up with the state of the art of one or another technology. One issue, for example, that has been of concern in Western Europe is whether transnational companies (IBM and DEC) will completely dominate the computer industry there or will leave room for a domestic producer such as Siemens as well.[26] In either case, there will be development and there will be some jobs created. In much of the world not even that is assured. So instead of the global village that Marshall McLuhan saw on the horizon we could be moving toward a global ghost town. What the long-term consequences of this will be for the collective happiness of our species is difficult to predict. But there is no reason to reject out of hand Hudson Institute founder Herman Kahn's dire prediction

> that outside of the 20 percent of the world that is expected to live in postin-dustrial societies in the year 2000, the other 80 percent of humanity is likely to be deeply preoccupied with various kinds of reactions that resulted from the process of more or less forced Westernization and then withdrawal.[27]

The percentages are just educated guesses. What is beyond question is that a substantial segment, perhaps a majority, of the human race has little or nothing to say about or even to do with technological progress. On the contrary, for every "advance" that gives some human beings still greater power, other human beings are likely to be exploited, disengaged, or even eliminated. Whether the mechanism of their marginalization is an occupation army, a colonial administration, a puppet government, or control of the internal economy through international debt and trade restrictions, the effect is essentially the same: a group of people who once determined their own destiny in a smaller world become pawns in a game over which others exercise effective control.

If revolution is a radical change in form of government, then for a society once relatively independent to become subservient to powerful outsiders is a revolution. Nor can those subdued be expected to react favorably to such a deterioration in their status. According to one perceptive analyst of colonialism, those colonized may despise themselves and strive to make themselves as inconspicuous as possible; adulate and seek to imitate and be accepted by those who control their lives; or despair of ever being fully accepted into the ranks of the controllers and in their despair resort to antagonizing their societal protagonists.[28] (The latter course is greatly facilitated if, as often happens, a major power sees reasons of its own to support an insurgency.)

The colonialism that was so much a part of the industrialization of western Europe came apart after Europe's colonial empires reached their paroxysm of futility in two world wars that affected every continent on this earth. Now the neocolonialism of the superstates, flying the banner of modernization, is achieving levels of control heretofore only dreamed of. And that very control is breeding dissent and open rebellion in many parts of the world.[29] In response, once hostile power elites find ways to cooperate with one another as privileged peers across national boundaries, usually to their mutual advantage but not necessarily to that of the masses of people in the countries affected.

As Erich Fromm once put it, a "revolution of hope" is possible only through a "humanization of technology."[30] But neither past nor present policies with regard to modernization support a belief that its humanization is likely to come about. If it does, it will be because of a concerted effort on the part of all who recognize any other alternative as intolerable. But, to take just one example, so long as the efforts of the oppressed in South Africa to control their own destiny are not effectively combined with those of others in the same region or continent, if not beyond, the transnational power elite will continue to share control exclusively among themselves, cosmetic adjustments to demands for divestment notwithstanding.[31]

The prosperity, even the survival, of many human beings on this planet depends on what a powerful few decide is in their own interest.[32] But as machines continue to substitute for and supersede the physical and even the intellectual labor of human beings, the latter may well be discarded like yesterday's technology. Their continued existence will be tolerated only so long as they accept their misfortune and withdraw into oblivion. This they are unlikely to do, at least not indefinitely. Rather will they resort to whatever means of retaliation the technology available to them makes possible. Such tactics as kidnapping, assassination, airplane hijacking, and bombing, though certainly dramatic, win no new bargaining rights in the world. But frustration and hatred may engender even more devastating behavior; and this could lead to "counterinsurgency" on an order of magnitude so awesome as to leave the ovens of Auschwitz in the Middle Ages of eugenics technology. The long-range consequences of this scenario: a century not of genocide but of paupercide: the indirect elimination of the nonproductive and the direct elimination of the counterproductive in many parts of the world.[33]

More positive prognostications are available. But they lack credibility to the extent that they disregard the level of global control that today's technology makes possible. The failure of each superpower in recent decades to determine a people's destiny militarily suggests that greater optimism is defensible. But such optimism is muted by the cycle of drought and famine in one long-exploited Third World country after another. Development, for some, is good by definition. But definitions have a way of leaving out what they do not include; and that is why some writers refuse to disregard marginalization when describing modernization. Another approach, in some ways far more promising, is to redefine development holistically and teleologically, so it refers to what it would be in its finest realization. To appreciate this approach, however, we must first acknowledge a neutralist view of development.

As with technology and technology transfer, so with development, defenders of a value-neutralist position would reject the question about development's benefits as inappropriate if not meaningless. They would not wish to be considered indifferent to the plight of people in whose midst development is to take place. But they would insist that such considerations are not susceptible to scientific, that is, quantitative, treatment, so must be left, as it were, to take care of themselves.[34] This insistence on treating development scientifically comes in two forms: the market approach and the Marxist approach. The market approach is, essentially, the libertarian doctrine globalized. The Marxist approach involves a globalization of dialectical, or conflict-centered, analysis.

From the viewpoint of a country targeted for development, these two approaches have much in common. Each insists that a reputable study of development can include only what can be analyzed quantitatively. They also agree that development is basically a kind of growth. They differ in the science they favor for studying development and in the results they expect development to bring about. For the market approach, the science of choice is economics; for the Marxist approach, it is political science. As for results, the market approach is aimed at maximum production; the Marxist, at global maintenance of a classless technostructure. The resulting blindness to local effects which these ideological opponents share is well expressed by perceptive Third World scholars in these words: Each approach (they say) tends to reduce

> the issue of distribution . . . to technoeconomic and historic rationality. . . . First, in both, structural change will inevitably bring about the liquidation of social groups, often necessitate violence and destruction, and result in political systems that are authoritarian and oppressive. These tend to be perceived as the necessary human costs of achieving the collective good. Second, in both, the main goal of structural change is the transformation of the productive and distributive system, which is seen as the basic determinant of the nature of people and society. The central societal problem is the sharing of material output.[35]

In other words, these reductionist characterizations of development are, however well-meaning, particularly congenial to the corporate interests in whose behalf they have been espoused.[36] But by virtue of their narrow focus on purely material growth they disregard other aspects of development which are not so easily disregarded by the people in a country undergoing "development." These other aspects have been increasingly emphasized in recent decades by Third World scholars and by global agencies such as the United Nations.[37] Even growth, they point out, must be understood to include "productive capacity, the technological capability for self-reliance, and ecologically sound management of resources." A country's development must be attentive to equity, which involves "distribution of growth, wealth and income, . . . the sharing of physical well-being, [and] the eradication of poverty." A third essential aspect of development involves "the political processes that ensure human rights and provide for a wide sharing of power," in short, participation and freedom.[38]

In this perspective, development can be a benefit to all concerned, but only if it is understood to include and to be responsive not only to material, meaning narrowly technological and economic, but also to social and political progress as well.

The Mythology of Progress

If the workers' representative does get past the dragon of development, there at once looms up the dragon of *progress,* whose prowess gives the first dragon its sense of importance. Thus in talking about development, or modernization, we referred almost as often to progress. When seriously confronted, in other words, development looks to progress for support. For progress, like development, is positive by definition. Its pedigree goes back into antiquity; but it is thought to be especially impressive by virtue of its being grounded, purportedly, in the very heart of biological science: in the theory of evolution. Evolution, as an empirically based concept, is, of course, supposed to be value-neutral. But when all decked out as a justification for certain social policies, it takes on other characteristics. It becomes a formidable dragon. According to chivalric tradition, that is no reason not to step forward with steadfast gait. So be it, then. But first a word about the conceptual terrain that must be traversed.

As noted, the concept of progress is no newcomer to the cultural scene. But until fairly recently it seems to have been more a focus of speculation than a justifier of action. In its speculative guise, as assiduously researched by Charles Van Doren, there were five key questions to be addressed, namely, (1) whether there is a pattern of change, and if so whether it is (2) discoverable, (3) irreversible, (4) advantageous to humans, and (5) within our power to evaluate. Writers who speculated about progress can also be categorized according to their views as to whether progress is necessary or contingent, whether it is unending, whether it involves only products and institutions or human nature as well, whether it is due to natural or to human agency, and if the latter whether this is due to social or collective memory or to inheritance of intellectual assets, notably reason. Events, however, have to some degree undermined such speculations. In the eighteenth and nineteenth centuries, theorists disagreed primarily about the mechanism and finality of progress: the Marquis de Condorcet and William Godwin and, with qualifications, Thomas Malthus, Auguste Comte, as well as Hegel and Marx, considered progress to be unending and, implicitly, knowable. In the twentieth century, scepticism has prevailed: philosophers R. G. Collingwood and Karl Popper deny that progress is knowable, and Carl Becker speaks only of "non-meliorative progress," which means only irreversible cumulative change.[39]

This retrenchment among thinkers has not, however, dampened corporate doers' enthusiasm for progress. In their vocabulary, progress is an untroublesome reality the very mention of which is thought to be enough to put critics on the defensive. For, their apologists note, the ever-burgeoning abundance of consumer goods is in and of itself incontrovertible evidence of progress. All sorts of other empirical data cause concern about the reliability of such a materialistic measure of progress. But these findings do not dissuade those who are committed to progress; so their commitment might better be thought of as a kind of faith or belief rather than a carefully reasoned position.[40] Of course, even a deeply held belief can be severely tested; and that, it has been argued, is happening in our own time to belief in progress.[41] But thus far defenders of corporate interests have not succumbed to this particular heresy; so progress still functions for them as a kind of court of last appeal.

Consider how progress enters (often surreptitiously) into their arguments. It might be introduced sedately, as above, to lend support to development. But it might also directly attack a proposal (such as those being made in this book) which calls for a change in the status quo. This might seem ironic, at first glance, since progress supposedly involves change. But there are, on this view, good changes and other changes. And one way to tell one from the other is to determine if any redistribution of wealth is at stake.

Here, in broad brush strokes, is how it works. Grant for the sake of discussion that there is injustice in the world, that wealth is unevenly distributed among human beings, and that there is no principled justification for such maldistribution. But by what formula or mechanism might redistribution correct the manifest inequities in the world? None to which all might agree can be found; so nothing needs to be done. This, however, is not as cruel as it sounds, because the problem, according to this belief, will take care of itself: progress eventually benefits everyone, even those who have to pay for it in some unpleasant way.

This principled acquiescence in other people's suffering is consistent with unmitigated egoism. But it is more likely to be rationalized by appealing to an economic version of utilitarianism, to the effect that the pain of labor (as "disutility") is outweighed by the ever more widespread possession of consumer goods (as "utility").[42] But if one acknowledges any responsibility for the present well-being of others, then no mere appeal to better times ahead (because, for example, what the rich currently enjoy will one day "trickle down" to the poor) can explain away the gross inequalities of which Ferdinand and Imelda Marcos were only caricatures. For, whether locally or globally, those who are doing most of the suffering constitute a majority of our species. So for those whose fate it is to live their lives in the present, pure progressivism of the sort here described does not have enough socially redeeming features to neutralize reasonable envy.[43]

With troubling thoughts such as these being entertained, the defenders of progress need to show more clearly than is their wont just what counts as progress and by what means it is to be achieved. The former, as noted, they tend to view as a matter of numbers. The latter is left up to competition. And the raison d'être of competition is likely to be sought in the very depths of nature: in our allegedly aggressive precursors, or in the bifurcation of our brain. Whatever the merits of these and other reductionist accounts, they share a tendency to disregard the fact that cooperation is at least as reliable an engine of progress as is competition. And, what is more, it is becoming increasingly apparent that cooperation is a necessary condition for socially advantageous progress. By offering reasons why this is so, we may neutralize yet another dragon on our way to community-oriented justice for workers.

To begin with, it is statistically demonstrable that the primary beneficiaries of liberty under capitalism are and, their defenders assure us, are expected to be the corporate owners. If, however, this is too crassly the case, social unrest may also be expected. So, as Rawls recognizes, some minimum standard of well-being is clearly advantageous even to owners, and, as such, ought to be appealing to libertarians. But, remaining true to their principles, they are unwilling to follow Rawls's lead in this regard. In response to any suggestion that government be responsible for correcting irregularities of the market, owners and their defenders appeal to the primacy of progress as end and to the unique instrumentality of competition for the attainment of that end—hence the sacred tradition of laissez-faire. But does competition really engender progress; and, if so, what is the nature of such oddly engendered progress?

The belief that progress requires competition seems to presuppose something like Newton's law of inertia, that any change in a body's momentum requires a force from without. As applied to human beings, this is superficially plausible. One's lethargy is challenged by the intrusion of an alarm clock, a concerned parent, a boss, a drill sergeant, a federal marshal, an avalanche. None of these intrusions, however, is an example of competition; for, though each involves an outside force, that force is not competitive.

What distinguishes competition from any other outside force? For one thing, if the outside force is competitive it seeks the same good that inspires you to action, be it a blue ribbon or a 50% share of a market. Moreover, your and your competitor's attraction to this good presupposes a value system that you have each internalized. For Georg Simmel, the German sociologist, competition is indirect conflict in which the opponents neither harm nor destroy one another but exert parallel efforts for the same prize.[44] Political scientists would add that the prize is not divisible or at least not evenly so. This is why, on their analysis, the multiple-player zero-sum game must have a winner and a loser. To this necessary condition must be added as a sufficient condition that the good sought is neither renewable nor expandable.

To the economist, when competition is totally absent (a monopoly) or almost totally absent (an oligopoly), demand generates profits for the supplier(s) without their need to minimize costs, assure quality, improve service, or even advertise. Perfect competition is a theoretically ideal state of affairs in which participants in a market are constrained by one another and by market conditions to provide a quality product or service at a reasonable price. Only in the unattainable ideal state of perfect competition is competition a catalyst for progress; and the progress here in question is indifferent to social well-being.[45]

Ever since Adam Smith empowered the Invisible Hand to bolster perfect competition, libertarians have relied on some version of this doctrine to defend laissez-faire as the best if not only way to serve the public interest. But, as Nobel laureate Paul Samuelson has noted, only if we added a number of welfarist constraints on the origin and maintenance of such a system would its results be socially beneficial in any ethically meaningful way. All that a "perfectly perfect competition" would achieve in a given market, says Samuelson, is an equilibrium *among competitors* with the efficiency property that "you can't make any one man better off without hurting some other man." [46] Until well into the present century, however, welfarist constraints were systematically excluded from justifications of competition; and yet, however inconsistently, competition was applauded as being good for society as a whole—in the long run.

In a context of laissez-faire, such an attribution of teleological efficacy to competition obviously needed justification, especially in view of the enduring support for such time-honored maxims as the Golden Rule. So Charles Darwin arrived on the scene in the nick of time. His evidence for a theory of natural selection seemed to show that competition is a fact of nature the ongoing result of which is "survival of the fittest." Both Herbert Spencer and Karl Marx accepted Darwin's "findings" in the natural order as foundational for their own "scientific" study of the laws of progress. But they arrived at contradictory recommendations about how humans should deal with evolution on the level of culture.

One might conclude from a conflict-based account of evolution that the process is immune from human intervention even on the level of culture, hence is best left entirely to its own devices. This, essentially, is the laissez-faire view of evolution, identified by Herbert Spencer as "social Darwinism." Implicit in this view is the assumption that laws of nature cannot be tampered with or, if they can, that such tampering will be more detrimental than advantageous to human interests.[47] Alternatively, one might conclude from a conflict-based account of evolution that one can facilitate, accelerate, and perhaps even direct the process by learning its laws and applying them systematically to social processes. This is how Marxists (and, they say, Marx) interpret Darwin, as they seek by means of the dialectic to achieve on the level of culture what Darwin accomplished on the level of nature.[48] Implicit in this view is the assumption that nature left to itself might not bring about a state of affairs congenial to human desires and aspirations.

This divergence between Spencer and Marx points to the hazards of applying to human activity models devised to account for natural processes. Moreover, it is only a theory and not an established fact that conflict is the driving force behind evolution. Many objections have been raised against the conflict-based account of evolution, three of which are especially relevant here: (1) that intraspecific conflict does not exist in nature; (2) that evolution and/or progress is constrained by finite resources; and (3) that progress is a value-laden concept which cannot be found in or founded upon nature.

The first objection: intraspecific conflict is not a causative factor in the processes of nature but has been read into these processes. Darwin, on this view, did not "find" conflict in nature, at least not within the same species; he found it in the writings of Thomas Malthus, through whose eyes he then proceeded to read nature. Pëtr Kropotkin, to be considered below, was an early spokesperson for this objection.

The second objection bypasses the causative question and notes instead that many resources essential to human survival are nonrenewable and diminishing, hence we leave progress up to nature at the expense of future generations. This view is associated with neo-Malthusians who call for "limits to growth" and even for "zero population growth" (ZPG). Their namesake had similar concerns and called for voluntary abstinence as the only moral means to achieve population control. His position suffered from an inability to imagine technological changes, especially in preservation and transportation, that would make possible global distribution of food to the hungry. (He also failed to imagine reliable contraceptives but presumably would have opposed these on moral grounds.) More generally, appeals for constraints on progress are typically answered by some expression of confidence that human ingenuity will find an adequate technological fix.

The third objection discredits the concept of progress as a value-laden vector found neither in nature nor in the facts of human history but only in the aspirations and expectations of human beings. In its positivist form, with facts isolated from values, this view is at the heart of the secular understanding of science, so vigorously under attack in recent years. Its virtues have been extolled by purist advocates of the scientific method and need not be repeated here. Of course, undermining the concept of progress does not solve the problem of distribution, but simply leaves distribution to conventional and not necessarily just arrangements. Distribution, however, is not a fatalistic outcome (or "destiny," in the language of Jean-Paul Sartre); it is an objective that we freely choose (an "interest").[49]

Given the non-Darwinian character of the Mendelian theory of evolution[50] the debate about conflict in nature is merely quaint; or so it would be were it not for sociobiologists and antiquarian economists. As for the former, Bernard de Mandeville was perhaps wiser in that he proposed only a *fable* of the bees, because real bees kill off their drones once the honey has been gathered, then live on it through the winter.[51] As for the latter, they still refer to "the Darwinian law of survival of the fittest" as the ultimate bogeyman for those unable to compete. Their references to this obsolete paradigm, however, are more a traditional rite than a basis for theory. Besides, this issue is moot if one finds a justification for competition not in nature but in culture.

The "translational" problems that arise when one tries to link human-level competition (not to mention conflict) with processes on the subhuman level are neatly avoided if one restricts the domain of concern to the level of culture. This is done, for example, by contract theories, such as John Locke's version with its labor theory of ownership. It is also true of Robert Nozick's entitlement theory, which requires for a just holding (of property) that both the original acquisition and all subsequent transfers of property were just. Milton Friedman, similarly, says holdings are just so long as the lottery by which they are acquired is impartial. These theories abstract from what Nozick calls "end state" considerations and justify present arrangements on the basis of a procedurally acceptable past. On such views (Locke's excepted) neither merit nor need constitutes a challenge to the way things are. Rawls's contractarian approach adheres to these restrictions as well. But unlike the others, he does try to build at least minimal redistribution into his theory, by means of a government agency that would effect appropriate transfers (as determined by the difference principle). The point here, however, is not whether such welfarist concerns are convincingly argued by their respective proponents but whether they are consistent with the concept of progress.

Progress and Social Welfare

These barbed comments about the moral indifference of competition are certainly an embarrassment to the dragon of progress. But it takes more than embarrassment to down a dragon. Progress in particular might simply parry the thrust by downplaying competition and endorsing cooperation as the key to social welfare.

As we have seen, views that link progress to competition do tend to understand progress as a change for the better not only in the competitors but in the society that nurtures them. In this way, social welfare is appealed to at least implicitly as a justification for competition. But, as we have also seen, neither business competition nor business progress necessarily contributes in any way to an improvement in social welfare. Inversely, progress advantageous to society as a whole is likely to be a result of cooperation. Thus are we invited to ask if cooperation might succeed where competition fails as an instrument of *socially* advantageous progress. And, indeed, a case for this claim can be made. I will here sketch this case first by noting that progress and cooperation are not inconsistent, then by postulating that cooperation not only contributes to but is a necessary condition for social welfare.

In the first place, as Prince Kropotkin argued against the Darwinists, there are many indications that the survival value of cooperation surpasses that of competition.[52] While acknowledging the presence of conflict in nature and in society, he shows, citing numerous examples, that "mutual aid" and "mutual support" contribute far more to species survival. This argument he bases on studies of animal behavior, on paleoanthropology, anthropology, and history, especially that of communitarian structures in the Middle Ages. And were he alive today he could also draw on the experience of numerous firms all over the world, not only internally with regard to their workforces but externally in their dealings with other firms. For even in an era of hostile takeovers, major companies of all kinds depend for their success on cooperative arrangements with suppliers, distributors, government, and at times even so-called competitors.

Second, the theory of evolution neither supports nor precludes an expectation of expanding cooperation among human beings. Before Darwin, a number of scholars, notably Dante and Immanuel Kant, envisioned the unification of mankind as the ultimate outcome of progress.[53] After Darwin, various scholars have tied evolution to this ultimate unification. Important in this regard is French paleoanthropologist Pierre Teilhard de Chardin. His *The Phenomenon of Man* contains a carefully reasoned argument by a respected evolutionist that the process of evolution is convergent. Human beings, notes Teilhard, are the most recent emergence within nature; but evolution has not been arrested or completed, it has only begun. The human race is in its infancy and, since attaining to consciousness, has in part taken over the process of evolution, which is moving toward a higher development of consciousness; and this higher level involves a vital unity among all human beings. This is a minority opinion among evolutionists, but it is a plausible extrapolation from known data.[54]

Third, cooperation is arguably a necessary condition for socially advantageous human progress. This belief is implicit in social arrangements as diverse as those of millenialist religious sects (the Joachimites and the Jehovah's Witnesses), guilds, utopian socialists, intercorporate joint ventures, military alliances, and transnational efforts to facilitate trade relations and to control such global problems as environmental pollution and the danger of nuclear annihilation. These latter tasks, as we will see, call for global solutions not generally possible through the instrumentality of nation-states.

In a word, the idea of progress is consistent with the idea of cooperation. But if progress through cooperation is to wear a human face, it must be measured in terms of social welfare. What this means may be indicated by comparing the views of several economists who have taken this issue seriously. First, however, a word about social welfare.

Social welfare is sometimes taken in the abstract to be the opposite of individual welfare. In practice, however, the two are not necessarily incompatible; but, unlike individual welfare, social welfare is unthinkable without some commitment to redistributing goods among the members of a society—in the interest of all, ideally, but ordinarily at greater cost to some individuals than to others. How this is done is a matter of public policy; how it is justified is a long-standing concern of social philosophy. At issue is what has traditionally been called distributive justice, the essence of which is a formula for allocating available resources which those involved accept as being fair. Among philosophers from Aristotle to Rawls this formula is understood as applying in some proportion to all members of society however situated. In economic parlance, however, a formula for distributive justice is understood more narrowly as a way to transfer goods from those better endowed to those less so.[55]

The economists' view of distributive justice is reflected in the common practice of representing allocation as a matter of slicing a pie with fixed and invariant dimensions. But there are obvious limitations to this sort of representation. In the first place, no matter how one slices a determinate pie (except in the ideal world of perfect competition), some may get more or less than they need or deserve. From the viewpoint of public policy, the size of the pie to be cut is itself an important, sometimes the most important, issue with regard to allocation. Besides, some crucial questions of distributive justice are not appropriately addressed in terms of allocation. These may involve either public goods or ethical issues. Public goods, as understood by economists, are nonexcludable, which means that they are not subject to distribution through the market but are available to all whether they have paid for them or not, such as clean air, national defense, and scientific discoveries.[56] Similarly, as Solomon showed in the disputed parentage case (1 Kings 3:16–28), ethical issues are not readily disposed of by allocation. This, however, has not prevented the U.S. Supreme Court from trying, as in certain well-known and much debated decisions regarding abortion and affirmative action.[57]

In short, there is more to distributive justice than just "divvying up" whatever is available for consumption. As Jean-Paul Sartre has stressed, any distribution among human beings takes place in a context of scarcity. So it is incumbent on us to defend rather than merely take for granted the policies and institutions through the instrumentality of which distribution is carried out. It is in this way that the *humane* advantages of cooperation over competition come to the fore.

With these general considerations in mind, consider first how American economist Lester Thurow tries to endorse distributive justice without sacrificing his belief in progress. In his *The Zero-Sum Society* (1980), Thurow raises some serious questions about distribution that he cannot answer using economists' traditional talk about competition; so he turns to the notion of a zero-sum game to make a case for cooperation.[58]

As noted, Thurow still looks to competition and growth as the solution to all sorts of economic problems, including labor costs. He berates those, such as smokestack industry leaders, who seek government protection instead of believing in competition as the true faith requires. And he argues that eliminating the income tax on corporations would improve their competitiveness on the world market.[59] Such objectives, apparently, are important to achieve to maintain growth; for, without growth, the hard decisions are even harder to make. These are the decisions that involve what he calls "a substantial zero-sum element."

Eschewing old-fashioned appeals to nature or culture, Thurow says this is a matter not of theory but of "algebraic necessity." Society's challenge, as he sees it, is to muster the political courage to do what the economists' numbers tell us has to be done. Typically, this involves making hard choices for long-term benefit that will inevitably have short-term negative effects on some individuals. These latter, among whom are workers displaced by the closing of an obsolete plant, he (to his credit) would have society assist. How might society muster this assistance? Thurow notes that income (and wealth even more) in the United States is concentrated among a comparatively small percentage of the population: two-thirds goes to the top two quintiles. Direct transfer payments to those in need would be "a pure zero-sum transfer" because "[e]very dollar given to the bottom 60 percent of the population must be taken away from the top 40 percent of the population." More generally, Thurow applies the zero-sum game analogy wherever there is a state of affairs any change in which will have effects that are costly for some members of society. For example, he refers both to inflation and to the relative income of different groups as "the paradigm zero-sum game." Other problems with zero-sum characteristics include distribution of jobs with a view to avoiding discriminatory practices, adopting zero economic growth (ZEG) as a social objective, removing government subsidies on agricultural products, and providing direct income transfers to needy individuals.[60]

So much, and not much more, can an apolitical economist say about social welfare at a time when there is not enough growth to sustain Keynesian benefits without redistribution. British economist John Maynard Keynes did not reject classical economic beliefs when, in *The End of Laissez-Faire*, he questioned the adequacy of the nineteenth-century doctrine (Say's Law) that general unemployment is impossible under conditions of flexible prices.[61] But he did show that its almost sacred "employment equilibrium" between capital and labor is entirely consistent with massive unemployment—in other words, that purely economic equilibrium can be indistinguishable from social disharmony. To prevent or at least minimize the effects of this happening, he said, government might need to intervene like an engineer to fix the system. The principal reason for this problem, he later argued, is that private savings decisions do not necessarily go where investments are needed; and the result is an *unemployment* equilibrium.[62] A world in the throes of the Great Depression was now prepared for his contention that government has to provide a corrective and, in so doing, become an indispensable protector of progress.[63]

Many governments in recent decades have practiced what Keynes preached, first with good results but now with some regret. The problem, according to the experts, seems to be that productivity is not improving rapidly enough to enable governments to continue priming the pump; so restructuring, rearrangement, and especially establishment of new markets have come to be viewed as inescapable. There is, however, a fundamental flaw in this crisis-prevention strategy. For if the engine will run efficiently only so long as productivity improves, then cost-cutting will continue to be sought by means of laborsaving devices and offshore production. As a result, some people will be hurt while others benefit.

This scenario is not intolerable from the perspective of consumerist utilitarianism. Technological and globalizational unemployment is a small price to pay, in terms of maximizing utility, if greater productivity results. But this only underlines the need to break what Dutch economist Bob Goudzwaard calls the "law of undiminished escalation of labor productivity." To do this, we must stop treating labor as a disutility and, the cautions of Chapter 5 notwithstanding, somehow build a society in which labor will have sufficient quality to be a utility, that is, a positive factor for happiness. How might this be done? Goudzwaard looks to a kind of religious conversion as a possible solution; and he is persuasive to the extent that he calls for disenchantment with the commodification of life. Even if we cannot follow him beyond this point, we can agree with his reason for going on, namely, that "the emptiness created by the death of the god of progress must be filled with something else." [64] Whatever else this might be, it will involve human beings in cooperative endeavors. And cooperation is what enables people to come to an agreement.

Rawlsian Justice: A Liberal Dose of Social Welfare

Even if the fire were out of development and progress, the way to community-oriented justice would still be blocked by a dragon known as *liberal justice*. This dragon is disarmingly hospitable. It has about it an air not of menace but of sweet reasonableness; and in recent years it has been talking a language familiar to people who think about labor relations. It invites the workers' representative into its lair, sets the table for tea, and sallies forth into sparkling conversation.

Distracted from concern about manifest inequities, the workers' representative is truly at risk—at risk of buying into this dragon's line that we are all, socially, politically, and economically, as close as can be to where we would rationally and without bias agree to be.

If, as suggested above, progress is not an end in itself and competition does not automatically lead to social welfare, then agreements to cooperate might be the best way we have to achieve social welfare. Of course, in the world as we know it, people and institutions do compete with one another; and, under certain circumstances, they may not see any alternative. But competition as such has no more inherent value than does a nuclear missile; and the former, over time, may be as destructive as the latter. For it is a paradox of free competition that the stiffer the competition, the greater the incentive to eliminate one's competitor. But the absence of competition is not a sufficient condition for cooperation. There is, in other words, more to social well-being than keeping a list of winners and losers. So the question we have come down to is this: should a workers' representative endorse a social system that glorifies competition as an instrument of progress or might the representative instead seek social welfare through principles that encourage cooperation?

John Rawls, for one, seems strongly committed to the latter response. And for this reason, one might expect his theory of justice to serve somehow in philosophy, as did Keynesianism in economics, as a bridge from libertarian laissez-faire to an endorsement of social welfare. He surely wants his theory to serve this purpose, and he fills the pages of his treatise with reasons for so interpreting the liberal tradition. But once the careful reader puts all the pieces of Rawls's learned puzzle together, the assembled picture is about what one might expect of a libertarian forced by circumstances to take charge of society and needing to explain this anomaly to friends of the strict observance. This I say, it should be clear by now, wishing it were otherwise and hoping one day so to be persuaded. But such persuasion will not come from the Rawlsian text itself.

Rawls's "liberalism" has the appearance of being more dedicated to social welfare than it in fact is, for several reasons. Chief among these, or at least the subject of the most commentary, is his difference principle, which on its face seems to preclude a society from making progress without taking into account the basic needs of the least advantaged. These least-advantaged members of society, Rawls suggests, might be defined either as the group with the lowest average income or as the group of unskilled laborers. Consistent with this concern for the needs of the least advantaged, moreover, is Rawls's opposition to utilitarianism precisely because, in his view, it allows a majority to benefit from decisions that cause or at least allow a minority to be harmed. And, third, Rawls insists that he adopts individualist assumptions only as a methodological point of departure on his way to a glowing endorsement of cooperative human relations in society.

With honorable objectives such as these in mind, he devotes some six hundred pages to defending them by arguing, first, that perfectly rational persons would so agree if they were intellectually and emotionally neutral and, second, that just such an agreement turns out to be in harmony with what people understand to be good for them.

Rawls's way to justice, in short, is clearly paved with good intentions; but at the end of the road is, I believe, a kind of utilitarianism for the elite. This may be shown, for the limited purposes of this book, by locating Rawls's contractarianism within the philosophical tradition, noting how contrived is his concept of justice, and seeing how he modifies this concept to accommodate delays in its realization.

Like Plato, Rawls thinks of society as arranged hierarchically, with those most advantaged effectively making the decisions for all others. And, like Aristotle, he considers this arrangement to be distributively just provided that everyone benefits proportionately to their importance to society. To show that this is the case, Rawls reactivates a long disregarded contractual approach that in previous centuries had been used to justify absolute monarchy (Hobbes), parliamentary democracy (Locke), and democratic egalitarianism (Rousseau). Persuaded by Hume that no ancient social contract, even if historical, can survive the pitfalls of time to justify present arrangements, Rawls takes it to be purely hypothetical. But the principles agreed to in this hypothetical contract serve as a kind of Kantian antidote against utilitarianism in that it mandates principles which safeguard the respect to which every person is entitled. The difference principle in particular functions somewhat as did Locke's restrictions on ownership, namely, that one not waste what is acquired and that one leave "enough, and as good" for others.[65]

Rawls's defense of what he calls justice as fairness (to emphasize his focus on procedures) is in many ways contrived. This alone does not make it unacceptable; but it does make it unconvincing.

First, he sets as his goal to "establish that, given the circumstances of the parties, and their knowledge, beliefs, and interests, an agreement on [the first principles of justice] is the best way for each person to secure his ends in view of the alternatives available" and indeed "the unique solution to the problem set by the original position," thereby to avoid egoism, which he says is "the no-agreement point."[66] But utilitarianism is the only alternative nonegoist theory he considers. So by what logic is the adoption of justice as fairness the "unique solution"? If neither justice as fairness nor utilitarianism is agreed to, why must egoism (rather than another altruistic theory) be "the no-agreement point"?

Second, since Rawls defines justice in terms of fair procedures, how can the resulting principles, however appropriate otherwise, be considered just? Out of many possible choices, Rawls allows the social contractors to consider only two (justice as fairness and utilitarianism), and their choice between these two is to "hold unconditionally."[67] Is this not "stacking the deck" against other possible arrangements? And is it not procedurally unfair to stack the deck?

Third, Rawls says he wants to achieve what he calls reflective equilibrium between the principles of justice as fairness and our "considered [moral] judgments." In other words, he does not claim to be offering a definitive proof of his theory but only the most reasonable view (more reasonable, at least, than utilitarianism), given the options he has elected to consider.[68] But since he does not consider all live options (socialism, for one, is only mentioned in passing), how can he claim to have achieved reflective equilibrium? Why, in other words, should people no longer think about or be motivated to consider options he has not even addressed? Besides, if Rawls's principles of justice are consistent with our basic moral convictions, as he claims they are, then why does he have to go to so much trouble to argue that they would be accepted by totally rational social contractors behind a "veil of ignorance"?

Fourth, to make sure that the social contractors will be impartial in their selection of principles of justice, Rawls carefully circumscribes their knowledge and their motivation.[69] He allows the social contractors to have increasingly detailed information about their society (by gradually "lowering the veil of ignorance") as they establish, consecutively, a constitution, laws, and institutions. But by the time an operative society is "up and running," the damage has been done if what was agreed upon at the foundations is inappropriate, unworkable, or whatever. And, as many critics have asked, is it plausible that anyone could arrive at principles applicable to a concrete situation on the basis of such scanty information and orientation? Might not this quest for hypothetical objectivity be just a way to disregard troublesome problems in the real world that demand to be considered in their own right?

Fifth, though the principles of justice are selected first, they are achieved last. They are a target at which people are to aim. Thus even a society that is approaching justice needs to implement processes, notably through education, that will assure its stability. And already "behind the veil" the social contractors are required to take future generations into account by adopting a just savings principle. But Rawls recognizes that earthlings cannot be counted on to jump at the chance to be just. So he lays down a few sketchy instructions on how to muddle through in the interim. He leaves it "importantly to intuition" to "measure" departures from the ideal and make the best of "less than favorable conditions." Thus might people's all-important liberty be constrained "in the common interest" or in cases where there is only "partial compliance." It might also be denied, he says, "to enhance the quality of civilization so that in due course the equal freedoms can be enjoyed by all."[70]

More urgent even than liberty is satisfaction of "basic wants" (a consumerist equivalent of needs?). This minimalist goal attained, however, Rawls would have us believe that people (especially if they have been properly educated) will derive so much vicarious self-esteem from "the publicly affirmed distribution of fundamental rights and liberties" that they will scarcely even notice gaping disparities in economic distribution. Even if tempted to feel "left out" at the present time, they (from the viewpoint of those who understand justice) have no grounds for complaint against "entrepreneurs" who are "building for the future." [71]

Rawls recognizes that the have-nots might make socially disruptive class comparisons; so he attempts to neutralize the import of such comparisons by focusing on a theoretically just ("well-ordered") society in which there is, by definition, no justifiable ("excusable general") envy.[72] But this is not an adequate response to anyone who says justice requires, if not the expeditious establishment of equality and common ownership of goods, then at least visible signs of progress in that direction. For this reason, his rationalization of maldistribution of goods amounts to a utilitarianism for the elite: it justifies the pain of the few (the poor of the present generation) by appealing to the happiness of the many (in some hazy tomorrow when conditions will at last be conducive to something better).

At one point, sixth, Rawls relates the principles of justice to individuals' natural duties (which apply to all) and obligations (which apply only to the ruling elite); and in this context he provides a role for protest (civil disobedience) and principled noncompliance (conscientious refusal). He justifies such behavior, provided it is within the bounds of propriety, because (as Rousseau had insisted) the people constitute a check against government excess. But having steered clear of the unjust society, he never has to consider at what point polite responses might without injustice spill over into "militant action and organized resistance." [73]

Rawls assumes at the outset, finally, that the social contractors are motivated only by individualist considerations, as in classical liberalism. But his goal, he says, is to justify a "social union of social unions." By this he means a network of special goal-oriented associations coexisting and cooperating in the same society; and this, to be sure, has a certain appeal. But Rawls does not really explain how the hypothetical individuals with whom he starts come to thrive in such togetherness. They are motivated to seek agreement on the principles because, as Hume had proposed, they are mutually disinterested in moderate scarcity: "circumstances of justice." [74] They do come together into associations, or social unions, but on an ad hoc, mutually self-interested, basis. The result is, as Michael Sandel has argued, not a prioritized ("constitutive") community but a social arrangement in which individuals draw reciprocal benefit from one another as they improve their prioritized individual well-being (in accordance with the virtue-favoring "Aristotelian principle").[75] Haskell Fain finds such attempts to build a society out of unrelated individuals foredoomed to failure; for, he argues, if they did not already constitute some sort of collective entity before entering into a contract, no contract as such can so transform them. The group—for example, a biological or cultural family—must exist as such, Fain insists, before an agreement is made whereby they commit themselves to accomplishing a task, in this case, the building of a society.[76]

Especially crucial to a consideration of work and justice is Rawls's altogether casual announcement that the social contractors behind the veil of ignorance might be understood to be firms, meaning companies, including presumably transnational corporations. In this way he aligns himself with the predilections of the traditional liberal, or libertarian, who wants corporations to be regarded as indistinguishable from other individuals and having the same rights and privileges, whatever those might be. Such institutional entities are incomparably more powerful than are "plain vanilla" individuals who weigh comparatively little on the socioeconomic scale. But, presumably, this for Rawls is no more troubling than is the inequality between individuals who, however great the difference between their respective situations, do not (justifiably) envy one another because the system that allows such difference is fair.

A masterful work of the power and complexity of Rawls's *A Theory of Justice* is neither explained nor a fortiori explained away in so few words. This, however, is not my purpose. As noted at the outset, I here wish only to indicate that anyone interested in dealing with the dragons that stand in the way of community-oriented justice for workers must eventually take on this dragon. And what makes this dragon so difficult to overcome is that it purports to stand for much of what chivalrous dragon-fighters take to be their concerns. It favors individual liberty and it favors the cohesion of groups. It favors progress; and when there is enough progress, it would transfer some of its benefits from the rich to the poor. But to anyone who has to deal with injustice here and now, it is on record only in behalf of a right, conceivably even a duty, to opt out or to express one's disapproval, with due restraint, in public. According to Rawls, who wrote these words at the peak of resistance to the Vietnam War, such noncompliance is grounded in laws governing the behavior of nations. This is not much of an invitation to reinterpret justice as fairness globally; but some have taken it to be an invitation nonetheless. Whence the appearance of *global justice*. It remains to be seen if this dragon has anything to offer a workers' representative who knows that workers in particular locations do not believe their interests are taken seriously by the corporate executives of global enterprise.

Global Justice and
Corporation-Community Relations

GLOBAL JUSTICE. It certainly sounds appealing! Like "a war to end all wars," or "one world," or "perfect harmony." Pollyanish, perhaps. But hope springs eternal, and our reach *should* exceed our grasp. This acknowledged, ideals do deserve serious consideration. But how can a responsible workers' representative distinguish global justice from pie-in-the-sky when the battles all seem to be fought in local communities, with dispensable workers on one side and mobile capital on the other? My answer to this question might be referred to as controlled utopianism and will be arrived at by means of a retrospective and reductionist analysis that leaves the community as the *experimentum crucis* of justice.

The *Dramatis Personae*

In reaching this point, we have discussed a wide variety of topics having to do with work. Though varied, they are all interconnected insofar as each sheds light on the relationships between worker and community, worker and corporation, and corporation and community. And these relationships, I contend, constitute the context within which a workers' representative must seek to establish the terms and conditions of justice for workers. But so far I have not explained as clearly as one might what is meant by the corporations or the communities that help constitute this context for justice. We have talked about communities, usually understanding a community to be a local constituency of people with shared interests. We have also discussed different aspects of corporations, including in particular the fact that the larger ones are usually not contained within any one community but extend their empire far and wide, often to every continent. This, in turn, suggests that the appropriate context of justice with regard to corporations is not local but nothing less than global. So before concluding our representative's philosophical briefing, we need to confront the dragon of global justice with our concerns about the interaction of corporations and communities.

256

First to be noted is that the term *corporation* has a number of different meanings, not all of which are mutually compatible. Remote from our concerns are usages that refer to types of national governance. More pertinent is the legal fiction of which I have been speaking throughout this book. It should be clear by now that I consider this vacuous usage harmful to community interests. Some whose concerns I share, however, think otherwise. The International Association of Machinists and Aerospace Workers (IAM), for example, sees the dependence of corporations on law for their existence as a justification for imposing social demands upon them.[1] In this way, they turn the vacuous concept into one that is normative, much as English businessman George Goyder once proposed that a well-behaving company be authorized to refer to itself as a "public company." In this vein, the IAM proposes a Rebuilding America Corporate Act in which corporations are defined as "entities doing business for the convenience and needs of the community, in the public interest, for benefit of the public and in expectation of benefit to the public." They then propose what might be considered a paradigm of such a public benefit corporation: federal legislation, which they call the Rebuilding America Inner Cities Act, would authorize establishing wherever needed "a locally administered not-for-profit Community Redevelopment Corporation." According to the provisions of this proposed federal statute, "[a]n incorporated municipality of 250,000 population or more" could apply for development fund assistance in behalf of one or more neighborhoods within its jurisdiction.[2] So though they do not specify what they mean by a community, they do indicate by this example and others that they are thinking of a local political entity. Thus they attempt to combine a somewhat quantitative concept of community with a normative concept of corporation. The intention is good; but if the results are to be good as well, further analysis of both terms is needed.

Outside of courtrooms, corporations are commonly analyzed in normative, although not usually ethical, terms. For example, the common statutory distinction between corporations organized for profit and those that are nonprofit, or not-for-profit, is manifestly based on purpose or objective. The financial evaluation of profit-seeking corporations is a booming industry of which stock market trading represents only the most visible component. More pertinent to the concerns of this study, domestic firms are distinguished from those that are transnational, or multinational, based on the scope of their endeavors. The latter are often further distinguished depending on the ethnic mix of their management or on the purpose for which they expand beyond their home borders.[3] Those that in effect acknowledge no one national allegiance Robert Reich calls "pure" multinationals, of which he says many American companies are examples. Those that expand beyond their home borders but with the purpose of improving the long-term well-being of their home country's workforce Reich calls "national" multinationals, of which he says Japanese companies and the Swedish company Volvo are examples.[4]

The key point here, quite simply, is that corporations are commonly characterized according to normative criteria. There is, then, no reason in principle not to
try to establish criteria for determining how justly corporations treat communities
with which they have dealings. But to accommodate distinctions now to be made
with regard to communities, it will be useful to distinguish between corporations
that are domestic (operating entirely within a given political unit's jurisdiction)
and those that are dispersed (operating not only within but also beyond a given
political unit's jurisdiction).

The list of different kinds of communities in which a corporation operates can
be made as long as one likes by introducing ever finer distinctions. But for our
purposes the only entities that need be considered are, on the one hand, the workplace and, on the other, the relevant local, national, regional, or global political
entities. In this book I have been identifying problems of justice for workers that
arise out of the relations between a corporation and each of the communities here
identified, although I have not always explicitly identified either the relationship
or its components along the way. Now it is time to be clear about the different
"turfs" on which or among which these issues have to be resolved.

Much has been said in preceding chapters about what rights workers should
have in or at the workplace, especially with regard to meaningful work, nondiscriminatory hiring and promotion policies, and union organizing. Still more
could be said with regard to workplace health and safety, child care facilities,
and so on. But we are not likely to hear the workplace referred to as a community. Robert Reich, who is no slouch in his expressions of concern for workers,
is an exception in this regard. He does speak about the negative impact of plant
closings on a community such as Detroit; but because, in his words, "geographic
communities cease to have real social significance for many citizens," he believes
that "[i]n a real sense, the work community is replacing the geographic community as the most tangible American social setting," by virtue of its being a
"unique community of skills and relationships within a work force." [5] Inasmuch
as workforce restructuring has become even more common than when Reich
wrote these words, I question whether there is enough stability in the American
corporate workplace to justify his usage. Besides, this telescoping of community
into corporation opens the way to a telescoping of ethics into corporate ethics,
which is yet another way to leave chicken-watching to the fox.[6] Accordingly,
what follows is concerned with relationships between a corporation and a local
community of which the corporation's workers may be members but not to the
exclusion of others. And, as a matter of fact, this is entirely consistent with
Reich's recognition of workers' need for what he calls "civic virtue." [7]

The notion of a local community is obvious, but ambiguous. It might refer
to a more or less well-organized ethnic or religious minority inhabiting a particular neighborhood in a city, or all the people organized into a political unit

as small as a village or as large as a multiborough metropolis like New York City. Historically, the significance of these units has been inversely proportional to the advance of technologies that facilitate nourishment, communication, and transportation, to mention a few. Athens, Rome, and Venice, each in its time, enjoyed political power as expansive as available technology permitted. And for comparable reasons guilds dominated trade in cities until in response to the needs of capitalism they were abolished. Reich goes the wrong way, however, in suggesting that the political power of cities should in effect be abolished as obsolete, as were guilds two centuries ago.

Accounts of the death of cities are greatly exaggerated. Their influence has indeed been undermined by the establishment of farther-reaching political entities; but the latter should facilitate rather than inhibit responsive government in cities. This, at least, is the sentiment of the people of New Delhi, who have petitioned the government of India to recognize their city as a state. Also, the city is often the principal victim of a plant closing, as in Youngstown, or the beneficiary of industrial development, be it worker-oriented, as in Mondragon, Spain, or capitalist-inspired, as in Singapore.

I have spoken about a number of views that associate a community with the largest effective unit of government, in particular, that of a nation-state. The nation-state is the locus of what John Dewey thought of as the Great Community. It was also the locus of the now abrogated social contract among representatives of business, labor, and government. For well over a century it has been the principal instrument of corporate hegemony. And it is responsible, especially in the United States, for the inability of local units of government to control their destinies vis-à-vis major corporations—both because of policies it adopts, for instance, opening the floodgates of deregulation, and because of policies it fails to adopt, such as not requiring federal incorporation. Such problems notwithstanding, it is just such a "democratic" nation-state that Rawls has in mind as he contemplates the conditions for justice in the world.[8]

Especially important in today's world is the community understood as an entire, even multinational, region. In some respects, the United States of America is a community in this sense, as witness the dominance of federal preemption over "states' rights." So is the Union of Soviet Socialist Republics, in spite of the manifest preference of many peoples in that amalgam for their own national sovereignty. Better examples of voluntarily established regional communities are the economic communities in Western Europe, including the European Coal and Steel Community, the European Atomic Energy Community, and the European Economic Community, this latter being now an increasingly cooperative organization of twelve sovereign nations, many of which fought bitter wars against one another in both the distant and the recent past. Now these countries are committed to the abolition of all trade barriers among them by the end of 1992. In the process, they will create the world's largest market to which domestic corporations will have privileged access.⁹

Important as are the foregoing candidates for being a community, the domain of reflection for a number of contemporary political philosophers is increasingly global: either the globe as a whole or, somewhat less ambitiously, the community of nations. The latter is institutionalized in a limited way in the United Nations. To the former there correspond no really effective political institutions; but ideas for such are not lacking. Moreover, their implementation in some fashion would seem to be urgent in view of the comparatively untrammeled advancement of corporate globalization. Thus the need to give some attention at this point to reflections on global justice. But in the end I will come back to the singular importance of building justice for workers from within one's local community, with assistance as feasible and as forthcoming from geographically more encompassing units of government.

Global Justice: An Offer That Can't Be Refused?

Theoretical interest in global justice has grown since the publication of Rawls's nation-oriented study. Social and political philosophers in particular are engaged in a great debate on the subject, albeit in fairly technical terms and at a high level of abstraction. The timeliness of this debate should be apparent, especially against a background of potential nuclear annihilation. But the participants seldom consider the role of TNCs, even though the latter's "global" behavior is largely responsible for creating the issues that now stretch old philosophical theories to their breaking point. Out of this ferment will eventually come theories significantly different from those we have chewed on since the rise of nation-states. Meanwhile, the informed representative of workers needs to appreciate one key issue in this debate: whether it is better to conceptualize global justice in unqualified global terms or in less than global (usually understood as national) terms.

If I may simplify without distortion, there are three kinds of questions to which the parties to this debate give different answers: as to what is desirable, what is feasible, and what is morally obligatory. For example, with regard to political institutions, scholars who agree that some form of global governance is desirable might part company on the question of feasibility or on that of obligation. Similarly, scholars who agree about the desirability of people helping one another regardless of political arrangements may part company on questions about the feasibility of doing so or on the question of obligation. In the global justice debate, there is a significant split between libertarians and liberals which replicates their disagreement at the intranational level but at the same time puts libertarians in the anomalous position of defending nation-states against the liberals. The latter aspire to global approaches while the former defend the autonomy of subglobal political units.

One possible starting point for a liberal theory of global justice is Rawls's approach. And he himself suggests this possibility in his original work. But the problems of adaptation appear to be intractable. Whatever the strengths of his approach, his redistributive principles are intended to be intranational, not international. He leaves the global economy to the law of nations. In particular, he has nothing of substance to say about one rationally crafted subglobal society benefiting from the resources of another rationally crafted subglobal society without paying a fair share of the costs.

Rawls has even less to say about the behavior of transnational corporations, wherever based, and individuals who act in their behalf. If his theory of justice is to take transnational interactions into account, it must be relocated in a global context within which transnational corporations are recognized as institutions and even as "moral persons." A global version of Rawlsian justice might, for example, apply his difference principle to various claims made against corporations by "least advantaged" communities around the world. Such, at least, is the approach Charles Beitz takes in attempting a globalized interpretation.[10]

This move is attractive on its face just because it promises to consider purportedly universal principles of conduct to be applicable beyond the confines of any one nation-state.[11] But few philosophers have found a palatable way to make the globe the geographical correlate of universality. Especially problematic for defenders of a global ethic is the inadequacy of global enforcement of standards. This some philosophers view as a compliance problem—important in its own right but secondary to the task of establishing universal (global) norms.[12] A more serious objection is that a global interpretation tends to disregard the moral significance of loyalty to less than global groups, be they families or nation-states or in particular local communities. This disregard is especially suspect when it endorses outside intervention.[13] The root cause of this flaw in the liberal model is, according to Onora O'Neill, that it requires an abstraction which idealizes and thereby distorts the realities of community. Thus, she says, "[i]t is beside the point to complain that an abstract liberal account of justice fails to take community seriously enough, since it is predicated on the view that in modern times a serious conception of justice cannot presuppose community."[14]

Toward correcting this distortion, I return to Julius Stone's concept of a justice-constituency, which involves "the claimants and beneficiaries of justice in concrete times and places, with their biological endowments and social environments, and their limited and tentative envisionings of the future."[15] I acknowledge his association of this concept with a nation-state and by extension to "mankind"; but, as noted in Chapter 1, I prefer to apply it to social units less complex than or even unrelated to any one or more nation-states. For in addition to the levels with which Stone was primarily concerned, the vital interests of more localized justice-constituencies need to be acknowledged. Moreover, for some purposes it makes more sense to define subglobal interests functionally, without regard to geographical units, for example, to deal with concerns about the environment (notably, the ocean floors) or about human rights. In short, a global ethic needs to be sophisticated enough to take into account interests and claims that have global import but are less than global in scope.[16]

An early example of such a global ethic is David Ricardo's justification of various transnational exchanges on the basis of "comparative advantage."[17] This doctrine came into play whenever there was a need to justify an unequal distribution of resources among different groups of people (colonizers and colonized, as often as not). So, though conceptualized in terms of market exchange, this doctrine of comparative advantage was a handy device for justifying exploitation. To avoid such a unilateral ethic, one must also consider the comparative *dis*advantage people must endure because of circumstances over which they have no control.

To spell out the full import of this last observation would require a disquisition over topics including at least colonialism and national sovereignty, with corporate intervention thrown in. In lieu of such thoroughness, let me cite just a few examples of how radically an exogenous force can destroy the equilibrium of a local community. Cortés's conquest of the Incas is a matter of common lore; but it is only one of many such intrusions that changed peoples' lives forever. The nomadic practices of peoples in the Sahel zone of West Africa were admirably suited to survival of humans and animals until French-imposed national boundaries severely limited their mobility and subjected them to ecological collapse and starvation. The inhabitants of Bikini Atoll had little choice but to submit to evacuation to another island for over a generation when the United States selected their home to test atomic weapons after World War II. An originally enslaved populace that concentrated on sugar production in Jamaica was transformed yet one more time when bauxite was discovered on the island in 1952 and began to be processed a few years later. Examples of this sort are not in short supply. But the thrust of the issue is well expressed, for example, in the novels of Ibo writer Chinua Achebe, notably *The Arrow of God*, in which a tribal religious leader retains his office only so long as he understands his role in terms compatible with the colonizers' perceived interests.

As noted above with regard to progress, those in controlling positions have a tendency to interpret events in a manner congenial to themselves, as with the disingenuous acceptance of "the white man's burden." This problem of bias notwithstanding, some theorists cut through the epistemological haze to insist on the importance of being obligated to do good. From the viewpoint of what is called virtue theory, moral obligation is not subject to limitation but is an open-ended function of one's changing capabilities. Ethicists concerned with legal ramifications, however, devote more attention to identifying the limits of obligation, whence the notion of "minimalist ethics." Consistent with the objectives of minimalist ethics are various attempts to establish basic human rights to which by definition every human being anywhere in the world is entitled.[18] A common formulation in this respect is to the effect that everyone is entitled at least to all basic needs for survival. The scope of these basic needs is very broadly stated in Article 25 of the proposed United Nations Charter of Economic Rights and Duties as including not only food, clothing, housing, and medical care but also a basic welfare safety net. Other formulations, including that of John Rawls in *A Theory of Justice*, are narrower with regard to physical needs and broader with regard to psychic needs. Whatever the formulation, through various chains of reasoning a number of ethicists conclude that the identification of a minimum allocation imposes a moral obligation on those able to contribute to its realization.[19]

According to Peter Singer, for example, each of us individually has an obligation to relieve world hunger up to the point beyond which we would fall to a worse state than that of those to whom we give of our resources.[20] The sentiment is noble; the appeal is moving. But (as Singer himself has come to acknowledge) it is not an adequate basis for solving the problem of world hunger. For if Singer may be said to favor *caring,* it can be shown that *not caring* may be no less humane in its effects.

According to Singer, I, as an individual, have an obligation to give of my resources to others in need up to the point that further giving would make my condition no better than that of the beneficiary(ies) of my giving. But on the assumption that this obligation is based on a utilitarian commitment to effect the greatest good for the greatest number, I may strive to achieve either the greatest good or some measure of good for the greatest number, but not both.

In quest of some measure of good for the greatest number, I assume as a principle of equality that each of the needy should count for one and none for more than one. Suppose next that I can identify 100 million individuals in the world whose access to food is insufficient to maintain the minimum daily standards of nutrition (however that is determined). Assume further that I can part with $10,000 without being myself reduced to a condition of having less than the minimum daily nutrition. Dividing 10,000 by 100 million, I determine that I should give one ten-thousandth of a U.S. dollar, or one one-hundredth of a cent, to each identified infrequent eater. We may disregard the fact that such an amount would make no appreciable difference to any of the recipients, because it is not possible to transfer such a small amount of money to them. Such, quite simply, are the constraints imposed by the international banking system, available monetary units of exchange, and available instrumentalities of transfer. From an obligation one cannot fulfill one must be excused or, if not excused, be granted a suspension until such time as it becomes possible to carry it out.

Nothing of moral import is changed by a (counterfactual) objection that there are, say, only 1 million certifiably hungry persons in the world. On this assumption, I would owe one U.S. cent to each hungry person. But the fees for international transfer of funds are such that it would cost me far more to effect each such transfer than these individuals would gain either individually or collectively from my largess. What is more, given that I had only the $10,000 to give to others, the added expense of effecting these transfers would render me ultimately worse off than they, taken individually or collectively. Thus again my alleged obligation should be excused or at least suspended.

In quest of the greatest good regardless of the numbers of persons benefited, I might single out one or several persons for my largess. Even apart from the nagging problem of targeting my philanthropic dollar effectively (which a utilitarian, unlike a Kantian, cannot ignore), should I help educate one healthy person, say, in agricultural economics or should I help provide medical treatment for several persons who are suffering the effects of malnutrition? A choice in this regard is inevitably subjective and so fails to address important concerns about fair distribution. What is more, it fails to address the very difficult background question of balancing population dynamics and resource availability—a problem that some neo-Malthusians would solve by a global application of triage.[21]

People's behavior in the wake of natural disasters lends some support to Singer's claim that we are morally obligated as individuals to do what we can for others in need. Independently of political or ideological differences, individual donations are plentiful for at least short periods of time after the occurrence of a major catastrophe, such as the recent famines in Bangladesh and Sudan, or the earthquakes in Colombia, Mexico City, and Armenia. But in all such instances fair allocation of the goods or services provided is hindered or even precluded by lack of, or deliberate interference with, appropriate procedures for implementation of assistance. In view of these and other related problems, philosopher Onora O'Neill, who has carefully examined the problem of world hunger, argues that talk about global obligations is but empty words in the absence of procedures to translate obligation into results.[22]

These complications seriously undermine Singer's claim on pragmatic grounds. But they do not affect his basic claim that we as individuals are morally obliged to do what we can to help people live at least minimally decent lives. This claim I do not dispute. But one's initiative in fulfilling such an obligation is better directed, as William Aiken argues, toward bringing about policy and, ultimately, institutional changes.[23] This strategy differs from Singer's in that it endorses cooperation as a sine qua non for eventual success. But at what level of political organization is such cooperation most feasible?

In view, for example, of people's inability to deliver transnational disaster aid expeditiously, some scholars argue that better global institutional arrangements are needed to deal with what they perceive to be global problems. Toward this end, they, individually and as teams, have begun the crucial but arduous task of delineating the structure of a truly just world order. Especially noteworthy in this regard is the work of the World Order Models Project (WOMP). WOMP teams of scholars have been established in Latin America, Japan, India, Africa, North America, Europe, the Soviet Union, and (to focus on transterritorial matters) Oslo, Norway. Under the general directorship of Saul H. Mendlovitz (cofounder of WOMP with Harry Hollins), each team has now published a report, the flavor of which is contained in a Mendlovitz-edited anthology entitled *On the Creation of a Just World Order* (1975).[24] These efforts share in common recognition of the trend toward globalization of our species and a desire to articulate a humane end state of this globalization. Most stress the need for certain functional institutions at the global level; but the African and, to some extent, the Japanese reports focus on cultural criteria for constructing a new world order.

Writing for WOMP/USA, Richard Falk proposes a global charter that would empower a "central guidance system" to implement a limited "global social contract." At the outset he identifies four WOMP/USA value preferences: minimization of large-scale collective violence; maximization of social and economic well-being; realization of fundamental human rights and conditions of political justice; and rehabilitation and maintenance of environmental quality, including the conservation of resources.[25] (Many would add, as a fifth value, participation in decision making.) Global attainment of these value preferences, Falk says, is impossible so long as "the logic of [the Peace of] Westphalia" continues to prevail. According to this logic, the world order system consists exclusively of the governments of states each of which is considered sovereign and equal independent of any higher authority within the world order system. Alternative logics are supranational (represented only minimally by, for example, agencies of the United Nations) and transnational: increasingly significant because of the activities of transnational corporations.

The transnational logic, according to Falk, is undermining not only "the constraining boundaries of the state" but even the basic ecosystems of the planet. In response to this challenge, he develops a set of possible models for world government, settles on a basically supranational model that would entrust heightened power to a reorganized United Nations, then turns to the problem of transition to such an arrangement. His objections to mainstream American foreign policy are somewhat muted, and his assessment of the role of TNCs is ambivalent and inconclusive. But he recognizes very well that the governments of developing countries, compromised as they often are by foreign corporations, do not necessarily represent the aspirations of their people.[26] To complete the picture, he need only have added that the governments of developed countries are hardly more immune to being compromised.[27]

This latter problem is well articulated by Gerald and Patricia Mische. According to them the policies and priorities of all existing nation-states, large and small, are driven by three "national security motors": balance-of-weapons competition, balance-of-payments competition, and competition over scarce resources. They show, for example, how these "motors" led to one global crisis after another in the early 1970s: U.S. President Richard Nixon's response to a war-generated balance-of-payments crisis by abruptly abrogating his country's commitment to the international agreement that had pegged the world's monetary system to a strong U.S. dollar (1971); the resulting oil embargo imposed by the Oil Producing and Exporting Countries (OPEC) in 1973; and U.S. President Gerald Ford's quest for "Energy Independence" for his country—which already depends on foreign sources for more than 50% of thirteen major natural resources and will for all of them (except phosphate) by the year 2000.[28] They show further how seven cabinet-level departments in the U.S. government—not only Defense and State but also Justice, Treasury, Commerce, Agriculture, and Transportation—must virtually ignore domestic needs to focus on the offshore priorities of the three national security motors by supporting major corporations that can produce and sell goods abroad.

Just months before the OPEC move, in July 1973, the Committee for Economic Development issued a prophetic report. It concluded, among other things, that unless "there is fundamental agreement [among nations] on the rules of the game and a basic willingness to abide by a central authority that will enforce these rules, . . . the world will be moving toward a system of economic warfare among increasingly separated regional trading blocs."[29]

Subsequent events corroborate these concerns, but not in the way foreseen. The only effective "regional trading bloc" that has emerged is not in the Middle East but involves the developed countries of Western Europe: the European Community. Developed countries have found ways to circumvent the worst effects of the OPEC embargo, in large part because they represent the principal consumers of oil as well as of everything else. LDCs, however, were thrown into economic chaos by the increase in oil prices, and their mounting indebtedness remains a global problem which lender banks in the developed countries can get around by judicious write-offs that actually improve the market value of their stocks. This differential impact reflects the extent to which the international monetary system is controlled by lending institutions in the Northern Hemisphere. Of course, many people in developed countries have also experienced a decline in their living standards because of corporate global activities. These activities are characterized, however, less by competition than by locally compromising arrangements that result in what Richard J. Barnet calls the "Global Factory."[30]

Apart from the phenomenon of worker displacement, Americans are witnessing some aspects of the Global Factory as foreign, especially Japanese, companies enter into joint ventures with American-based companies, open assembly (not production) plants in the United States, buy American buildings and businesses, and invest so heavily in the American market that some analysts have begun to worry that these wealthy foreigners might be in a position to determine by their investment decisions whether Americans will maintain their present standard of living. Meanwhile, American scholars are debating whether the United States is still competitive in the world market. Those who say we are disagree with those who say we are not, in part because the former assume that the American people will tolerate an annual decline of 1% in their standard of living.[31]

Community: If Not in Cities, Where?

The gravity of such problems on a less than global level leads many scholars to support the idea of global justice in principle while working to achieve justice within one's own community. For example, Kai Nielsen, having considered the arguments for a more global concept of justice, agrees that we should maintain a global perspective but recommends that we concentrate our efforts on solving the problems we face in our own communities. Richard Barnet, after following corporations and resources all over the world, has come to the conclusion that our survival depends on, among other things, the local community. In the words of Herman R. van Gunsteren, "The way to work toward globalism is to work with local pieces."[32] This encouragement of local initiative provides, I believe, the very key to achieving justice for workers in the world today. Elaborating its implications will accordingly be a suitable way to bring our reflections into final focus. At issue is still the question of corporate-community relations, first with regard to justice and then with regard to the relationships themselves.

In particular, work and justice will remain incompatible if there is no significant input into corporate decision making at the local level. In their single-minded quest for profit, corporations make restructuring decisions that entail multiple transactions, operations, and installations with minimal regard to local, national, and regional borders. Often, where local government is weak, pliable, and undemocratic, corporate moves are consummated without even consulting the people of the communities most directly affected. What can a contractarian theory tell us about the justice of such arrangements if they are not society-building in intent or in fact? John Rawls does contend that an arrangement detrimental to the least advantaged is suspect, and he identifies the least advantaged with unskilled laborers and those below them economically. But how can this have a bearing on the arrangements of a globalizing enterprise? Globalization might harm semi-skilled or even skilled laborers in one place but arguably benefit unskilled laborers somewhere else. Moreover, those arguably benefiting might be primarily female, while those harmed might be primarily male. But what follows from these or any other globe-hopping observations? If only bordered entities operate on the basis of originating agreements, and these agreements are binding altogether and only within that entity, then social contracts are irrelevant when it comes to debating what corporations ought to be doing globally. For from the viewpoint of the TNC (unlike that of the astronaut) the globe is not a big blue marble with billowy clouds; it is a strategic map into which pins representing facilities are pushed one day and removed another. It is, if you will, the philosophically fabled state of nature.

What is needed, then, is a way to ameliorate this unqualified "global" perspective without endorsing an unqualified "local" perspective (neither of which is realistic) and, in the process, confront the allegedly spaceless and timeless business decision with the "solidarity" of human groups. A useful guide for this purpose would be the analyses carried out by Jean-Paul Sartre in his *Critique of Dialectical Reason*. Also useful would be a consideration of the concept of honor, not only in so-called heroic societies but in various traditional communities in the contemporary world, especially in Africa and East Asia. In lieu of such a detailed account, I will merely appeal to the fertile hints that can be gleaned from Haskell Fain's rethinking of the grounds for normative politics, which he defines as "an inquiry into the morality of power." [33]

Fain seeks to remedy the inability of available theories of international law to help solve global problems that call for cooperation across, and in spite of, national borders. Included among such problems are, primordially, the preservation of the human race (if not life of any kind) on this planet and also environmental protection, peaceful conflict resolution, world population control, management of resources of the sea, and Antarctica. Other, more controversial, problems include poverty in the Third World, the relationship between the world political community and its constituent nation-states, ideological antagonisms, and the unregulated operations of TNCs.

To justify solving such global problems through law, Fain views the very existence of urgent transnational tasks as pointing to the existence of a noncentralized community of nations. In developing his task-oriented theory, he claims that a biological (not an artificial) community, inherently able and morally entitled to act, must exist *as the foundation for* mutually binding agreements. To support this view of the mutually enabling origins of agreements, Fain adds to the obligation-making power that of permission, or permission-exemption, powers: it is permissions with regard to tasks, and not rules, that constitute a political community.[34]

As noted, Fain takes this position because he believes other approaches to normative politics fail to mandate the solution of global problems. The requirement that the community be *morally* entitled to act rules out reality politics, which in effect equates right with force. Traditional contract theories, including that of John Rawls, canonize the legal autonomy and isolation of the nation-state. (Charles Beitz's proposal to remedy this shortcoming by adding a difference principle on the global level fails, in Fain's opinion, because of the harshly diverse fates of First and Third World countries.) In agreement with Hans Kelsen's legal conceptualism, Fain takes international law to be paramount; but rather than accepting, as does Kelsen, whatever happens to be the (positive) law, Fain seeks "the intersection of desirability and authority at the foundational level of the law." [35] By contrast, complete rejection of Kelsen's internationalism (common among Anglo-American jurists) favors the autonomy of the nation-state vis-à-vis international agreements. Against such presumed autonomy, Fain contends that states should be understood as being by definition in a "field" with other states so in effect having two constitutions, one of which arises out of agreements with other states, and that these agreements are binding (*pacta sunt servanda*) even if not domestically convenient. [36]

This principled prioritizing of international law is, in Fain's own words, "a dangerous and unpleasant doctrine." But the theoretical alternatives offer much less hope of our ever transcending the fatalism of global chaos. So on a very elemental level the reader—this one, at least—wants Fain's analyses to be persuasive. On a theoretical level, this will require further attention to the difficult task of clarifying the respective etiological importance of tasks, permissions, communities, and what Fain at one point calls simply "contemporary dependencies." [37] But in practice, as Jean-Paul Sartre liked to argue, a difficulty is for the most part in the eye of the would-be achiever. And, as I have been arguing, one task that needs to be carried out is that of achieving stable, mutually advantageous relationships between corporations and communities. Taking a cue, then, from Fain's prioritizing of a biological group's permissions, I should like to sketch what is at issue in developing a system of community permissions for corporate activities.

For a start, recall that a community may be understood politically to be any level of human organization, be it global, regional, national, provincial, or local. Following Fain's lead, and mindful of the work of sociobiologists, I suggest that the principal biological community in the world today is the city. Accordingly, the principal locus of corporate-community relations should also be the city. Having discussed this point, I will turn to conclusions and leave the rest to our workers' representative.

Once upon a time, as many writers like to note, the family was the primordial human organization. Acceptance of this as a fact caused Locke to envision a kinder, gentler state of nature than had Hobbes before him. Locke, in turn, proved all too prophetic as early capitalism "incorporated" the family as a unit

into the production process. Well into the nineteenth century, many socialists
contend, the earlier arrangement gave way to a split between work (the realm
of the male) and life (the narrowly circumscribed domain of the female). Thus
the focus of early, especially socialist, feminist reaction: anti-life (in the sense of
domestic confinement) and pro-work (in the sense of greater involvement).[38] This
analysis is unquestionably insightful. Quite unintentionally, it even supports current efforts to redefine the meaning of family so that couples other than traditional
heterosexual mates can benefit from employer-provided benefits. But its scope is
essentially limited to the bourgeoisie in developed nations. It is rendered almost
quaint by the multifaceted complexity of the Global Factory. The city, however,
can transcend this limitation.

Today, all over the world, the city is becoming not only the center but the
very embodiment of the corporation. The focal point of the ancient city (Chi-
chen Itza, Kuala Lumpur, Jerusalem, Athens) was its principal religious temple.
The focal point of the medieval city (Edinburgh, Paris, Cologne) was a principal
church or castle. In early modern cities (Berlin, Brussels, Boston) commerce and
government are relatively coequal foci. But in the contemporary city that is rising
out of the ruins of past arrangements, the skyscrapers of commerce dominate
not only the view but also the activity of, and satellite services provided by, the
surrounding community.

The city, then, is in many respects a satellite for corporate needs; but a satellite is not superfluous. The city and its people constitute the community on which
a corporation and its people are most immediately and directly dependent. Indeed, the city's people and the corporations' people are to some extent one and
the same, transfers notwithstanding. Corporate employees are community residents, citizens, parents. Their children attend community schools. All use the
community's facilities and benefit from its amenities.

The name of this game is mutual need satisfaction. Business needs skills. The
city provides education that prepares, and amenities that attract and hold, people
with needed skills. Business needs infrastructure; the city provides it. Business
claims to need flexibility, including institutional mobility; but it can enjoy this
only if cities provide stability (generally speaking, there must be places to go
from and to).

Smaller political units may also be loci for living to some degree, but they
are essentially disempowered except in and through their links with the city. Even
the so-called bedroom communities are not unrelated to the city. One-fourth or
more of a suburb's population may turn over in the course of a year as corporations move their management people about. The corporations enjoy the luxury
of this flexibility, however, only so long as the core city remains stable with all
its services, including the airport.

Towns and villages survive and, if fortunate, thrive only because their residents have access to the full-service city. The once vital downtown of Atchison, Kansas, is decaying; but its people, many of whom work out of the Kansas City airport, still have access to metropolitan shopping and entertainment. Isuzu Motors has located an assembly plant in the minuscule village of Dayton, Indiana, to which its employees come from miles around. Its Japanese managers benefit from the engineering resources of West Lafayette's Purdue University and from sushi restaurants in Indianapolis, all nearby. Many onetime village and farm properties in France and Great Britain now function as second home refuges for harried urbanites.

The old-style one-company town is obsolete for similar reasons. At least in developed countries, people are increasingly less willing to depend solely on one company or industry for the quality of their lives. People in Kenosha, Wisconsin, so recently demoralized by Chrysler's decision to close an antiquated plant, are now "taking their destiny in their own hands" and have begun to believe that there can be life after cars.[39] After years of deadening endurance, the people of Houston are discovering that there is life after oil (as after cotton and rice).[40] Philosopher John McDermott, an easterner transplanted to Texas, describes the city as a wasteland of "sky-buildings" surrounded by "enervated neighborhoods."[41] But a spirited rejuvenation built on biotechnology, aerospace, chemicals, and to a lesser extent health care and computers gives Mayor Kathy Whitmire an image of rebuilder of lost dreams. This fiscal conservative accountant, occupant of an art deco office dating from the pre–World War II days of agricultural opulence, personifies a new era in which women's traditional nurturing role is expanding beyond the family, beyond volunteerism, to encompass the community whose locus and center is the city. And as president of the nationwide Conference of Mayors (in 1989–90) she symbolizes the recognition among city government leaders of their common interests and concerns.[42]

In so acclaiming the city as principal agent of nurturing, I am not unmindful of the potential for corruption exemplified by a Tammany Hall; or, for brutality exemplified by "Bull" Connor of Birmingham, Alabama, in the days of civil rights protests; or, for exclusivity, by the guilds at the height of their power and in our times by Oak Park, Illinois, and, more recently, Yonkers, New York. Cities, as everyone knows, are not problem-free, even apart from such rhetorically targeted issues as crime, drugs, abortion, and homelessness. This, in spite of the traditional dislike of intellectuals for cities,[43] is an inescapable consequence of the fact that cities are where most people, at least in developed countries, live. Cities even more so are where most people work.

This being the case, our failure to solve the problem of fair exchange for work is most immediately and most terribly manifested by the declining level and variety of services and amenities available to people in our cities. The practice on the national level of draining resources from cities for the sake of those corporate subsidies called "national defense" is only randomly of benefit to cities. It is clearly detrimental on balance, when, without lowering people's taxes, it results in lower levels of funding (meaning nonraiding of resources) of cities in the name of local autonomy. For as every politician soon learns, there is a limit to how much taxation people can endure. It is time, then, to stop blaming the urban victims of our grotesque distortion of priorities.

The source of the problems of our cities will be found less in the latest crime statistics than in the balance sheets of major corporations that thrive on building the instruments of our national insecurity with resources that only selectively benefit people's lives. And to the extent that workers are caught up in this barbarous equation of good with guns, they too have chosen, in Freud's terms, Thanatos over Eros. But they are victims more than instigators of this travesty, which is why their more enlightened leaders are calling for "economic conversion." It is at this point, however, that they must begin to see how their interests intersect those of others in the city.

This is admittedly a delicate and difficult thesis for a workers' representative to accept, precisely because the history of our cities chronicles corporate dominance of civic institutions and, through them, of workers' interests. In the nineteenth century, communities came to be sharply divided into classes. But promise of upward mobility, as expressed in the idea of free labor, enabled business spokespersons to persuade many workers of the preeminence of community consciousness over class consciousness. The hegemony of this view of reality did not prevent workers from transforming their legacy of artisan protest into ongoing commitment to equality. But it was effective enough that labor leader Samuel Gompers could distinguish American labor's sense of fellow feeling (*Klassengefühl*) from European labor's more radical intellectual understanding of itself as an oppressed class (*Klassenbewustzein*).[44] This newly emerging view of that period has led labor historian Brian Greenberg to describe workers' perceptions of the social order in nineteenth-century Albany, New York, as having "evolved through a dialectic between the dominant free labor belief and the workers' own awareness of themselves as a class." They never realized their ideal of a "cooperative commonwealth," but many continued to pursue an alternative to capitalist industrialization.[45]

The wisdom of that divided allegiance has become more apparent in the course of the twentieth century as corporate manipulation of workers' interests is exercised through all levels of government. In particular, workers cannot expect their interests to be defended by urban leaders who cannot distinguish these interests from often incompatible corporate priorities. But the fulfillment of our potential as human beings is unattainable if communities do not support workers, not against corporations as such but against the complex of interests (including those of national government) that view local workers as mere pawns on the great game board of power and privilege.

Quite obviously, the structure and distribution of economic and political power are not conducive to a worker-sensitive alliance of local interests. But it is not impossible to achieve. In the United States, at least, the common concerns of local government are considered and pursued through such umbrella organizations as the Conference of Mayors, the much larger National League of Cities (whose membership is open to all city government officials), and, of comparable interest, the Conference of Governors. None of these or other related organizations has any constitutional status in our national government. But neither do the lobbyists who represent the Fortune 500 in our nation's capital. They have already become and must continue to be even more a force to be reckoned with, a voice to be heard. But their voice will be all the easier to hear, even by a patrician, the more they and the representatives of workers are able to see their interests as being at least compatible if not convergent. Perspectives will differ, sometimes sharply; but the concerns, say, of the Conference of Mayors are, or at least should be, the concerns of organized labor as well.[46]

No one, of course, agrees without regret to bite the hand that provides wherewithal; but this should not discourage the quest for alternative sources of sustenance. Draining people's lives for the sake of "national interests" indistinguishable from corporate greed could reduce civilization to the worst-case scenario of the most pessimistic sci-fi novel. But the opportunity for reversing this trend will never be better; and an important step in that direction is a commitment on the part of all concerned to justice in corporate-community relations.

The notion of community, it should be apparent, is not simply being equated with that of the city. A city cannot become or even contain community by fiat. But the tendency of many scholars to denigrate community as an obsolete way of life that must yield to the impersonal ways of modern society is an unfounded and ultimately destructive bias. The formal relationships that are so characteristic of modern life need not obliterate the interpersonal cooperation of community. Life and work, *Gemeinschaft* and *Gesellschaft,* can coexist. This, in fact, is what Alfred Tönnies was trying to say a century ago, before his interpreters reduced his message to a mere report on the demise of traditional ways of caring about one another.[47] Clearer today than when Tönnies examined the problem, the rise of corporate polities has made it urgent that people not allow themselves to be treated exclusively as placeless individual workers. Rather, must they find ways to do their work and relate to their employers in the context of the lives they live together, in community.

John Dewey, in conclusion, was right after all. We do need a Great Community to sustain our well-being in the world. His only mistake was to search for it principally at the level of nationalist abstractions. The Great Community is the city or, at least, is the potential of the city. (This, all too ironically, seems better recognized by those who aim guided missiles than by those responsible for improving people's lives.) Its realization in every part of the globe, with the encouragement of corporate enterprise and the protection of all levels of government, might well be the best and brightest hope for the working people of the world.

Conclusions

THE ARGUMENT DEVELOPED in this book leads through a labyrinth of particular concerns to three principal conclusions, one factual, one hortatory, and one theoretical.

I. The factual conclusion is this: *the social contract involving business, labor, and government is no longer tenable "as written," because business now exercises de facto sovereignty over the other two parties to the contract.*

To say that this conclusion is factual is, of course, controversial. It has in its favor, however, everything that has been brought to bear on the subject in this book. (The notion of sovereignty is considered below, in regard to the theoretical conclusion.)

II. The hortatory conclusion is this: *workers will be able to counterbalance the concentrated power of corporations only to the extent that they and the communities in which they live come to see their interests as intertwined and learn to defend these interests cooperatively.*

There are three corollaries of this conclusion, each of which focuses on one of the three principal *dramatis personae* in the book:

1. *Representatives of corporations,* including the transnationals, will deserve respect in the human community only if their ability to control people's lives at all levels of government is tempered by a recognition of social responsibility to the communities in which they locate.
2. *Workers' representatives* must expand their long-standing recognition that the interests of workers and employers are not identical into a more deliberate and open alignment of workers' interests, identities, and raison d'être with those of the local communities in which they live.
3. *Representatives of local communities* will discharge their duties more responsively and merit support at the polls as they come to identify the interests, identity, and raison d'être of the community less with corporations and more with local employees of, and others in the community who depend on, those corporations for their well-being.

277

The reasoning that leads to the hortatory conclusion and its three corollaries may be restated by focusing, in order, on corporations, workers, and communities.

CORPORATIONS

The corporation has evolved, historically, from joint ventures of fully liable individuals into limited-liability legal nonentities. Legal fictions aside, corporations are as real as, and frequently more powerful than, most nation-states. A corporation thus envisaged is a complex organization whose agents make decisions in its behalf that significantly affect the natural and social environment of people all around the world. In this way, corporations at least collectively control both the workers and the communities they touch.

Corporations control not only their own workers (to be discussed below) but many other persons who are ostensibly employed by other entities, including various units or branches of government. One or more corporation(s) may be the wholesaler of the products they sell at retail, or the principal buyer of their products or services, or the source or conduit of the products and services they, as government workers, are supposed to help regulate or facilitate. Regardless of what line of work people are in, the power of corporations extends to them and makes them the corporations' subjects.

Corporations control not only workers but communities. They dominate communities directly to the extent that they control their basic structure and indirectly by dominating the basic structure of traditional political entities at provincial ("state"), national, regional, and international levels.

WORKERS

Rousseau had it right when he said that everywhere people are in chains. What is surprising is that he thought they were born free.

People are more inclined to play than to work. This inclination to play may blossom into creative work that is literally invaluable. But more basic needs tend to call for sustained and, often, unsatisfying consumption of energy. That is why some human beings force others to work. Directly forcing others to work is enslavement. The art of indirectly leading others to work is known as management. Management may in some circumstances be indistinguishable from slaveholding. But in the better places it is more likely to motivate workers by plugging their presumed aspirations into such instrumental values as those of a work ethic.

An underlying assumption of the management relationship to others has been that the others have limited learning potential, so their labor must be divided to maximize productivity. With this in mind, each individual worker's job assignment and its accompanying responsibilities have been deliberately limited. As the variety of assignments increases and the market for resulting products and services multiplies, however, management's need for more limited-assignment workers expands. This intensifies the competition among employers for special-assignment workers; and this competition results in better fringe benefits, either on an individual basis or collectively, through a union.

To overcome its dependency on the skills of the workforce, management has responded by drawing as much of its workforce as possible from the cheapest labor that can provide the needed skills; automating as many jobs as possible, while keeping automation-tending assignments as simple as possible; cutting fringes as much as possible by requiring employees, through copayments and taxes, to bear more of the cost of the benefits; assigning as many jobs as possible, whatever their degree of complexity, to nonemployee workers, who are not eligible for employer-paid fringes; exploiting the skills of their downsized workforce by assigning them larger portions of "meaningful work"; using bankruptcy, plant relocation, and other devices that undercut the leverage of workers who are unionized or have union-avoiding benefits or have skills not easily duplicated, to force them, as a group, to outdo other groups of workers in job-saving concessions; and emphasizing the importance of maintaining an educated workforce, thereby transforming education into limited-skill acquisition and putting most of the burden of acquisition on the workers themselves, through tuition and taxes.

COMMUNITY

Historically, the notion of community has been associated with the closely tied relationships of *Gemeinschaft*. Contrary to Alfred Tönnies's expectations, however, *Gemeinschaft* is commonly considered doomed, and rightly so, to be replaced by the more efficient, depersonalized interactions of isolated individuals that is characteristic of "modern" *Gesellschaft*. *Gesellschaft* being considered the norm, *community* is redefined to refer to any cooperative interaction, such as a nation-state, or a group of nation-states (notably, the European Community), or even all nation-states. In this way, the notion of community has shifted in meaning, from a naively to a belligerently local system of face-to-face, interpersonal relationships, then to a consciously impersonal centralized system that treats individual human beings with uniform indifference.

In accordance with this "modern" approach to human relationships, sociopolitical issues are increasingly formulated in national, international, and even global terms. This totalizing perspective is reflected in the strategy of American unions to concentrate their efforts at the level of the nation-state in regard to lobbying, bargaining, and even support for foreign policy. A comparable focus has prevailed in some West European countries, such as Sweden and West Germany, where the nation-state functions as the principal arena for addressing the concerns of workers. In Soviet bloc countries, the state is viewed theoretically as the apparatus of workers while at the same time, however inconsistently, it functions as their ultimate employer.

There are indications that the modern tendency toward political and economic totalization has, in some respects, reached its apogee and is now in decline. The reverse dynamic of decentralization, long an issue in countries with distinct ethnic minorities, such as France, Canada, and Spain, is finding some degree of support in virtually every country. Tibetans challenge the Chinese monolith; ethnic Albanians resist Yugoslavian authority; the ethnic nationalism of particular Soviet republics challenges the hegemony of the overarching state.[1] In the United States, two kinds of reversal in direction are under way, one corporationist and the other populist.

The ideological commitment of recent federal administrations to "antifederalism" has been translated into significant deregulation in the areas of communication and transportation, which the media have noticed, and in housing, environmental management, and labor relations as well. The ultimate significance of this process is that it shifts even more power, more openly, to the major corporations.

The populist reversal in direction is, by contrast, the very opposite of government acquiescence in corporate hegemony. It is, in fact, a still unorganized movement to protect social welfare against centralized, community-indifferent corporations—precisely because of the failure of government to take responsibility in this area.

Employer-employee relations, pensions, health care insurance, air and water pollution, including radiation damage, are in principle regulated at the state or federal level. Attempts over the past century to localize such control have been repeatedly aborted by appeals to interstate commerce, national defense, and the all-purpose generic doctrine of state and federal preemption, which benefit none so handsomely as they do the major corporations. But people are becoming less able to believe what is contradicted, in so many ways, by their own experience. As a result, local response to local problems is challenging the mythology of totalized omnicompetence. Corporate hegemony is under challenge. Communities are standing up for their interests, as they have in the past with regard to shareholders' rights, toxic waste, and unsafe nuclear plants.[2]

This groundswell of populist response to the tyranny of the marketplace should reach out to include plant closings, bankruptcies, and strikebreaking. But so far it seldom has. Why not? Because there is still a widespread belief, generally supported by the corporate-controlled media, that large groups of people are no different than isolated individuals when it comes to not getting along with their employers: the victim is still blamed. It is possible to trace radiation in the atmosphere or carcinogens in the water to corporate causes. The connection is not as obvious when it comes to housing gluts, boarded-up storefronts, divorces, or even suicides. Even less obvious is the connection between corporate demands and government-collected taxes. But corporate power is ever-present as a principal factor in many of these community-draining phenomena.

III. The theoretical conclusion is this: *Social and political philosophy will remain irrelevant to a major social and political issue so long as its practitioners do not deal with the fact that corporations are becoming the world's most powerful de facto bearers of sovereignty.*

This conclusion is not meant in any normative sense to add authority to corporate power. Nor is it meant to reintroduce any long-disputed theory of legal or governmental sovereignty in behalf of a claim that corporations should be recognized theoretically as the final arbiters of social policy. What it does mean is that corporations, especially the transnationals, have a practical, or political, relationship with "official" governments that is comparable in its effects to a relationship that theorists have attributed to some nation-states' military forces.[3] As expressed by Stanley I. Benn, a recognized expert on the subject of sovereignty, this notion might refer to "a person, or a body or a class of persons, said to exercise supreme power in a state, as distinct from authority, in the sense that their wills can usually be expected to prevail against any likely opposition."[4] This just happens to be a fairly accurate description of the "political influence" of corporations on some nation-states that are thought to be sovereign.

Where this kind of relationship exists, governments are to corporations as priests once were to the warrior class: they are responsible for the ritual that lends respectability to the power. And workers, on whatever level, are like vassals in the service of a suzerain: they give of themselves, of their lives, of their substance, in return for the privilege of being allowed to continue serving. Any political philosophy that does not address this most dominant political fact of our age is in that respect better designated a theology: it studies not what is there but only hallowed texts that lead people to see what is not there.

In this book I have attempted to study what is there, for anyone to see. Others may not see it, or want to see it, as I do. But this may be just a matter of degree. For no one denies that corporations can and often do have a significant impact on government (at all levels), on communities, and on the workforce. Those who list this impact only under benefits will not find my assessment congenial. Those who do recognize some negative impacts, but believe government can and will make it right, will consider my analysis unduly pessimistic. Only those who share my doubts about the independent judgment and social concern of national governments are likely to come with me down the path to community power. And even some of them will leave us when they realize that we see our goal not as an exclusive alternative but as an enriching and empowering counterforce.[5] This perhaps leaves me in the position of having preached only to the converted. But others (such as residents of Niagara, New York, or Valdez, Alaska, users of the Dalkon Shield or DES, and employees of Union Carbide in Bhopal) may in time be joining us.

Notes and Index

Notes

Abbreviations used in the notes:

BW	Business Week	NLJ	National Law Journal
ITT	In These Times	NYT	New York Times
IS	Indianapolis Star	WSJ	Wall Street Journal

INTRODUCTION

1. See Arnold Thurman, "The Personification of Corporation," in his *The Folklore of Capitalism* (New Haven: Yale University Press, 1937), pp. 185–206. I do not mean to suggest that the only way our laws characterize a corporation is as a person or as a commodity, but only that these two characterizations are typical of the way in which the full social (and political) reality of corporations is routinely denied or camouflaged. David T. Bazelon, a corporate attorney who later became a federal judge, contended decades ago that corporations in the United States are essentially illegal but are at the same time the principal political powers of our times (something political philosophers still have not noticed). See his *The Paper Economy* (New York: Vintage, 1963), pp. 360, 397, and *passim*. Christopher Stone thinks tort law and criminal law do impinge, albeit ineffectually, on corporate behavior (*Where the Law Ends: The Social Control of Corporate Behavior* [New York: Harper & Row, 1975]). Ralph Nader, at that time, wanted to federalize if not internationalize corporations (*Constitutionalizing the Corporation* [Washington, D.C.: Corporate Accountability Research Group, 1976]). But Robert Hessen, articulating the conservative view, replied that *modern* corporations do not exist by government "concession," that government's role with regard to incorporation is no greater than with regard to marriages, that is, to record the fact (*In Defense of the Corporation* [Stanford: Hoover Institution, 1979]). Bazelon and Hessen are in basic agreement about the status of the corporation before the law; they just read the results through different political spectacles.

2. See Clive Jenkins and Barrie Sherman, *The Collapse of Work* (London: Eyre Methuen, 1979).

3. See Michael Lessnoff, *Social Contract* (Atlantic Highlands, N.J.: Humanities, 1986), esp. p. 94.

4. John Rawls, *A Theory of Justice* (Cambridge, Mass.: Belknap Press of Harvard University Press, 1971), pp. 264, 563, 523, 525, 527, 529. In chapter 8, "The Sense of Justice," in which Rawls considers moral development as progressing from a morality of authority to one of association and then one of principles, he endorses the latter's "independence from the accidental contingencies of our world" as an expression of Kantian

285

maturity, but understands this to mean not indifference to one's situation but the basis for both establishing and expanding just institutions "for the good of the larger community" (*ibid.*, pp. 474–75).

5. See, however, Elizabeth H. Wolgast, *The Grammar of Justice* (Ithaca: Cornell University Press, 1987), and my review forthcoming in *Nous.*

6. For introductory accounts, see Alan Brown, "The Contractarian Conception of Justice," in his *Modern Political Philosophy* (New York: Viking Penguin, 1986), pp. 55–86; Robert Paul Wolff, *Understanding Rawls* (Princeton: Princeton University Press, 1977); and Brian Barry, *The Liberal Theory of Justice* (Oxford: Clarendon, 1973).

7. See Jan Narveson, *The Libertarian Idea* (Philadelphia: Temple University Press, 1989).

8. See Terry Pinkard, *Democratic Liberalism and Social Union* (Philadelphia: Temple University Press, 1987).

9. Michael J. Sandel, *Liberalism and the Limits of Justice* (Cambridge: Cambridge University Press, 1982).

10. See Charles Beitz, *Political Theory and International Relations* (Princeton: Princeton University Press, 1979); Steven Luper-Foy, ed., *Problems of International Justice* (Boulder: Westview, 1988); *Ethics* 98 (July 1988): Symposium on Duties beyond Borders.

11. See Pinkard, *Democratic Liberalism*, ch. 3: "Civil Obligation and Social Union."

12. Elizabeth Wolgast approaches the interests of a subgroup (namely, women offended by pornography) in a similar way (Grammar of Justice, ch. 5). But she argues only for a right to be heard and leaves it up to "the rest of the community" to decide the matter. This implies the existence in a community of privileged policy makers. I prefer to think of the community as a collection of groups (and individuals) each of which has interests that persist whether or not they are effectively acknowledged by others.

13. The issue of constraints on a representative has been much debated over the years. See *ibid.*, ch. 4: "Sending Someone Else."

14. By way of qualification, I do not reject out of hand the idea, well articulated by Peter F. Drucker, that managers are also workers. See his *Management: Tasks, Responsibilities, Practices* (New York: Harper & Row, 1973), pp. 4, 32–33, 47–48, and *passim.*

15. Onora O'Neill, *Faces of Hunger* (London: Allen & Unwin, 1986), p. 127. The objective of action-oriented reasoning is to bring about a convergence of "uplifted" politics and applied ethics by both acknowledging and expanding people's "present categories and boundaries" (*ibid.*, p. 45). See also *ibid.*, ch. 3, regarding "standards for practical reasoning."

16. Recent works that contribute in various ways to an elucidation of this issue, but which I was unable to consider in this book, include Marcus R. Raskin, *The Common Good: Its Politics, Policies and Philosophy* (New York: Routledge & Kegan Paul, 1986); Larry May, *The Morality of Groups* (Notre Dame: University of Notre Dame Press, 1988); and Jon Elster, *The Cement of Society* (New York: Cambridge University Press, 1989).

CHAPTER 1

1. This issue of comparative economic advantage is thoughtfully addressed by Bernard Gendron in *Technology and the Human Condition* (New York: St. Martin's, 1977), ch. 12.

2. John Rawls, *A Theory of Justice* (Cambridge, Mass.: Belknap Press of Harvard University Press, 1971), pp. 378–79.

3. Charles Beitz, *Political Theory and International Relations* (Princeton: Princeton University Press, 1979).

4. Julius Stone, "Approaches to the Notion of International Justice," in *The Future of the International Legal Order*, ed. Richard A. Falk and Cyril E. Black (Princeton: Princeton University Press, 1969), quoted in Moorhead White, "Reflections on Injustice and International Politics," in *Ethics and International Relations*, ed. Anthony Ellis (Manchester: Manchester University Press, 1986), pp. 213–21.

5. This definition of *community* is intended to apply to corporations Robert Dahl's Principle of Affected Interests: "Everyone who is affected by the decisions of a government should have the right to participate in that government" (quoted by Kirkpatrick Sale, *Human Scale* [New York: Coward, McCann and Geoghegan, 1980], p. 377). I am grateful to Caroline Whitbeck for having steered me away from a more abstract definition.

6. Gus Edgren, "Employment Adjustment to Trade under Conditions of Stagnating Growth," in *Employment Outlook and Insights*, ed. D. H. Freedman (Geneva: International Labour Organisation, 1979), p. 7.

7. Auto industry data are from *Automotive News, 1988 Market Data Book Issue*, pp. 6, 23, and 32; and *The Value Line Investment Survey*, 30 Dec. 1988, pp. 101–13.

8. Barry Bluestone and Bennett Harrison, *The Deindustrialization of America* (New York: Basic Books, 1982), p. 143.

9. *Ibid.*, pp. 145–47.

10. "The Hollow Corporation," *BW*, 3 March 1986, p. 58.

11. *Ibid.* Regarding semiconductors see "Is It Too Late to Save the U.S. Semiconductor Industry?" *BW*, 18 Aug. 1986, pp. 62–67; Thomas G. Donlan, "Can This Be Silicon Valley?" *Barron's*, 30 March 1987, pp. 8ff.

12. "The Hollow Corporation," p. 62. See also Stephen S. Cohen and John Zysman, *Manufacturing Matters: The Myth of the Post-Industrial Economy* (New York: Basic Books, 1987).

13. See the paternalistic rationale for secrecy in *General Motors Corp. (GMC Truck & Coach Division)*, 191 N.L.R.B. 951, 952 (1971). Included in the Omnibus Trade and Competitiveness Act of 1987 is a requirement that employers give employees sixty-day notice of any planned closing or large-scale layoffs.

14. See *BW*, 15 May 1989, pp. 45–46, 3 March 1986, p. 72.

15. *BW*, 16 June 1986, p. 101.

16. See Edmund F. Byrne, "The Laborsaving Device: Evidence of Responsibility?" in *Philosophy and Technology* IV, ed. Paul T. Durbin (Dordrecht: Reidel, 1988), pp. 63–85.

17. I owe much of this information to William C. Baker. For dollars-and-cents details, see Julia Flynn Siler, " 'Big Steel' Bets the Future on the Indiana Mills," *NYT*, 25 Dec. 1988, p. F5.

18. *IS*, July–Dec. 1986, *passim*.

19. *Ibid.*, 5–8 July 1987; "The Quiet Coup at Alcoa," *BW*, 27 June 1988, p. 61. The traditional employment-at-will doctrine (a firing may be for any reason or for no reason) that benefited Cummins is now subject to an exception for breach of contract. See *Romack v. Public Service Co. of Indiana*, Supreme Court of Indiana No. 22S04-8708-CV-765 (1987), upholding in part *Romack v. Public Service Co. of Indiana*, 499 N.E.2d 768 (Ind.App. 4 Dist. 1986).

20. *IS*, 26 March, 15 April, and 13 June 1988.

21. *First English Evangelical Lutheran Church of Glendale (Calif.) v. County of Los Angeles*, 107 S.Ct. 2378 (1987). See "Court Tilts Scales towards Property Owners, *NLJ*, 22 June 1987, pp. 5ff. See also Noel Peirce, "Placing Constraints on Property Rights," *IS*, 21 June 1987, p. F7.

22. The Van Nuys story is dramatically recounted in Eric Mann, *Taking on General Motors: A Case Study of the* UAW *Campaign to Keep GM Van Nuys Open* (Los Angeles: University of California Center for Labor Research and Education, Institute of Industrial Relations, 1987). The others, in Joseph B. White, "Factory Towns Start to Fight Back Angrily When Firms Pull Out," *WSJ*, 8 March 1988; "Digesting AMC: So Far, So Good," *BW*, 22 Feb. 1988. For Chrysler chairman Lee Iaccoca's compensation, see *BW*, 1 May 1989, p. 53. Not surprisingly, Chrysler employees in other plants resent the "special treatment" shown to Kenosha workers. See "Chrysler Contract Pits Plant against Plant," *News & Letters*, June 1988, p. 3.

23. *IS*, 14 Feb. 1989, p. 1.

24. Tim Smart et al., "More States Are Telling Raiders: Not Here, You Don't," *BW*, 13 Feb. 1989, p. 28.

25. See Philip A. Miscimarra, *The* NLRB *and Managerial Discretion: Plant Closings, Relocation, Subcontracting, and Automation*, Labor Relations and Public Policy Series No. 24 (Philadelphia: Wharton School, University of Pennsylvania, 1983).

26. See James B. Atleson, *Values and Assumptions in American Labor Law* (Amherst: University of Massachusetts Press, 1983).

27. Martin Tolchin and Susan Tolchin, *Buying into America: How Foreign Money Is Changing the Face of Our Nation* (New York: New York Times Books, 1988).

28. Bill Koenig, "Culture Clash: Many Have Second Thoughts about Luring Foreign Firms," *IS*, 12 July 1988, sec. C; "Why Mitsubishi Is Right at Home in Illinois," *BW*, 30 May 1988, p. 45; Siler, " 'Big Steel.' " A unitary tax (now in force in only three states) is one based on the global rather than the state income of a transnational corporation.

29. See, for example, Leslie Wayne, "The Coming Foreign Raiders," *NYT*, 27 Nov. 1987; "Will the Auto Glut Choke Detroit?" *BW*, 7 March 1988, pp. 54–56; "Japan's Clout in the U.S.," *BW*, 11 July 1988, pp. 64–75.

30. "U.S. Exporters That Aren't American," *BW*, 29 Feb. 1988, pp. 70–71.

31. For background analysis see Vine Deloria, Jr., *Behind the Trail of Broken Treaties: An Indian Declaration of Independence* (Austin: University of Texas Press, 1985); Vine Deloria, Jr., and Clifford M. Lytle, *The Nations Within: The Past and Future of American Indian Sovereignty* (New York: Pantheon, 1984); Ward Churchill, ed., *Marxism and Native Americans* (Boston: South End Press, 1984).

32. See Onora O'Neill's argument that the cultural values (*Sittlichkeit*) of one society cannot be transferred elsewhere without translation ("Ethical Reasoning and Ideological Pluralism," *Ethics* 98 [July 1988]: 705–22). For the Hegelian background of her terminology, see William Maker, ed., *Hegel on Economics and Freedom* (Macon, Ga.: Mercer University Press, 1987), esp. Shaun Gallagher, "Interdependence and Freedom in Hegel's Economics," pp. 159–81.

33. David Hume, "Of the Original Social Contract," in *Social Contract*, ed. Ernest Barker (New York: Oxford University Press, 1960), p. 151; John Locke, "An Essay concerning the True Origin, Extent and End of Civil Government," *ibid.*, pp. 103–15; Jean-Jacques Rousseau, "The Social Contract," *ibid.*, pp. 214, 216.

34. Rawls, *Theory of Justice*, p. 197.

35. Alan Riding, *Distant Neighbors: A Portrait of the Mexicans* (1984; rpt. New York: Vintage, 1986), pp. 32–33, 51–52, 262, 420–21; Linda Schele and Mary Ellen Miller, *The Blood of Kings: Dynasty and Ritual in Maya Art* (New York: Braziller, 1986). Special thanks to Sandy Hall, resident of Palenque.

36. The situation here described is based on numerous on-site interviews and extensive reading. See, for example, *Nova Scotia Sun* (Antigonish), 28 March and 20 June 1973; *Chronicle-Herald* (Halifax), 3, 7, 11, 19, and 25 April 1973. Especially helpful was research done by a courageous group of professors at St. Francis Xavier University, Antigonish, who referred to themselves collectively as SARA: Strait Advanced Research Association. The quotation is from David Bentley, *ibid.*, 7 April 1973.

37. Noam Chomsky and Edward S. Herman, *The Washington Connection and Third World Fascism* (Boston: South End, 1979), pp. 129–204. See also pp. 205–17.

38. Armand Mattelart, *Transnationals and the Third World: The Struggle for Culture*, tr. D. Buxton (South Hadley, Mass.: Bergin & Garvey, 1983), pp. 107–8.

39. Maria Shao, "Why Taiwan's Doors Should Swing Open," *BW*, 3 Aug. 1987, p. 41; Douglas R. Sears, "Taiwan's Export Boom to U.S. Owes Much to American Firms," *WJ*, 27 May 1987, pp. 1, 12; "America's New-Wave Chip Firms," *ibid.*, p. 30; "Taiwan's Wealth Crisis: Its \$53 Billion Cash Hoard Is Economic Poison," *BW*, 13 April 1987, pp. 46–47.

40. Mattelart, *Transnationals*, p. 106; Richard J. Barnet, *The Lean Years: Politics in the Age of Scarcity* (New York: Simon & Schuster, 1980), p. 249.

41. See Michael Novak, "Two Views on Helping Latin American Poor," *IS*, 14 June 1987, p. 10; see also David Collier, *Squatters and Oligarchs: Authoritarian Rule and Policy Change in Peru* (Baltimore: Johns Hopkins University Press, 1976); and Alejandro Portes and John Walton, *Labor, Class, and the International System* (New York: Academic, 1981), pp. 79–97.

42. Obiora F. Ike, *Value, Meaning and Social Structure of Human Work* (New York: Peter Lang, 1986), pp. 148–55, 160–62, 165–66, 170–71, 176, 182–86, 337.

43. Mattelart, *Transnationals*, p. 111; Riding, *Distant Neighbors*, pp. 417–20; "The Magnet of Growth in Mexico's North," *BW*, 6 June 1988, pp. 48–50; "Mexico Looks Better and Better to Japan," *BW*, 8 June 1987, p. 58. See also NACLA, "Hit and Run: U.S. Runaway Shops on the Mexican Border," *Latin America and Empire Report* 9 (July–Aug. 1975): 2–30.

44. Pablo Neruda, "The United Fruit Company," tr. Ben Belitt, in *How the Other Third Lives*, ed. Margaret B. White and Robert N. Quigley (Maryknoll, N.Y.: Orbis Books, 1977), pp. 33–34. (Date assigned to poem is possible, but it may have been written earlier.)

45. "The End of Corporate Loyalty?" *BW*, 4 Aug. 1986, pp. 42–49. See also David Pauly, "Retailing's Hard Times," *Newsweek*, 8 Aug. 1988, pp. 46–47.

46. See John Gibbons, *Tenure and Toil* (Philadelphia: Lippincott, 1888), pp. 148–49, 183–91; Stanley Buder, *Pullman: An Experiment in Industrial Order and Community Planning, 1830–1930* (New York: Oxford University Press, 1967); Alfred Winslow Jones, *Life, Liberty, and Property* (New York: Lippincott, 1941); Barbara Dinham and Colin Hines, *Agribusiness in Africa* (Trenton, N.J.: Africa World, 1984).

47. Judith Lichtenberg, one of the few philosophers to deal with plant closings as a moral issue, arrives at a similar conclusion but is more supportive of workers at point-of-departure plants by extending Locke's labor theory of property to them and deciding that a utilitarian calculus gives them the nod in the long run. See her "On Alternatives to Industrial Flight: The Moral Issues," in *Moral Rights in the Workplace*, ed. Gertrude Ezorsky (Albany: State University of New York Press, 1987), pp. 200–208. Henry Shue's "Transnational Transgressions," in *Just Business*, ed. Tom Regan (New York: Random House, 1984), is more favorable to Third World interests but falters by acknowledging that "[b]y 'living' in many places at the same time, [a transnational corporation] 'lives' nowhere in particular" (p. 272).

48. Not all stockholders are at all times treated with respect. For a case study to the contrary, see Benjamin J. Stein, "The Art of the Dubious Deal: How Donald Trump Snookered His Own Shareholders," *Barron's*, 9 Jan. 1989, pp. 6–7, 29.

49. At least in the short run, the People's Republic of China has been able to make both Volkswagen AG and Chrysler Corporation sensitive to such concerns—to the amazement of Western bottom-liners. See Julia Leung, "Socialism Burdens a Chinese Car Venture: Welfare Tasks Absorb 80% of Giant Auto Plant's Work Force," *WSJ*, 13 April 1989, p. A14.

CHAPTER 2

1. See Linda Schele and Mary Ellen Miller, *The Blood of Kings: Dynasty and Ritual in Maya Art* (New York: Braziller, 1986), ch. 5. See also ch. 4.

2. *Ibid.*, ch. 6; Alan Riding, *Distant Neighbors: A Portrait of the Mexicans* (1984; rpt. New York: Vintage, 1986), chs. 2, 10, 14.

3. Aristotle, *Politics*, Bk. I, especially 1252b, 1253b–1255b, 1256b, 1259b–1260b.

4. Such considerations, which are well developed in contract and tort law, are, according to Terry Pinkard, legitimate expressions of Rawls's "social union." See his *Democratic Liberalism and Social Union* (Philadelphia: Temple University Press, 1987), pp. 106–21.

5. David Brion Davis, *Slavery and Human Progress* (New York: Oxford University Press, 1984), p. xvii.

6. *Ibid.*, pp. 276, 278, 309. For emancipation dates, see pp. 116, 224, 274, 280–81, 284–85, 288–89, 299, 319.

7. See, for example, David Lyons, "Nature and Soundness of the Contract and Coherence Argument," in *Reading Rawls*, ed. Norman Daniels (Oxford: B. Blackwell, 1975), pp. 141–67, esp. 148–49, cited approvingly by J. J. C. Smart, "Distributive Justice and Utilitarianism," in *Justice and Economic Distribution*, ed. John Arthur and William H. Shaw (Englewood Cliffs, N.J.: Prentice-Hall, 1978), pp. 106–7. Such waffling on the question of slavery is sometimes justified on the grounds that we know too little about history to be able to compare viable alternatives—a fallacious argument from ignorance that would undermine any attempt to evaluate a set of conditions in the actual world. R. M. Hare avoids this fallacy by arguing that the evil of slavery can be shown empirically, on utilitarian grounds ("What Is Wrong with Slavery?" *Philosophy and Public Affairs* 8 [Winter 1979]: 103–21).

8. Robert Nozick, *Anarchy, State, and Utopia* (New York: Basic Books, 1974), pp. 169–72. Nozick is unnecessarily precious about just what his supporting argument proves (p. 169n.) because it is vitiated in its entirety by his assertion that in a free society one can sell oneself into slavery (p. 331), even if one seldom sells one's entire self (p. 283).

9. *Ibid.*, pp. 263–64. The next step would be to argue, as did George Fitzhugh in the nineteenth century, that some people are better off as chattel slaves than they would be as industrial wage slaves. See R. E. Ewin, *Liberty, Community, and Justice* (Totowa, N.J.: Rowman & Littlefield, 1987), pp. 170–80. Nozick does not take this step; but he does blur the distinction between chattel slavery and citizenship under a democratic form of government by arguing that one cannot identify the point at which a progressively liberated slave ceases to be a slave (*Anarchy*, pp. 290–92).

10. Jacques LeGoff, *Time, Work, and Culture in the Middle Ages*, tr. Arthur Goldhammer (Chicago: University of Chicago Press, 1980), p. 84.

11. Karl de Schweinitz, *England's Road to Social Security, 1349 to 1947* (Philadelphia: University of Pennsylvania Press, 1947), p. 6.

12. John Pound, *Poverty and Vagrancy in Tudor England* (Burnt Mill, Eng.: Longman, 1971), pp. 3–38.

13. Kenneth M. Stampp, *The Peculiar Institution: Slavery in the Ante-Bellum South* (New York: Vintage, 1956), pp. 34–42. I thank John Bonsignore for this reference.

14. Barry Jones, *Sleepers, Wake! Technology and the Future of Work* (Melbourne: Oxford University Press, 1982), p. 19.

15. Aristotle, *Politics*, Bk. I, ch. 4, 1253b:35.

16. David F. Noble, *Forces of Production* (New York: Knopf, 1984), p. 76.

17. Norbert Wiener, *The Human Use of Human Beings* (1950; rpt. New York: Avon Discus, 1967), p. 220.

18. The original German edition was published in Switzerland in 1944; the English edition in 1950. Citations are to Johan Huizinga, *Homo Ludens: A Study of the Play Element in Culture* (Boston: Beacon, 1967). More recent philosophical attention to play, especially in Europe, has tended to focus on alternatively objective and subjective concepts. See Richard Detsch, "A Non-Subjective Concept of Play—Gadamer and Heidegger versus Rilke and Nietzsche," *Philosophy Today* 29 (Summer 1985): 156–72; Drew A. Hyland, *The Question of Play* (Lanham, Md.: University Press of America, 1984).

19. Huizinga, *Homo Ludens*, p. 28.

20. *Ibid.*, p. 6.

21. *Ibid.*, pp. 14, 6, 52, 210. Huizinga leaves unresolved and problematic the relationship between seriousness and play. For more recent attempts to clarify this relationship see Leslie Wright, "The Distinction between Play and Intrinsically Worthwhile Activities," *Journal of the Philosophy of Education* 19 (July 1985): 65–72; Randolph Feezell, "Play and the Absurd," *Philosophy Today* 28 (Winter 1984): 319–28; and John Darling, "Is Play Serious?" *Journal of the Philosophy of Education* 17 (1983): 103–10.

22. Huizinga, *Homo Ludens*, pp. 10–12.

23. *Ibid.*, pp. 7, 58, 67.

24. *Ibid.*, pp. 13, 9, 51, 200.

25. Robert Rimmer, in his novel *The Byrdwhistle Option* and in "The Play Ethic," *Free Inquiry* 3 (Winter 1982–83): 11–16, thinks productivity might be improved just by redefining much of our work as play!

26. Huizinga, *Homo Ludens*, p. 64.

27. From Marge Piercy, *To Be of Use* (Garden City, N.Y.: Doubleday, 1973), reprinted in *Circles in the Water: Selected Poems of Marge Piercy* (New York: Knopf, 1982), p. 106.

28. François Rabelais, *Gargantua*, XXIII, XXIV.

29. Johann Fichte, *Sittenlehre*, sec. 20.

30. See Charles Woolfson, *The Labour Theory of Culture: A Reexamination of Engels's Theory of Human Origins* (London: Routledge & Kegan Paul, 1982). Lewis Mumford disagrees. See his *Technics and Human Civilization* (New York: Harcourt, Brace Jovanovich, 1967), esp. pp. 22–26.

31. Arts. 3 and 18 of the constitutional charter of 10 July 1918; see Adriano Tilgher, *Work*, 1st English ed. of *Homo Faber* (1930), tr. Dorothy Canfield Fisher (New York: Arno Press, 1977), chs. 14 and 15.

32. Yves Simon, *Work, Society and Culture*, ed. Vukan Kuic (New York: Fordham University Press, 1971), pp. 111–12.

33. David J. Cherrington, *The Work Ethic: Working Values and Values That Work* (New York: ANACOM, 1980); Lee Smith, "Cracks in the Japanese Work Ethic," *Fortune* 109 (14 May 1984): 162–68; and Susan Field, "Egypt's Worst Enemy May Be Euphoria," *Euromoney* (UK), April 1979, pp. 77–82.

34. Michael Rose, *Reworking the Work Ethic* (London: Batsford Academic, 1985). See also E. Jordan Blakely, *Work Ethic: Pride, or Mental Illness*, ed. M. Sarah Ross (Flint, Mich.: Jordan Blakely, 1985); and Blakely, *Work Ethic: An Analytical View, 1983*, (Madison, Wisc.: Industrial Research Association, 1983).

35. Jacques LeGoff, *Time, Work, and Culture*, pp. 53–58.

36. *Ibid.*, pp. 112–21.

37. See, for example, Thorstein Veblen, *The Theory of the Leisure Class* (1899; rpt. New York: Modern Library, 1934), pp. 22, 535, 83.

38. By utopia I mean a proposed happiness-inducing state of affairs. By happiness I mean at least self-satisfaction if not self-actualization. And by work I mean an activity or status by virtue of which one achieves survival if not self-satisfaction.

39. Nathan D. Grundstein, *The Managerial Kant* (Cleveland: Case Western Reserve University Press, 1981).

40. Michael Maccoby, *The Leader* (New York: Simon & Schuster, 1981), p. 26. For

historical perspective see Carl Bridenbaugh, *The Colonial Craftsman* (1950; rpt. Chicago: University of Chicago Phoenix, 1961).

41. Cherrington, *Work Ethic*, p. 106.

42. This distinction between a communitarian and an authoritarian tradition with regard to work parallels in some respects Ferdinand Tönnies's distinction between two types of social organization, *Gemeinschaft* (usually translated as community) and *Gesellschaft* (usually translated as society). See Tönnies, *Community and Society* (1887), tr. and ed. Charles P. Loomis (New York: Harper Torchbook, 1963). See also Chapter 11, below.

43. See also the distinctions made by J. P. Day: "Locke on Property," in *Life, Liberty, and Property*, ed. Gordon J. Schochet (Belmont, Calif.: Wadsworth, 1971), p. 123.

44. U.S. Congress, Office of Technology Assessment, *Computerized Manufacturing Automation: Employment, Education, and the Workplace* (Washington, D.C.: U.S. Government Printing Office, 1984).

45. Robert Theobald, "Toward Full Unemployment," in *The World of Work*, ed. Howard F. Didsbury, Jr. (Bethesda, Md.: World Future Society, 1983), p. 54.

46. See Barry Bluestone and Bennett Harrison, *The Deindustrialization of America* (New York: Basic Books, 1982); Ian Benson and John Lloyd, *New Technology and Industrial Change: The Impact of the Scientific-Technical Revolution on Labour and Industry* (London: Kogan Page, 1983); Barry Jones, *Sleepers, Wake! Technology and the Future of Work* (Melbourne: Oxford University Press, 1982).

47. David Macarov, *Work and Welfare: The Unholy Alliance* (London: Sage, 1980).

48. Hannah Arendt, *The Human Condition* (1958; rpt. Garden City, N.Y.: Doubleday Anchor, 1959).

49. Thomas More, *Utopia*, tr. H. V. S. Ogden (New York: Appleton-Century-Crofts, 1949), p. 34.

50. Frank E. Manuel and Fritzie P. Manuel, *Utopian Thought in the Western World* (Cambridge, Mass.: Belknap Press of Harvard University Press, 1979), p. 274.

51. *Ibid.*, p. 372.

52. Adam Ferguson, *An Essay on the History of Civil Society*, pt. 1, secs. 1 and 7, in the ed. by D. Forbes (Edinburgh, 1966), pp. 7, 42, quoted by John Passmore, *The Perfectibility of Man* (New York: Scribner, 1970), p. 48. See also *ibid.*, pp. 297–98.

53. Friedrich Engels, *Socialism Utopian and Scientific* (1880), tr. Edward Aveling (Chicago: Charles H. Kerr, 1908), pp. 51–75; Manuel and Manuel, *Utopian Thought*, pp. 684, 697–716.

54. Manuel and Manuel, *Utopian Thought*, pp. 594, 601, 632, 647 (Saint-Simon); 658, 667, 681 (Fourier); 680, 681, 686, 690 (Owen).

55. Payton E. Richter, ed., *Utopias: Social Ideals and Communal Experiments* (Boston: Holbrook, 1971), pp. 54 and 125 (Ripley and Emerson on Brook Farm), 143 (Charles Nordhoff on Oneida). The organization of work in these communities was as often as not a class-based authoritarianism. See Mark Holloway, *Heavens on Earth: Utopian Communities in America, 1680–1880*, 2d ed. (New York: Dover, 1966), pp. 111–12, 191–92.

56. Manuel and Manuel, *Utopian Thought*, pp. 769, 743, 746.

57. B. F. Skinner, *Walden Two* (1948; rpt. New York: Macmillan, 1976), pp. 45–59, 147–48, 150–51, 159, 160, 165, 203–6, 213.

58. David Dickson, *The Politics of Alternative Technology* (New York: Universe, 1975), pp. 103–4. Why this invalidation of the notion of unemployment is not a way to ignore the chronic poverty of a New Delhi or a Lima-Callao is not specified. A comparable utopia by fiat is proclaimed by Theobald, "Toward Full Unemployment." Such modish projections render quaint the distinctions made by Paul Weiss in his "A Philosophical Definition of Leisure," in *Leisure in America: Blessing or Curse?* ed. James C. Charlesworth (Philadelphia: American Academy of Political and Social Science, 1964), p. 21. See also Bernard Lefkowitz, *Breaktime: Living without Work in a Nine-to-Five World* (Baltimore: Penguin, 1980).

59. See Richard J. Barnet and Ronald E. Muller, *Global Reach: The Power of Multinational Corporations* (New York: Simon & Schuster Touchstone, 1974), p. 171; Derek Llewellyn-Jones, *Human Reproduction and Society* (New York: Pitman, 1974), pp. 377–79.

60. See United Nations Economic and Social Council, *Transnational Corporations: Issues in the Formulation of a Code of Conduct* (New York: United Nations, 1976), p. 27, no. 110.

61. *BW*, 26 March 1984, p. 108. Progress will be redefined in Chapter 10, below.

CHAPTER 3

1. Max Weber, *The Protestant Ethic and the Spirit of Capitalism* (1904–5), tr. Talcott Parsons (1930; rpt. New York: Scribners, 1958). See also James B. Gilbert, *Work without Salvation* (Baltimore: Johns Hopkins University Press, 1977).

2. R. H. Tawney criticized Weber's individualist bias and argued for communitarian values in his *Religion and the Rise of Capitalism* (1926; rpt. New York: Mentor, 1954).

3. Weber, *Protestant Ethic*, p. 53.

4. See, for example, Francis L. K. Hsu, "Filial Piety in Japan and China: Borrowing, Variation and Significance," *Journal of Comparative Family Studies* 2 (Spring 1971): 67–74; J. Elder, "The Gandhian Ethic of Work in India," in *Religious Ferment in Asia*, ed. Robert J. Miller (Lawrence: University of Kansas Press, 1974); and Winston L. King, "A Christian and a Japanese-Buddhist Work-Ethic Compared," *Religion* 11 (July 1981): 207–26. For a more general view of the culture-specific role of a work ethic, see Erik von Kuehnelt-Leddihn, "La morale du travail: Un problème mondial," *Cahiers de Sociologie Economique* 2 (Dec. 1971): 215–27.

5. Weber, *Protestant Ethic*, pp. 55, 57–59, see also pp. 251, 159, 169, 139, 175, 179. See also Robert Cummings Neville, *The Puritan Smile* (Albany: State University of New York Press, 1987).

6. Karl de Schweinitz, *England's Road to Social Security, 1349 to 1947* (Philadelphia: University of Pennsylvania Press, 1947), chs. 1–3; Weber, *Protestant Ethic*, pp. 134, 138–48; see also p. 235.

7. Christopher Hill, *Society and Puritanism in Pre-Revolutionary England*, 2d ed. (New York: Schocken, 1967), p. 127.

8. Hill, *Society and Puritanism*, pp. 127–37.

9. Paschal Larkin, *Property in the Eighteenth Century with Special Reference to England and Locke* (1930; rpt. New York: Howard Fertig, 1969), pp. 72, 54ff.; C. B. Macpherson, *The Political Theory of Possessive Individualism, Hobbes to Locke* (Oxford: Clarendon Press, 1972), pp. 194–217; Maurice Cranston, *John Locke: A Biography* (New York: Macmillan, 1957), pp. 424–27. Bob Frye suggested these references.

10. David Hume, *Essays*, New Universal Library, 1905), pt. 2, no. 8, "Taxes," p. 247; cf. Larkin, *Property in the Eighteenth Century*, pp. 98–99. Hume's severity with regard to the domestic poor is counterbalanced to some extent by his openness to the possibility that poor countries might eventually catch up with rich countries, a view Adam Smith both shared and advanced. See W. W. Rostow, "The Rich Country–Poor Country Problem," in *Rich Countries and Poor Countries* (Boulder: Westview, 1987), pp. 49–78.

11. Results of a study by William O'Hare published in *Population Today*, as reported in *BW*, 21 March 1988, p. 16. See also Alan L. Otten, "Poor Will Find Many Jobs Will Be Out of Reach as Labor Market Shrinks, Demands for Skills Rise," *WSJ*, 27 May 1987, p. 56.

12. Reprinted in John J. McDermott, ed., *A Cultural Introduction to Philosophy* (New York: Knopf, 1985), pp. 41–42 from "The Rule of St. Benedict" (tr. E. F. Henderson, *Select Historical Documents of the Middle Ages* [London: George Bell & Sons, 1896]).

13. Jacques Le Goff, *Time, Work, and Culture in the Middle Ages*, tr. Arthur Goldhammer (Chicago: University of Chicago Press, 1980), p. 84.

14. Thomas Aquinas, *Summa Theologica* II–II, q. 66, a. 7.

15. Remi Breyer, *Catechisme des riches*, as reviewed by Larkin, *Property in the Eighteenth Century*, pp. 184–85.

16. *Ibid.*, pp. 185, 206, 192, 223–24.

17. Le Goff, *Time, Work, and Culture*, p. 79.

18. Andrew Ure, *The Philosophy of Manufactures or an Exposition of the Scientific, Moral and Commercial Economy of the Factory System of Great Britain* (London: C. Knight, 1835), p. 423. See also Richard Thain's description of the "new Calvinists" in *Think Twice Before You Take That Job* (New York: Dow-Jones-Irwin, 1986).

19. Frank E. Manuel and Fritzie P. Manuel, *Utopian Thought in the Western World* (Cambridge, Mass.: Belknap Press of Harvard University Press, 1979), p. 771; and André Gorz, "The Tyranny of the Factory: Today and Tomorrow," in *The Division of Labor*, ed. Gorz (Sussex, Eng.: Harvester, 1976), p. 58.

20. Herbert Marcuse, *One-Dimensional Man* (Boston: Beacon, 1964), pp. 35–37. See also pp. 445, 59, 231–32, 235. See below, note 59.

21. See David Lane and Felicity O'Dell, *The Soviet Industrial Worker: Social Class, Education and Control* (Oxford: Martin Robinson, 1978). For a renowned example of how difficult it could be to harmonize the democratic ideology with state-mandated productivity, see Miklòs Haraszti, *A Worker in a Worker's State*, tr. Michael Wright (New York: Universe Books, 1978), esp. pp. 159–75, and Michael Burawoy, *The Politics of Production* (London: Verso, 1985), ch. 4.

22. See Andrew Pollack, "High-Tech Entrepreneurs: New Doubt on a U.S. Ideal," *NYT*, 14 June 1988, p. 1+.

23. Tracy Kidder, *The Soul of a New Machine* (Boston: Little, Brown, 1981). For a

less "high-tech" interpretation, see D. M. Dooling, ed., *A Way of Working* (Garden City, N.Y.: Doubleday Anchor, 1979).

24. Leo Marx, *The Machine in the Garden* (Oxford: Oxford University Press, 1964).

25. E.g., E. F. Schumacher, in *Small Is Beautiful: Economics as if People Mattered* (New York: Harper & Row, 1975) and *Good Work* (New York: Harper & Row, 1979).

26. David J. Cherrington, *The Work Ethic: Working Values and Values That Work* (New York: AMACOM, 1980), pp. 43, 49–51, 62.

27. Claude Lévi-Strauss, "The Sorcerer and His Magic," in *Magic, Witchcraft, and Curing*, ed. John Middleton (Garden City, N.Y.: Natural History, 1967), pp. 31–35, reprinted from Lévi-Strauss, *Structural Anthropology* (New York: Basic Books, 1963). See also Ronald P. Rohner and Evelyn C. Rohner, *The Kwakiutl Indians of British Columbia* (New York: Holt, Rinehart and Winston, 1970).

28. Le Goff, *Time, Work, and Culture*, p. 115.

29. Mircea Eliade, *The Forge and the Crucible*, tr. Stephen Corrin (London: Rider & Co., 1962).

30. Le Goff, *Time, Work, and Culture*, pp. 77–79, 82–83. See also Louis I. Dublin and Alfred J. Lotka, *The Money Value of a Man* (New York: Ronald Press, 1946).

31. *The Autobiography of Benvenuto Cellini*, tr. John A. Symonds (Garden City, N.Y.: Garden City Publishing, 1927), p. 30.

32. Jean-Jacques Rousseau, *Emile*, tr. Allan Bloom (New York: Basic Books, 1979), pp. 195–201.

33. *Ibid.*, pp. 201–3.

34. Karl Marx, *Capital*, vol. I, intro. Ernest Mandel, tr. Ben Fowkes (New York: Vintage, 1977), ch. 7, pp. 283–84; ch. 14, pp. 479–84; ch. 15, pp. 492ff., App. II, pp. 1029–31; ch. 15, pp. 545–50, 557–58, 617.

35. Jean-Paul Sartre, *Critique of Dialectical Reason* (1960), ed. Jonathan Ree, tr. Alan Sheridan-Smith (London: Verso Books, 1976), p. 52.

36. *Ibid.*, pp. 95, 445–62. Jan Douwe van der Ploeg has shown, analogously, that farmers subject to economic and technological innovation may still demonstrate craftsmanship ("Patterns of Farming Logic, Structuration of Labour and Impact of Externalization: Changing Dairy Farming in Northern Italy," *Sociologia Ruralis* 25, no. 1 [1985]: 5–25).

37. Sartre, *Critique*, pp. 110, 238–49; see also p. 153. For the equivalent development in the United States see David Montgomery, *The Fall of the House of Labor* (Albany: State University of New York Press, 1987).

38. II Baruch 74:1 in *The Apocrypha and Pseudepigrapha of the Old Testament in English*, 2 vols., ed. Robert H. Charles (Oxford: Clarendon, 1913), 2:518.

39. Manuel and Manuel, *Utopian Thought*, pp. 73–74.

40. *Ibid.*, p. 36.

41. *Ibid.*, pp. 67–73, 83–84.

42. Aristotle, *Metaphysics*, tr. W. D. Ross, in *Introduction to Aristotle*, ed. Richard McKeon (New York: Modern Library, 1947), Bk. I, ch. 1.

43. Sir Alfred Zimmern, *The Greek Commonwealth*, 5th ed. (London: Oxford University Press, 1961), pp. 272–73.

44. Xenophon, *Oeconomicus*, tr. Carnes Lord, IV, 2, 3, in Leo Strauss, *Xenophon's Socratic Discourse* (Ithaca: Cornell University Press, 1970); and *Plutarch's Lives* (New

York: Modern Library, 1932), p. 183; as cited by Melvin Kranzberg and Joseph Gies, *By the Sweat of Thy Brow* (New York: Putnam's Capricorn, 1975), pp. 27, 28.

45. Josef Pieper, *Leisure the Basis of Culture* (1947), tr. Alexander Dru (New York: Random House, 1963), pp. 72–74.

46. Thorstein Veblen, *The Theory of the Leisure Class* (1899; rpt. New York: Modern Library, 1934), p. 5.

47. *Ibid.*, pp. 22–24, 28. Two years earlier Herbert Spencer had published a somewhat more balanced account along similar lines in *The Principles of Ethics* (New York: D. Appleton, 1897), vol. 1, pt. 2, ch. 11: "Industry," pp. 422–34.

48. Veblen, *Theory of the Leisure Class*, p. 54.

49. *Ibid.*, pp. 81, 85.

50. *Ibid.*, pp. 342, 361, 359–60. See also p. 244.

51. "Japan's Secret Economic Weapon: Exploited Women," *BW*, 4 March 1985, pp. 54–55.

52. Bertrand Russell, "In Praise of Idleness," in *In Praise of Idleness and Other Essays* (London: Unwin, 1984).

53. Dennis Gabor, *Inventing the Future* (London: Penguin, 1964), pp. 19–20.

54. Frijthof Bergmann, Lecture, South Bend, Ind., 22 Oct. 1982. See his *On Being Free* (South Bend: University of Notre Dame Press, 1979). See also Gabriel Vahanian, "Utopia as Ethic of Leisure," *Humanitas* 8 (Nov. 1972): 347–65.

55. Georges Friedmann, *The Anatomy of Work* (1961), tr. Wyatt Rawson (New York: Free Press of Glencoe, 1964), pp. 119, 155.

56. Kranzberg and Gies, *By the Sweat of Thy Brow*, p. 218.

57. Robert Boguslaw, *The New Utopians* (Englewood Cliffs, N.J.: Prentice-Hall, 1965), esp. pp. 2–4, 114, 126, 202. Comparable concerns have been expressed by Martin Buber, André Gorz, and Gordon Rattray Taylor. See Taylor, *Rethink* (Baltimore: Penguin Pelican, 1974), pp. 324 and 327. David Dickson goes beyond Boguslaw to say that even lifestyle is subject to design (*The Politics of Alternative Technology* [New York: Universe Books, 1974], p. 100). For a more skeptical interpretation of Boguslaw's "stern warning," see Langdon Winner, *Autonomous Technology* (Cambridge, Mass.: MIT Press, 1977), p. 143.

58. Dickson, *Politics of Alternative Technology*, pp. 55–56, and, in general, 41–62. See also Bernard Gendron, *Technology and the Human Condition* (New York: St. Martin's, 1977). Taylor's methodology is considered in Ch. 5, below.

59. See above, n. 20. Marcuse bases his optimism on a passage from Marx's *Grundrisse der Kritik der politischen Oekonomie* in which Marx declares that labor time will eventually cease to be the measure of wealth. Adam Schaff, however, thinks Marx's early dream of an "end of labor" was a "youthful folly" that he categorically rejected in *Capital*. According to Schaff, "utopian prophecies" about what automation might accomplish "do not take us a single step further in the organization of our life today" (*Marxism and the Human Individual*, tr. Olgierd Wojtasiewicz, ed. Robert S. Cohen [New York: McGraw-Hill, 1970], pp. 124–26, 134–35).

60. Sigmund Freud, *The Future of an Illusion*, tr. W. D. Robson-Scott (1928; rpt. Garden City, N.Y.: Doubleday Anchor, 1955), pp. 5–6, 15.

61. Sigmund Freud, *Civilization and Its Discontents* (1930), tr. James Strachey (New

York: Norton, 1962), p. 2 (note). See Friedmann, *Anatomy of Work*, p. 126; Philip Rieff, *Freud: The Mind of the Moralist*, 3d ed. (Chicago: University of Chicago Press, 1979), p. 245.

62. Erich Fromm, *The Sane Society* (New York: Rinehart, 1955), pp. 288–89; quoted by Friedmann, *Anatomy of Work*, pp. 154–55.

63. E. F. Schumacher, "Social and Economic Problems Calling for the Development of Intermediate Technology" (mimeograph, n.d.), quoted by Dickson, *Politics of Alternative Technology*, p. 153.

64. Murray Bookchin, *Post-Scarcity Anarchism* (Berkeley: University of California Press, 1971), p. 132. Such nostalgia for craftsmanship Thorstein Veblen considered mere leisure class preference for "honorific crudeness" that would set their goods apart from mass-produced items available to all (*Theory of the Leisure Class*, pp. 158–60, 162).

CHAPTER 4

1. David Braybrooke, "Work: A Cultural Ideal Ever More in Jeopardy," in *Midwest Studies in Philosophy* VII, ed. Peter A. French et al. (Minneapolis: University of Minnesota Press, 1982), pp. 321–41.

2. Frances Fox Piven and Richard A. Cloward elucidate the relationship between welfare policy and work in *Regulating the Poor: The Functions of Public Welfare* (New York: Vintage, 1971). For historical background see Karl de Schweinitz, *England's Road to Social Security, 1349 to 1947* (Philadelphia: University of Pennsylvania Press, 1947); Martha J. Soltow and Susan Gravelle, *Worker Benefits: Industrial Welfare in America, 1900–1935* (Metuchen, N.J.: Scarecrow, 1983). Two philosophers have addressed the question of welfare rights in some detail: Nicholas Rescher looks for criteria in *Welfare Rights: The Social Issues in Philosophical Perspective* (Pittsburgh: University of Pittsburgh Press, 1972); and Carl Wellman proceeds more analytically in *Welfare Rights* (Totowa, N.J.: Rowman & Littlefield, 1982). Of only marginal interest in these studies is the burgeoning issue of what to do should work no longer be a generally attainable path to welfare.

3. Nozick includes in his entitlement theory a requirement that unjust acquisitions be rectified; but in lieu of attempting to establish his theory together with the rectification principle, he merely appeals to a Lockean proviso that precludes monopolizing resources and then turns his attention to a critique of Rawls. See *Anarchy, State, and Utopia* (New York: Basic Books, 1974), ch. 7. See also Alan Brown, *Modern Political Philosophy: Theories of the Just Society* (New York: Viking Penguin, 1986), ch. 4.

4. See *Unemployment Insurance: Global Evidence of Its Effects on Unemployment* (Vancouver: Fraser Institute, 1978).

5. See J. Douglas Brown, *An American Philosophy of Social Security* (Princeton: Princeton University Press, 1972), p. 55.

6. See, for example, "Benefits to Unemployed Persons," *Labor Lawyer*, 4 (Summer 1988): 644–68; Rosa W. King, "The Worsening Ills of Workers' Comp," *BW*, 12 Oct. 1987, p. 46; Ken Hyder, "Jobless Facing 'Try Harder' Rule," *Observer* (London), 16 July 1989, p. 9. UI is short for unemployment insurance.

7. Brown, *American Philosophy of Social Security*, pp. 82–83.

8. *Ibid.*, p. 84.

9. *Ibid.*, p. 102–4.

10. Aron Bernstein, "Benefits Are Getting More Flexible—But Caveat Emptor," *BW*, 8 Sept. 1986, pp. 64, 66; E. Ehrlich et al., "Putting the Traditional Pension Out to Pasture," *BW*, 5 May 1986, pp. 102–3; Susan B. Garland, "The Crisis in Health Benefits," *BW*, 15 June 1987, p. 36.

11. Hay/Huggins Co. survey, reported in *BW*, 8 Aug. 1988, p. 18.

12. "A Pile of Cash That Doesn't Stack Up to a Raise," *BW*, 23 Dec. 1985, p. 33.

13. "Pensions after 2000: A Granny Crisis Is Coming," *Economist* 19 (May 1984): 59–60, 62. See also Jean-Jacques Rosa, ed., *The World Crisis in Social Security* (Paris: Fondation nationale d'économie politique, and San Francisco: Institute for Contemporary Studies, 1982).

14. See "Why Late Retirement Is Getting a Corporate Blessing," *BW*, 16 Jan. 1984, pp. 69, 72.

15. See "Can Washington Keep Its Hands Off Social Security's Bulging Coffers?" *BW*, 21 March 1988, p. 61; Alan S. Blinder, "Congress Should Keep Its Hands Off This Nest Egg," *BW*, 4 July 1988, p. 20; Robert Kuttner, "What Makes the Debate over Social Security so Curious," *BW*, 8 Aug. 1988, p. 14.

16. See Paul Magnusson, "We Are Plundering the Social Security Till," *BW*, 18 July 1988, p. 92.

17. See Jane Bryant Quinn, "Your Precarious Pension," *Newsweek*, 21 May 1984, p. 74; "Pension Plans Get More Flexible," *BW*, 8 Nov. 1982, p. 87; "Inflation Is Wrecking the Private Pension System," *BW*, 12 May 1980, pp. 92–99; "Rescuing 2,000 Pension Plans," *BW*, 28 April 1980, pp. 60, 66; Alvin D. Lurie, "The Once and Future Pension Reform," *BW*, 21 April 1980, p. 25; "The Vital Pension Funds That ERISA May Kill," *BW*, 26 Nov. 1977, p. 124.

18. See, however, observations of Cyril F. Brickfield, executive director of AARP, in *Modern Maturity*, Oct.–Nov. 1985, p. 19.

19. Gunnar Myrdal, *Beyond the Welfare State* (New Haven: Yale University Press, 1960).

20. Susan Katz Hoffman, "Litigation over Multiemployer Pension Plans," *NLJ*, 24 Sept. 1984, pp. 20–21.

21. "The Pension Cookie Jar," NBC-TV, Aug. 1988.

22. "Why More Companies Are Terminating Their Pension Plans," *BW*, 25 June 1984, p. 21.

23. Alicia M. Kershaw, "COBRA Puts New Bite into Pension Terminations," *NLJ*, 5 May 1986, pp. 15, 18.

24. John Hoerr, "Saving the Agency That Saves Workers' Pensions," in *BW*, 2 Nov. 1987, p. 118.

25. Otis Bowen, U.S. secretary of health and human services, speaking to Americans for Generational Equity, C-Span II, 29 July 1988.

26. See Oscar W. Cooley, *Paying Men Not to Work* (Caldwell, Ida.: Caxton, 1964).

27. Illustrative of the tendency among philosophers to assume (or even rationalize) the status quo with regard to employment are two anthologies: Marshall Cohen, Thomas

Nagel, and Thomas Scanlon, eds., *Equality and Preferential Treatment* (Princeton: Princeton University Press, 1976); and Barry Gross, ed., *Reverse Discrimination* (Buffalo, N.Y.: Prometheus, 1977). More balanced than works by Nicholas Capaldi and Alan H. Goldman on this subject is Robert K. Fullinwider, *The Reverse Discrimination Controversy: A Moral and Legal Analysis* (Totowa, N.J.: Rowman & Littlefield, 1980). The issue of immigration rights is addressed in *The Border That Joins: Mexican Migrants and U.S. Responsibility*, ed. Peter G. Brown and Henry Shue (Totowa, N.J.: Rowman & Allanheld, 1982). Serious philosophical consideration of employment rights should take into account the data studied in Jonathan H. Turner and Charles E. Starnes, *Inequality: Privilege and Poverty in America* (Santa Monica, Calif.: Goodyear, 1976), the reflections on equality in *The Concept of Equality*, ed. William T. Blackstone (Minneapolis: Burgess, 1969), the meticulous analysis by Douglas Rae et al., *Equalities* (Cambridge, Mass.: Harvard University Press, 1981), and the legal survey by Kent Greenawalt, *Discrimination and Reverse Discrimination* (New York: Knopf/Borzoi, 1983).

28. Lawrence C. Becker, "The Obligation to Work," *Ethics* 91 (Oct. 1980): 325–49; James W. Nickel, "Is There a Human Right to Employment?" *Philosophical Forum* 10 (Winter–Summer 1978–79): 149–70.

29. Patricia Werhane, *Persons, Rights and Corporations* (Englewood Cliffs, N.J.: Prentice-Hall, 1985); Thomas Donaldson, *Corporations and Morality* (Englewood Cliffs, N.J.: Prentice-Hall, 1982). See also Milton Snoeyenbos, Robert Almeder, and James Humber, eds., *Business Ethics* (New York: Prometheus, 1983).

30. Donaldson, *Corporations and Morality*, p. 30. See also *Corrigible Corporations and Unruly Laws*, ed. Brent Fisse and Peter A. French (San Antonio: Trinity University Press, 1985).

31. Among numerous examples of the most strident opposition are William Safire, "Drawing the Line at Plant Closings," NYT News Service, in *IS*, 14 May 1988; "Jobs in Perpetuity: That's What Advance Notification of Plant Closings Is All About," *Barron's*, 20 June 1988, pp. 9, 36. Less worried were writers for *BW*, e.g., 30 May 1988, p. 22; 6 June 1988, p. 19; and (an editorial) 13 June 1988, p. 118.

32. "Shortcomings of Management," in *More Construction for the Money: Summary Report of The Construction Industry Cost Effectiveness Project* (New York: Business Roundtable, 1983), pp. 21–30. Compare "Union Workers May Really Be More Productive," *BW*, 22 Aug. 1983, p. 22; Charles Brown and James Medoff, "Trade Unions in the Production Process," *Journal of Political Economy* 86 (1978): 355–78; William F. Maloney, "Productivity Bargaining in Contract Construction," 1977 *Labor Law Journal* 532–38.

33. There is precedent for just this sort of rethinking the realities in the recent U.S. Supreme Court decision in *Container Corp. of America v. [California] Franchise Tax Board*, which frees states to tax the *global* profits of a corporation operating within its borders. See "Now States Can Really Put the Bite on Business," *BW*, 11 July 1983, p. 90.

34. See Deborah Groban Olson, "Union Experiences with Worker Ownership: Legal and Practical Issues Raised by ESOP's, TRASOP's, Stock Purchases and Co-Operatives," 1982 *Wisconsin Law Review* 732–823; Zachary D. Fasman, "Legal Obstacles to Alternative Work Force Designs," *Employee Relations Law Journal* 8 (1982): 256–81; "Worker Ownership and Section 8(a)(2) of the National Labor Relations Act," *Yale Law Journal* 91 (1982): 615–33; Harold J. Krent, "Collective Authority and Technical Expertise: Reexam-

ining the Managerial Employee Exclusion," *New York University Law Review* 56 (1981): 694–741; Jan Stiglitz, "Union Representation in Construction: Who Makes the Choice?" *San Diego Law Review* 18 (1981): 583–632; Lizanne Thomas, "Predatory Intent Is an Essential Element of a Union's Antitrust Violation," *Washington and Lee Law Review* 38 (1981): 450–99; "Determining Breach of Fiduciary Duty under the Labor-Management Reporting and Disclosure Act: *Gabauer v. Woodcock,*" *Harvard Law Review* 93 (1980): 608–17; Baker A. Smith, "Landrum-Griffin after Twenty-One Years: Mature Legislation or Childish Fantasy?" 1980 *Labor Law Journal* 273–81; Barry A. Macey, "Does Employer Implementation of Employee Production Teams Violate Section 8(a)(2) of the National Labor Relations Act?" *Indiana Law Journal* 20 (1974): 516–37; "New Standards for Domination and Support under Section 8(a)(2)," *Yale Law Journal* 82 (1973): 510–32; Ralph K. Winter, Jr., "Collective Bargaining and Competition: The Application of Antitrust Standards to Union Activities," *Yale Law Journal* 73 (1963): 14.

35. Ian Benson and John Lloyd, *New Technology and Industrial Change: The Impact of the Scientific-Technical Revolution on Labour and Industry* (London: Kogan Page, 1983), p. 200; Andrew Levison, *The Full Employment Alternative* (New York: Coward, McCann & Geoghegan, 1980), pp. 66–67.

36. See above, n. 34, esp. Fasman, "Legal Obstacles," and Olson, "Union Experiences."

37. "The Unions Balk at a Quick Sale of Conrail," *BW,* 27 Feb. 1984; "On Track for Conrail: Union Ownership," *BW,* 20 June 1983, p. 184. See also *ibid.,* p. 194; *BW,* 5 April 1982, pp. 72–79.

38. Levison, *Full Employment Alternatives,* pp. 134–35.

39. Benson and Lloyd, *New Technology and Industrial Change,* pp. 124–27; Ira C. Magaziner and Robert B. Reich, *Minding America's Business* (New York: Vintage, 1983), pp. 261–327.

40. Levison, *Full Employment Alternative,* pp. 110–11, 207–9.

41. Magaziner and Reich, *Minding America's Business,* pp. 210–15. See Levison, *Full Employment Alternative,* pp. 83–87, regarding the impact of mechanization on the workforce in industries such as meat packing after World War II.

42. "A Risky Operation in the Bloated Welfare State," *BW,* 17 Oct. 1983, pp. 56–57.

43. Kevin R. Hopkins, "How to Adjust to the Coming Worker Shortage," *IS,* 17 Feb. 1989, p. A8.

44. Explaining to employers the legal advantages of having independent contractors rather than employees is something of a growth industry. In addition to seminars, there are handy manuals and even a publication known as the *Independent Contractor Report.*

45. See, for example, Gene Koretz, "How the Hispanic Population Boom Will Hit the Work Force," *BW,* 20 Feb. 1989, p. 21.

CHAPTER 5

1. See Adina Schwartz, "Meaningful Work," *Ethics* 92 (1982): 634–46; and Gerald Doppelt, "Conflicting Paradigms of Human Freedom and the Problem of Justification," *Inquiry* 27 (1984): 51–86. In "Meaningful Work and Market Socialism," *Ethics* 97 (1987):

517–45, Richard J. Arneson finds arguments for mandating MW not persuasive but believes it would be achieved under market socialism. But his definition of meaningful work, at pp. 522–23, requires levels of both job satisfaction and workplace democracy attainment of which would practically require worker ownership. David Schweickart doubts that the market, however structured, can be trusted to achieve MW (American Philosophical Association, Eastern Division Meeting, Dec. 1985).

2. Robert Nozick, *Anarchy, State, and Utopia* (New York: Basic Books, 1974), pp. 246–50.

3. Studs Terkel, *Working* (1972; rpt. New York: Avon, 1975), pp. xxix, xxx.

4. Quoted, *ibid.*, p. xxviii.

5. Paul Dickson, *The Future of the Workplace* (New York: Weybright and Talley, 1975), pp. 24–33. See also Paul Harrison, "Humanizing Factories," *Human Behavior*, Aug. 1976, pp. 40–43; and for earlier examples, see David Jenkins, *Job Power* (New York: Doubleday, 1973), chs. 10–13.

6. See John A. Byrne, "Business Fads: What's In—and Out," *BW*, 20 Jan. 1986, pp. 52–61; John Hoerr, "Human Resources Managers Aren't Corporate Nobodies Anymore," *BW*, 2 Dec. 1985, pp. 58–59. See also Dickson, *Future of the Workplace*, pp. 20–24.

7. Bruce R. McBrearty, "Improved Employee Productivity Accomplished with 'Deskilling' " (advertisement), *Barron's*, 3 Dec. 1984, p. 77; Everett M. Rogers and Judith K. Larson, *Silicon Valley Fever: Growth of High-Technology Culture* (New York: Basic Books, 1986).

8. Joan M. Greenbaum, *In the Name of Efficiency: Management Theory and Shopfloor Practice in Data-Processing Work* (Philadelphia: Temple University Press, 1979), p. 163.

9. Pamela Patrick, *Health Care Worker Burnout* (Chicago: Blue Cross Inquiry Books, 1981).

10. Suzanne Daley, "Hospitals Bracing for New Rules on Work Hours," *NYT*, 19 June 1988, p. Y17.

11. Michael A. Pollock and Aaron Bernstein, "Why Air Controllers Are Talking Union Again," *BW*, 27 May 1985, pp. 124, 126; Tom Morgenthau, "Can We Keep the Skies Safe?" *Newsweek*, 30 Jan. 1984, pp. 24–31; William Serrin, "Workers' Demands Tied to Technology," *Virginia Pilot*, 17 Aug. 1981, p. A2.

12. Tracy Kidder, *The Soul of a New Machine* (1981; rpt. New York: Avon, 1982).

13. John A. Byrne et al., "Caught in the Middle: Six Managers Speak Out on Corporate Life," *BW*, 12 Sept. 1988, pp. 80–88; "The Feminization of the Professional Work Force," *BW*, 17 Feb. 1986, p. 21.

14. "The Growing Disaffection with 'Workaholism,' " *BW*, 27 Feb. 1978, p. 97.

15. David J. Cherrington, *The Work Ethic: Working Values and Values That Work* (New York: AMACOM, 1980).

16. "The Revival of Productivity," *BW*, 13 Feb. 1984, pp. 92–100.

17. Francine Waskowicz, written assignment in correspondence course on Philosophy of Work taught by the author. Quoted with permission.

18. Terkel, *Working*, p. 456.

19. See Barry Maley, Dexter Dumphy, and Bill Ford, *Industrial Democracy and Worker Participation* (a bibliography) (Kensington: University of New South Wales Press, 1982); Daniel Zwerdling, *Workplace Democracy* (New York: Harper & Row, 1980); Paul

Blumberg, *Industrial Democracy: The Sociology of Participation* (New York: Schocken, 1968); Frederick Emery and Einer Thorsrud, *Democracy at Work* (Leiden: Martinus Nijhoff Social Sciences Division, 1966). See also the journal *Workplace Democracy*.

20. Alfred Diamant, "Workplace Democracy: Some Thoughts on Organizational Culture," paper presented at the Midwest Political Science Association, Chicago, April 1986. Diamant calls attention to a working-class hegemonic system that failed ("red Vienna," 1918–34) and to the "rediscovery" of corporatism, as described in two Sage publications edited by Gerhard Lehmbruch and Philippe C. Schmitter: *Patterns of Corporatist Policy Making* (1982) and *Trends towards Corporatist Intermediation* (1983).

21. See above, n. 1, with regard to Richard J. Arneson.

22. A worker's obligation to participate in performance-enhancing programs, at least those of the "New Age" variety, is being challenged in court under Title VII of the 1964 Civil Rights Act. See Martha Brannigan, "Employers' 'New Age' Training Programs Lead to Lawsuits over Workers' Rights," *WSJ*, 9 Jan. 1989.

23. See Erich Fromm's introduction to the Early Manuscripts in *Marx's Concept of Man* (New York: Ungar, 1961).

24. Kostas Axelos focuses on Marx in *Alienation, Praxis and Techne in the Thought of Karl Marx*, tr. Ronald Bruzina (Austin: University of Texas Press, 1976). The Marxist literature is reviewed by Richard Schacht in his *Alienation* (New York: Doubleday Anchor, 1971). Two international, cross-disciplinary conferences (a third is scheduled for 1989) resulted in proceedings edited by R. Felix Geyer and David Schweitzer, *Theories of Alienation* (The Hague: Nijhoff, 1976), and *Alienation: Problems of Meaning, Theory and Method* (London: Routledge & Kegan Paul, 1981).

25. Joachim Israel, "Alienation from Work: A Conceptual Analysis," *Philosophical Forum* 10 (Winter–Summer 1978–79): 265–305, including responses. See also Frederick M. Gordon, "Marx's Concept of Alienation and Empirical Sociological Research," *ibid.*, 242–64. André Gorz, *Alienation: From Marx to Modern Sociology: A Macro-Sociological Analysis* (Boston: Allyn and Bacon, 1971).

26. Technology is seen as the cause of alienation by David M. Gordon, Richard Edwards, and Michael Reich, *Segmented Work, Divided Workers: The Historical Transformation of Labor in the United States* (Cambridge: Cambridge University Press, 1982). The best-known defense of technology as a cure for alienation is that of Robert Blauner, *Alienation and Freedom* (Chicago: University of Chicago Press, 1964). For more socioeconomically conscious accounts, see Michael Burawoy, *The Politics of Production: Factory Regimes under Capitalism and Socialism* (London: Verso, 1985); Bernard Gendron, *Technology and the Human Condition* (New York: St. Martin's, 1977), ch. 8; and Adam Schaff, *Marxism and the Human Individual* (New York: McGraw-Hill, 1970), ch. 2.

27. See Simon Marcson, *Automation, Alienation and Anomie* (New York: Harper & Row, [1970]), and Jon M. Shepard, *Automation and Alienation: A Study of Office and Factory Workers* (Cambridge, Mass.: MIT Press, 1971).

28. Eileen Power, *Medieval People* (Garden City, N.Y.: Doubleday Anchor, 1954), pp. 17–19.

29. *Ibid.*, p. 22.

30. Jacques Le Goff, *Time, Work and Culture in the Middle Ages*, tr. Arthur Goldhammer (Chicago: University of Chicago Press, 1980), pp. 83–86.

31. From "The Pleasant Historie of John Winchcomb, . . . The famous and Worthy Clothier of England; declaring . . . how hee set continually five hundred poore people at work, to the great benefite of the Common-wealth (London, 1626; rpt. in *The Works of Thomas Deloney*, ed. Francis O. Mann [Oxford: Clarendon, 1912]), pp. 20–21 (punctuation adapted to modern conventions).

32. Michael Maccoby, *The Leader* (New York: Simon & Schuster, 1981), pp. 26, 29–30.

33. See Barbara Dinham and Colin Hines, *Agribusiness in Africa* (Trenton, N.J.: Africa World, 1984); Andrew M. Kamarck, *The Economics of African Development* (New York: Praeger, 1967); Frantz Fanon, *The Wretched of the Earth*, tr. Constance Farrington (New York: Ballantine, 1963).

34. Alison Jaggar in *Feminist Politics and Human Nature* (Totowa, N.J.: Rowman & Allanheld, 1983) discusses the different ways in which radical, socialist, and liberal feminists, respectively, account for women's subordination in terms of reproduction. In Zillah R. Eisenstein, ed., *Capitalist Patriarchy and the Case for Socialist Feminism* (New York: Monthly Review, 1979), socialist feminists trace work relationships in the home to capitalist patriarchy. Eisenstein in *The Radical Future of Liberal Feminism* (New York: Longman, 1981) charges liberal feminists with accepting patriarchy and thereby committing the working mother to a "double day." Arguments in support of androgynous cosharing of sex roles are presented by Mary O'Brien, *The Politics of Reproduction* (Boston: Routledge & Kegan Paul, 1981); Nancy Chodorow, *The Reproduction of Mothering: Psychoanalysis and the Sociology of Gender* (Berkeley: University of California Press, 1978; and Dorothy Dinnerstein, *The Mermaid and the Minotaur: Sexual Arrangements and Human Malaise* (New York: Harper & Row, 1976).

35. Carolyn Merchant uncovers some pseudo-scientific macho underpinnings in *The Death of Nature* (New York: Harper & Row, 1979). Mircea Eliade explores the sexual symbolism of ancient mining and metallurgy in *The Forge and the Crucible*, tr. Stephen Corrin (London: Rider, 1962).

36. Aaron Bernstein et al., "The Double Standard That's Setting Worker against Worker," *BW*, 8 April 1985, pp. 70–71.

37. Michael A. Pollock and Aaron Bernstein, "The Disposable Employee is Becoming a Fact of Corporate Life," *BW*, 15 Dec. 1986, pp. 52–56; Carol Kleiman, "Temporary Help a Full-Time Service," *Chicago Tribune*, 13 April 1986, sec. 8, p. 1; Deborah C. Wise et al., "Part-Time Workers: Rising Numbers, Rising Discord," *BW*, 1 April 1985, pp. 62–63; Eric Gelman with Richard Sandza, "The Boom in Worker Leasing," *Newsweek*, 14 May 1984, p. 55; William Serrin, "Up to a Fifth of U.S. Workers Now Rely on Part-Time Jobs," *NYT*, 14 Aug. 1983, pp. 1, 22.

38. See David Kelley, "In Praise of Homework," *Barron's*, 3 Dec. 1984, pp. 11, 46; Doug Stewart, "What Ever Happened to the Electronic Cottage?" *Popular Computing*, July 1985, pp. 65–67+; Sharon Rubinstein, "These 'Temps' Don't Just Answer the Phone," *BW*, 2 June 1986, p. 74. For the feminization of part-time work, see Veronica Beechey and Tessa Perkins, *A Matter of Hours: Women, Part-time Work, and the Labour Market* (London: Polity, 1987).

39. Barbara McIntosh, "Employee Leasing Issues: Employer Determination and Lia-

bility Considerations," 1987 *Labor Law Journal* 11–20; Richard A. DuRose, "Management's Right to Subcontract Being Restricted," *NLJ*, 9 Dec. 1985, p. 20; David P. Radelet, "Using 'Rented' Employees: Look Before You Lease," *NLJ*, 1 April 1985, pp. 18–19.

40. "Swapping Work Rules for Jobs at GE's 'Factory of the Future,' " *BW*, 10 Sept. 1984, pp. 43–44. See also Michael A. Pollock et al., "Construction Unions Try to Shore Up a Crumbling Foundation," *BW*, 4 Feb. 1985, pp. 52, 54.

41. See the following, all in *BW*: John Hoerr et al., "Management Discovers the Human Side of Automation," 29 Sept. 1986, pp. 70–75; "How Power Will Be Balanced on Saturn's Shop Floor," 5 Aug. 1985, pp. 65–66; "Swapping Work Rules for Jobs at GE's 'Factory of the Future,' " 10 Sept. 1984, pp. 43, 46; "A Work Revolution in U.S. Industry: More Flexible Rules on the Job Are Boosting Productivity," 16 May 1983, pp. 100–110; "Can GM Change Its Work Rules?" 26 April 1982, pp. 116, 119; "Detroit Gets a Break from UAW," 30 Nov. 1981, pp. 94, 96. For Diesel Allison, see Will Higgins, "Harmony Gives Way to Strife at Allison as Labor Talks Fail," *Indianapolis Business Journal*, 7–13 April, 1986; Bill Koenig, "Allison Workers Split on Work-Rule Changes," *IS*, 27 March 1986, p. 41.

42. See Dale D. Buss, "GM vs. GM: Unions Say Auto Firms Use Interplant Rivalry to Raise Work Quotas," *WSJ*, 7 Nov. 1983.

43. Adam Smith, *The Wealth of Nations* (1776), ed. Andrew Skinner (New York: Penguin, 1970), pp. 112, 115–16.

44. Herbert Spencer, *The Principles of Ethics* (New York: Appleton, 1897), 1: 142, 146.

45. Emile Durkheim, *The Division of Labor in Society* (5 eds., 1893–1926), tr. George Simpson (New York: Macmillan Free Press, 1933), pp. 270, 310–12, 371–73, 375–89.

46. Georges Friedmann, *The Anatomy of Work: Labor, Leisure, and the Implications of Automation*, tr. Wyatt Rawson (New York: Free Press, 1964), pp. 74, 75–81.

47. Harris L. Sussman, Digital Equipment Corporation personnel expert, quoted in "Experts Divided on Jobs in the 90's," *NYT*, 16 April 1989, p. F31.

48. Job control should not be confused with worker control, which has to do with on-the-job authority and responsibility. See David Montgomery, *Workers' Control in America* (Cambridge: Cambridge University Press, 1979); Wolfgang Abendroth, *A Short History of the European Working Class* (New York: Monthly Review, 1972); and Alejandro Portes and John Walton, *Labor, Class, and the International System* (New York: Academic, 1981).

49. For example, it refers to the work product of a composer, whose musical compositions are numbered in chronological order. A sculptor or painter may identify one of his or her works simply as an opus with a number. Writers may refer to their most important work as a magnum opus (great work). And the complete works of a writer are sometimes referred to by the Latin equivalent: *opera omnia*.

50. Intransitively, it suggests the exercise of force or influence, the achieving of an effect; transitively, it calls to mind responsible oversight of something as challenging as a machine or even a railroad.

51. As the novels of John Le Carre illustrate, even in regard to spies the term *operative*, like *agent*, implies an antiwork bias that demeans those who carry out the orders of others, especially when referring to industrial workers.

52. This view is frequently espoused these days, e.g., in the set of articles published in *BW*, 19 Sept. 1988, pp. 100–141, under the collective title "Human Capital: The Decline of America's Work Force."

53. William H. Mobley, "Where Have All the Golfers Gone?" *Personnel Journal*, July 1977. Maureen Turnbull brought this article to my attention.

54. See Susantha Goonatilake, *Aborted Discovery: Science and Creativity in the Third World* (London: Zed Books, 1984); Paolo Freiere, *Pedagogy of the Oppressed*, tr. Myra Bergman Ramos (New York: Seabury Continuum, 1970).

CHAPTER 6

1. Reflective equilibrium, as used by John Rawls, is the result of a kind of dialectic between theoretically postulated principles of justice and "our firmest convictions" about what justice involves. "By going back and forth" between the two and adjusting one to the other we eventually "find a description of the initial situation that both expresses reasonable conditions and yields principles which match our considered judgments duly pruned and adjusted" (*A Theory of Justice* [Cambridge, Mass.: Belknap Press of Harvard University Press, Harvard Belknap, 1971], pp. 19–20).

2. Reinhard Bendix, *Work and Authority in Industry: Ideologies of Management in the Course of Industrialization* (1956; rpt. Berkeley: University of California Press, 1974), pp. 108–16. Labor historians have discerned a similar dialectic in nineteenth-century America in spite of owners' appeals to the "free labor values" of "community consciousness." See Brian Greenberg, *Worker and Community* (Albany: State University of New York Press, 1985), p. 1. See also below, Chapter 11.

3. See Paschal Larkin, *Property in the Eighteenth Century* (1930; rpt. New York: Howard Fertig, 1969), p. 233.

4. Russell A. Smith, Leroy S. Merrifield, and Theodore J. St. Antoine, *Labor Relations Law: Cases and Materials*, 5th ed. (Indianapolis: Bobbs-Merrill, 1974), pp. 1–49. Regarding change in British law (1875) see Sidney Webb and Beatrice Webb, *The History of Trade Unionism* (1894; 2d ed. 1920; rpt. New York: Augustus M. Kelley, 1965), pp. 71–108, 282, 291.

5. See, for example, *Coppage v. Kansas*, 236 U.S. (1914), 14–17.

6. Richard B. Freeman and James L. Medoff, *What Do Unions Do?* (New York: Basic Books, 1984), ch. 10. For a statement of the wage inflation argument, see George H. Hildebrand, *American Unionism* (Reading, Mass.: Addison-Wesley, 1979), ch. 5.

7. See Orme W. Phelps, *Introduction to Labor Economics*, 4th ed. (New York: McGraw-Hill, 1967), p. 511.

8. See Bill Powell, "Boosting Shop-Floor Productivity by Breaking All the Rules," *BW*, 26 Nov. 1984, pp. 100, 104; Otis Port et al., "The Productivity Paradox," *BW*, 6 June 1988, pp. 100–114.

9. Charles Brown and James Medoff, "Trade Unions in the Production Process," *Journal of Political Economy* 86, no. 3 (1978): 377.

10. Freeman and Medoff, *What Do Unions Do?* chs. 11–12.

11. *Columbus Dispatch*, 14 Oct. 1984, p. F1; Alex Kotlowitz, "Rebuilding Demand for Union Bricklayers," *WSJ*, 24 Aug. 1987. See also William F. Maloney, "Productivity Bargaining in Contract Construction," 1977 *Labor Law Journal*: 532–38.

12. See "Why a Strike May Shatter Coal's Newfound Peace," *BW*, 9 July 1984, p. 104; Godfrey Hodgson, "Britain's Do-or-Die Strike," *NYT Magazine*, 30 Sept. 1984, pp. 28+.

13. See Aaron Bernstein and Sandra D. Atchison, "How OSHA Helped Organize the Meatpackers," *BW*, 29 Aug. 1988, p. 82; "A Silver Bullet for the Union Drive at Coors?" *BW*, 11 July 1988, pp. 61–62.

14. See Catherine Yang and David Zigas, "A New Strain of Merger Mania," *BW*, 21 March 1988, pp. 122–25.

15. This argument was already being articulated by British laborites in the nineteenth century. See Webb and Webb, *History of Trade Unionism*, pp. 292–98.

16. Herbert Spencer, *Social Statics* (1850) and *Man versus the State* (1884) (Caldwell, Ida.: Caxton, 1940), rpt. in E. Wight Bakke et al., eds., *Unions, Management and the Public*, 3d ed. (New York: Harcourt, Brace & World, 1967), p. 28. See also *ibid.*, pp. 125ff., and Spencer, *The Principles of Ethics*, vol. 2 (New York: Appleton, 1897), ch. 3: "Restraints on Free Contract," pp. 287–97.

17. Selig Perlman, *A Theory of the Labor Movement* (1928; rpt. New York: Augustus Kelley, 1949), p. 275, quoted in Philip Taft, "Theories of the Labor Movement," in *Interpreting the Labor Movement*, Industrial Relations Research Association, Publication No. 9 (Madison, Wisc.: Industrial Relations Research Association, 1952), p. 31.

18. Alexis de Tocqueville, *Democracy in America*, tr. George Lawrence, ed. J. P. Mayer and Max Lerner (New York: Harper & Row, 1966), pp. 558–59, 488, and *passim*.

19. An indirect employer is defined as factors that exert a "determining influence on the shaping both of the work contract and, consequently, of just and unjust relationships in the field of human work" (*Laborem exercens*, English ed. [On human work] [London: Catholic Truth Society, 1981], nn. 16–17).

20. See, however, Charles Landesman's definition of political unionism in "The Union Movement and the Right to Organize," in *Moral Rights in the Workplace*, ed. Gertrude Ezorsky (Albany: State University of New York Press, 1987), p. 157.

21. Sidney Webb and Beatrice Webb, *Industrial Democracy* (London: Longmans, Green, 1920), pp. 840–50, rpt. in Bakke et al., eds., *Unions, Management and the Public*, Webb and Webb, pp. 39–42; *The History of Trade Unionism*, rev. ed. extended to 1920 (New York: Longmans, Green, 1935), pp. 6, 10–11, 41–56. See also Taft, "Theories of the Labor Movement," pp. 3–6, 14–17.

22. John Dewey, *Liberalism and Social Action* (1935; rpt. New York: Capricorn, 1963), p. 54. See also Edmund F. Byrne, "Workplace Democracy for Teachers: John Dewey's Contribution," in *Philosophy and Technology VI*, ed. Paul T. Durbin (Dordrecht: Kluwer Academic, forthcoming).

23. Tomsky favored union plant management; Trotsky favored their intervention on the level of the national economy. Lenin adopted a combination of both perspectives but insisted on punitively enforced absolute obedience to the will of the manager in the interest of technical efficiency. See Bendix, *Work and Authority*, pp. 192–97.

24. Clark Kerr and Abraham Siegel, "The Structuring of the Labor Force in Industrial Society," *Industrial and Labor Relations Review*, Jan. 1955; rpt. in Bakke et al., eds., *Unions, Management and the Public*, pp. 61–66.

25. These two opposed formulations of freedom track fairly neatly Isaiah Berlin's famous distinction between "Two Concepts of Liberty," in *Essays on Liberty* (London: Oxford University Press, 1969), pp. 118–38.

26. Anthony Skillen, "The Politics of Production," ch. 2, in Skillen, *Ruling Illusions: Philosophy and the Social Order* (Atlantic Highlands, N.J.: Humanities, 1978).

27. Sidney Webb and Beatrice Webb, *The History of Trade Unionism* (1894); 2d ed. 1920; rpt. New York: Augustus M. Kelley, 1965), p. 15. The role of the medieval guild merchant, or body of traders who gained local advantages over foreigners, is also relevant to and to some extent incorporated into this account of the craft guild. See J. L. Bolton, *The Medieval English Economy, 1150–1500* (Totowa, N.J.: Rowman & Littlefield, 1980); John Richard Green, *A Short History of the English People*, new ed. (London: Macmillan, 1888), pp. 193–201.

28. Webb and Webb, *History of Trade Unionism* (1965), pp. 1, 6, 14, and 41.

29. Howard Dickman, *Industrial Democracy in America: Ideological Origins of National Labor Relations Policy* (La Salle, Ill.: Open Court, 1987).

30. George Unwin, *The Gilds and Companies of London* (1908; 4th ed. New York: Barnes & Noble, 1963), pp. 108–9, 165–66, 170, 176–216.

31. *Ibid.*, pp. 75–76, 168, 217–42, 249–63.

32. Guilds were abolished in France in 1791 and in Belgium and the Netherlands when they came under French control, in Spain and Portugal in 1839–40, in Austria and Germany in 1859–60, and in Italy in 1864. See *ibid.*, p. 1.

33. *Ibid.*, pp. 264–65. See also Webb and Webb, *History of Trade Unionism* (1965), pp. 28–41.

34. Bendix, *Work and Authority*, pp. 57, 108–16.

35. Adam Smith, *The Wealth of Nations* (1776), ed. Andrew Skinner (1970; rpt. New York: Penguin, 1977), Bk. I, ch. viii, p. 169.

36. James B. Atleson, *Values and Assumptions in American Labor Law* (Amherst: University of Massachusetts Press, 1983).

37. Deborah Groban Olson, "Union Experiences with Worker Ownership: Legal and Practical Issues Raised by ESOP's, TRASOP's, Stock Purchases and Co-Operatives," 1982 *Wisconsin Law Review* 795. For a more complete account of a union's agenda, see James Wallihan, *Union Government and Organization* (Washington, D.C.: Bureau of National Affairs, 1985).

38. See John Hoerr, "Move Over Boone, Carl, and Irv—Here Comes Labor," *BW*, 14 Dec. 1987, pp. 124–25; Donald Liddle, "A Union Man Runs Unimar," *NYT*, 18 Sept. 1988, p. F11. See also John Hoerr and William C. Symonds, "A Brash Bid to Keep Steel in the Mon Valley," *BW*, 11 Feb. 1985, p. 30.

39. See Donald I. Baker, "Sale of Conrail Is Latest Chapter in Sad History of Railroad Mergers," *NLJ*, 22 April 1985, pp. 18–21; and the following articles in *BW*: "Conrail Management Strives to Stay in Control," 19 Nov. 1984, p. 48; "The For-Sale Sign on Conrail Starts Attracting Serious Bidders," 16 April 1984, pp. 74ff.; "Conrail's Workers

Get a Powerful New Ally," 14 May 1984, p. 157; "An 'Investment Banker' for Labor," 25 June 1984, pp. 137, 140.

40. Keith Bradley and Alan Gelb, *Worker Capitalism: The New Industrial Relations* (Cambridge, Mass.: MIT Press, 1985), pp. 43–46, 108–20. In Great Britain, they say, worker ownership is usually destined to fail for strategic and ideological reasons. More successful are worker-servicing businesses run by unions in West Germany. See "The Stain on German Unions," *BW*, 12 April 1982, pp. 128ff.

41. 444 U.S. 672.

42. 231 N.L.R.B. 1108 and 231 N.L.R.B. 1232.

43. *Hertzka and Knowles v. N.L.R.B.*, 503 F.2d 625 (9th Cir. 1974), *cert. den.* 423 U.S. 875 (1975).

44. *N.L.R.B. v. Silver Spur Casino*, 623 F.2d 571 (9th Cir. 1980).

45. *Spark's Nugget, Inc.*, 230 N.L.R.B. 275 (1977).

46. 221 F.2d 165.

47. Section 2 (12), 29 U.S.C. section 152 (12).

48. Section 2 (11), 29 U.S.C. section 152 (11).

49. *N.L.R.B. v. Yeshiva University*, 444 U.S. 672, 687, 689 (1980).

50. *Id.* at 697. Subsequent consideration of broader social implications support what Brennan believed the statute already allows. See John Hoerr, "America's Labor Laws Weren't Written for a Global Economy," *BW*, 13 Jan. 1986, p. 38, and "Power-Sharing between Management and Labor: It's Slow Going," *BW*, 17 Feb. 1986, p. 37; Roger B. Jacobs, "Worker Committees and the NLRA: 'Domination' or Sound Management?" *NLJ*, 17 March 1986, pp. 23–24, 31; "A Post-Yeshiva Victory," (AFT) *On Campus*, April 1986, p. 3.

51. Section 4; 15 U.S.C. s. 15.

52. *Bausch & Lomb Optical Company and United Optical and Instrumental Workers of America, Local 678*, 108 N.L.R.B. 1555 (1954).

53. *N.L.R.B. v. David Buttrick Co.*, 361 F.2d 300 (1st Cir., 1966).

54. *Connell Construction Co. v. Plumbers & Steamfitters*, 421 U.S. 616, 95 S.Ct. 1830, 44 L.Ed.2d 418.

55. *Meat Cutters, Local 576 v. Wetterau Foods*, 597 F.2d 133, 136 (8th Cir. 1979) (emphasis added).

56. *California State Council of Carpenters and Carpenters 46 v. Associated General Contractors of California, Inc.*, 648 F.2d 527 (1980).

57. *Id.* at 536–37, 538.

58. *Associated General Contractors of California, Inc., v. California State Council of Carpenters*, 459 U.S. 519; 103 S.Ct. 897, 913 (1983). Because this eight-to-one ruling was based on procedural technicalities, it left open the possibility that a better-articulated union claim might be better received. See Rowland L. Young, "Union Is Not a Person under the Clayton Act: Associated General Contractors, Inc. v. Calif. State Council of Carpenters, 103 S.Ct. 897 (Feb. 22, 1983)," *American Bar Association Journal* 69 (May 1983): 666.

CHAPTER 7

1. For relevant literature, see above, Chapter 4, n. 27. Efforts in much of this literature to defend the civil rights of a racial minority are seriously challenged by a number of recent U.S. Supreme Court decisions, including *City of Richmond v. Croson* (23 Jan. 1989), 57 U.S.L.W. 4132.

2. See the companion cases *Board of Regents v. Roth*, 408 U.S. 564 (1971) and *Perry v. Sindermann*, 408 U.S. 593 (1972). For a brief review of constitutional theories that might be applied to democratize the workplace, see Robert Ellis Smith, *Workrights* (New York: Dutton, 1983), pp. 30–37.

3. U.S.C. s. 703(h).

4. Equal Employment Opportunity Commission, *Guidelines on Employment Testing Procedures* (Washington, D.C.: U.S. Government Printing Office, 1966).

5. U.S.C. ss. 1604–7.

6. U.S.C. s. 1607.5(b)(4).

7. 401 U.S. 421.

8. *McDonnell-Douglas Corp. v. Green* (1973), 411 U.S. 792, 802–5. An example of a case applying an economic theory of business necessity is *Green v. Missouri Pacific RR Co.*, 381 F.Supp. 992, 996 (E.D. Mo., 1974).

9. 422 U.S. 405, 434, 95 S.Ct. 2362, 2379 (1975).

10. See Irving Thalberg, "Themes in the Reverse-Discrimination Debate," *Ethics* 91 (Oct. 1980): 138–50, a review of five books that address particular cases, especially the *Bakke* case, and their broader implications.

11. See Samuel Bowles and Herbert Gintis, *Schooling in Capitalist America* (New York: Basic Books, 1976).

12. "Thatcher: Put More to Work by Shrinking the Safety Net," *BW*, 12 Sept. 1983, p. 60; "Why Welfare Rolls May Grow," *BW*, 29 March 1982, pp. 165–66; "A Frantic Rush to Prop Up Unemployment," *BW*, 26 Feb. 1979, pp. 58–59.

13. See "Meat Packers Fight Automation, Firings," *News & Letters*, 10 April 1987; "The GM Settlement Is a Milestone for Both Sides," *BW*, 8 Oct. 1984, pp. 160–62; "Seniority Squeezes Out Minorities in Layoffs," *BW*, 5 May 1975, pp. 66–67. For Supreme Court rulings on seniority see *Memphis Firefighters Local 1784 v. Stotts*, 467 U.S. 561, 104 S.Ct. 2576 (1984); *County of Los Angeles v. Davis*, 440 U.S. 625, 99 S.Ct. 1379 (1979); *Franks v. Bowman Transportation Co.*, 424 U.S. 747, 96 S.Ct. 1251 (1976).

14. See John Hoerr, "Why Job Security Is More Important Than Income Security," *BW*, 21 Nov. 1983, p. 86; All Things Considered, PBS, 29 May 1984 (seniority and overtime among auto workers and longshoremen); William Serrin, "Recovery Irrelevant to Workers Left Behind," *NYT*, 4 Sept. 1983, pp. 1, 83; "Displaced Workers May Have to Face Lower Wages," *BW*, 19 Sept. 1983, p. 22; "Fears of Higher Unemployment in Europe" *BW*, 3 Aug. 1981, p. 66.

15. See Edward Yemin, "Comparative Survey," in *Workforce Reductions in Undertakings*, ed. Yemin (Geneva: International Labour Office, 1982), p. 14; Roger Kaufman, "Why the U.S. Unemployment Rate Is So High," in *Unemployment and Inflation*, ed. M. J. Piore (White Plains, N.Y.: M. E. Sharpe), p. 160; Ira C. Magaziner and Robert B.

Reich, *Minding America's Business* (New York: Vintage, 1983), pp. 12–18, 143–54, 211–14, 271–76, 333–34.

16. *Negotiating Technological Change* (Brussels: European Trade Union Institute, pp. 50–51. For historical background to this development, see Ira Benson and John Lloyd, *New Technology and Industrial Change* (London: Kegan Paul, 1983).

17. Gary E. Murg and Clifford Scharman, "Employment at Will: Do the Exceptions Overwhelm the Rule?" *Boston College Law Review* 23 (March 1982): 329–30, nn. 1–2, p. 337, nn. 48–50.

18. Charles A. Brake, Jr., "Limiting the Right to Terminate at Will—Have the Courts Forgotten the Employer?" *Vanderbilt Law Review* 35 (1982): 203, n. 10; Murg and Scharman, "Employment at Will," pp. 343–44, nn. 87–88.

19. See Werner Sengenberger, "Federal Republic of Germany," in *Workforce Reductions in Undertakings*, ed. Yemin, pp. 85–101; *Economic Dislocation: Plant Closings, Plant Relocations and Plant Conversion*, Joint Report of Labor Union Study Tour Participants, May 1, 1979, ch. 3 and App. 3.

20. Paul O'Higgins, *Workers' Rights* (London: Arrow Books, 1976), pp. 62–78; Jeremy McMullen, *Rights at Work: A Workers' Guide to Employment Law*, 2d impression (with supplement) (London: Pluto Press, 1979), pp. 144–208, 324–34, Supplement; G. J. Anderson, "Limits on the Right to Claim for Unjustified Dismissal," 1982 *New Zealand Law Journal* 59–64. See also *Cessation de la relation de travail à l'initiative de l'employeur* (Geneva: Bureau International du Travail, 1980).

21. "It's Getting Harder to Make a Firing Stick," *BW*, 27 June 1983, pp. 104–5; "Fire Me? I'll Sue!" *American Bar Association Journal* 69 (June 1983): 719. Compare O'Higgins, *Workers' Rights*, pp. 62–72; McMullen, *Rights at Work*, pp. 144–84.

22. Faye L. Calvey, "Termination of the At Will Employee: The General Rule and the Wisconsin Rule," *Marquette Law Review* 65 (Summer 1982): 652; Brake, "Limiting the Right to Terminate at Will," p. 204; Murg and Scharman, "Employment at Will," p. 340, n. 67, pp. 343ff., 357; Comment, "Employment at Will and the Law of Contracts," *Buffalo Law Review* 23 (1973): 212–16.

23. For the reactionary view see Brake, "Limiting the Right to Terminate at Will," pp. 204–5; for the more favorable view see Murg and Scharman, "Employment at Will," p. 339, n. 63, 355, 369; Calvey, "Termination of the At Will Employee," p. 652. See also Eric Isbell-Sirotkin, "Defending the Abusively Discharged Employee: In Search of a Judicial Solution," *New Mexico Law Review* 12 (Spring 1982): 711–45. The minimalist view is articulated by J. Ronald Petrikin, "In Defense of Employment at Will," *Oklahoma Bar Journal* 53 (1982): 2209–14.

24. Aaron Bernstein, "More Dismissed Workers Are Telling It to the Judge," *BW*, 17 Oct. 1988, pp. 68–69. See also p. 112.

25. Karl Marx and Friedrich Engels, *The Communist Manifesto* (1847), pt. I, 2d ed. (New York: Pathfinder, 1987), pp. 19–20, 27, 6.

26. Leland Matthew Goodrich, "United Nations," in *Encyclopaedia Britannica*, vol. 18 (1982), p. 900. (The cooperative movement in the Third World also benefits from a comparable training program at the Coady International Institute in Antigonish, Nova Scotia.)

27. Bruce Vandervort, "ILO Shaken by American Departure," *ITT*, 23–29 Nov. 1977, p. 10.

28. Michael A. Pollock, "Is Big Labor Playing Global Vigilante?" *BW*, 4 Nov. 1985, pp. 92–96.

29. Richard J. Barnet and Ronald E. Muller, *Global Reach: The Power of the Multinational Corporations* (New York: Simon & Schuster, 1974), p. 313.

30. "PATCO's Spotty Aid Abroad," *BW*, 31 Aug. 1981, p. 86.

31. "Common Market: A Call for Multinationals to Tell Labor Their Plans," *BW*, 12 Jan. 1981, p. 40; "Slapping Down Labor's Demand for Disclosure," *BW*, 1 Nov. 1982, p. 48; *European Communities* (N.p.: Price Waterhouse, 1987), pp. 58, 87–88.

32. Dick Barry, "Labor Unity," in *Labor Confronts the Transnationals* (New York: International Publishers, 1984), p. 101.

33. Alain Stern, "Trade Union Unity," *ibid.*, pp. 97–99; Barnet and Muller, *Global Reach*, pp. 315–16.

34. Barnet and Muller, *Global Reach*, pp. 314–15.

35. "International Labor Brews a Boycott of Coke," *BW*, 23 April 1984, p. 43.

36. Barnet and Muller, *Global Reach*, ch. 11 and p. 317.

37. Barbara Buell, "Why Japanese Workers Got Underwhelming Raises," *BW*, 25 April 1988, p. 82.

38. Laxmi Nakarmi, "What Kind of Korea Will the New Labor Movement Build?" *BW*, 12 Oct. 1987, pp. 56–57; and "Korean Labor's New Voice Is Saying: 'More,' " *BW*, 2 May 1988, pp. 45–46.

39. "Honda's U.S. Unit to Export Cars to South Korea," *WSJ*, 15 June 1988, p. 7; and the following from *BW*: "Detroit Is Bracing for a One-Two Punch," 16 Nov. 1987, pp. 136–37; William J. Holstein, "Japan Is Winning Friends in the Rust Belt," 19 Oct. 1987, p. 54, and "Honda Is Turning Red, White, and Blue," 5 Oct. 1987, p. 38; Marilyn Edid et al., "Why Mazda Is Settling in the Heart of Union Territory," 9 Sept. 1985, pp. 94–95.

40. *IS*, 12–16 Sept. 1983, *passim*.

41. See Bowles and Gintis, *Schooling in Capitalist America*.

42. See Steve Lohr, "The Japanese Challenge: Can They Achieve Technological Supremacy?" *NYT Magazine*, 8 July 1984, pp. 18–23+.

43. See the following, all from *BW*: "The Tightening Squeeze on White-Collar Pay," 12 Sept. 1977, pp. 82–94; "The Middle Ranks Get Furious Over Low Raises," 5 Nov. 1979, p. 158; "A New Target: Reducing Staff and Levels," 21 Dec. 1981, pp. 69–73; "More Professionals Pound the Pavement," 1 Feb. 1982, p. 28; Marilyn A. Harris, "A Lifetime at IBM Gets a Little Shorter for Some," 29 Sept. 1986, p. 40; Bill Symonds, "You Got the Ax. Now What Should You Do?" 23 Jan. 1989, pp. 110–11.

44. "10 Million Workers Displaced since '83," Associated Press, *IS*, 13 Dec. 1988, p. C4. Such data render suspect earlier projections that service-sector wages would be high enough to prevent the middle class from falling off the edge of the earth: "The Myth of the Vanishing Middle Class," *BW*, 9 July 1984, pp. 83, 87. See also David H. Freedman, ed., *Employment Outlook and Insights* (Geneva: International Labour Office, 1979), pp. 48, 96.

45. Personal communication, Daniel Cerezuelle, Bordeaux, France.

46. Ian Benson and John Lloyd, *New Technology and Industrial Change: The Impact of the Scientific-Technical Revolution on Labour and Industry* (London: Kogan Page, 1983), pp. 165–84.

47. A particularly pointed example involves the manufacture of machine tools. See European Trade Union Institute, *Negotiating Technological Change*, p. 13.

48. See Benson and Lloyd, *New Technology and Industrial Change*, pp. 49–55; David Wheeler, "Is There a Phillips Curve?" in *Unemployment and Inflation*, ed. Piore, pp. 46–57.

CHAPTER 8

1. To my knowledge, Rawls does not actually use the Supreme Court's timetable expression for achieving desegregation, but it is consistent with his timetable for justice as fairness in *A Theory of Justice* (Cambridge, Mass.: Belknap Press of Harvard University Press, 1971), sec. 82, pp. 541–48.

2. Jasia Reichardt, *Robots: Fact, Fiction, and Prediction* (New York: Penguin, 1978), p. 120.

3. The following description of robots and their capabilities is based on *ibid.*, pp. 140–41.

4. For a more sophisticated comparison between human and robot capabilities, see U.S. Congress, Office of Technology Assessment, *Automation and the Workplace: A Technical Memorandum* (Washington, D.C.: U.S. Government Printing Office, 1983), p. 16.

5. Desmond Smith, "The Robots (Beep. Click) Are Coming," *Pan Am Clipper*, April 1981, p. 33; Ed Janicki, "Is There a Robot in Your Future?" *IS Magazine*, 22 Nov. 1981, p. 55.

6. See below, notes 27 and 28.

7. "Russian Robots Run to Catch Up," *BW*, 17 Aug. 1981, p. 120; "The Push for Dominance in Robotics Gains Momentum," *BW*, 14 Dec. 1981, p. 108; Smith, "The Robots (Beep. Click) Are Coming." See also *Metalworkers and New Technology: Results of IMF Questionnaire on Industrial Robots*, IMF Document 81-13 (Geneva: n.p., 1981), pp. 37–38.

8. According to the San Jose, California, market research firm Dataquest. Investment in all forms of automation in the United States was about $16 billion in 1986 and is expected to grow through 1991 by 12% a year. See Hank Gilman, "The Age of Caution," in *WSJ.*, Special Report on Technology in the Workplace, 12 June 1987, p. 23D.

9. Reichardt, *Robots*, pp. 138, 140; "Racing to Breed the Next Generation," *BW*, June 9, 1980, pp. 73, 76; "The Push for Dominance in Robotics Gains Momentum," p. 108.

10. Warren P. Seering, "Who Said Robots Should Work Like People?" *Technology Review*, April 1985, pp. 59–67.

11. "Fanuc Edges Closer to a Robot-Run Plant," *BW*, 24 Nov. 1980, p. 56; "The Speedup in Automation," *BW*, 3 Aug. 1981, pp. 58–59. See also David Fleischer, "Robot-Built Robots," *Science Digest*, Dec. 1981, p. 44.

12. "GM's Ambitious Plan to Employ Robots," *BW*, 16 March 1981, p. 31; Harley Shaiken, "The Brave New World of Work in Auto," *ITT*, Sept. 19–25, 1979, p. 13.

13. "Racing to Breed the Next Generation," p. 76; "GM's Ambitious Plan to Employ Robots"; Janicki, "Is There a Robot in Your Future?" pp. 54–55; Ronald Taggiasco et al., "A Launching Pad for Automating Europe's Plants," *BW*, 10 Dec. 1984, pp. 57, 60.

14. "General Motors: What Went Wrong?" *BW* 16 Mar. 1987, pp. 103, 105.

15. "How Robots Are Cutting Costs for GE," *BW* 9 June 1980, p. 68. See also "General Electric: The Financial Wizards Switch Back to Technology," *BW*, 16 March 1981, pp. 112–13.

16. See Herb Brody, "U.S. Robot Makers Try to Bounce Back," *High Technology Business*, Oct. 1987, pp. 18–24. This article is the source of my information about several recent developments.

17. See Langdon B. Winner, *Autonomous Technology* (Cambridge, Mass.: MIT Press, 1977); John Cohen, *Human Robots in Myth and Science* (New York: Allen & Unwin, 1967).

18. See George Terborgh, *Automation Hysteria* (New York: Norton, 1966); Henry Elsner, Jr., *Technocrats: Prophets of Automation* (Syracuse, N.Y.: Syracuse University Press, 1967).

19. David J. Cherrington, *The Work Ethic: Working Values and Values That Work* (New York: ANACOM, 1980), p. 106.

20. "Labor Can't Scratch Racetrack Automation," *BW*, 19 March 1979, pp. 35–36.

21. Hugh Aldersey-Williams et al., "Robots Head for the Farm," *BW*, 8 Sept. 1986, pp. 66–67.

22. "Revamping Air Traffic Control," *BW*, 18 Jan. 1982, pp. 100–101.

23. Guenter Friedrichs and Adam Schaff, eds., *Microelectronics and Society: A Report to the Club of Rome* (New York: NAL Mentor, 1983), pp. 115–202; Christopher Evans, *The Micro Millenium* (New York: Washington Square, 1979), pp. 121–45; Tom Stonier, *The Wealth of Information* (London: Thames Methuen, 1983), pp. 99–122.

24. *Negotiating Technological Change* (Brussels: European Trade Union Institute, 1982), pp. 8–11, 16; Ian Benson and John Lloyd, *New Technology and Industrial Change: The Impact of the Scientific-Technical Revolution on Labour and Industry* (London: Kogan Page, 1983), pp. 39–43; Roy Rothwell and Walter Zegfeld, *Technical Change and Employment* (New York: St. Martin's, 1979); Paul Stoneman, *Technological Diffusion and the Computer Revolution* (London: Cambridge University Press, 1976), p. 177.

25. *Negotiating Technological Change*, pp. 12–18, 20. The terms *skilled* and *nonskilled* translate into American usage ETUI's terms *qualified* and *nonqualified*. With regard to exacerbation of the division of labor see Harry Braverman, *Labor and Monopoly Capital: The Degradation of Work in the Twentieth Century* (New York: Monthly Review, 1974). See also Benson and Lloyd, *New Technology and Industrial Change*, pp. 31–47. Regarding impact on women, see Barbara Drygulski Wright, ed., *Women, Work, and Technology* (Ann Arbor: University of Michigan Press, 1987); Ursula Huws, *Your Job in the Eighties: A Woman's Guide to New Technology* (London: Pluto, 1982). See below, nn. 39–41.

26. James Womack and Daniel Jones, "The Fourth Transformation in Autos," *Technology Review*, Oct. 1984, pp. 29–37.

27. H. Allan Hunt and Timothy L. Hunt, *Human Resource Implications of Robotics* (Kalamazoo, Mich.: W. E. Upjohn Institute for Employment Research, 1983), p. x.

28. *Ibid.*, pp. 111–12, 172. For more pollyanish projections, see Donald N. Smith and Peter Heytler, Jr., *Industrial Robots Forecast and Trends: A Second Edition Delphi Study* (Ann Arbor: Society of Manufacturing Engineers and University of Michigan, 1985), pp. 9–10.

29. Larry Hirschhorn, *Beyond Mechanization: Work and Technology in a Postindustrial Age* (Cambridge, Mass.: MIT Press, 1984), p. 158.

30. Harley Shaiken, *Work Transformed: Automation and Labor in the Computer Age* (Lexington, Mass.: Heath Lexington Books, 1986), p. 119. Computer-based analogic part programming is already eliminating humans from this job (*ibid.*, pp. 121–23). The range of possible impacts of technology on work can be gleaned from Annette Harrison, *Bibliography on Automation and Technological Change and Studies of the Future*, Rand Paper P-3365-3 (Santa Monica, Calif.: Rand, 1967; Springfield, Va.: Clearinghouse for Federal Scientific and Technical Information, U.S. Department of Commerce, 1968); and from ROBOMATICS, a microfiche service available in technical libraries and accessible via indexes and abstracts.

31. Ichiro Saga, "Japan's Robots Produce Problems for Workers," *WSJ*, 28 Feb. 1983, p. 19.

32. Seering, "Who Said Robots Should Work Like People?" p. 67; U.S. Congress, Office of Technology Assessment, *Computerized Manufacturing Automation: Employment, Education, and the Workplace* (Washington, D.C.: U.S. Government Printing Office, 1984), pp. 143–44.

33. See, for example, Colin Gill, *Work, Unemployment and the New Technology* (Oxford: B. Blackwell, 1985).

34. Daniel Bell, *The Coming of Post-Industrial Society* (New York: Basic Books, 1973); Stephen Hill, *Competition and Control at Work: The New Industrial Sociology* (Cambridge, Mass.: MIT Press, 1981); Claus Offe, *Disorganized Capitalism: Contemporary Transformations of Work and Politics* (Cambridge, Mass.: MIT Press, 1985), pp. 129–50.

35. H. J. Habbakuk, *American and British Technology in the Nineteenth Century: The Search for Labor Saving Inventions* (Cambridge: Cambridge University Press, 1962). For subsequent debate over Habbakuk's thesis, see Michael Burawoy, *The Politics of Production* (London: Verso, 1985), pp. 117–18, n. 54.

36. Leon Bagrit, *The Age of Automation* (New York: Mentor, 1965); George Terborgh, *Automation Hysteria* (New York: Norton, 1966); *The Impacts of Robotics on the Workforce and Workplace* (Pittsburgh: Carnegie-Mellon University Press, 1981).

37. The alarm was sounded already in the nineteenth century, not only by Marx but by such writers as John Cameron Simonds and John T. McEnnis (1887) and Henry George (1879). In the twentieth century George E. Barnett showed the impact of mechanization on the printing, stonecutting, and bottling industries (1926); Elliott Dunlap Smith (1939), Stuart Chase (1943), and Georges Friedmann (1955) expressed concern about the long-term implications of automation. More recently, such concerns are being expressed at more frequent intervals, for instance, by Ben B. Seligman (1966), Joan M. Greenbaum (1979), Robert Howard (1985), Harley Shaiken (1986), and Shashona Zuboff (1988).

38. Illustrative of union responses are the following: the European Trade Union Insti-

tute's *The Impact of Microelectronics on Employment in Western Europe in the 1980s* (Brussels: ETUI, 1979) and *Negotiating Technological Change* (1982); two 1981 publications of the AFL-CIO Department for Professional Employees: *Technological Change Clauses in Collective Bargaining Agreements* and *Cooperation or Conflict*; *European Experiences with Technological Change in the Workplace*; and Edward Yemin, ed., *Workforce Reductions in Undertakings* (Geneva: International Labour Organisation, 1982) and *Technological Change: The Tripartite Response* (Geneva: International Labour Organisation, 1985). See also Benjamin Sollow Kirsh, *Automation and Collective Bargaining* (New York: Central Book, 1964); and, for purposes of comparison, Milton J. Nadworny, *Scientific Management and the Unions, 1900–1932* (Cambridge, Mass.: Harvard University Press, 1955).

39. Illustrative of this concern are female-specific impact studies, e.g., Heather Menzies, *Women and the Chip: Case Studies of the Effects of Informatics on Employment in Canada* (Montreal: Institute for Research and Public Policy, 1981); studies of home-targeted technologies, e.g., Ruth Cowan, *More Work for Mother* (New York: Basic Books, 1983); and labor pool analyses, e.g., Veronica Beechey and Tessa Perkins, *A Matter of Hours: Women, Part-time Work, and the Labour Market* (London: Polity, 1987). See also Joan Rothschild, ed., *Machina ex Dea* (New York: Pergamon, 1983).

40. Asoka Bandarage, "Victims of Development," *Women's Review of Books* 5 (Oct. 1987): 3.

41. Kathryn B. Ward, *Women in the World-System* (New York: Praeger, 1984), pp. 16–18, 24–29. See also Barbara Ehrenreich and Annette Fuentes, "Life on the Global Assembly Line," *MS* 9, no. 7 (1981): 52–59, 71; Maria P. Fernández-Kelly, *For We Are Sold: I and My People: Women and Industry in Mexico's Frontier* (Albany: State University of New York Press, 1983), and Fernández-Kelly, "The 'Maquila' Women," *NACCA Report on the Americas* 14, no. 5 (1980): 14–19; R. Grossman, "Women's Place in the Integrated Circuit," *Pacific Research* 9 (1978–79): 2–17; Janet W. Salaff, *Working Daughters of Hong Kong* (Cambridge: Cambridge University Press, 1981); Helen I. Safa, "Runaway Shops and Female Employment: The Search for Cheap Labor," *Signs* 7, no. 2 (1981): 418–33; Nadia Haggag Youssef, *Women and Work in Developing Societies* (Berkeley: University of California Press, 1974); and Bandarage, "Victims of Development," p. 4.

42. See Charles Edquist and Staffan Jacobsson, *Flexible Automation: The Global Diffusion of New Engineering Technology* (Cambridge: B. Blackwell, 1988); Gerald K. Helleiner, *International Economic Disorder* (Toronto: University of Toronto Press, 1983).

43. Andrew Ure, *The Philosophy of Manufactures or An Exposition of the Scientific, Moral, and Commercial Economy of the Factory System of Great Britain* (1835; rpt. London: Frank Cass, 1967), pp. 23, 20, 19. See also pp. 16, 40–41, 331, 368–70.

44. See Habbakuk, *American and British Technology*, pp. 134, 152–53, 195, 198–99.

45. Karl Marx, *The Poverty of Philosophy* (1847), in Karl Marx and Friedrich Engels, *Collected Works* (London: Lawrence and Wishart, n.d.), 7:207, 393–94. See Jon Elster, *Explaining Technical Change* (Cambridge: Cambridge University Press, 1983), pp. 163–71.

46. David Dickson, *The Politics of Alternative Technology* (New York: Universe, 1975), pp. 72–73, 181–82.

47. Robert L. Heilbroner, "The Impact of Technology: The Historic Debate," in *Automation and Technological Change*, ed. John T. Dunlop (Englewood Cliffs, N.J.: Prentice-Hall Spectrum, 1962), pp. 11–14.

48. Frederick W. Taylor, "Shop Management," in *The Principles of Scientific Management* (New York: Harper & Brothers, 1903), p. 32.

49. See Rex Maus and Randall Allsup, *Robotics: A Manager's Guide* (New York: Wiley, 1986), pp. 27, 189–200. See also *The Impacts of Robotics on the Workforce and Workplace*, p. 49.

50. Joseph Engelberger, Society of Manufacturing Engineers Technical Paper, MS 74-167, 1974.

51. "Industrial Uses of the Microprocessor," in *The Microelectronics Revolution*, ed. Tom Forester (Oxford: B. Blackwell, 1980), p. 144 (originally published in *Science*, 18 March 1977).

52. Otis Port, "High Tech to the Rescue," *BW*, 16 June 1986, p. 101. See also "Artificial Intelligence: The Second Computer Age Begins," *BW*, 8 March 1982, pp. 66–75; "A New Target: Reducing Staff and Levels," *BW* 21 Dec. 1981, pp. 69–73.

53. Shaiken, *Work Transformed*, pp. 140–55; Melvin Blumberg and Donald Gerwin, "Coping with Advanced Manufacturing Technology," paper presented at conference on Quality of Work Life in the 80s, Toronto, 1981, p. 12.

54. "The Speedup in Automation," *BW*, 3 Aug. 1981, pp. 62–67; "Technology Challenges Postal Union," *ITT*, 17–23 Aug. 1977, p. 8.

55. See Otis Port, "High Tech to the Rescue," *BW*, 16 June 1986, pp. 100–103; William J. Hampton, "GM Bets an Arm and a Leg on a People-Free Plant," *BW*, 12 Sept. 1988, pp. 72–73.

56. Brody, "U.S. Robot Makers Try to Bounce Back," p. 20.

57. "Thinking Ahead Got Deere in Big Trouble," *BW*, 8 Dec. 1986, p. 69.

58. Kathleen Deveny, "As John Deere Sowed, So Shall It Reap," *BW*, 6 June 1988, pp. 84, 86; Kathryn M. Welling, "Bitter Harvest," *Barron's*, 27 June 1988, pp. 6ff.

59. William M. Bulkeley, "Uncovering the Hidden Costs," *WSJ*, Special Report on Technology in the Workplace, 12 June 1987, p. 14D. The ultimate cost might well be the job of the manager who becomes dependent on technically skilled employees. See Peter Waldman, "Those Dangerous Liaisons," *ibid.*, p. 16D. Compare Catherine L. Harris et al., "Office Automation: Making It Pay Off," *BW*, 12 Oct. 1987, pp. 134–38ff.

60. "Machine Parts: It Really May Pay to Buy American," *BW*, 30 May 1988, p. 101.

61. Quoted in Michael Connolly, "From IBP to Hormel: Meatpackers Fight Companies, Union Bureaucrats," *News & Letters* 32 (10 April 1987): 8.

62. Amit Bhaduri, "A Study in Agricultural Backwardness under Semi-Feudalism," *Economic Journal* 83 (1973): 120–37. See also Stephen A. Marglin, "What Do Bosses Do?" in *The Division of Labour*, ed. André Gorz (Hassocks: Harvester, 1978), pp. 13–54.

63. Habbakuk, *American and British Technology*, pp. 139–40.

64. See, for example, Wendy Zellner, "GM's New 'Teams' Aren't Hitting Any Homers," *BW*, 8 Aug. 1988, pp. 46–47.

65. Miklòs Haraszti, *A Worker in a Worker's State*, tr. Michael Wright (New York: Universe, 1978), pp. 35, 40.

66. Michael Wright, "About the Author," *ibid.*, pp. 15–17.

67. P. K. Edwards and Hugh Scullion, *The Social Organization of Industrial Conflict: Control and Resistance in the Workplace* (Oxford: B. Blackwell, 1982), ch. 7.

68. Harry Braverman, *Labor and Monopoly Capital* (New York: Monthly Review, 1974), pp. 188, 193–94, 199, 227–28, 205.

69. *Ibid.*, pp. 196–206.

70. Shaiken, *Work Transformed*, pp. 108–9.

71. U.S. Congress, Office of Technology Assessment, *Computerized Manufacturing Automation*, pp. 142–43.

72. Machine Tool Task Force, *Executive Summary, Technology of Machine Tools*, 1:17; see also David F. Noble, *Forces of Production* (New York: Knopf, 1984).

73. See, for example, Andrew Zimbalist, ed., *Case Studies on the Labor Process* (New York: Monthly Review, 1979); and Les Levidow and Bob Young, eds., *Science, Technology and the Labour Process: Marxist Studies*, 2 vols. (London: Free Association Books, and Atlantic Highlands, N.J.: Humanities, 1981 and 1985). Historical studies in this perspective include Dan Clawson, *Bureaucracy and the Labor Process: The Transformation of U.S. Industry, 1860–1920* (New York: Monthly Review, 1980); and David F. Noble's studies of the engineering profession in *America by Design* (New York: Knopf, 1980) and of numerical machine control in *Forces of Production*.

74. Stephen Wood, ed., *The Degradation of Work? Skill, Deskilling and the Labour Process* (London: Hutchinson, 1982). Michael Burawoy develops a stronger and yet more appreciative critique of Braverman, which faults him for analyzing work relationships from within capitalism without any external reference, for example, to pre- or noncapitalist systems (*Politics of Production*, esp. pp. 21–41).

75. *Project Utopia*, film produced by California Newsreels, San Francisco, 1987.

76. Braverman says this is because the complexity of reasons why there has been a "transformation of the labor process" does not lend itself to a "unitary answer" (*Labor and Monopoly Capital*, p. 169).

77. Dickson, *Politics of Alternative Technology*, pp. 72–73, 181–82.

78. Peter Drucker, "The Changed World Economy," *Foreign Affairs*, Spring 1986, p. 768.

79. For Ure's views on the need for machines to outdo foreign competition, see *Philosophy of Manufactures*, pp. 31–32, 329. For the view of Coventry textile manufacturers, see sign in Coventry Textile Museum, reprinted in Edmund F. Byrne, *Philosophy of Work* (Bloomington: Indiana University Division of Extended Studies, 1986), at pp. 112–13.

80. George Unwin, *The Gilds and Companies of London* (1908; 4th ed. New York: Barnes & Noble, 1963), pp. 137–39, 246–50.

81. *NYT*, 6 July 1984. This and two subsequent quotations I owe to Jeff Robbins.

82. "The Hollow Corporation," *BW*, 3 March 1986, p. 72.

83. "Are America's Manufacturers Finally Back on the Map?" *BW*, 17 Nov. 1986, pp. 92ff.; Peter Engardio, "Textile Imports Are Swamping Even the Best Companies," *BW*, 16 Sept. 1985, pp. 50–54.

84. James B. Treece et al., "Can Ford Stay on Top?" *BW* 28 Sept. 1987, pp. 78–82, 86.

85. M. M. Barash et al., "Optimal Planning of Computerized Manufacturing Systems (CMS)," paper presented at NSF Grantees' Conference on Production Research and Technology, West Lafayette, Ind., 27–29 Sept. 1978, p. E-1.

86. Marvin Minsky, ed., *Robotics* (Garden City, N.Y.: Doubleday Anchor, 1985), Introduction.

87. Noble, *Forces of Production*, pp. 71–76.

88. Norbert Wiener, *God and Golem, Inc.* (Cambridge, Mass.: MIT Press, 1966), pp. 52–53, 64.

89. Robert Boguslaw, *The New Utopians* (Englewood Cliffs, N.J.: Prentice-Hall, 1965).

90. "The Productivity Paradox," *BW*, June 6, 1988, pp. 100–108. See also Sal Nuccio, "Accounting for Automation," *High Technology Business*, Aug. 1988, pp. 38–39.

91. Jeffrey Zygmont, "Guided Vehicles Set Manufacturing in Motion," *High Technology*, Dec. 1986, pp. 16–21; "The Productivity Paradox," pp. 104, 108.

92. Maureen Dowd, "Brock Says Fewer Workers Have Skill for Current Jobs," *NYT*, 14 Jan. 1987, p. Y9; John Templeman et al., "Europe's Other Employment Problem," *BW*, 30 June 1986, pp. 48–49; James Barron, "Gaps in Retraining Are Seen in Era of Industrial Change," *NYT*, 10 Aug. 1986, pp. 1+.

CHAPTER 9

1. Thomas Hobbes, *Leviathan*, ed. Francis B. Randall (New York: Washington Square, 1964), ch. xv, p. 98; Ernest Barker, ed., *Social Contract* (New York: Oxford University Press, 1960), pp. 23, 28, 55–56, 77 (Locke), 186–89 (Rousseau).

2. See Lawrence Becker, "Property: A Select Bibliography," *Philosophy and Law Newsletter* (American Philosophical Association), Winter 1987, pp. 3–5.

3. Gottfried Dietz, *In Defense of Property* (1963; rpt. Baltimore: Johns Hopkins University Press, 1971), p. 69.

4. *Ibid.*, pp. 78–84.

5. Pierre Joseph Proudhon, *What Is Property?* tr. Benjamin R. Tucker (New York: Fertig, 1966 [first published in English c. 1890]), p. 368.

6. Dietz, *In Defense of Property*, pp. 98–99, 100–108.

7. For current philosophical discussion of corporate responsibility see above, Chapter 4, nn. 29–30. See also Clarence Walton, ed., *The Ethics of Corporate Conduct* (Englewood Cliffs, N.J.: Prentice-Hall, 1977).

8. This is because the courts respect the managerial prerogative of determining where and how to invest corporate wealth. See Philip A. Miscimarra, *The NLRB and Managerial Discretion: Plant Closings, Relocation, Subcontracting, and Automation*, Labor Relations and Plant Policy Series No. 24 (Philadelphia: Wharton School, University of Pennsylvania, 1983).

9. Judge Thomas Lambros, quoted in Staughton Lynd, "What Happened to Youngstown," *Radical America* 15 (July–August 1981): 43–44. See *Local 1330, et al. v. U.S.*

Steel, 492 F.Supp. 1 (N.D. Ohio 1980), *aff'd in part and rev'd in part*, 631 F.2d 1264 (6th Cir. 1980); and discussion of theories of case in Lynd, *The Fight against Shutdowns: Youngstown's Steel Mill Closings* (San Pedro, Calif.: Singlejack, 1982), pp. 139–46, 160, 162–65, 175–76, 178–79.

10. On this subject I am deeply indebted to Peter d'Errico for sharing with me his insightful analysis of the ideological underpinnings of American corporate law.

11. Robert Reinhold, "Oil Company Town, Facing Eviction, Digs in for Legal Battle," *NYT*, 23 Feb. 1986, p. 1.

12. Morning Edition, PBS, 20 Oct. 1988.

13. James C. Goodale, "Ninth Circuit Case May Have Impact on Constitutionality of Cable Act," *NLJ*, 25 March 1985, pp. 23–25. The Reagan veto was effective 6 November 1988. This mercantile view of First Amendment rights is touted by Michael Gartner, *Advertising and the First Amendment* (Winchester, Mass.: Unwin Hyman, 1988).

14. Nova, PBS, 15 April 1986.

15. John Hoerr, " 'We're Not Going to Sit Around and Allow Management to Louse Things Up,' " *BW*, 18 May 1987, p. 107.

16. Aaron Bernstein et al., "The Secondary Boycott Gets a Second Wind," *BW*, 27 June 1988, p. 82.

17. See the following, all in *BW*: Aaron Bernstein, "The Unions are Learning to Hit Where It Hurts," 17 March 1986, pp. 112, 114; "The Picket Line Gives Way to Sophisticated New Tactics," 16 April 1984, pp. 116, 118; "The Ripples Spreading from the Stevens Pact," 3 Nov. 1980, pp. 107, 110; "Embattled Unions Strike Back at Management," 4 Dec. 1978, pp. 54–58ff.

18. Adolf A. Berle and Gardiner C. Means, *The Modern Corporation and Private Property* (1932; rev. ed. New York: Harcourt, Brace & World Harvest, 1967).

19. Beth Mintz and Michael Schwartz, *The Power and Structure of American Business* (Chicago: University of Chicago Press, 1985), pp. 22–27.

20. Bruce Nussbaum and Judith H. Dobrzynski, "The Battle for Corporate Control," *BW*, 18 May 1987, pp. 102–09. See also Christopher Power and Vicky Cahan, "Shareholders Aren't Just Rolling Over Anymore," *BW*, 27 April 1987, pp. 32–33.

21. See Sarah Bartlett, "From Boone Pickens, Another Popular (and Profitable?) Cause," *BW*, 7 July 1986, pp. 64–65; Chuck Hawkins and Gregory L. Miles, "Carl Icahn: Raider or Manager?" *BW*, 27 Oct. 1986, pp. 98–104.

22. Mintz and Schwartz, *Power and Structure of American Business*, pp. 27–30.

23. *Ibid.*, pp. 30–44, 57.

24. "The End of Corporate Loyalty?" *BW*, 4 Aug. 1986, pp. 42–49.

25. Mintz and Schwartz, *Power and Structure of American Business*, p. 87.

26. See John Gibbons, *Tenure and Toil, Or Rights and Wrongs of Property and Labor* (Philadelphia: Lippincott, 1888), pp. 148–49, 183–91; Stanley Buder, *Pullman: An Experiment in Industrial Order and Community Planning, 1830–1930* (New York: Oxford University Press, 1967); Alfred Winslow Jones, *Life, Liberty, and Property* (New York: Lippincott, 1941); Barbara Dinham and Colin Hines, *Agribusiness in Africa* (Trenton, N.J.: Africa World, 1984).

27. See Dinham and Hines, *Agribusiness in Africa*; Richard J. Barnet and Ronald E.

Muller, *Global Reach: The Power of the Multinational Corporations* (New York: Simon & Schuster, 1974), pp. 254–302.

28. Among the innumerable studies of slavery, see in particular the Marxist analysis in Elizabeth Fox Genovese and Eugene D. Genovese, *Fruits of Merchant Capital: Slavery and Bourgeois Property in the Rise and Expansion of Capitalism* (New York: Oxford University Press, 1983); and the religious analysis in David Brion Davis, *The Problem of Slavery in Western Culture* (Ithaca: Cornell University Press, 1966).

29. "Airline Wages Are Set for a Long Slide," *BW*, 9 April 1984, pp. 127–28.

30. "For Better or for Worse?" *BW*, 12 Jan. 1987, p. 39.

31. See Jeffrey M. Laderman, "What Does Equity Financing Really Cost?" *BW*, 7 Nov. 1988, pp. 146, 148.

32. "The Growing Apprehension about Takeovers," King Features Syndicate, *IS*, 9 Nov. 1988.

33. David Pauly, "A Mountain of Debt," *Newsweek*, 7 Nov. 1988, p. 80.

34. Christopher Farrell, "Learning to Live with Leverage," *BW*, 7 Nov. 1988, p. 141.

35. This expression is the title of a book by Jeff Madrick: *Taking America* (New York: Bantam, 1987).

36. See, for example, Richard McKenzie, *Restrictions on Business Mobility* (Washington, D.C.: American Enterprise Institute, 1979); John Heckman and John Strong, "Is There a Case for Plant Closing Laws?" *New England Economics Review*, July–Aug. 1980, pp. 34–51.

37. Judith Lichtenberg, "Workers, Owners and Factory Closings," *Report from the Center for Philosophy and Public Affairs* (College Park: University of Maryland) 4 (Fall 1984): 12.

38. Early responses to this reality include "Plant Shutdowns: States Take a New Tack," *BW*, 24 Oct. 1983, pp. 72, 76; David Moberg, "Unions, Communities Wage Uphill Battle against Plant Closings," *ITT*, 18–24 July 1979, pp. 7–8; *A Guide for Communities Facing Plant Closings* (Northeast-Midwest Institute, 1982).

39. Quoted in Stephen Labaton, "For the States, a Starring Role in the Takeover Game," *NYT*, 3 May 1987, p. 8F.

40. *Edgar v. MITE*, 457 U.S. 624 (1982).

41. *C.T.S. Corp. v. Dynamics Corp. of America*, 481 U.S. 69 (1987).

42. Kirk Victor, "Steam May Be Building for a Counterrevolution in Antitrust," *NLJ*, 4 May 1987, pp. 1, 26.

43. See Paula Dwyer et al., "Takeover Artists Take a Direct Hit," *BW*, 4 May 1987, p. 35; David Penticuff, "Study Blasts Hoosier Anti-Takeover Law," *Indianapolis Business Journal*, 16–22 May 1988, p. 4A.

44. "The High Court's Raid on the Raiders," *BW*, 11 May 1987, p. 170.

45. Kirk Victor, "States Flex Muscles on Takeovers," *NLJ*, 1 June 1987, pp. 1, 35; Sharon Pamepinto and James E. Heard, "New State Regulation of Corporate Takeovers," *NLJ*, 21 Sept. 1987, pp. 26–28.

46. See Catherine Yang and Joseph Weber, "Is Delaware About to Harpoon the Sharks?" *BW*, 25 Jan. 1988, p. 34; Sherry R. Sontag, "Court Challenges to Delaware Takeover Law Begin," "Battle Begins over Takeover Law," and "A Takeover Law Grows

in Delaware," *NLJ*, 15 Feb. 1988, p. 37; 29 Feb. 1988, pp. 3, 8; 11 April 1988, pp. 1, 19–20.

47. Mary J. Pitzer, "An Acid Test for Antitakeover Laws," *BW*, 28 Sept. 1987, p. 31.

48. In *Ozark Trailers, Inc.*, 161 N.L.R.B. 561, 566.

49. E. F. Schumacher, *Small Is Beautiful: Economics as if People Mattered* (New York: Harper & Row, 1975).

50. R. H. Tawney, *The Acquisitive Society* (New York: Harcourt, Brace, 1920).

51. "What's Missing from the Debate about Takeovers?" *BW*, 15 Dec. 1986, p. 16.

52. See J. F. C. Harrison, *Quest for the New Moral World: Robert Owen and the Owenites in Britain and America* (New York: Scribner's, 1969), pp. 2–3, 48–49, 51–53, 61–62.

53. John Gibbons, *Tenure and Toil*, pp. 294–95. See also pp. 115, 131, 148–55, 167–71, 180–91, 198, 262–70.

54. See Edmund F. Byrne, "Workplace Democracy for Teachers: John Dewey's Contribution," in *Philosophy and Technology* VI, ed. Paul T. Durbin (Dordrecht: Kluwer Academic, forthcoming).

55. John Dewey, *The Public and Its Problems* (1927), in *John Dewey: The Later Works, 1925–1953*, Vol. 2: *1925–1927*, ed. Jo Ann Boydston (Carbondale: Southern Illinois University Press, 1984), pp. 296, 367.

56. John Dewey, *Liberalism and Social Action* (1935; rpt. New York: Capricorn, 1963), pp. 20–21, 25, 61, 64. See also Dewey, *The Public and Its Problems* (Chicago: Gateway, 1946), pp. 109, 190.

57. Dewey, *The Public and Its Problems* (Gateway ed.), pp. 212–13, 216, 211.

58. Percival Goodman and Paul Goodman, *Communitas: Means of Livelihood and Ways of Life* (1947; rpt. New York: Vintage, 1960); Robert Nisbet, *The Social Philosophers: Community and Conflict in Western Thought* (New York: Crowell, 1973).

59. Kirkpatrick Sale, *Human Scale* (New York: Coward, McCann & Geoghegan, 1980).

60. These environmentalist ideas are based to some extent on the work of Christopher Stone, *Should Trees Have Standing?* (Los Altos, Calif.: William Kaufman, 1974). See also Edith B. Weiss, "The Planetary Trust: Conservation and Intergenerational Equity," *Ecology Law Quarterly* 17, no. 4 (1984): 500ff.

61. This question was raised in *City of Oakland v. Oakland Raiders*, 32 Cal. 3rd 60, 646 P.2d 835, 183 Cal. Rptr. 673 (1982). The California Supreme Court decided that the Commerce Clause of the U.S. Constitution would be violated if such a constraint were imposed. See below, n. 83.

62. John E. Cribbett, William F. Fitz, and Corwin W. Johnson, *Cases and Materials on Property*, 3d ed. (Mineola, N.Y.: Foundation, 1972), pp. 1065–80.

63. Spencer H. MacCallum, *The Art of Community* (Menlo Park, Calif.: Institute for Humane Studies, 1970).

64. See Michele Galen, "Suits Target High Cost of Summer Fun," *NLJ*, 15 June 1987, pp. 3, 10; and compare *Nollan v. California Coastal Commission*, 107 S.Ct. 3141 (1987) and *Keystone Bituminous Coal Assoc. v. DeBenedictis*, 107 S.Ct. 1232 (1987).

65. Satisfactory resolution of the difficult and controversial question of just compensation will here be assumed. See William Michael Treanor, "The Origins and Original

Significance of the Just Compensation Clause of the Fifth Amendment," *Yale Law Journal* 94 (Jan. 1985): 674–716.

66. *Bloodgood v. Mohawk Hudson RR Co.* (N.Y. 1837), 18 Wend. 9.

67. *Scudder v. Trenton Delaware Falls Co.*, 1 N.J. Eq. 694 (1832).

68. See, e.g., *Fallbrook Irrigation District v. Bradley*, 164 U.S. 112 (1896).

69. See, e.g., *Ryerson v. Brown*, 35 Mich. 332 (1877).

70. 270 N.Y. 333, 1 N.E.2d 153.

71. 348 U.S. 28.

72. 12 N.Y.2d 379, 190 N.E.2d 402 (1963).

73. 410 Mich. 616, 304 N.W.2d 455 (1981). See "Pushing the Boundaries of Eminent Domain," *BW* 4 May 1981, p. 174.

74. 104 S.Ct. 2321 (1984). See also *City and County of San Francisco v. Ross*, 44 Cal.2d 52, 279 P.2d 529 (1955); *Karech v. City Council*, 271 S.C. 339, S.E.2d 342 (1978); *In re The Westlake Project, City of Seattle*, 96 Wash.2d 616, 638 P.2d 549 (1981).

75. *Hawaii Rev. Stat.* par. 516-1 to 83 (1976 and Supp. 1982).

76. 702 F.2d at 798.

77. 104 S.Ct. at 2330.

78. *Id.* at 2329–30.

79. *First English Evangelical Church v. County of Los Angeles*, 107 S.Ct. 2378 (1987).

80. See Eugene J. Morris, "Supreme Court Land Use Decisions Uncertain in Defining a 'Taking,' " *NLJ*, 7 Sept. 1987, p. 20; "Court Tilts Scales toward Property Owners," *NLJ*, 22 June 1987, pp. 5, 32; Stuart Taylor, Jr., "High Court Backs Rights of Owners in Land-Use Suit," *NYT*, 9 June 1987, pp. 1, 17; David W. Dunlap, "Ruling May Dampen Ardor of Local Planners," *ibid.*, p. 17.

81. *Pennell v. City of San Jose*, 86–753, decided 24 Feb. 1988.

82. *NLJ*, 25 April 1988, p. 5.

83. *City of Oakland v. Oakland Raiders*, 32 Cal. 3d 60, 646 P.2d 835, 183 Cal. Rptr. 673 (1982), *cert. den.*, 30 June 1986. See Susan Crabtree, "Public Use in Eminent Domain: Are There Limits after *Oakland Raiders* and *Poletown*?" *California Western Law Review* 20 (Spring 1984): 82, 88–90. Some legal scholars, such as Charles Reich, Frank Michelman, and Joseph Sax, have argued that even entitlements, e.g., under social security, should be protected as property. See Gregory S. Alexander, "The Concept of Property in Private and Constitutional Law: The Ideology of the Scientific Turn in Legal Analysis," *Columbia Law Review* 82 (Dec. 1982): 1545–99. This step, which would add a valuable tool to the communitarian chest, the Supreme Court has been unwilling to take. See *Flemming v. Nestor*, 363 U.S. 603 (1960); *Board of Regents v. Roth*, 408 U.S. 564 (1972). Compare *Pennsylvania Coal Co. v. Mahon*, 260 U.S. 393 (1922).

84. "Memorandum of Law in Opposition to Production Incorporated's Motion for an Order Restraining a Massachusetts Municipality from Taking Its Plant by Eminent Domain," prepared by Donald Siegel and Paul Bamberger for the legal committee of the Northeast Region, Jewish Labor Committee, 33 Harrison Avenue, Boston, Mass. 02111.

85. These recommendations parallel those in Barry Bluestone and Bennett Harrison, *The Deindustrialization of America* (New York: Basic Books, 1982), pp. 231–62. See also *ibid.*, Table 6.7, p. 163.

86. Written in 1888, published in James Bryce, *The American Commonwealth, Selec-*

tions from (Chicago: University of Chicago, 1946; rpt. from 1910 Macmillan ed.), p. 647.

87. Mintz and Schwartz, *Power Structure of American Business*, p. 61.

CHAPTER 10

1. See Joseph Margolis, "The Technological Self," in *Technological Transformation: Contextual and Conceptual Implications*, ed. Edmund F. Byrne and Joseph C. Pitt (Dordrecht: Kluwer Academic, 1989), pp. 1–15.

2. See my review of this work in *Nature and System* 1 (Dec. 1979): 283–86.

3. See in this regard Edmund F. Byrne, "Can Government Regulate Technology?" in *Philosophy and Technology*, ed. Paul T. Durbin and Friedrich Rapp (Dordrecht: Reidel, 1983), pp. 17–33.

4. See my review of Ellul's *The Technological System* in *Nature and System* 3 (Sept. 1981): 184–88.

5. See Edmund F. Byrne, "U.S. Domsat Policy: A Case Study of Economic Constraints on Technology Assessment," *Prace Naukoznawcze i Prognostyczne* (Papers on Science of Science and Forecasting) 1–2 (Wrocław, Poland, 1981): 71–86.

6. See Byrne and Pitt, eds., *Technological Transformation*, esp. Stanley R. Carpenter, "What Technologies Transfer: The Contingent Nature of Cultural Responses," pp. 163–77.

7. See George H. Nadel and Perry Curtis, eds., *Imperialism and Colonialism* (New York: Macmillan, 1964); and for contemporaneous concerns see Karl Marx and Friedrich Engels, *On Colonialism* (New York: International Publishers, 1972).

8. The neo-Malthusian mentality here alluded to permeates most of the pages of *Lifeboat Ethics: The Moral Dilemmas of World Hunger*, ed. George R. Lucas, Jr., and Thomas W. Ogletree (New York: Harper & Row, 1976), originally published in the Spring and Summer 1976 issues of *Soundings*. See also Garrett Hardin, *Exploring New Ethics for Survival* (Baltimore: Penguin, 1973).

9. The paternalistic tone is illustrated by publications such as L. C. Graves, *Modern Production among Backward Peoples* (1935; rpt. New York: Augustus M. Kelley, 1968).

10. The most monumental study of its kind, on which I have drawn for many insights, is Gunnar Myrdal, *Asian Drama: An Inquiry into the Poverty of Nations*, 3 vols. (New York: Pantheon, 1968). (A one-volume abridged edition was published by Random House: New York: Vintage, 1972.)

11. See Godfrey Gunatilleke et al., eds., *Ethical Dilemmas of Development in Asia* (Lexington, Mass.: Heath Lexington Books, 1983), p. 37, nn. 18–22; Lars Anell and Birgitta Nygren, *The Developing Countries and the World Economic Order* (London: Methuen, 1980).

12. See Jeffrey Harrod, *Power, Production, and the Unprotected Worker* (New York: Columbia University Press, 1987), vol. 2 of a 4-volume series.

13. Myrdal, *Asian Drama*, 2:1134–136.

14. See Elias Mendelievich, ed., *Children at Work* (Geneva: International Labour Office, [1979]). Because poverty is the common factor that induces families to allow their

children to be exploited, this exploitation is by no means unique to the TNC in the Third World; it is just as likely to be indigenous there or in developed countries to which the poor migrate. See Roger Sawyer, *Children Enslaved* (London: Routledge, 1988). What Sawyer and others fail to consider, however, is the role of TNCs (and their colonial predecessors) in creating these conditions of poverty.

15. See, for example, Barbara Dinham and Colin Hines, *Agribusiness in Africa* (Trenton, N.J.: Africa World, 1984).

16. See Martin Ravallion, *Markets and Famines* (New York: Oxford University Press, 1987); William A. Dando, *Geography of Famine* (New York: Halsted, 1980).

17. See H. J. Duller, *Development Technology* (London: Routledge & Kegan Paul, 1982), esp. pp. 75–77.

18. See Noam Chomsky and Edward S. Herman, *The Washington Connection and Third World Fascism* (Boston: South End, 1979); and Alexander R. Magno's analysis of the Philippines under Marcos: "Technocratic Authoritarianism and the Dilemmas of Dependent Development," in *Ethical Dilemmas of Development in Asia*, ed. Gunatilleke et al., pp. 179–203.

19. Gerald K. Helleiner, *International Economic Disorder; Essays in North-South Relations* (Toronto: University of Toronto Press, 1981).

20. See Wilbert E. Moore, *Social Change* (Englewood Cliffs, N.J.: Prentice-Hall, 1963); and Moore, *Man, Time and Society* (New York: Wiley, 1963). Compare Eric Hoffer, *The Ordeal of Change* (New York: Harper & Row, 1963).

21. See Florian Znaniecki, *The Social Role of the Man of Knowledge* (New York: Harper Torchbooks, 1968); E. O. James, *The Nature and Function of Priesthood* (New York: Barnes & Noble, 1955); Claude Lévi-Strauss, *The Savage Mind* (Chicago: University of Chicago Press, 1966).

22. As Wilbert E. Moore points out in *Social Change*, pp. 40–42, 89–112, modernization and progress are not interchangeable concepts. Human values, in particular, tend to be undermined by merely technological advancement. See Eric Josephson and Mary Josephson, eds., *Man Alone* (New York: Dell Laurel, 1962); Erich Fromm, ed., *Socialist Humanism* (Garden City, N.Y.: Doubleday Anchor, 1966).

23. See Peter L. Berger and Thomas Luckmann, *The Social Construction of Reality* (Garden City, N.Y.: Doubleday Anchor, 1967), pp. 92–128; Vittorio Lanternari, *The Religions of the Oppressed* (New York: Mentor, 1965); James Mooney, *The Ghost-Dance Religion and the Sioux Outbreak of 1890* (Chicago: Phoenix, 1965); Richard A. Schermerhorn, *Society and Power* (New York: Random House, 1961), pp. 53–69.

24. See, for example, Andrew M. Kamarck, *The Economics of African Development* (New York: Praeger, 1967), p. 233.

25. Anibal Quijano Obregón, "Tendencies in Peruvian Development and in the Class Structure," in *Latin America: Reform or Revolution?* ed. James Petras and Maurice Zeitlin (Greenwich, Conn.: Fawcett Premier, 1968), p. 327; David S. Landes, *Prometheus Unbound* (Cambridge: Cambridge University Press, 1969), pp. 34–35; Kamarck, *Economics of African Development*, p. 163.

26. In the wake of negotiation, cooperative arrangements, and transfer of businesses back and forth, this issue remains unresolved as the European Community prepares to

eliminate internal trade barriers. See, in *BW*: John J. Keller, "IBM Takes a Big Step Away from PBXs," 26 Dec. 1988, p. 65; Richard A. Melcher, "DEC: Making the Most of Vanishing Borders," 12 Dec. 1988, p. 60; "Special Report: Reshaping the Computer Industry," 16 July 1984, pp. 84–111; "Suddenly U.S. Companies Are Teaming Up," 11 July 1983, pp. 71ff.

27. Herman Kahn, as quoted in *The Management of Information and Knowledge* (Washington, D.C.: U.S. Government Printing Office, 1970), p. 27.

28. Albert Memmi, *The Colonizer and the Colonized*, tr. Howard Greenfield (Boston: Beacon, 1967).

29. Robert L. Heilbroner, *The Future as History* (1960; rpt. New York: Harper Torchbooks, 1968).

30. Erich Fromm, *The Revolution of Hope* (New York: Bantam, 1968).

31. See Desaix Myers III, *U.S. Business in South Africa: The Economic, Political, and Moral Issues* (Bloomington: Indiana University Press, 1980); Reginald H. Green and Ann Seidman, *Unity or Poverty? The Economics of Pan-Africanism* (Baltimore: Penguin African Library, 1968); and Jim Donahue, "Senators' Investments Linked to South Africa," *Multinational Monitor*, Sept. 1988, p. 6.

32. Jagdish Bhagwati, *The Economics of Underdeveloped Countries* (New York: World University Library, 1966), pp. 205–44; Green and Seidman, *Unity or Poverty?* pp. 99–131; Petras and Zeitlin, eds., *Latin America*, pp. 1–144.

33. As Landes notes (*Prometheus Unbound*, p. 38), there is ample precedent for such paupercide in the history of European expansionism; and it has not been unknown between peoples who are at least geographically more closely related, e.g., in the Middle East, in sub-Saharan Africa, and in Southeast Asia.

34. The following discussion is based on ideas articulated by Godfrey Gunatilleke, "The Ethics of Order and Change: An Analytical Framework," in Gunatilleke et al., eds., *Ethical Dilemmas of Development in Asia*, pp. 1–39.

35. *Ibid.*, p. 12.

36. See Helleiner, *International Economic Disorder*, pp. 4–8.

37. See above, n. 11.

38. Gunatilleke, "Ethics of Order and Change," p. 16.

39. Charles Van Doren, *The Idea of Progress* (New York: Praeger, 1967), pp. 13–16, 33–193, 210–17, 225–28. See Carl Becker, *Progress and Power* (New York: Vintage, 1965).

40. See Bob Goudzwaard, *Capitalism and Progress* (Grand Rapids, Mich.: Eerdmans, 1979); John Baillie, *The Belief in Progress* (London: Oxford University Press, 1950); Christopher Dawson, *Progress and Religion* (London: Sheed & Ward, 1929).

41. Goudzwaard, *Capitalism and Progress*, p. 248.

42. *Ibid.*, pp. 30–31.

43. Reference here is to a major concern of John Rawls, to be considered in the final section of this chapter.

44. Georg Simmel, *Conflict and the Web of Group-Affiliations*, tr. Kurt Wolff and Reinhold Bendix (New York: Macmillan Free Press, 1955), p. 57.

45. Economist John Kenneth Galbraith says perfect competition is an utterly arcane

and useless technical exercise for mathematical economists (*Economics in Perspective* [Boston: Houghton Mifflin, 1987], pp. 260, 285). In the real world, people pay for what technical exercises disregard. See K. William Kapp, *The Social Costs of Private Enterprise* (1950; rpt. New York: Schocken, 1971); Frederick C. Thayer, *An End to Hierarchy! An End to Competition!* (New York: New Viewpoints, 1973), pp. 84–100.

46. Paul Samuelson, *Economics*, 6th ed. (New York: McGraw-Hill, 1964), p. 621.

47. In Charles Van Doren's opinion, Spencer's arguments for progress show only adaptability, (*Idea of Progress*, pp. 301–2); but neither Spencer nor his entrepreneurial fans were content with any such narrow interpretation. See Galbraith, *Economics in Perspective*, pp. 121–23; and see also n. 52, below.

48. This Marxist interpretation of Marx is contested by, among others, Michel Henry. See his *Marx: A Philosophy of Human Reality*, tr. Kathleen McLaughlin (Bloomington: Indiana University Press, 1983), p. 6.

49. Jean-Paul Sartre, *Critique of Dialectical Reason*, tr. Alan Sheridan-Smith (London: Verso, 1982), pp. 197–219, esp. p. 213.

50. See, for example, Jay M. Savage, *Evolution* (New York: Holt, Rinehart and Winston, 1963).

51. For this information I thank beekeeper James R. East.

52. Pëtr Kropotkin, *Mutual Aid: A Factor of Evolution* (London: Heinemann, 1910). John Dewey took a similar position, thereby setting himself apart from most social scientists of his day and from the likes of John D. Rockefeller and Andrew Carnegie, who found true inspiration in Spencer's ideas. Carnegie and Spencer, in fact, became intimate friends. See John Dewey and James H. Tufts, eds., *Ethics*, rev. ed. (New York: Henry Holt, 1932), pp. 368–75; Richard Hofstadter, *Social Darwinism in American Thought*, rev. ed. (Boston: Beacon, 1955), pp. 45–46.

53. See Thomas J. Schlereth, *The Cosmopolitan Ideal in Enlightenment Thought* (Notre Dame: University of Notre Dame Press, 1977); Van Doren, *Idea of Progress*, pp. 379–87.

54. Pierre Teilhard de Chardin, *The Phenomenon of Man* (New York: Harper, 1959; rev. ed., 1965). See also Bernard Delfgaauw, *Evolution: The Theory of Teilhard de Chardin*, tr. H. Hoskins (London: Fontana, 1969). Anthropologist Julian Huxley, for one, agrees with Teilhard de Chardin at least in a general way.

55. See, for example, Clair Wilcox, *Toward Social Welfare* (Homewood, Ill.: Richard D. Irwin, 1969); also the classic work in this field, Arthur C. Pigou, *The Economics of Welfare* (London: Macmillan, 1920).

56. James D. Gwartney and Richard Stroup, *Economics: Private and Public Choice*, 2d ed. (New York: Academic, 1980), pp. 71, 716–22.

57. Fred Frohock, *Public Policy: Scope and Logic* (Englewood Cliffs, N.J.: Prentice-Hall, [1967]), pp. 5–7.

58. Lester Thurow, *The Zero-Sum Society* (New York: Basic Books, 1980).

59. *Ibid.*, pp. 99, 125–26. See also Thurow, *The Zero-Sum Solution* (New York: Simon & Schuster, 1985), pp. 103, 123.

60. Thurow, *Zero-Sum Society*, pp. 42, 162, 189, 91, 118, 157.

61. John Maynard Keynes, *The End of Laissez-Faire* (London: Hogarth, 1926). Keynes's critique did not occur in a vacuum but continued a movement toward greater

realism in economic theory. See Paul J. McNulty, *The Origins and Development of Labor Economics* (Cambridge, Mass.: MIT Press, 1980), chs. 3–7; Paul Samuelson, *Economics: An Introductory Analysis*, 6th ed. (New York: McGraw-Hill, 1964), pp. 340–42.

62. John Maynard Keynes, *The General Theory of Employment, Interest and Money* (London: Macmillan, 1936).

63. Goudzwaard, *Capitalism and Progress*, pp. 102–5; John Kenneth Galbraith, *Economics and the Public Purpose* (Boston: Houghton Mifflin, 1973); and Galbraith, *Economics in Perspective*, pp. 221–36. The end result of this government attention, according to Frederick C. Thayer, is that Say's Law has become a matter of policy (*An End to Hierarchy!* pp. 100–101).

64. Goudzwaard, *Capitalism and Progress*, pp. 242, 249.

65. John Locke, "An Essay concerning the . . . End of Civil Government," in Ernest Barker, ed., *Social Contract* (London: Oxford University Press, 1960), pp. 18 and 23.

66. John Rawls, *A Theory of Justice* (Cambridge, Mass.: Belknap Press of Harvard University Press, 1971), pp. 119 and 136. See also p. 141.

67. *Ibid.*, pp. 123–25.

68. *Ibid.*, pp. 20, 46–51, 581, 586–87.

69. *Ibid.*, pp. 92, 128–29, 137, 138, 142, 144–45.

70. *Ibid.*, pp. 128, 284–93, 245–48.

71. *Ibid.*, pp. 542–45, 78, 80, 99.

72. *Ibid.*, sections 80–81.

73. *Ibid.*, p. 363.

74. *Ibid.*, pp. 129, 192, 264–65, 520–29, 126, n. 3, 127–28.

75. Michael Sandel, *Liberalism and the Limits of Justice* (Cambridge: Cambridge University Press, 1982), pp. 59–65.

76. Haskell Fain, *Normative Politics and the Community of Nations* (Philadelphia: Temple University Press, 1987), pp. 92–105.

CHAPTER 11

1. International Association of Machinists and Aerospace Workers (IAM), *Let's Rebuild America* (Washington, D.C.: Kelly, 1984), p. 107. See also Thomas Donaldson, *Corporations and Morality* (Englewood Cliffs, N.J.: Prentice-Hall, 1982), ch. 3.

2. IAM, *Let's Rebuild America*, pp. 113, 190–95. See also p. 108. George Goyder's proposal will be found in his *The Responsible Company* (Oxford: B. Blackwell, 1961).

3. Howard V. Perlmutter classifies transnational corporations into those with home-grown management (ethnocentric), local management (polycentric), or globally dispersed management (geocentric). See Hans Gunter, ed., *Transnational Industrial Relations* (London: Macmillan St. Martin's, 1972), pp. 18–19, 21–50, 117–32.

4. Robert Reich, *The Next American Frontier* (New York: Penguin, 1983), pp. 260–62.

5. *Ibid.*, pp. 251–52. No less defeatist and apologetic in this respect is Neil W. Chamberlain, *The Limits of Corporate Responsibility* (New York: Basic Books, 1973).

6. This view, obviously congenial to corporate interests, is espoused by Norman Bowie, "The Moral Obligation of Multinational Corporations," in *Problems of International Justice*, ed. Steven Luper-Foy (Boulder: Westview, 1988), pp. 97–113.

7. Reich, *Next American Frontier*, p. 280.

8. For additional reflections on this usage of community, see Benedict Anderson, *Imagined Communities: Reflections on the Origin and Spread of Nationalism* (London: Verso, 1983); Anthony D. Smith, *The Ethnic Origins of Nations* (Oxford: B. Blackwell, 1986).

9. See Philip Revzin, "Europe Will Become Economic Superpower as Barriers Crumble," *WSJ*, 29 Nov. 1988, pp. 1ff.; "1992," *IS*, 23 Oct. 1988, p. F5; Scott Sullivan, "Who's Afraid of 1992?" *Newsweek*, 31 Oct. 1988, pp. 32–33; "Europe 1992: A Truly Common Market?" *Barron's*, 3 Oct. 1988, pp. 8ff. For broader background, see *European Communities* (Price Waterhouse, 1987); *The Community Today* (Luxembourg. Commission of the European Communities, 1979); and C. G. Bamford and H. Robinson, *Geography of the EEC* (Estover: Macdonald & Evans, 1983).

10. See Charles Beitz, *Political Theory and International Relations* (Princeton: Princeton University Press, 1979); Beitz, "Cosmopolitan Ideals and National Sentiments," *Journal of Philosophy* 80 (1983): 591–600; and Beitz, "International Distributive Justice," in *Problems of International Justice*, ed. Luper-Foy, pp. 27–54.

11. See Anthony Ellis, ed., *Ethics and International Relations* (Manchester: Manchester University Press, 1986), esp. James Fishkin, "Theories of Justice and International Relations," pp. 1–23; and Brian Baxter, "The Self, Morality, and the Nation-State," pp. 113–26. See also Beitz, "Cosmopolitan Ideals and National Sentiment"; and Edmund F. Byrne, "The Depersonalization of Violence," *Journal of Value Inquiry* 7 (Fall 1973): 161–72.

12. Brian Barry, "Can States Be Moral? International Morality and the Compliance Problem," in *Ethics and International Relations*, ed. Ellis, pp. 61–84.

13. See Jeff McMahon, "The Ethics of International Intervention," in *Ethics and International Relations*, ed. Ellis, pp. 24–51; David Miller, "The Ethical Significance of Nationality," *Ethics* 98 (July 1988): 675; Michael Walzer, "The Moral Standing of States," in *International Ethics*, ed. Charles R. Beitz et al. (Princeton: Princeton University Press, 1985), p. 224; and Onora O'Neill, "Ethical Reasoning and Ideological Pluralism," *ibid.*, pp. 705–22. For arguments supporting intervention, see "Replies to Walzer," *Philosophy and Public Affairs* 9 (Summer 1980): 385–403.

14. O'Neill, "Ethical Reasoning," p. 714.

15. Julius Stone, "Approaches to the Notion of International Justice," in *The Future of the International Legal Order*, vol. 1, *Trends and Patterns*, ed. Richard A. Falk and Cyril E. Black (Princeton: Princeton University Press, 1969), quoted in Moorhead Wright, "Reflections on Injustice and International Politics," in *Ethics and International Relations*, ed. Ellis, pp. 213–21. See also Thomas Scanlon, "Contractualism and Utilitarianism," in *Utilitarianism and Beyond*, ed. Amartya Sen and Bernard Williams (Cambridge: Cambridge University Press, 1982), pp. 103–28.

16. See Herman R. van Gunsteren, "Admission to Citizenship," *Ethics* 98 (July 1988): 732, 735.

17. IAM, *Let's Rebuild America*, pp. 12–18, 74.

18. Because basic rights are commonly thought of as inhering (or not) in individuals, they do not include collective or social rights as such. See, for example, Richard A. Malanson, "Human Rights and the American Withdrawal from the ILO," *Universal Human Rights* 1 (Jan.–March 1979): 43–61. Recent studies that are broader in scope include Henry Shue, *Basic Rights* (Princeton: Princeton University Press, 1980); *Human Rights*, ed. J. Roland Pennock (New York: New York University Press, 1981); Alan S. Rosenbaum, ed., *The Philosophy of Human Rights: International Perspective* (Westport, Conn.: Greenwood Press, 1980).

19. Compare, for example, the arguments of Onora O'Neill and William Aiken regarding world hunger in *Problems of International Justice*, ed. Luper-Foy, pp. 67–96.

20. Peter Singer, *Practical Ethics* (Cambridge: Cambridge University Press, 1979), pp. 158–81; Singer, "Famine, Affluence, and Morality," in C. H. Sommers, ed., *Vice and Virtue in Everyday Life* (New York: Harcourt Brace Jovanovich, 1985), pp. 590–600.

21. See Richard J. Barnet, *The Lean Years: Politics in the Age of Scarcity* (New York: Simon & Schuster, 1980), pp. 302–5.

22. O'Neill, "Hunger, Needs, and Rights," in *International Justice*, ed. Luper-Foy, p. 82. See also her commentary on Singer's evolving position in *Faces of Hunger* (London: Allen & Unwin, 1986), pp. 56–63.

23. William Aiken, "World Hunger, Benevolence, and Justice," in *International Justice*, ed. Luper-Foy, pp. 84–96.

24. Saul H. Mendlovitz, ed., *On the Creation of a Just World Order* (New York: Free Press, 1975).

25. Richard A. Falk, *A Study of Future Worlds* (New York: Free Press, 1975), p. 11.

26. *Ibid.*, pp. 136–37, 380–96, 405–6.

27. Barnet describes this problem in considerable detail, especially with regard to the military-industrial complex (*Lean Years*, pp. 216–35).

28. Gerald Mische and Patricia Mische, *Toward a Human World Order* (New York: Paulist, 1977), pp. 113–31.

29. *Strengthening the World Monetary System*, A Statement on National Policy by the Research and Policy Committee for Economic Development (July 1973), p. 10.

30. See Barnet, *Lean Years*, pt. 3. Regarding North-South division, John Maynard Keynes sought to prevent Northern dominance of the International Monetary Fund. See *ibid.*, p. 288. See also *North-South: A Programme for Survival*, Report of Independent Commission on International Development Issues (London: Pan Books, 1980).

31. Lester M. Thurow, *The Zero-Sum Solution* (New York: Simon & Schuster, 1985), pp. 95–103. For a more theoretical analysis of these issues, especially with regard to employment opportunities, see Claus Offe, *Disorganized Capitalism* (Cambridge, Mass.: MIT Press, 1985).

32. Kai Nielson, "World Government, Security, and Global Justice," in *Problems of International Justice*, ed. Luper-Foy, pp. 269–70; Barnet, *Lean Years*, pp. 306–13; van Gunsteren, "Admission to Citizenship," p. 732.

33. Haskell Fain, *Normative Politics and the Community of Nations* (Philadelphia: Temple University Press, 1987), p. 1.

34. *Ibid.*, p. 110. Fain devotes two chapters to articulating the centrality of tasks and permissions, respectively. His conclusions in this regard are consistent with those of Frederick C. Thayer, who draws upon organization theory to defend a "consensus plan" for involving all levels of government in solving local problems (*An End to Hierarchy! An End to Competition!* [New York: New Viewpoints, 1973], pp. 171–74).

35. Fain, *Normative Politics*, p. 211.

36. Fain spices his exposition with a well-proportioned mixture of meticulous philosophical analysis on the one hand and case studies on the other. Some of the cases are real, others hypothetical. Examples of the former include transformation of the Jewish Settlement in Palestine into the State of Israel, the so-called "cod war" dispute between the United Kingdom and Iceland, U.S. refusal to accept the jurisdiction of the World Court over its disagreement with Nicaragua, and evolution of the EEC into a supranational community of nations. Examples of the latter are the Lone Ranger as law enforcer (Nozick's parable reinterpreted) and—what deserves the status of a classic—an engaging account of alien beings, called Rafters, whose settlement out on the ocean fails to qualify as a legal state under the standard definition used by international lawyers because they have no defined territory and do not choose to enter into relations with other states.

37. Fain, *Normative Politics*, pp. 213, 179.

38. See Eli Zaretsky, *Capitalism, the Family, and Personal Life* (New York: Harper Torchbook, 1976); also Seyla Benhabib and Drucilla Cornell, eds., *Feminism as Critique: On the Politics of Gender* (Minneapolis: University of Minnesota Press, 1987). The theoretical implications of this position are brilliantly articulated in a contractarian mode by Carole Pateman, *The Sexual Contract* (Stanford: Stanford University Press, 1988). See also Virginia Held, "Non-Contractual Society: A Feminist View," in *Science, Morality and Feminist Theory*, ed. Marsha Hanen and Kai Nielsen (Calgary: University of Calgary Press, 1987).

39. Doron P. Levin, "Kenosha Looks Beyond Chrysler," *NYT*, 22 Dec. 1988, pp. Y29, 36.

40. Mark Ivey, "Houston's Sick Economy Is Taking a Little Nourishment," *BW*, 16 January 1989, pp. 102–3. That Houston set itself up for the downturn is suggested by Barry Bluestone and Bennett Harrison, *The Deindustrialization of America* (New York: Basic Books, 1982), pp. 83–92.

41. John J. McDermott, "The Aesthetic Drama of the Ordinary," in *Technology as a Human Affair*, ed. Larry A. Hickman (New York: McGraw-Hill, forthcoming).

42. The election of women as governors and even as presidents or prime ministers of nation-states is a more complicated matter, inasmuch as the constituencies of those levels of government are so predominantly corporate as distinguished from communitarian. So at this level the woman leader is far more likely to be a mere figurehead.

43. See Morton White and Lucia White, *The Intellectual versus the City* (1962; rpt. New York: Oxford University Press, 1977). This generalization is wonderfully contradicted by Lewis Mumford. See his *The City in History: Its Origins, Its Transformations, Its Prospects* (New York: Harcourt, Brace and World, 1961).

44. Alan Dawley, *Class and Community: The Industrial Revolution in Lynn* (Cambridge, Mass.: Harvard University Press, 1976), pp. 223, 225–26, 229, 239.

45. Brian Greenberg, *Worker and Community: Responses to Industrialization in a Nineteenth-Century American City, Albany, New York, 1850–1884* (Albany: State University of New York Press, 1985), pp. 3, 160.

46. See *Projects and Services of the United States Conference of Mayors* (Washington, D.C.: U.S. Conference of Mayors, 1987). See also *The National League of Cities Handbook: A Guide to Services and Participation*, 2d ed. (Washington, D.C.: National League of Cities, 1987). Many helpful publications and services are available through either organization, each of which offers associate membership to organizations other than city governments.

47. See Thomas Bender, *Community and Social Change in America* (New Brunswick, N.J.: Rutgers University Press, 1978).

Conclusions

1. See Gérard Chaliand, ed., *Minority Peoples in the Age of Nation-States*, tr. Tony Berrett (London: Pluto Press, 1989).

2. See David Vogel, *Lobbying the Corporation: Citizen Challenges to Business Authority* (New York: Basic Books, 1978).

3. This assessment of military forces is attributed to British theorist Lord Bryce. See Stanley I. Benn, "The Uses of 'Sovereignty,' " in *Political Philosophy*, ed. Anthony Quinton (Oxford: Oxford University Press, 1967), p. 66. For an initial approach to the political analysis of corporations, see Frederick Thayer's view of economic theory as political anarchy, *An End to Hierarchy! An End to Competition!* (New York: New Viewpoints, 1973), pp. 100–105.

4. Stanley I. Benn, "Sovereignty," in *The Encyclopedia of Philosophy*, vol. 7 (New York: Macmillan, 1967), p. 501. See also Benn, "Uses of 'Sovereignty,' " pp. 79–81.

5. I am thinking here in particular of Robert Paul Wolff's proposal "to break the American economy down into regional and subregional units of manageable size" in *In Defense of Anarchism* (New York: Harper Torchbook, 1970), p. 82.

Index

in the future, according to: Frijthof Bergmann, 81; Robin Clarke, 60; André Gorz,
69; Melvin Kranzberg and Joseph Gies,
81; Herbert Marcuse, 69, 82–83; Robert
Theobald, 56
in Greek and Roman literature, 77
in Judaeo-Christian mythology, 68, 77
as labor process, 199
obligation to engage in, 37, 45–57, 69–70
papal encyclicals on, 143–44
as servile, 50
and shirking, 54, 67–68, 83
as status, 54, 55
and vagrancy, 42, 58, 68
Work, value of, 70, 126–27
according to: Thomas Aquinas, 67; Saint
Benedict, 58, 66–67, 68; Murray Bookchin, 84; Calvinism and Puritanism, 59,
63–64, 68–69; Christian Socialists, 67;
Adam Ferguson, 59; Benjamin Franklin,
51; Sigmund Freud, 83, 272; Eric Fromm,
83, 239; Jesus, 65, 66; Martin Luther,
68; David Macarov, 56; Norman Mailer,
71; Cotton Mather, 51; Claus Offe, 190;
Saint Paul, 63, 65; Marge Piercy, 48;
François Rabelais, 48; Adriano Tilgher,
50; Voltaire, 48–49
Work ethic(s), 8, 9, 45, 53, 57, 61, 62–84
according to: David J. Cherrington, 50, 52,
71, 187; Octave Mirbeau, 49; Michael
Rose, 50; Max Weber, 63–64, 69, 220
as manifested in: workaholism, 118, worker
burnout, 117
Worker control, 106–7
Worker displacement, 6, 55, 106, 109, 187–91
protection against, 165–77
Worker ownership, 153–54
and Employee Stock Ownership Plans
(ESOPs), 153, 214
as proposed for Conrail, 107, 154
Workers, 286 n. 14
and class consciousness, 272
coercion of, 42, 278–79
mobility of, 9, 42, 99, 110
Workers' representative, 11–12, 27, 37, 45,
158, 159, 176, 182, 205, 209, 241
Workers' rights, 9, 13, 20, 182, 209–10. *See
also* Liberty; Unions, in general (*and*) in
particular

under "right to work" statutes, 137
in views of: Lawrence C. Becker, 99;
James W. Nickel, 99; Patricia Werhane,
100
Workforce:
contingent, 127
restructuring of, 13, 14, 15, 16, 20, 26, 204
women in, 79, 80, 127, 191, 270, 271
sarily representative):
in Anaheim, California, 204
in Austin, Minnesota, 196–97
in Canada, 168
in Dominican Republic, 30
in Flint, Michigan, 186
in France, 116
in Fremont, California, 186
in Glaris, Switzerland, 221
in Great Britain, 146, 168, 170, 198
in Hungary, 198
in India, 91, 197
in Indiana, 20–22, 25, 28–29
in Italy, 185
in Japan, 175, 189
in Louisville, Kentucky, 186
in Malaysia, 191
on medieval monastic estate, 123–24
in New Zealand, 170
in Nigeria, 30–31, 191
in Norway, 116, 168, 200
in People's Republic of China, 60
in Soviet Union, 48, 49, 167, 184
in South Korea, 29, 175
in Sweden, 90, 93, 116, 127, 168, 188, 200
in Taiwan, 29
in Tazmania, 191
in Thailand, 191
in West Germany, 90, 102, 127, 166, 169–
70, 188, 194
Workplace democracy, 120, 223
Workplace therapy, 115–16
World Order Models Project (WOMP), 265–66

Xenophon, 78

Yellow-dog contracts, 138

Zero-sum game, 243–44, 249